READINGS ABOUT INDIVIDUAL
AND GROUP DIFFERENCES

READINGS
ABOUT
INDIVIDUAL
AND GROUP
DIFFERENCES

EDITED BY

Lee Willerman
The University of Texas at Austin

Robert G. Turner
Pepperdine University

W. H. Freeman and Company
San Francisco

Library of Congress Cataloging in Publication Data

Main entry under title:

Readings about individual and group differences.

(A Series of books in psychology)
Bibliography: p.
Includes index.
1. Difference (Psychology) 2. Intelligence levels.
3. Nature and nurture. 4. Individuality. 5. Psy-
chology, Pathological. 6. Sex differences (Psychology)
I. Willerman, Lee, 1939–   II. Turner, Robert
Gerald, 1945–
BF697.R38   155.2′2   78-13079
ISBN 0-7167-1015-3
ISBN 0-7167-1014-5 pbk.

Printed in the United States of America

9 8 7 6 5 4 3 2

Contents

V EDUCATIONAL PROCESSES

VI PERSONALITY

VII PSYCHOPATHOLOGY

VIII MENTAL RETARDATION AND OTHER HANDICAPS

IX GENIUS AND CREATIVITY

X SEX DIFFERENCES

XI INTELLIGENCE AND AGING

XII RACE AND ETHNICITY

Preface

The topic of individual and group differences is a fascinating one. It is of interest not only to researchers in many disciplines in the natural and social sciences but to the general public as well. As any careful observer can attest, humans exhibit a wide range of differences for almost any characteristic under consideration. This volume presents readings on a variety of topics that continue to capture the interest of researchers directly investigating individual and group differences.

Perusal of the table of contents reveals that the nature and nurture of intelligence is a central concern of the field of individual and group differences, often called differential psychology. However, differential psychology is also concerned with individual differences in personality and psychopathology and group differences such as sex, age, and ethnicity.

Most of the articles in this volume are of relatively recent vintage. The purpose of emphasizing contemporary articles is to acquaint the reader with the issues and research areas that are now receiving the greatest attention and that are likely to receive continued attention in the future.

A more representative selection would also have included articles dealing exclusively with methodology. The solution of many of the problems under investigation by differential psychologists is often obstructed by failure to identify the major behaviors that should be measured as well as by failure to determine how these behaviors can be measured once they are identified. The literature dealing with methodology usually requires fairly sophisticated knowledge to be understood and thus is excluded here. However, by paying close attention to how the authors of the articles approach the problems they are investigating, the student can see the basic issues in psychological measurement revealed in more digestible form.

Most of the articles in this collection have been edited fo delete analyses or subtopics that are not of general interest and to keep the book at a manageable length. We hope that these editorial deletions will make for smooth reading without misrepresenting the major theses of the authors. We have written a brief introduction to each of the articles to familiarize the student with the problem addressed by the author or authors.

September 1978

Lee Willerman
Robert G. Turner

READINGS ABOUT INDIVIDUAL
AND GROUP DIFFERENCES

I

HISTORY

This selection from the work of Sir Francis Galton is regarded by many as having founded and set the tone for the field of individual differences. Among the points on which to focus are Galton's claims about the prepotence of hereditary factors in the attainment of eminence and the notion that differences among individuals are best revealed when the task is at the appropriate level of difficulty for the sample under investigation. Examine carefully the logical basis for his arguments about hereditary factors. Are they convincing? What competing hypotheses can be offered to account for the findings?

1

Classification of Men According to Their Natural Gifts

FRANCIS GALTON

I have no patience with the hypothesis occasionally expressed, and often implied, especially in tales written to teach children to be good, that babies are born pretty much alike, and that the sole agencies in creating differences between boy and boy, and man and man, are steady application and moral effort. It is in the most unqualified manner that I object to pretensions of natural equality. The experiences of the nursery, the school, the University, and of professional careers, are a chain of proofs to the contrary. I acknowledge freely the great power of education and social influences in developing the active powers of the mind, just as I acknowledge the effect of use in developing the muscles of a blacksmith's arm, and no further. Let the blacksmith labour as he will, he will find there are certain feats beyond his power that are well within the strength of a man of herculean make, even although the latter may have led a sedentary life. Some years ago, the Highlanders held a grand gathering in Holland Park, where they challenged all England to compete with them in their games of strength. The challenge was accepted, and the well-trained men of the

Galton, Francis. "Classification of Men According to Their Natural Gifts." From *Hereditary Genius*, 1869, pp. 56–66.

hills were beaten in the foot-race by a youth who was stated to be a pure Cockney, the clerk of a London banker.

Everybody who has trained himself to physical exercises discovers the extent of his muscular powers to a nicety. When he begins to walk, to row, to use the dumb bells, or to run, he finds to his great delight that his thews strengthen, and his endurance of fatigue increases day after day. So long as he is a novice, he perhaps flatters himself there is hardly an assignable limit to the education of his muscles; but the daily gain is soon discovered to diminish, and at last it vanishes altogether. His maximum performance becomes a rigidly determinate quantity. He learns to an inch, how high or how far he can jump, when he has attained the highest state of training. He learns to half a pound, the force he can exert on the dynamometer, by compressing it. He can strike a blow against the machine used to measure impact, and drive its index to a certain graduation, but no further. So it is in running, in rowing, in walking, and in every other form of physical exertion. There is a definite limit to the muscular powers of every man, which he cannot by any education or exertion overpass.

This is precisely analogous to the experience that every student has had of the working of his mental powers. The eager boy, when he first goes to school and confronts intellectual difficulties, is astonished at his progress. He glories in his newly-developed mental grip and growing capacity for application, and, it may be, fondly believes it to be within his reach to become one of the heroes who have left their mark upon the history of the world. The years go by; he competes in the examinations of school and college, over and over again with his fellows, and soon finds his place among them. He knows he can beat such and such of his competitors; that there are some with whom he runs on equal terms, and others whose intellectual feats he cannot even approach. Probably his vanity still continues to tempt him, by whispering in a new strain. It tells him that classics, mathematics, and other subjects taught in universities, are mere scholastic specialities, and no test of the more valuable intellectual powers. It reminds him of numerous instances of persons who had been unsuccessful in the competitions of youth, but who had shown powers in afterlife that made them the foremost men of their age. Accordingly, with newly furbished hopes, and with all the ambition of twenty-two years of age, he leaves his University and enters a larger field of competition. The same kind of experience awaits him here that he has already gone through. Opportunities occur—they occur to every man—and he finds himself incapable of grasping them. He tries, and is tried in many things. In a few years more, unless he is incurably blinded by self-conceit, he learns precisely of what performances he is capable, and what other enterprises lie beyond his compass. When he reaches mature life, he is confident only within certain limits, and knows, or ought to know, himself just as he is probably judged of by the world, with all his unmistakeable weakness and all his undeniable strength. He is no longer tormented into hopeless efforts by the fallacious promptings of overweening vanity, but he limits his undertakings to matters below the level of his reach, and finds true moral repose in an honest conviction that he is engaged in as much good work as his nature has rendered him capable of performing.

There can hardly be a surer evidence of the enormous difference between the intellectual capacity of men, than the prodigious differences in the numbers of marks obtained by those who gain mathematical honours at Cambridge. I therefore crave permission to speak at some length upon this subject, although the details are dry and of little general interest. There are between 400 and 450 students who take their degrees in each year, and of these, about 100 succeed in gaining honours in mathematics, and are ranged by the examiners in strict order of merit. About the first forty of those who take mathematical honours are distinguished by the title of wranglers, and it is a decidedly creditable thing to be even a low wrangler; it will secure a fellowship in a small college. It must be carefully borne in mind that the distinction of being the first in this list of honours, or what is called the senior wrangler of the year, means a vast deal more than being the foremost mathematician of 400 or 450 men taken at haphazard. No doubt the large bulk of Cambridge men are taken almost at haphazard. A boy is intended by his parents for some profession; if that profession be either the Church or the Bar, it used to be almost requisite, and it is still important, that he should be sent to Cambridge or Oxford. These youths may justly be considered as having been taken at haphazard. But there are many others who have fairly won their way to the Universities, and are therefore selected from an enormous area. Fully one-half of the wranglers have been boys of note at their respective schools, and, conversely, almost all boys of note at schools find their way to the Universities. Hence it is that among their comparatively small number of students, the Universities include the highest youthful scholastic ability of all England. The senior wrangler, in each successive year, is the chief of these as regards mathematics, and this, the highest distinction, is, or was, continually won by youths who had no mathematical training of importance before they went to Cambridge. All their instruction had been received during the three years of their residence at the University. Now, I do not say anything here about the merits or demerits of Cambridge mathematical studies having been directed along a too narrow groove, or about the presumed disadvantages of ranging candidates in strict order of merit, instead of grouping them, as at Oxford, in classes, where their names appear alphabetically arranged. All I am concerned with here are the results; and these are most appropriate to my argument. The youths start on their three years' race as fairly as possible. They are then stimulated to run by the most powerful inducements, namely, those of competition, of honour, and of future wealth (for a good fellowship is wealth); and at the end of the three years they are examined most rigorously according to a system that they all understand and are equally well prepared for. The examination lasts five and a half hours a day for eight days. All the answers are carefully marked by the examiners, who add up the marks at the end and range the candidates in strict order of merit. The fairness and thoroughness of Cambridge examinations have never had a breath of suspicion cast upon them.

Unfortunately for my purposes, the marks are not published. They are not even assigned on a uniform system, since each examiner is permitted to employ his own scale of marks; but whatever scale he uses, the results as to proportional merit are the same. I am indebted to a Cambridge examiner for a copy of his marks in respect to two examinations, in which the scales of marks were so alike as to make it easy, by a slight proportional adjustment, to compare the two together. This was, to a certain degree, a confidential communication, so that it would be improper for me to publish anything that would identify the years to which these marks refer. I simply give them as groups of figures, sufficient to show the enormous differences of merit (Table 1.1). The lowest man in the list of honours gains less than 300 marks; the lowest wrangler gains about 1,500 marks; and the

Table 1.1

Scale of merit among the men who obtain
mathematical honours at Cambridge

Number of marks obtained by candidates	Number of candidates in the two years, taken together, who obtained those marks
Under 500	24
500 to 1,000	74
1,000 to 1,500	38
1,500 to 2,000	21
2,000 to 2,500	11
2,500 to 3,000	8
3,000 to 3,500	11
3,500 to 4,000	5
4,000 to 4,500	2
4,500 to 5,000	1
5,000 to 5,500	3
5,500 to 6,000	1
6,000 to 6,500	0
6,500 to 7,000	0
7,000 to 7,500	0
7,500 to 8,000	1
	200

The results of two years are thrown into a single table. The total number of marks obtainable in each year was 17,000. I have included in this table only the first 100 men in each year. The omitted residue is too small to be important. I have omitted it lest, if the precise numbers of honour men were stated those numbers would have served to identify the years. For reasons already given, I desire to afford no data to serve that purpose.

senior wrangler, in one of the lists now before me, gained more than 7,500 marks. Consequently, the lowest wrangler has more than five times the merit of the lowest junior optime, and less than one-fifth the merit of the senior wrangler.

The precise number of marks obtained by the senior wrangler in the more remarkable of these two years was 7,634; by the second wrangler in the same year, 4,123; and by the lowest man in the list of honours, only 237. Consequently, the senior wrangler obtained nearly twice as many marks as the second wrangler, and more than thirty-two times as many as the lowest man. I have received from another examiner the marks of a year in which the senior wrangler was conspicuously eminent. He obtained 9,422 marks, whilst the second in the same year—whose merits were by no means inferior to those of second wranglers in general—obtained only 5,642. The man at the bottom of the same honour list had only 309 marks, or one-thirtieth the number of the senior wrangler. I have some particulars of a fourth very remarkable year, in which the senior wrangler obtained no less than ten times as many marks as the second wrangler, in the "problem paper." Now, I have discussed with practised examiners the question of how far the numbers of marks may be considered as proportionate to the mathematical power of the candidate, and am assured they are strictly proportionate as regards the lower places, but do not afford full justice to the highest. In other words, the senior wranglers above mentioned had more than thirty, or thirty-two times the ability of the lowest men on the lists of honours. They would be able to grapple with problems more than thirty-two times as difficult; or when dealing with subjects of the same difficulty, but intelligible to all, would comprehend them more rapidly in perhaps the square root of that proportion. It is reasonable to expect that marks would do some injustice to the very best men, because a very large part of the time of the examination is taken up by the mechanical labour of writing. Whenever the thought of the candidate outruns his pen, he gains no advantage from his excess of promptitude in conception. I should, however, mention that some of the ablest men have shown their superiority by comparatively little writing. They find their way at once to the root of the difficulty in the problems that are set, and, with a few clean, apposite, powerful strokes, succeed in proving they can overthrow it, and then they go on to another question. Every word they write tells. Thus, the late Mr. H. Leslie Ellis, who was a brilliant senior wrangler in 1840, and whose name is familiar to many generations of Cambridge men as a prodigy of universal genius, did not even remain during the full period in the examination room: his health was weak, and he had to husband his strength.

The mathematical powers of the last man on the list of honours, which are so low when compared with those of a senior wrangler, are mediocre, or even above mediocrity, when compared with the gifts of Englishmen generally. Though the examination places 100 honour men above him, it puts no less than 300 "poll men" below him. Even if we go so far as to allow that 200 out of the 300 refuse to work hard enough to get honours, there will remain 100 who, even if they worked hard, could not get them. Every tutor knows how difficult it is to drive abstract conceptions, even of the simplest kind, into the brains of most people—how feeble and hesitating is their mental grasp—how easily their brains are mazed—how incapable they are of precision and soundness of knowledge. It often occurs to persons familiar with some scientific subject to hear men and women of mediocre gifts relate to one another what they have picked up about it from some lecture—say at the Royal Institution, where they have sat for an hour listening with delighted attention to an admirably lucid account, illustrated by experiments of the most perfect and beautiful character, in all of which they expressed themselves intensely gratified and highly instructed. It is positively painful to hear what they say. Their recollections seem to be a mere chaos of mist and misapprehension, to which some sort of shape and organisation has been given by the action of their own pure fancy, altogether alien to what the lecturer intended to convey. The average mental grasp even of what is called a well-educated audience, will be found to be ludicrously small when rigorously tested.

In stating the differences between man and man, let it not be supposed for a moment that mathematicians are necessarily one-sided in their natural gifts. There are numerous instances of the reverse, of whom the following will be found, as instances of hereditary genius, in the appendix to my chapter on SCIENCE. I would especially name Liebnitz, as being universally gifted; but Ampere, Arago, Condorcet, and D'Alembert, were all of them very far more than mere mathematicians. Nay, since the range of examination at Cambridge is so extended as to include other subjects besides mathematics, the differences of ability between the highest and the lowest of the successful candidates is yet more glaring than what I have already described. We still find, on the one hand, mediocre men, whose whole energies are absorbed in getting their 237 marks for mathematics; and, on the other hand, some few senior wranglers who are at the same time high classical scholars and much more besides. Cambridge has afforded such instances. Its lists of classical honours are comparatively of recent date, but other evidence is obtainable from earlier times of their occurrence. . . . Since 1824, when the classical tripos was first established, the late Mr. Goulburn (son of the Right Hon. H. Goulburn, Chancellor of the Exchequer) was second wrangler in 1835, and senior classic of the same year. But in more recent times, the necessary labour of preparation, in order to acquire the highest mathematical places, has become so enormous that there has been a wider differentiation of studies. There is no longer time for a man to acquire the necessary knowledge to succeed to the first place in more than one subject. There are, therefore, no instances of a man being absolutely first in both examinations, but a few can be found of high eminence in both classics and mathematics, as a reference to the lists published in the *Cambridge Calendar* will show. The best of these more recent degrees appears to be that of Dr. Barry, late Principal of Cheltenham, and now Principal of King's College, London (the son of the eminent architect, Sir Charles Barry, and brother of Mr. Edward Barry, who succeeded his father as architect). He was fourth wrangler and seventh classic of his year.

In whatever way we may test ability, we arrive at equally enormous intellectual differences. Lord Macaulay (see under LITERATURE for his remarkable kinships) had one of the most tenacious of memories. He was able to recall many pages of hundreds of volumes by various authors, which he had acquired by simply reading them over. An average man could not certainly carry in his memory one thirty-second—ay, or one hundredth—part as much as Lord Macaulay. The father of Seneca had one of the greatest memories on record in ancient times (see under LITERATURE for his kinships). Porson, the Greek scholar, was remarkable for this gift, and, I may add, the "Porson memory" was hereditary in that family. In statesmanship, generalship, literature, science, poetry, art, just the same enormous differences are found between man and man; and numerous instances recorded in this book, will show in how small degree, eminence, either in these or any other class of intellectual powers, can be considered as due to purely special powers. They are rather to be considered in those instances as the result of concentrated efforts, made by men who are widely gifted. People lay too much stress on apparent specialities, thinking over-rashly that, because a man is devoted to some particular pursuit, he could not possibly have succeeded in anything else. They might just as well say that, because a youth had fallen desperately in love with a brunette, he could not possibly have fallen in love with a blonde. He may or may not have more natural liking for the former type of beauty than the latter, but it is as probable as not that the affair was mainly or wholly due to a general amorousness of disposition. It is just the same with special pursuits. A gifted man is often capricious and fickle before he selects his occupation, but when it has been chosen, he devotes himself to it with a truly passionate ardour. After a man of genius has selected his hobby, and so adapted himself to it as to seem unfitted for any other occupation in life, and to be possessed of but one special aptitude, I often notice, with admiration, how well he bears himself when circumstances suddenly thrust him into a strange position. He will display an insight into new conditions, and a power of dealing with them, with which even his most intimate friends were unprepared to accredit him. Many a presumptuous fool has mistaken indifference and neglect for incapacity; and in trying to throw a man of genius on ground where he was unprepared for attack, has himself received a most severe and unexpected fall. I am sure that no one who has had the privilege of mixing in the society of the abler men of any great capital, or who is acquainted with the biographies of the heroes of history, can doubt the existence of grand human animals, of natures pre-eminently noble, of individuals born to be kings of men. I have been conscious of no slight misgiving that I was committing a kind of sacrilege whenever, in the preparation of materials for this book, I had occasion to take the measurement of modern intellects vastly superior to my own, or to criticise the genius of the most magnificent historical specimens of our race. It was a process that constantly recalled to me a once familiar sentiment in bygone days of African travel, when I used to take altitudes of the huge cliffs that domineered above me as I travelled along their bases, or to map the mountainous landmarks of unvisited tribes, that loomed in faint grandeur beyond my actual horizon.

I have not cared to occupy myself much with people whose gifts are below the average, but they would be an interesting study. The number of idiots and imbeciles among the twenty million inhabitants of England and Wales is approximately estimated at 50,000, or as 1 in 400. Dr. Seguin, a great French authority on these matters, states that more than thirty percent of idiots and imbeciles, put under suitable instruction, have been taught to conform to social and moral law, and rendered capable of order, of good feeling, and of working like the third of an average man. He says that more than forty percent have become capable of the ordinary transactions of life, under friendly control; of understanding moral and social abstractions, and of working like two-thirds of a man. And, lastly, that from twenty-five to thirty percent come nearer and nearer to the standard of manhood, till some of them will defy the scrutiny of good judges, when compared with ordinary young men and women. In the order next above idiots and imbeciles are a large number of milder cases scattered among private families and kept out of sight, the existence of whom is, however, well known to relatives and friends; they are too silly to take a part in general society, but are easily amused with some trivial, harmless occupation. Then comes a class of whom the Lord Dundreary of the famous play may be considered a representative; and so, proceeding through successive grades, we gradually ascend to mediocrity. I know two good instances of hereditary silliness short of imbecility, and have reason to believe I could easily obtain a large number of similar facts.

To conclude, the range of mental power between—I will not say the highest Caucasian and the lowest savage—but between the greatest and least of English intellects, is enormous. There is a continuity of natural ability reaching from one knows not what height, and descending to one can hardly say what depth.

This article laid the groundwork for the objective measurement of intelligence. The scale that Alfred Binet and Theodore Simon proposed was the forerunner of the now famous Stanford-Binet Intelligence Scale, still widely used for the same purpose. The most important features to note in this article are their attempts to obtain a relatively objective measure of intellectual function and to devise test items that were relatively independent of school experience.

2

The Development of Intelligence in Children

ALFRED BINET AND THEODORE SIMON

Upon the Necessity of Establishing a Scientific Diagnosis of Inferior States of Intelligence

We here present the first rough sketch of a work which was directly inspired by the desire to serve the interesting cause of the education of subnormals.

In October 1904, the Minister of Public Instruction named a commission which was charged with the study of measures to be taken for insuring the benefits of instruction to defective children. After a number of sittings, this commission regulated all that pertained to the type of establishment to be created, the conditions of admission into the school, the teaching force, and the pedagogical methods to be employed. They decided that no child suspected of retardation should be eliminated from the ordinary school and admitted into a special class, without first being subjected to a pedagogical and medical examination from which it could

Binet, Alfred, and Simon, Theodore. "The Development of Intelligence in Children," *L'Année Psychologique*, 1905, pp. 163–244. In T. Shipley (ed.), *Classics in Psychology*. New York: Philosophical Library, 1961. Copyright © 1961 by Philosophical Library, Inc., and reprinted by permission.

be certified that because of the state of his intelligence, he was unable to profit, in an average measure, from the instruction given in the ordinary schools.

But how the examination of each child should be made, what methods should be followed, what observations taken, what questions asked, what tests devised, how the child should be compared with normal children, the commission felt under no obligation to decide. It was formed to do a work of administration, not a work of science.

It has seemed to us extremely useful to furnish a guide for future Commissions' examination. Such Commissions should understand from the beginning how to get their bearings. It must be made impossible for those who belong to the Commission to fall into the habit of making haphazard decisions according to impressions which are subjective, and consequently uncontrolled. Such impressions are sometimes good, sometimes bad, and have at all times too much the nature of the arbitrary, of caprice, of indifference. Such a condition is quite unfortunate because the interests of the child demand a more careful method. To be a member of a special class can never be a mark of distinction, and such as do not merit it, must be spared the record. Some errors are excusable in the beginning, but if they become too frequent, they ruin the reputation of these new institutions. Furthermore, in principle, we are convinced, and we shall not cease to repeat that the precision and exactness of science should be introduced into our practice whenever possible, and in the great majority of cases it is possible.

The problem which we have to solve presents many difficulties both theoretical and practical. It is a hackneyed remark that the definitions, thus far proposed, for the different states of subnormal intelligence, lack precision. These inferior states are indefinite in number, being composed of a series of degrees which mount from the lowest depths of idiocy, to a condition easily confounded with normal intelligence. *Alienists*** have frequently come to an agreement concerning the terminology to be employed for designating the difference of these degrees; at least, in spite of certain individual divergence of ideas to be found in all questions, there has been an agreement to accept *idiot* as applied to the lowest state, *imbecile* to the intermediate, and *moron* (debile)† to the state nearest normality. Still among the numerous alienists, under this common and apparently precise terminology, different ideas are concealed, variable and at the same time confused. The distinction between idiot, imbecile, .

---

* An alienist is a psychiatrist.—ED.

† The French word *débile* (weak) is used by Binet to designate the highest grade of mental defectives, called in England feeble-minded. In America the term feeble-minded has been used in the same sense, but unfortunately it is also applied generically to the entire group of mental defectives. To obviate this ambiguity, we coined the word *Moron* (Greek Moros, foolish) to designate the highest grade of mental defect. We have accordingly translated *débile* by moron, except in a few instances where the context requires a different term.—ED. [T. Shipley]

and moron is not understood in the same way by all practitioners. We have abundant proof of this in the strikingly divergent medical diagnoses made only a few days apart by different alienists upon the same patient.

. . .

We cannot sufficiently deplore the consequence of this state of uncertainty recognized today by all alienists. The simple fact, that specialists do not agree in the use of the technical terms of their science, throws suspicion upon their diagnoses, and prevents all work of comparison. We ourselves have made similar observations. In synthesizing the diagnoses made by M. Bourneville upon patients leaving the Bicetre, we found that in the space of four years only two feeble-minded individuals have left his institution although during that time the Bureau of Admission has sent him more than thirty. Nothing could show more clearly than this change of label, the confusion of our nomenclature.

What importance can be attached to public statistics of different countries concerning the percentage of backward children if the definition for backward children is not the same in all countries? How will it be possible to keep a record of the intelligence of pupils who are treated and instructed in a school, if the terms applied to them, feebleminded, retarded, imbecile, idiot, vary in meaning according to the doctor who examines them? The absence of a common measure prevents comparison of statistics, and makes one lose all interest in investigations which may have been very laborious. But a still more serious fact is that, because of lack of methods, it is impossible to solve those essential questions concerning the afflicted, whose solution presents the greatest interest; for example, the real results gained by the treatment of inferior states of intelligence by doctor and educator; the educative value of one pedagogical method compared with another; the degree of curability of incomplete idiocy, etc. It is not by means of a priori reasonings, of vague considerations, of oratorical displays, that these questions can be solved; but by minute investigation, entering into the details of fact, and considering the effects of the treatment for each particular child. There is but one means of knowing if a child, who has passed six years in a hospital or in a special class, has profited from that stay, and to what degree he has profited; and that is to compare his certificate of entrance with his certificate of dismissal, and by that means ascertain if he shows a special amelioration of his condition beyond that which might be credited simply to the considerations of growth. But experience has shown how imprudent it would be to place confidence in this comparison, when the two certificates come from different doctors, who do not judge in exactly the same way, or who use different words to characterize the mental status of patients.

It might happen that a child, who had really improved in school, had received in the beginning the diagnosis of moron (debile), and on leaving, the prejudicial diagnosis of imbecile, simply because the second doctor spoke a different language from the first. If one took these certificates literally, this case would be considered a failure. On the contrary, the appearance of amelioration would be produced if the physician who delivered the certificate of dismissal had the habit of using higher terms than the one who furnished the certificate of entrance. One can even go further. The errors which we note, do not necessarily emanate from the disagreement of different physicians. It would suffice for the same physician to deliver the two certificates, if he did not employ for each one the same criterion; and it would certainly be possible for him to vary unconsciously after an interval of several years if he had nothing to guide him but his own subjective impressions. Might not the same thing also happen if his good faith as a physician happened to be in conflict with the interests of the institution which he directed? Might he not unconsciously as it were, have a tendency to lower the mental status of patients on entering and to raise it on dismissal, in order to emphasize the advantages of the methods which he had applied? We are not incriminating anyone, but simply calling attention to methods actually in use which, by their lack of precision, favor the involuntary illusions of physicians and relatives, in a word, of all those who, having an interest in the amelioration of the condition of the defective child, would have a tendency to confound their desires with the reality.

Perhaps someone will raise an objection and say this uncertainty has no special application to diagnosis of the degrees of mental debility; it is also to be found in mental pathology and, in a general way, in the diagnosis of all maladies; it is the result of the empirical nature which is characteristic of clinical studies. It might be added, that, if anyone took the trouble to make a statistical study of the divergence in the diagnosis of different physicians upon the same patient, it would probably be found that the percentage of disagreement is very great in all branches of medicine.

We believe it worth while to examine their objection because it permits us to enter more deeply into the analysis of the question. The disagreements of practitioners might come from three very different classes of causes:

1. Ignorance, that is, the lack of aptitude of certain physicians. This is an individual failure, for which abstract science is not responsible. It is certain that, even when the symptoms of a disease are absolutely clear, such a physician might fail to recognize them through incapacity. There are many accountants who make mistakes in calculation, but these errors do not discredit mathematics. A physician might not be able to recognize a "p. g." if he is himself a "p. g."

2. The variable meaning of terms. Since the same expression has a different sense according to the person who uses it, it is possible that the disagreement of diagnosis may be simply a disagreement of words, due to the use of different nomenclature.

3. Lack of precision in the description of the symptoms which reveal or which constitute a certain particular malady; different physicians do not examine the same patient in the same manner and do not give the symptoms

the same importance; or, it may be they make no effort to find out the precise symptoms, and no effort to analyze carefully in order to distinguish and interpret them.

Of these three kinds of error, which is the one that actually appears in the diagnosis of inferior states of intelligence? Let us set aside the first. There remain the faults of nomenclature, and the insufficiency of methods of examination.

The general belief seems to be that the confusion arises wholly from an absence of a uniform nomenclature. There is some truth in this opinion. It can be proved by a comparison of terms used by authors belonging to the different countries. Even in France the terms differ somewhat according to the physician, the order of the admitted subdivisions not being rigorously followed. The classification of Magnan is not that of Voisin, and his, in turn, differs from that of Bourneville. Undoubtedly it would be a good work to bring about a unification of this nomenclature as has been done for the standard of measurements and for electric units. But this reform in itself is not sufficient and we are very sure that they deceive themselves who think that at bottom this is only a question of terminology. It is very much more serious. We find physicians who, though using the same terminology, constantly disagree in their diagnosis of the same child. The examples cited from M. Blin prove this. There the doctors had recourse to the terminology of Morel, who classifies those of inferior intelligence as idiots, imbeciles and "debiles." Notwithstanding this use of the same terms, they do not agree in the manner of applying them. Each one according to his own fancy, fixes the boundary line separating these states. It is in regard to the facts that the doctors disagree.

In looking closely one can see that the confusion comes principally from a fault in the method of examination. When an alienist finds himself in the presence of a child of inferior intelligence, he does not examine him by bringing out each one of the symptoms which the child manifests and by interpreting all symptoms and classifying them; he contents himself with taking a subjective impression, an impression as a whole, of his subject, and of making his diagnosis by instinct. We do not think that we are going too far in saying that at the present time very few physicians would be able to cite with absolute precision the objective and invariable sign, or signs, by which they distinguish the degrees of inferior mentality.

A study of the historical side of the question shows us very clearly that what is lacking is a *precise basis for differential diagnosis.*

New Methods for the Diagnosis
of the Intellectual Level of Subnormals

. . .

To what method should we have recourse in making our diagnosis of the intellectual level? No one method exists, but there are a number of different ones which should be used cumulatively, because the question is a very difficult one to solve, and demands rather a collaboration of methods. It is important that the practitioner be equipped in such a manner that he shall use, only as accessory, the information given by the parents of the child, so that he may always be able to verify this information, or, when necessary, dispense with it....

The organization of methods is especially important because, as soon as the schools for subnormals are in operation, one must be on his guard against the attitude of the parents. Their sincerity will be worth very little when it is in conflict with their interests. If the parents wish the child to remain in the regular school, they will not be silent concerning his intelligence. "My child understands everything," they will say, and they will be very careful not to give any significant information in regard to him. If on the contrary, they wish him to be admitted into an institution where gratuitous board and lodging are furnished, they will change completely. They will be capable even of teaching him how to simulate mental debility. One should, therefore, be on his guard against all possible frauds.

In order to recognize the inferior states of intelligence we believe that three different methods should be employed. We have arrived at this synthetic view only after many years of research, but we are now certain that each of these methods renders some service. These methods are:

1. *The medical method,* which aims to appreciate the anatomical, physiological, and pathological signs of inferior intelligence.

2. *The pedagogical method,* which aims to judge of the intelligence according to the sum of acquired knowledge.

3. *The psychological method,* which makes direct observations and measurements of the degree of intelligence.

From what has gone before it is easy to see the value of each of these methods. The medical method is indirect because it conjectures the mental from the physical. The pedagogical method is more direct; but the psychological is the most direct of all because it aims to measure the state of the intelligence as it is at the present moment. It does this by experiments which oblige the subject to make an effort which shows his capability in the way of comprehension, judgment, reasoning, and invention.

THE PSYCHOLOGICAL METHOD

The fundamental idea of this method is the establishment of what we shall call a measuring scale of intelligence. This scale is composed of a series of tests of increasing difficulty, starting from the lowest intellectual level that can be observed, and ending with that of average normal intelligence. Each group in the series corresponds to a different mental level.

This scale properly speaking does not permit the measure of the intelligence, because intellectual qualities are not superposable, and therefore cannot be measured as linear surfaces are measured, but are on the contrary, a classification, a hierarchy among diverse intelligences; and for the necessities of practice this classification is equivalent to a measure. We shall therefore be able to know, after studying two individuals, if one rises above the other and to how many degrees, if one rises above the average level of other individuals considered as normal, or if he remains below. Understanding the normal progress of intellectual development among normals, we shall be able to determine how many years such an individual is advanced or retarded. In a word we shall be able to determine to what degrees of the scale idiocy, imbecility, and moronity correspond.

The scale that we shall describe is not a theoretical work; it is the result of long investigations, first at the Salpetriere, and afterwards in the primary schools of Paris, with both normal and subnormal children. These short psychological questions have been given the name of tests. The use of tests is today very common, and there are even contemporary authors who have made a specialty of organizing new tests according to theoretical views, but who have made no effort to patiently try them out in the schools. Theirs is an amusing occupation, comparable to a person's making a colonizing expedition into Algeria, advancing always only upon the map, without taking off his dressing gown. We place but slight confidence in the tests invented by these authors and we have borrowed nothing from them. All the tests which we propose have been repeatedly tried, and have been retained from among many, which after trial have been discarded. We can certify that those which are here presented have proved themselves valuable.

We have aimed to make all our tests simple, rapid, convenient, precise, heterogeneous, holding the subject in continued contact with the experimenter, and bearing principally upon the faculty of judgment. Rapidity is necessary for this sort of examination. It is impossible to prolong it beyond twenty minutes without fatiguing the subject. During this maximum of twenty minutes, it must be turned and turned about in every sense, and at least ten tests must be executed, so that not more than about two minutes can be given to each....

Another consideration. Our purpose is to evaluate a level of intelligence. It is understood that we here separate natural intelligence and instruction. It is the intelligence alone that we seek to measure, by disregarding in so far as possible, the degree of instruction which the subject possesses. He should, indeed, be considered by the examiner as a complete ignoramus knowing neither how to read nor write. This necessity forces us to forego a great many exercises having a verbal, literary or scholastic character. These belong to a pedagogical examination. We believe that we have succeeded in completely disregarding the acquired information of the subject. We give him nothing to read, nothing to write, and submit him to no test in which he might succeed by means of rote learning. In fact we do not even notice his inability to read if a case occurs. It is simply the level of his natural intelligence that is taken into account.

But here we must come to an understanding of what meaning to give to that word so vague and so comprehensive, "the intelligence." Nearly all the phenomena with which psychology concerns itself are phenomena of intelligence; sensation, perception, are intellectual manifestations as much as reasoning. Should we therefore bring into our examination the measure of sensation after the manner of the psycho-physicists? Should we put to the test all of his psychological processes? A slight reflection has shown us that this would indeed be wasted time.

It seems to us that in intelligence there is a fundamental faculty, the alteration or the lack of which, is of the utmost importance for practical life. This faculty is judgment, otherwise called good sense, practical sense, initiative, the faculty of adapting one's self to circumstances. To judge well, to comprehend well, to reason well, these are the essential activities of intelligence. A person may be a moron or an imbecile if he is lacking in judgment; but with good judgment he can never be either. Indeed the rest of the intellectual faculties seem of little importance in comparison with judgment. What does it matter, for example, whether the organs of sense function normally? Of what import that certain ones are hyperesthetic, or that others are anesthetic or are weakened? Laura Bridgman, Helen Keller and their fellow-unfortunates were blind as well as deaf, but this did not prevent them from being very intelligent. Certainly this is demonstrative proof that the total or even partial integrity of the senses does not form a mental factor equal to judgment. We may measure the acuteness of the sensibility of subjects; nothing could be easier. But we should do this, not so much to find out the state of their sensibility as to learn the exactitude of their judgment.

The same remark holds good for the study of the memory. At first glance, memory being a psychological phenomenon of capital importance, one would be tempted to give it a very conspicuous part in an examination of intelligence. But memory is distinct from and independent of judgment. One may have good sense and lack memory. The reverse is also common. Just at the present time we are observing a backward girl who is developing before our astonished eyes a memory very much greater than our own. We have measured that memory and we are not deceived regarding it. Nevertheless that girl presents a most beautifully classic type of imbecility.

As a result of all this investigation, in the scale which we present we accord the first place to judgment; that which is of importance to us is not certain errors which the subject commits, but absurd errors, which prove that he lacks judgment. We have even made special provision to encourage people to make absurd replies. In spite of the accuracy of this directing idea, it will be easily understood that it has been impossible to permit of its regulating exclusively our examinations. For example, one can not make tests of judgment on children of less than two years when one begins to watch their first gleams of intelligence. Much is gained when one can discern in them traces of coordination, the first delineation of attention and memory. We shall therefore bring out in our lists some tests of memory; but so far as we are able, we shall give these tests such a turn as to invite the subject to make absurd replies, and thus under cover of a test of memory, we shall have an appreciation of their judgment.

II

INTELLIGENCE DESCRIBED

This article by John L. Horn provides a good description of the theory of fluid and crystallized intelligence first proposed by Raymond B. Cattell. Fluid intelligence is related to "natural capacities," whereas crystallized intelligence develops out of the interaction of fluid intelligence with the culture in which the individual happens to be reared. Thus, crystallized intelligence is very culture-bound, formed by such factors as schooling and other culture-specific experiences. The two forms of intelligence tend to be correlated with each other, but they can be distinguished by means of various factor-analytic techniques and experimental designs that can trace changes in the two broad types of ability as people get older. Erudition is often mistaken for high general intelligence, whereas it probably is more closely related to the component of crystallized intelligence.

3

Intelligence—Why It Grows, Why It Declines

JOHN L. HORN

One of the oldest and most thoroughly studied concepts in psychology is the concept of intelligence. Yet the term "intelligence" still escapes precise definition. There are so many different kinds of behavior that are indicative of intelligence that identifying the essence of them all has seemed virtually impossible. However, some recent research indicates that much of the diversity seen in expressions of intelligence can be understood in terms of a relatively small number of concepts. What's more, this research has also given us insight into understanding where intelligence originates; how it develops; and why and when it increases or decreases.

Studies of the interrelationships among human abilities indicate that there are two basic types of intelligence: *fluid* intelligence and *crystallized* intelligence. Fluid intelligence is rather formless; it is relatively independent of education and experience; and it can "flow into" a wide variety of intellectual activities. Crystallized intelligence, on the other hand, is a precipitate out of experience. It results when fluid intelligence is "mixed" with what can be called "the intelligence of the culture." Crystallized intelligence increases with a person's experience, and with the education that provides new methods and perspectives for dealing with that experience.

These two major kinds of intelligence are composed of more elementary abilities, called "primary" mental abilities. The number of these primaries is small. Only about 30 can be accepted as really well-established. But with just these 30 primaries, we can explain much of the person-to-person variation commonly observed in reasoning, thinking, problem-solving, inventing, and understanding. Since several thousand tests have been devised to measure various aspects of intelligence, this system of primaries represents a very considerable achievement in parsimony. In much the same way that the chemical elements are organized according to the Periodic Law, these primary mental abilities fall into the patterns labeled fluid and crystallized intelligence.

Fluid Intelligence

What follows are some examples of the kinds of abilities that define fluid intelligence—and some of the tests that measure this kind of intelligence.

Induction is the ability to discover a general rule from several particular incidents and then apply this rule to cover a new incident.

For example, if a person observes the characteristics of a number of people who are members of a particular club or lodge, he might discover the rule by which membership is determined (even when this rule is highly secret information). He might then apply this rule to obtain an invitation to membership!

Among the tests that measure induction ability is the letter series. Given some letters in a series like

A C F J O—

the task is to provide the next letter. Of course, the test can be used only with people who know the alphabet, and this rules out illiterates and most children. We can't eliminate the influence of accumulated learning from even the purest examples of fluid intelligence.

Figural Relations refers to the ability to notice changes or differences in shapes and use this awareness to identify or produce one element missing from a pattern (Figure 3.1).

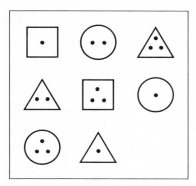

Figure 3.1
What figure fits into the lower right? (Answer: a square with two dots.)

. . .

Span of Apprehension is the ability to recognize and retain awareness of the immediate environment. A simple test is memory span: Several digits or other symbols are presented briefly, and the task is to reproduce them later, perhaps in reverse order. Without this ability, remembering a telephone number long enough to dial it would be impossible.

Other primary abilities that help define fluid intelligence include:

General Reasoning (example: extimating how long it would take to do several errands around town);

Semantic Relations (example: enjoying a pun on common words);

Deductive Reasoning, or the ability to reason from the general to the particular (example: noting that the wood of fallen trees rots and concluding that one should cover—for example, paint—wooden fence posts before inserting them into the ground);

Associative Memory, or the ability to aid memory by observing the relationships between separate items (example: remembering the way to grandmother's house by associating various landmarks en route, or remembering the traits of different people by association with their faces).

Crystallized Intelligence

Most of what we call intelligence—for example, the ability to make good use of language or to solve complex technical problems—is actually crystallized intelligence. Here are some of the primary abilities that demonstrate the nature of this kind of intelligence:

Verbal Comprehension. This could also be called general information, since it represents a broad slice of knowledge. Vocabulary tests, current-events tests, and reading-comprehension tests all measure verbal comprehension, as do other tests that require a person to recall information about his culture. The ability is rather fully exercised when one quickly reads an article like this one and grasps the essential ideas. Verbal comprehension is also called for when a person reads news items about foreign affairs, understands their implications, and relates them to one another and to their historical backgrounds.

Experiential Evaluation is often called "common sense" or "social intelligence." Experiential evaluation includes the ability to project oneself into situations, to feel as other people feel and thereby better understand interactions among people. Everyday examples include figuring out why a conscientious foreman is not getting good results from those under him, and why people disobey traffic laws more at some intersections than at others.

One test that measures experiential evaluation in married men is the following:

> Your wife has just invested time, effort, and money in a new hairdo. But it doesn't help her appearance at all. She wants your opinion. You should:
>
> 1. try to pretend that the hairdo is great;
> 2. state your opinion bluntly;
> 3. compliment her on her hairdo, but add minor qualifications; or,
> 4. refuse to comment.
>
> Answer 3 is considered correct—on the grounds that husbands can't get away with answers 1 and 4, and answer 2 is likely to provoke undue strife.

Formal Reasoning is reasoning in ways that have become more or less formalized in Western cultures. An example is the syllogism, like this one:

> No Gox box when in purple socks.
> Jocks is a Gox wearing purple socks.
> Therefore: Jocks does not now box.

The task is to determine whether or not the conclusion is warranted. (It is.)

An everyday example of formal reasoning might be to produce a well-reasoned analysis of the pros and cons of an issue presented to the United Nations. Formal reasoning, to a much greater extent than experiential evaluation or verbal comprehension, depends upon dealing with abstractions and symbols in highly structured ways.

Number Facility, the primary ability to do numerical calculations, also helps define crystallized intelligence, since to a considerable extent it reflects the quality of a person's education. In a somewhat less direct way, this quality is also represented in the primary abilities called mechanical knowledge, judgment, and associational fluency.

Semantic Relations and General Reasoning, listed as primary aspects of fluid intelligence, are also—when carrying a burden of learning and culture—aspects of crystallized intelligence. This points up the fact that, although fluid and crystallized intelligence represent distinct patterns of abilities, there is some overlap. This is what is known as *alternative mechanisms* in intellectual performance. In other words, a given kind of problem can sometimes be solved by exercise of different abilities.

Consider the general-reasoning primary, for example. In this, typical problems have a slightly mathematical flavor:

> There are 100 patients in a hospital. Some (an even number) are one-legged, but wearing shoes. One-half of the remainder are barefooted. How many shoes are being worn?

We may solve this by using a formal algebraic equation. Set x equal to the number of one-legged patients, with $100 - x$ then being the number of two-legged patients, and $x + \frac{1}{2}(100 - x)2$ being the number of shoes worn. We don't have to invent the algebraic techniques used here. They have been passed down to us over centuries. As Keith Hayes very nicely puts it, "The culture relieves us of much of the burden of creativity by giving us access to the products of creative acts scattered thinly through the history of the species." The use of such products is an important part of crystallized intelligence.

But this problem can also be solved by a young boy who has never heard of algebra! He may reason that, if half the two-legged people are without shoes, and all the rest (an even number) are one-legged, then the shoes must average one per person, and the answer must be 100. This response, too, represents learning—but it is not so much a product of education, or of the accumulated wisdom passed from one generation to the next, as is the typical product of crystallized intelligence. Fluid intelligence is composed of such relatively untutored skills.

Thus the same problem can be solved by exercise of *either* fluid intelligence *or* crystallized intelligence. We can also see the operation of such alternative mechanisms in these two problems.

ZEUS—JUPITER:	:ARTEMIS—?			
	Answer:	Phidias	Coria	*Diana*
HERE—NOW:	:THERE—?			
	Answer:	Thus	Sometimes	*Then*

The first problem is no harder to solve than the second, *provided* you have acquired a rather sophisticated knowledge of mythology. The second problem requires learning too, but no more than simply learning the language—a fact that puts native-born whites and Negroes on a relatively equal footing in dealing with problems of this sort, but places Spanish-speaking Puerto Ricans or Mexican-Americans at a disadvantage. As measures of fluid intelligence, both items are about equally good. But the first involves, to a much greater extent, crystallized intelligence gleaned from formal education or leisure reading.

Because the use of alternative mechanisms is natural in the play of human intelligence, most intelligence tests provide mixed rather than pure measures of fluid or crystallized abilities. This only reflects the way in which we usually go about solving problems—by a combination of natural wit and acquired strategies. But tests can be devised in which one type of intelligence predominates. For example, efforts to devise "culture fair" intelligence tests that won't discriminate against people from deprived educational or cultural backgrounds usually focus on holding constant the effect of crystallized capabilities—so that fluid capabilities can be more fully represented.

Now that we have roughly defined what fluid and crystallized intelligence are, let us investigate how each of them develops over time.

The infant, whose reasoning powers extend little beyond the observation that a determined howl brings food, attention, or a dry diaper, becomes the man who can solve legal problems all day, execute complicated detours to avoid the five o'clock traffic on his way home, and deliver a rousing speech to his political club in the evening. But how? To understand the intertwined development of the fluid and crystallized abilities that such activities require, we need to consider three processes essential to the development of intelligence: *anlage function*, the *acquisition of aids*, and *concept formation*.

Anlage function, which includes the complex workings of the brain and other nervous tissue, provides the physical base for all of the infant's future mental growth. ("Anlage" is a German word meaning "rudiment.") The second two factors—the aids and concepts the child acquires as he grows up—represent the building blocks that, placed on the anlage base, form the structure of adult intelligence.

The anlage function depends crucially and directly upon physiology. Physiology, in turn, depends partly on heredity, but it can also be influenced by injury, disease, poisons, drugs, and severe shock. Such influences can occur very early in life—often even in the womb. Hence it is quite possible that an individual's anlage functioning may have only a remote relationship to his hereditary potential. All we can say for sure is that the anlage process *is* closely tied to a physiological base.

A good everyday measure of a person's anlage functioning is his memory span (provided we can rule out the effects of anxiety, fatigue, or mental disturbance). Given a series of letters or numbers, most adults can immediately reproduce only about six or seven of them in reverse order. Some people may be able to remember 11, others as few as four, but in no case is the capacity unlimited or even very great. Memory span increases through childhood—probably on account of the increasing size and complexity of the brain—but it is not much affected by learning. This is generally true of other examples of anlage functioning.

Short-cuts to Learning

Aids are techniques that enable us to go beyond the limitations imposed by anlage functioning. An aid can, for example, extend our memory span. For example, we break up a telephone or social security number with dashes, transforming long numbers into short, more easily recalled sets, and this takes the strain off immediate memory.

Some aids, like the rules of algebra, are taught in school. But several psychologists (notably Jean Piaget) have demonstrated that infants and children also invent their own aids in their untutored explorations of the world. In development, this process probably continues for several years.

Concepts are categories we impose on the phenomena we experience. In forming concepts, we find that otherwise dissimilar things can be regarded as "the same" in some sense because they have common properties. For instance, children learn to distinguish the features associated with "bike"—two wheels, pedaling, riding outside, etc.—from those associated with "car." Very early in a child's development, these categories may be known and represented only in terms of his own internal symbols. In time, however, the child learns to associate his personal symbols with conventional signs—that is, he learns to use language to represent what he "knows" from direct experience. Also, increased proficiency in the use of language affords opportunities to see new relations and acquire new concepts.

The concepts we possess at any time are a residue of previous intellectual functioning. Tests that indicate the extent of this residue may, therefore, predict the level of a person's future intellectual development. A large vocabulary indicates a large storehouse of previously acquired concepts, so verbal ability itself is often taken as a good indication of ability to conceptualize. Many well-known tests of intelligence, especially of crystallized intelligence, are based on this rationale.

However, language is really only an indirect measure of concept awareness. Thus verbally oriented tests can be misleading. What about the child raised in an environment where language is seldom used, but which is otherwise rich in opportunity to perceive relationships and acquire concepts (the backwoods of Illinois, or by a pond in Massachusetts): At the extreme, what about a person who never hears the spoken word or sees the written word? He does not necessarily lack the awareness that we so glibly represent in language. Nor does he necessarily lack intelligence. A child who doesn't know the spoken or written word "key" surely understands the concept if he can distinguish a key from other small objects and use it to open a lock.

What is true of conventional language is also true of conventional aids. Lack of facility or familiarity with aids does not mean that a child has failed to develop intellectually, even though it may make him *appear* mentally slow on standard intelligence tests. Just as verbally oriented tests penalize the child who has not had the formal schooling or proper environment to develop a large vocabulary, many tests of so-called mathematical aptitude rely heavily on the use of conventional aids taught in school—on algebraic formulas, for example. Someone who has learned few of these conventional aids will generally do poorly on such tests, but this does not mean that he lacks intelligence.

We cannot overlook the fact that an intelligent woodsman may be just as intelligent, in one sense of this term, as an intelligent college professor. The particular combination of primary abilities needed to perform well may differ in the two cases, but the basic wherewithal of intellectual competence can be the same—adequate anlage functioning, plus an awareness of the concepts and a facility with the aids relevant to dealing with the environment at hand. Daniel Boone surely needed as much intelligence to chart the unexplored forests of the frontier as today's professor needs to thread his way through the groves of academe.

Education and Intelligence

It is obvious, then, that formal education is not essential to the development of important aspects of intelligence. Barring disruption of anlage functioning by accident or illness, the child will form concepts and devise aids to progressively expand his mental grasp as he grows up, and this will occur whether he goes to school or not.

Where formal instruction is significant is in making such development easier—and in passing along the concepts and aids that many people have deposited into the intelligence of a culture. The schools give children awareness of concepts that they may not have had the opportunity to gain from first-hand experience—the ability to recognize an Australian platypus, for example, without ever having seen one, or a knowledge of how the caste system works in India. Aids, too, are taught in school. A child well-armed with an array of mathematical formulas will likely be able to solve a problem faster and more accurately than one who must work it out completely on his own. Indeed, some problems simply cannot be solved without mathematical aids. Since the acquisition of both concepts and aids is cumulative, several years of formal education can put one child well ahead of another one, unschooled, who has roughly the same intellectual potential.

The Declining Years

Both fluid and crystallized intelligence, as we have just seen, develop with age. But intelligence also declines with age. This is especially true of the fluid kind. Looked at in terms of averages, fluid intelligence begins to decline before a person is out of his twenties. Crystallized intelligence fares better, however, and generally continues to increase throughout life. Because crystallized intelligence usually increases in this fashion, the decline in fluid abilities may not seriously undermine intellectual competence in people as they mature into middle age and even beyond. But let us look at these matters more analytically.

The graph (Figure 3.2) . . . represents results from several studies, each involving several hundred people. Notice, first, that the curves representing fluid intelligence (FI) and crystallized intelligence (CI) are at first indistinguishable, but become separate as development proceeds. This represents the fact that both are products of development. It also illustrates the fact that it is easier to distinguish between fluid intelligence and crystallized intelligence in adults than in children.

The maturation curve (M) summarizes evidence that the physical structures and processes that support intellect (the brain, for instance) grow and increase in complexity until the late teens or the early twenties. Development is rapid but decelerating. Since both fluid and crystallized intelligence depend on maturation, their curves more or less follow it.

But maturation accounts for only part of the change in the physical structures that support intelligence. They are also affected by injuries, such as birth complications, blows to the head, carbon monoxide poisoning, intoxication, and high fever. Such injuries are irreversible and thus cumulative. In the short run, they are difficult to discern, and their effects are masked during childhood by the rising curves of learning and maturation. In the long run, however, injuries resulting from the exposures of living take their toll. The older the person, the greater the exposure. Thus, part of the physiological base for intellectual functioning will, on an average, decrease with age (curve PB).

The sum of the influences represented by M and PB form the physiological base for intellectual processes at any particular time. In the early years, the effects of one compensate for the effects of the other. But as the

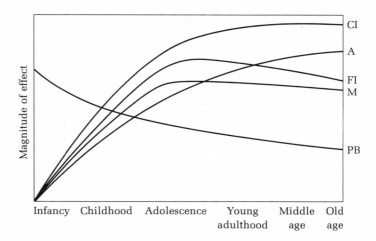

Figure 3.2

Development of fluid intelligence (FI) and crystallized intelligence (CI) in relation to effects produced by maturation (M), acculturation (A), and loss of physiological base (PB) as a result of injury.

M curve levels off in young adulthood and the PB curve continues downward, the total physiological base drops. Those intellectual abilities that depend very directly upon physiology must then decline.

The effects of brain tissue loss are variable, however. At the physiological level, an ability is a complex network of neurons that "fire" together to produce observable patterns of behavior. Such networks are overdetermined—not all of the neurons in the network need to "fire" to produce the behavior. And some networks are much more overdetermined than others. This means that when a loss of brain tissue (that is, a loss of neurons) occurs, some networks, and hence some abilities, will be only minimally affected. Networks that are not highly overdetermined, though, will become completely inoperative when a critical number of neurons cease to fire.

The crystallized abilities apparently correspond to highly overdetermined neural networks. Such abilities will not be greatly affected by moderate loss of neurons. The fluid abilities, on the other hand, depend much more significantly upon anlage functions, which are represented by very elementary neural networks. These abilities will thus "fall off" with a loss of neurons.

Curve A in the graph shows how, potentially at least, the effects of acculturation and positive transfer may accumulate throughout a lifetime. On this basis alone, were it not for neural damage, we might expect intelligence to increase, not decline, in adulthood.

Whether intellectual decline occurs or not will depend upon the extent of neuron loss, ,and upon whether learning new aids and concepts can compensate for losing old skills. For example, the anlage capacity to keep six digits in immediate awareness may decline with loss of neurons. But the individual, sensing this loss, may develop new techniques to help him keep a number in mind. Thus the overall effect may be no loss of ability. What the evidence does indicate, however, is that, with increasing age beyond the teens, there is a steady, if gentle, decline in fluid intelligence. This suggests that learning new aids and concepts of the fluid kind does not quite compensate for the loss of anlage function and the loss of previously learned aids and concepts.

On a happier note, and by way of contrast, the evidence also shows that crystallized intelligence *increases* throughout most of adulthood. Here alternative mechanisms come into play. Compensating for the loss of one ability with the surplus of another, the older person uses crystallized intelligence in place of fluid intelligence. He substitutes accumulated wisdom for brilliance, while the younger person does the opposite.

A word of caution about these results. They represent averages, and averages can be affected by a relatively few extreme cases. For example, if only a relatively few individuals experience brain damage, but the effect is rather pronounced in each case, this will show up in the averages. If such damage occurs more frequently with older people than with younger people, a corresponding decline of abilities with age will show up—even though such decline may not be an inevitable aspect of aging for everyone. But even though these cautions must be kept in mind, we should not lose track of the fact that the FI curve parallels the PB in adulthood.

Intelligence tests that measure mixtures of fluid and crystallized intelligence (and most popular ones do) show varying relationships between aging and intelligence in adulthood. If fluid tests predominate, decline is indicated. If crystallized intelligence is well represented, then there is no apparent decline.

Intellectual performance in important jobs in life will depend on both kinds of intelligence, and may be represented by a composite curve (FI and CI in the graph in Figure 3.3).

Notice that the peak of this curve occurs later than the peak of the FI curve below it. If fluid intelligence reaches its peak in the early twenties, intelligence in overall performance, influenced by the cultural accretion, may peak in the thirties. The evidence indicates that the greatest intellectual *productivity* tends to occur in the thirties or early forties, although the most *creative* work often is accomplished earlier. For example, half of the

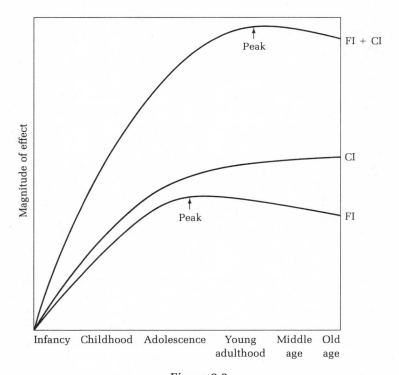

Figure 3.3

Fluid intelligence, crystallized intelligence, and the effect of the two added together.

52 greatest discoveries in chemistry (as judged by chemists) were made before the innovator had reached age 29, and 62 percent were made before he was 40. It would seem that creativity and productivity represent somewhat different combinations of fluid and crystallized intelligence, with productivity being relatively more affected by cultural factors.

The age at which the combined FI and CI function peaks varies from one person to another, depending on the development of new concepts and aids, the amount of brain damage, and other factors such as diet and general health.

Perhaps the most interesting result of all this recent work is the questions it provokes. What are the factors producing the apparent decline in fluid intelligence? Are they intrinsic to aging, or do they merely reflect the hazards of living? Are they associated with the hazards of different occupations? Do auto mechanics, for example, who are repeatedly exposed to carbon monoxide, show more decline in fluid intelligence than cement finishers, who work in the open air?

Most important of all, what experiences in infancy and childhood have favorable or unfavorable effects on the future growth of fluid intelligence? Of crystallized intelligence? Of both? Do experiences that affect fluid intelligence always affect crystallized intelligence, too? We are still far from finding firm and comprehensive answers to these questions, but they very clearly hold massive implications for our child-rearing practices, for our educational system, and for the whole complex of fields that bear on the development and management of human potential.

In this article, Drs. Hunt, Lunneborg, and Lewis write from the perspective of experimental cognitive psychology, which views the individual as an information processor. This branch of psychology tries to identify the various processes that are necessary for the registration, storage, and retrieval of information by breaking down cognitions into their component parts. This is done by devising experimental techniques that control for all components of information processing except for the component under investigation. You will see in the article that this approach leads to insights about the underlying features that enter into a wide variety of intellectual performances. Do not be discouraged if you find this article challenging reading. The article is hard to read, but it is of sufficient importance to merit the effort needed for comprehension.

4

What Does It Mean to Be High Verbal?

EARL HUNT, CLIFFORD LUNNEBORG, AND JOE LEWIS

Almost twenty years ago Cronbach (1957) deplored the existence of two disciplines of scientific psychology; the psychometrician who measures differences between individuals without much concern for the process by which subjects attack tests, and the experimental psychologist who studies processes in general, without regard for the differences between individuals. At the time Cronbach wrote, intelligence tests, based on a sophisticated theory of multidimensional measurement, were often heralded as psychology's greatest technological achievement. There were several theories of how man processes information in general (e.g., the Gestalt view and various adaptations of S-R learning theory), but within experimental psychology the study of cognition was not considered a rapidly developing area. In hindsight, the psychometricians of the 1940s and 1950s were probably quite correct in being disinterested in expla-

Hunt, E. B., Lunneborg, C., and Lewis, J. "What Does It Mean to Be High Verbal?" *Cognitive Psychology*, 1975, Vol. 7, pp. 194–227. Copyright © by Academic Press, Inc., and reprinted by permission.

nations of individual differences based on the then-current theories of cognition.

Today the situation is drastically changed. Cognitive psychology has shifted its philosophical position to a world view of man as an information processor, and as a result it is a thriving field of scientific investigation. Psychometrics, by contrast, has remained fairly static. The dominant social attitude toward intelligence has changed from one of approval to one of censure. This, however, must reflect a change in society's values since little new evidence concerning the tests themselves has been obtained.

These observations present a challenge to scientists interested in the study of cognition. On both scientific and social philosophical grounds, it seems a dubious procedure to base decisions on a measure, without a theory of how the measure works. We ought to measure cognitive power by use of an instrument whose design is based on our understanding of the cognitive process. The current article addresses this point, but somewhat indirectly. Directly we address ourselves to a related point. Does the present intelligence test (actually a composite of several specialized subtests) differentiate between individuals who also differ in ways in which a modern cognitive psychologist will find theoretically interesting? If they do, is this finding more than a tautology? Clearly we would have discovered little if we found that the tests a cognitive psychologist devises are, on their face, only slightly changed variants of the subtests of the present intelligence test. It would be more interesting if we found that the psychometric tests require one sort of ability, and the cognitive psychologist's tasks require another, but the same individuals who possess (or lack) one set of abilities possess or lack the other.

Intelligence is too global a term for such a discussion, since psychometrically defined intelligence consists of a number of separate factors. Guilford and Hoepfner (1971) distinguish more than 100 separate components, and virtually all psychometric theories distinguish at least two kinds of intelligence. We shall report studies of the information processing capabilities of people with varying degrees of *verbal ability* as defined by the Washington Pre-College Test (WPCT), a standard, group-administered test used to evaluate the academic potential of high school juniors in the state of Washington.* The WPCT consists of several subtests, whose scores are combined in varying ways to yield different composites. The verbal composite score is a weighted sum of four subtests; English Usage, Spelling, Reading Comprehension, and Vocabulary. English Usage requires the student to detect errors in capitalization, punctuation, grammar, usage, diction, and idiom; Spelling calls for the recognition of misspellings; Reading Comprehension presents the student with a series of paragraphs, each followed by a set of questions relating to the content of the para-

---

* For all practical purposes, the WPCT is interchangeable with the Educational Testing Service's more widely used Scholastic Achievement Test (SAT), the "College Board."

graph; and Vocabulary asks that a synonym be selected from among a set of alternatives for each of a series of stem words. Each test is in multiple choice format. The composite "verbal ability" score is defined by

$$
\begin{aligned}
(1)\ \text{Verbal Composite} = \ &(.22)\ \text{English Usage} \\
&+ (.33)\ \text{Spelling} \\
&+ (.29)\ \text{Reading Comprehension} \\
&+ (.33)\ \text{Vocabulary} \\
&- 8.94
\end{aligned}
$$

Each of the four contributing scores is in standard form with a mean of 50 and standard deviation of 10 for the high school normative population. The resulting verbal composite is in that same metric. The weights are based upon a factor analysis of the WPCT, and define a verbal factor. Verbal Composite scores so defined are generally the best single predictors of academic success (Lavin, 1965). When we refer to "verbal ability" our operational definition will be the composite defined by (1).

Intuitively, a person with "high verbal ability" should be glib of tongue, quick to pick up nuances in the language, and generally alert to information conveyed by either written or oral speech. We also expect the "high verbal" to show superior performance in the basic perceptual and motor skills involved in speech. A contrasting, less pleasant picture can be drawn for the low verbal. But let us consider the operational definition of verbal ability. Performance in the subtests of (1) is determined largely by what a person knows; the meaning of words, syntactic rules, and semantic relations between concepts denoted by words. None of the subtests measure aptitudes for recognizing letters or other highly overlearned codes, since all people taking the tests recognize these codes perfectly. The emphasis is on tests of knowledge.

In experimental psychology, by contrast, studies of cognition are usually designed so that extra-experimental knowledge will not be a factor in performance. The paradigm developed by Posner, Boies, Eichelman and Taylor (1969) is a good example. This task requires that the subject identify two printed letters as being "same" or "different" in accordance with their name, regardless of type case (e.g., A is the same as a.) The only thing a subject must know is the alphabet, in upper and lower case. This information is possessed by a substantial majority of American university students.

Experimental psychologists do deal at considerable length with the processes by which people detect stimuli, locate them in time and space, and coordinate them with respect to stored representations of highly overlearned codes. Experimental psychologists also study the process by which people integrate sequences of stimuli over time to form a stable percept, and how they operate upon this percept, coordinate it with stored percepts, transform it during problem solving, and eventually abstract information from the percept and place it in long-term memory. Let us refer to all these processes, collectively, as *Current Information Processing* (CIP). CIP obviously makes use of the particular information stored in long-term memory (LTM), but experiments are generally designed so that performance depends only on LTM information held by all subjects.

CIP has been described by analogy to sets of memory buffers and attached processors in a computer system (Atkinson and Shiffrin, 1968; Atkinson and Westcourt, 1974; Hunt, 1971, 1973; Hunt and Poltrock, 1974). Very generally, these theorists see information as being received simultaneously on several channels, each of which has its attached buffer memories. The channel buffers may make direct, and parallel, contact with LTM to arouse learned codes describing the current stimuli, e.g., during the translation from an acoustic signal to a recognized word. At some point the stimulus will be coded to a level at which it enters conscious short-term memory (STM). At this point a "time tag" is assigned to the perceived code. As items are assembled into STM they are temporally integrated into a coherent whole, as in the recognition of the meaning of a sentence. The argument is particularly striking for speech, although similar effects have been reported for other stimuli, including the perceptions built up from a sequence of visual scenes (Neisser, personal communication). Further manipulation of the internal representation may occur after the percept is formed, as in the transformation of mental images which occurs during certain types of spatial problem solving (Cooper and Shepard, 1973).

We shall focus our attention on the following characteristics of CIP activity; (a) the sensitivity of overlearned codes to arousal by incoming stimulus information, (b) the accuracy with which temporal tags can be assigned, and hence order information can be processed, and (c) the speed with which the internal representations in STM and intermediate-term memory (ITM, memory for events occurring over minutes) can be created, integrated, and altered.* The remainder of this article reports several studies relating these three CIP activities to one's verbal ability, as computed by Equation (1). There are two reasons for expecting to find relationships between psychometric intelligence and CIP capability. One is the intuitive expectation that, even if the intelligence test is not a direct measure of information processing, somehow we think that the more intelligent are also the more alert. We repeat our basic point. This may well be the case, but if so, it is an empirical fact to be established. The conclusion does not follow from a straightforward examination of psychometric intelligence tests. The second reason for expecting a relationship is more pro-

---

* We use the term intermediate-term memory (ITM) to refer to the process of holding information for a period of minutes. It would be consistent with much current usage to refer to this as long-term memory (LTM), but we prefer to reserve the latter term for the storage of information over days and even years. For elaboration of this viewpoint, see Hunt (1971, 1973) and Anderson and Bower (1973).

saic; preliminary work has indicated that such a relationship exists (Hunt, Frost, and Lunneborg, 1973). We shall first review the earlier studies, and then present some more complete data.

General Procedure

Our general procedure has been to contrast groups of university students of varying intelligence. "High verbal" subjects were defined as those students scoring in the upper quartile of WPCT verbal composite scores in the University of Washington freshman class for 1971–1972 or 1972–1973. "Low verbals" were similarly defined by the lower quartile. Since the University of Washington's student body is generally selected for scholastic ability, "high verbals" as identified by us can be considered to be high verbal with respect to the general population. Our "low verbal" subjects are better described as being of average verbal ability with respect to the population at large. This is shown in Figure 4.1, which depicts the distribution of verbal ability scores for all college bound high school seniors in Washington state. Our "high" and "low" ranges are superimposed on this distribution.*

Students eligible to serve as subjects were contacted by telephone or mail, and offered employment at the prevailing hourly rate for unskilled student help. The amount of money each participant earned depended upon the particular experiments in which they served as subjects.

Overview of Previous Results

Hunt et al. (1973) found that high verbal subjects appeared to manipulate information in STM more rapidly than low verbals. They based their conclusion on an experiment using Sternberg's (1975) memory scanning paradigm. In this task the subject is shown from one to five characters, displayed simultaneously for three seconds. Following this a probe character is shown. The subject's task is to indicate whether or not the probe was a member of the original set of characters. Many studies have found that reaction time (RT) is a linear function of n, the number of items in the original display. The slope of this function is interpreted as a measure of the time required to access and examine a single character stored in STM. Hunt et al. (1973) found that the slope of the RT for high verbals was reliably less than for low verbals (approximately 60 msec vs 80 msec per item). They took this as an indication that high verbals could search STM faster than low verbals. A puzzling aspect of their study, however,

---

* As there is probably self selection of the high school students who take the WPCT, the distribution of Figure 4.1 is itself biased toward containing fewer low scores than would be expected in a random sample of all high school juniors.

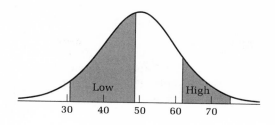

Figure 4.1

Ranges of low and high verbal university freshman in the
normal distribution of college-bound high school juniors.

was that the values of the slopes for both groups were much higher than
the range of slopes typically found using this paradigm. Most studies in
the literature report reaction times in the range of 30–50 msec per item.
Although the discrepancy may be because Hunt et al. did not use prac-
ticed subjects, as is typically done, the failure to find values comparable to
those obtained in many other laboratories is disturbing.

The order in which stimuli are observed is important in life. "John
loves Mary" is not the same as "Mary loves John." Estes (1972) has shown
that retention of the identity of items in STM and retention of the order of
their presentation are experimentally separable processes. Hunt et al.
(1973) report an experiment by Nix indicating that high verbals are especially sensitive to order information. Nix's procedure was based on the
release from proactive inhibition (PI release) phenomenon investigated by
Wickens and his associates (Wickens, 1972). In a PI release study subjects
are shown three words, then required to count backwards or do some other
interfering task for several seconds, and finally to recall the words presented in their correct order. If this procedure is repeated for several trials,
each trial using words in the same semantic category (e.g., vegetable
names), recall will be very good on the first trial but will progressively
decline. By the fourth trial recall is typically very poor. This is interpreted
as a demonstration of proactive inhibition, since stimuli presented on the
first n trials interfere with recall of those presented on the n + 1st trial.
Now suppose that the procedure just described is followed for the first
three trials, but on the fourth trial the semantic class of the stimuli is
changed (e.g., from vegatables to occupations). PI release is observed if
correct recall jumps to a higher level of performance than would be observed if the semantic class had not been changed. The phenomenon is
often a striking one, with recall jumping from near zero (for the fourth trial
of a control group) to near perfect following the change of categories.

Nix found that on the fourth trial of a PI release study high verbals
displayed PI release phenomenon markedly, while low verbals did not.
This difference was only shown, however, if the data were scored for recall

of the words in the correct order. When responses were scored as correct if they contained the appropriate words, regardless of order, then both groups showed the PI release effect. Nix's data clearly showed that the high verbals were more proficient than low verbals in retaining order information. On the other hand, this superiority was revealed by the manipulation of a semantic variable. It is not clear why changing semantic category should have any effect at all on one's ability to retain information about the order of presentation of words.

The question of differential sensitivity to semantic information was attacked directly in a third study, based on a procedure developed by Posner, Boies, Eichelman, and Taylor (1969). The subject is shown two letters which may vary either in identity (A or B) or type case (A or a) or both (A or b). The task is to identify the letters as "same" or "different." In the *physical identity* condition the subject is instructed to respond "same" only if the two letters are exactly identical, i.e., one of the pairs (AA,aa,BB,bb). In the *name identity* condition characters are to be identified as identical if they refer to the same letter, regardless of type case. Posner et al. (1969) have found that it requires about 70 msec longer for a subject to make a name identification than a physical identification. This presumably reflects the added time required to retrieve the name associated with each character. Hunt et al. (1973) found that the corresponding values were 33 msecs for high verbal subjects and 86 msecs for low verbals. If reliable, this is an extremely interesting result, for it indicates that high verbals can access highly overlearned material in LTM more rapidly than can low verbals. (It does not seem reasonable to maintain that "low verbal" college students do not know the alphabet.) Unfortunately, Hunt et al. (1973) used very few subjects in their study, and the data were only marginally significant ($p < .08$ for the crucial comparison).

In summary, the sheer number of results of Hunt et al. (1973) indicates that there is a relation between psychometrically defined intelligence and information processing. The specific experiments can be accepted only with reservations. Our first concern, therefore, was to attempt to reach the same conclusions as Hunt et al. (1973), but by using either different techniques or technically more reliable designs. Our second concern was to gain further information about the relationship between psychometrically defined verbal ability and information processing capacity.

EXPERIMENTS ON NAME ACCESSING AND CODE AROUSAL

"Being verbal" implies an ability to interpret arbitrary stimuli as part of the speech system. In dealing with written speech one must make a translation from an arbitrary visual code to its name. We regarded the Posner et al. (1969) name vs physical identity paradigm as the most direct test of this ability, and therefore our first concern was to repeat the experiment of Hunt et al. (1973) using this paradigm, in order to establish the reliability of their results.

The second experiment explored the ability to arouse long-term codes in a slightly different way. We asked if subjects with high verbal ability were more adept at arousing a "name code" in a situation in which the code was created by integrating two different stimuli over time.

Experiment 1. Experiment 1 was basically a repetition of the previous study using the Posner et al. (1969) paradigm. A second condition of the experiment offered us a chance to draw the same sort of conclusion using a different experimental procedure.

SUBJECTS. The subjects were twenty high and twenty low verbals recruited in the manner described previously.

PROCEDURE. The experiment consisted of two separate parts which, although they used the same subjects and were addressed to the same question, can logically be thought of as two distinct experiments.

The *computer display* data were from a replication of the Posner et al. (1969) *name instruction* condition, using both physically identical and name identical stimuli. That is, the subject was instructed to call two letters "identical" if they had the same name. The stimuli presented included physically identical (AA), name identical (aA) and different (aB) pairs. Posner et al. (1969) have found that the difference in the reaction time to physically and name identical stimuli appears in this situation. Using the name identity instructions has the added advantage that the subject cannot adopt a "set" toward name or physical identification and still optimize performance.

The stimuli were presented on a computer driven display screen. Responses were made by pressing two keys marked "same" or "different." The subject's preferred hand rested on top of the keys as the stimuli were presented. Prior to beginning the experiment, subjects were given 40 practice trials, followed by 320 trials containing 80 name identical pairs, 80 physical identity pairs, and 160 trials with letter pairs that were not physically or name identical (i.e., a B and an A in either upper or lower case). Median reaction times (RTs) for each subject were computed for physical and name identical trials.

In the *card sorting* study, which followed immediately, subjects sorted 3 × 5 in. cards with two letters (A,B,a,b, as before) on each card. The cards were to be sorted into "identical" and "different" piles under either physical identity or name identity instructions. Cards were sorted in decks of twenty, chosen to have an equal number of "identical" and "nonidentical" pairs under the appropriate instructions. Each deck was sorted three times in succession, with the experimenter rearranging the cards after each sorting. The first two decks were sorted under physical identity in-

Table 4.1

Means of median reaction time for same–different
identifications using computer-controlled display (msec)

Subjects	(1) Name identical trials	(2) Physically identical trials	(1)–(2)
High verbals	588.1	524.5	63.6
Low verbals	631.7	542.8	88.9

structions. The data from the first deck were disregarded, to weaken practice effects. The third deck was sorted under name identity instructions. The data reported are based on average times to sort each deck computed over three sortings.

RESULTS.   Fewer than 5% errors were made in the identification of letter pairs in the computer display phase. No differences across type of subject were noted. Table 4.1 shows the means of the median reaction times for correct name and physical identity identifications. Table 4.2 shows similar data for the time required to sort card decks under name or physical identity instructions. Accuracy in card sorting was virtually perfect. In both cases an analysis of variance showed that the interaction between type of identity or instruction and verbal ability was significant at less than the .05 level. Combining these results with the previous work of Hunt et al. (1973) there can be little doubt about the statistical reliability of the phenomenon.

. . .

EXPERIMENTS ON SPEED OF PROCESSING

The next two experiments [one experiment deleted] represent direct tests of the proposition that high verbal subjects are more rapid at processing information in simple verbal tasks where knowledge is not a problem. For the most part speed was the only question in the tasks we used, for the subjects were all quite capable of perfect information processing if time

Table 4.2

Mean time in seconds to sort 20 cards under varying instructions

Subjects	(1) Name identification	(2) Physical identification	(1)–(2)
High verbals	14.74	13.68	1.06
Low verbals	16.07	14.35	1.72

pressures were removed. We assert this because all our subjects were university students and, as will be seen, the accuracy demands of these tasks were quite low.

*Experiment 6: The Sunday + Tuesday Task.** A number of investigators have used reaction times in mental arithmetic as indicators of complex information processing. Consider the simple task of adding two numbers, $N1 + N2$, where $N1$ and $N2$ are both decimal digits. To make the analysis more complete, imagine that the task is as follows:

a. Present $N1$. Wait until the subject indicates he is ready.

b. Present $N2$. The subject responds with the sum of $N1$ and $N2$. The subject is required to go through the following internal steps.

1. Convert $N1$ into its internal representation.

2. Similarly, convert $N2$ on its presentation.

3. Add the two internal representations. If the sum exceeds the modulus of the number system being used, mark a carry bit and determine the amount by which the modulus has been exceeded.

4. Convert the answer from an internal representation to an external representation, and respond.

The above account is logical, from a computer-oriented viewpoint, but is probably too simplistic for college students and simple arithmetic. It is likely that many subjects will simply have memorized the sums of all pairs of digits, so that "mental arithmetic" becomes a test of long-term retention of paired associates. Also, decimal mental arithmetic involving small integers is so rapid in adults that it may be hard to time. We therefore altered the task in two significant ways. First, we forced subjects to do arithmetic in base 7, 12, or 26. Second, we used nonnumeric ordered lists (the days of the week, the months, and the alphabet) as external representations. Subjects were asked to think of the days of the week and/or the letters as representing integers, and then to add them. To illustrate, suppose one is asked to add MONDAY + THURSDAY. The presumed steps are as follows:

1. Enter the list of days. Locate MONDAY = 1.

2. Retain the internal representation of 1.

3. Locate THURSDAY = 4.

4. Find the internal representation of 4.

5. Add $4 + 1 = 5$.

6. Is $5 < 7$? Yes.

7. Locate the fifth item (FRIDAY) on the list of days.

8. Output FRIDAY.

---

* This experiment was designed and conducted by John Bolland. Clifford Lunneborg conducted the data analysis.

Note that if the answer had been "No" at step 6 it would have been necessary to subtract 7 from the answer to determine which item was to be located on the list of days.

The essence of this task is that it requires a number of data manipulation steps, involving searches of both LTM and STM. All the long-term memory information (order of days, months, letters) is certainly highly overlearned by college student subjects. Therefore any difference in performance between high and low verbals can reasonably be assigned to differences in speed of information processing rather than differences in knowledge.

PROCEDURE.   The subjects in this experiment were the same forty-nine subjects who participated in Experiment 3....

The equipment arrangement was the same as in Experiment 5. Each problem was presented on three slides. The first was a blank fixation slide, which appeared for three seconds. The second slide presented the first addend, which subjects were instructed to examine until they were ready for the second addend. At this time the subject pushed the button, which activated the projector and presented the second slide. The subject then spoke the sum, activating the voice key on the throat microphone. The experimenter recorded the response at this point. The next warning (blank) slide was then presented. The two times recorded were the time of exposure of the first slide (T_1) and the time from exposure of the second slide until the subject produced the sum (T_2).

Problems were presented in five sets. The first set of ten problems consisted of number pairs, with numbers varying from 1 to 10. The second through fourth set of problems consisted of eleven addition problems involving either days, months, or letters. The six possible orderings of problems were systematically varied across subjects within levels of verbal ability. The final set of problems consisted of blocks of six problems each of the number, day, month, and letter type. All 24 possible orderings of blocks within this set were used. The various counterbalancings can be summarized by noting that all subjects saw the same 67 problems (16 number, 17 each for day, month, and letter problems) but in different orders, with no two subjects within a verbal ability level group seeing the same order.

RESULTS.   Analysis of gross reaction times $(T_1 + T_2)$ and errors indicated that the high verbals were both more accurate and more rapid than the low verbals in day, month, and letter addition. There were no differences between groups in the (very easy) number addition problems. Furthermore, the advantage displayed by the high verbals increased as the problems became more difficult, i.e., as the base of the number system increased, from days to months to letters. These results are summarized by the point biserial correlations shown in Table 4.3.

In order to understand the greater processing speed of high verbals, the

Table 4.3

Point biserial correlations between verbal ability, time
to solve addition problems and accuracy of solution

Variable	Point biserial correlations
$T_1 + T_2$, "days" addition	−.29
$T_1 + T_2$, "months" addition	−.34
$T_1 + T_2$, "letters" addition	−.38
Proportion problems correct, "days" addition	.10
Proportion problems correct, "months" addition	.23
Proportion problems correct, "letters" addition	.31

data for this study were analyzed on the basis of a model of problem
solution which states that (a) the subject first accesses the appropriate
ordered list (digits, letters, days, or months) and determines the correct
numerical values and (b) then performs the addition numerically, doing a
subsidiary numerical subtraction if the base is exceeded, and, finally, re-
converts the numerical answer to the appropriate code. This model suggested that relevant differences in task demand among the 67 problems
could be captured by the following variables:

X_1—Days variable, taking the value 1 for problems involving the addition
of days and the value 0 for other problems;

X_2—Months variable, taking the value 1 for month addition problems and
0 otherwise;

X_3—Letters variable, taking the value 1 for letter addition problems and 0
otherwise;

X_4—Size of first addend, given by the position of the addend in the appropriate ordered list (Wednesday = 3, October = 10, W = 23);

X_5—Size of the second addend;

X_6—Amount by which first addend exceeds the second (0 if second
addend is larger);

X_7—Amount by which second addend exceeds the first (0 if first addend is
larger);

X_8—Carry variable, taking the value 1 if the sum of the addends exceeds
the base and 0 otherwise; and

X_9—Size of sum (if no carry) or of remainder (if carry is required). (Variables X_6 and X_7, though not explicit in the model, were included to tap the
effect of any shift in adding strategy dependent upon a discrepancy between
the terms.)

Variables X_1–X_9 (or a subset) were then used as independent variables
in a series of intra-individual linear regression analyses. Separate analyses
were conducted for each subject, taking encoding time (T_1), solution time

(T_2), and total problem time $(T_1 + T_2)$ as successive dependent variables. Each analysis defines a set of multiplicative constants or weights for the independent variables and an additive constant. The size of a particular weight can be interpreted as indicating the importance to the subject of the associated variable in accounting for differences between problems in response time. Our interest here was not in the individual weights but in contrasting the weights for the low and high verbal subjects.

Table 4.4 reports point biserial correlations between verbal group (high–low) and the regression or weighting constants for the three series of analyses. Negative correlations reflect larger weights (i.e., more responsiveness to the variable being weighted) in the low verbal group.

Group differences on T_1 (time to code the first addend) were slight, although there is the suggestion that this difference increases as the base of the addend increases, at least beyond days or, perhaps, months. The differences in total response times between verbal groups noted in Table 4.3 are almost entirely due to differences in T_2 (time during which computations actually take place). In terms of the model underlying these analyses, the strongest effects on verbal group response times are due to type of code and the presence or absence of a carry.

The larger additive constant for high verbals in the T_2 and $T_1 + T_2$ analyses reflects a greater consistency in their performance. They were less affected than low verbals by change in the form of a problem.

Analysis of total time to solution indicated that the high verbal subjects had a relatively greater advantage as the problems became harder. If this is so, the difference should be most apparent where there is a "quantum jump" in problem difficulty. Intuitively we would expect two such jumps in this task. The first would come when we change from the highly over-

Table 4.4*

Independent variable	Dependent variable		
	T_1	T_2	$T_1 + T_2$
Days (X_1)	.04	−.35	−.29
Months (X_2)	−.11	−.52	−.47
Letters (X_3)	−.27	−.28	−.37
Size A_1 (X_4)	−.18		·.00
Size A_2 (X_5)		−.25	−.25
$A_1 - A_2$ Difference (X_6)		−.12	−.08
$A_1 - A_2$ Difference (X_7)		−.23	−.23
Carry (X_8)		−.27	−.30
Size of Remainder (X_9)		−.02	−.16
Additive Constant	−.02	.31	.40

* Point biserial correlations between verbal group and regression coefficients for predicting addition task response times ($|r| \geq .27$, $p < .05$; $|r| \geq .36$, $p < .01$).

Table 4.5

Point biserial correlations
between verbal ability and the
difference between times on
different pairs of problem types

Days–numbers	−.35
Months–days	−.32
Letters–months	.02

learned number addition to some form of coded addition. The second jump should occur when we increase the base of the code above the familiar base 10. (Note that this is an assumption about the importance of arithmetic processes in the model, and states that the length of the list of code items is a relatively minor effect). These hypotheses can be tested by determining the point biserial correlations between verbal ability and the difference in total solution times for different pairs of problem types. The appropriate data are reported in Table 4.5, and clearly supports the hypotheses. Changing from months to letters has essentially no differential impact on the two groups.

These results are based on an analysis of response times for all trials. A similar analysis of response times on the (variable number of) trials on which the correct answer was reported produced coefficients which did not differ significantly from those reported here.

Discussion

University students who obtain high scores on a conventional paper and pencil test of verbal ability do unusually well on a variety of CIP tasks. We conclude that although a verbal intelligence test is directly a measure of what people know, it is indirectly a way of identifying people who can code and manipulate verbal stimuli rapidly in situations in which knowledge per se is not a major factor.

One of the most interesting superior abilities displayed by the high verbal is the ability to make a rapid conversion from a physical representation to a conceptual meaning, e.g., to recognize a particular visual pattern as a word or letter. Atkinson and Westcourt (1974) remark that this is a basic step in cognition, since the world impinges on us with physical stimuli, but our cognition is based on the manipulation of concepts. Another interesting superior ability of the high verbal is the ability to retain in STM information about the order of stimulus presentation. We have not explored the ramifications of this to any great extent. We do note, however, that this ability is assumed and used heavily in all psycholinguistic models of speech comprehension (e.g., Schank, 1973). We do not claim that "low verbals" cannot retain order information, for they obviously can. To do so, however, low verbals may have to spend more time recovering order information from the context of the situation, while the high verbals can rely on an internally assigned time tag. This would allow the high verbal subjects more time to deploy their mental machinery upon the task of extracting meaning from the input. Finally, the high verbal subjects appear to be more rapid in the manipulation of data in short term memory, as evidenced by their performance on scanning and simple computational tasks. Considering the number of such transformations that speech requires, this is certainly a useful ability.

Many of the tasks we have used conform to the classical "Donders task," in that they consist of a base component and, in some conditions, an added component. The physical identification-name identification task is a good example. Before retrieving a name code one clearly must recognize a physical code. Our interest has focused upon the interaction between groups of subjects and the increased amount of information processing required by the "added component" task. It should be noted that we consistently find small, though not statistically significant differences, between high and low verbal subjects on the base task as well as upon the added component. This is not in conflict with the classical finding that intelligence is not related to "simple" reaction time, because each of our base tasks typically contain an element of choice. Keele has speculated that although motor reaction times are not correlated with intelligence, choice reaction times may be (Keele, 1973, p. 80). Our data are certainly not compelling evidence for this speculation, but they are consistent with it.

It apparently would be possible to distinguish low verbal university students from high verbals by the use of information processing tasks alone. It is hard to see why one would do this, since presently available psychometric measures are quite adequate for this purpose and much easier to administer. Using an information processing test to identify verbal ability seems to us to be putting the cart before the horse. As Carroll (1974) has pointed out, verbal ability as we have defined it is not a factorially pure measure. Besides, we regard information processing capacity as being a more basic mental ability than the composite of skills lumped under the title "verbal aptitude."

This brings us to some speculations which, we believe, follow from our research. The first concerns the meaning of intelligence test scores. We know that these scores are, for some reason, moderately successful predictors of success in a variety of situations (Herrnstein, 1973). The statistical fact is hardly in doubt, although there is great controversy concerning the reason behind it. In our terms verbal intelligence tests *directly* tap a person's knowledge of the language, and *indirectly* tap CIP ability. Success in different tasks is probably dependent upon a host of factors, including both acquired knowledge and CIP ability. In many situations success may be achieved either by relying on prior knowledge or CIP ability to do the current task. We note that in the psychometric literature a similar distinction has been made by Cattell (1971), who argues that with increasing age cognitive style appears to shift from the fixing of new information (his "fluid intelligence") to the utilization of old information ("crystallized intelligence").

It seems plausible to believe that high verbal subjects know more about the linguistic aspects of their culture because they are more rapid in CIP tasks, rather than the reverse. To illustrate, imagine two individuals, one with high CIP abilities and one with low abilities, both of whom are given the same exposure to linguistic information. Unless the exposure is such that the low CIP individual can abstract all the information from this presentation, the high CIP individual will fix more information in long-term memory. If, by contrast, the initial exposure of information were individualized so that both persons were brought to the same level of immediate information fixation, then long-term retention should be equated. Indeed, we have previously reported that there is no correlation between verbal ability and retention of information over a period of weeks, providing that individual learning is equated (Hunt et al., 1973).

Another question which arises from our research is "What does it mean to know something?" At face value, "knowing something" is an either/or state of affairs. Either a piece of information is in long-term memory or it is not. This, of course, is too naive a view, since on occasion information can be recovered only with the aid of prompts. The amount of prompting required will vary from individual to individual and from time to time. Our results on differential accessibility of codes (e.g., the names of letters) indicate that even highly overlearned codes may be differentially available. At present there is no information to indicate whether this is because certain people have better "machinery" for retrieving information, suggesting a biological explanation, or because they have learned better coding and retrieval schemes.

Because of the interest in the social aspects of intelligence testing, we further point out that the results we have reported here have no implications for the debate over either social class or racial determinants of intelligence. None of our studies have contrasted CIP abilities in different racial or social groups. We have argued that given roughly comparable cultural experiences, differences in the amount of linguistic knowledge acquired and tested directly in an intelligence test are associated with differences in CIP abilities. If the cultural backgrounds of subjects are not comparable, then we would expect the correlation between CIP abilities and intelligence test scores to be reduced unless the groups involved also differed in CIP abilities. Whether such differences exist is an open question.

Although we would not advocate using the information processing tasks we have described as replacements for conventional scholastic aptitude tests, we do feel that such tasks have an important role in the measurement of individual differences. A test of current information processing ability should be useful in determining the manner in which information should be presented to a specific person, in order to maximize the probability of the information's being retained. We believe that the aptitude treatment interactions much sought after by educators are more likely to be found if "aptitude" is defined by the parameters of the information processing process than if it is defined by one's relative standing in a population. We also believe that information processing measures appear more suitable than psychometric instruments in assessing the effects of inter-individual differences, such as sex or age, and intra-individual differences, such as stress or drug intake, upon cognitive functioning. We hope that these conjectures will shortly be reexamined in the light of the data that must be obtained.

III

INTELLIGENCE
AND
GENETICS

This classic study by Alice Leahy utilizes one of the most powerful designs for separating genetic and environmental influences on a behavioral trait. Children adopted early into homes were compared with control children (reared by their own biological parents) to see whether control children resemble their parents more closely than do adopted children and their adopted parents. The results are straightforward and compelling, namely, that parents and children sharing a genetic connection more closely resemble each other than do those parents and children not having genes in common. Note that the results may be limited to the range of environments and range of genetic potentials in the two groups. This reminder is more than an academic caveat, for if relevant environmental differences are restricted in the two groups, the only things that can lead to differences among individuals are genetic factors.

5

Nature-Nurture and Intelligence

ALICE M. LEAHY

Introduction

THE PROBLEM

Variation in human intelligence is universally recognized. But experimentation to discover the causes which affect this variation has moved slowly. The reasons are obvious. First, conditions which permit the control of either heredity or environment are difficult to secure, and secondly, our tools for measurement are limited and crude. Although identical twins provide an absolute control of heredity, their separate location in diverse environment is rare. Experimentation involving the control of environment, on the other hand, is not entirely possible. Measures are avail-

Leahy, Alice M. "Nature-Nurture and Intelligence." *Genetic Psychology Monographs Supplement*, 1935, Vol. 16, pp. 235–308. Copyright © 1937 by The Journal Press and reprinted by permission.

able for only certain of its features. For its dynamic attributes we have no measures. Hence, what may appear to be similar environments are only approximately identical. However, the individual mental examination has been demonstrated to be fairly reliable of what may be called test intelligence.

The present investigation approaches the problem by a comparison of two groups of children living in approximately identical environments. In one group, the children are unrelated by blood or marriage to the persons shaping the environment. They are adopted children. In the other group, the children are the offspring of the persons who have shaped the environment. Both heredity and environment are operative in the latter group, while in the former, only environment.

Resemblance as expressed by means of the correlation between attributes in the home and test intelligence of child will constitute one type of analysis. Presumably the magnitude of the correlation between adopted children and their foster homes is a function of environment. In the case of parents and true children, it is a function of heredity and environment combined.

A comparative analysis of mean intelligence with cultural levels will constitute a second type of analysis. Since, as will subsequently be shown, the mean intelligence of the two groups of children is almost identical, marked contrasts in intelligence under constant environmental conditions would place the burden of causation on heredity.

If random placement of adopted children exists in each social stratum then variation from the mean intelligence of the group may be assigned to environmental diversity. Since the homes in both groups of children represent an equal spread on the cultural scale from high to low, we may assume that the nurture factor is equally potent in the determination of final variation in IQ. If the genetic variation in intelligence of each group of children corresponds to the variation measured by our test of intelligence, then the contribution of environment toward final variability in IQ of adopteds would be definitely increased, since they are somewhat less variable than the children reared by their own parents.

It should be emphasized that whatever trends and conclusions can be found in this study are valid only for populations as homogeneous in racial extraction, social standards, and educational opportunities as that from which our subjects are taken. The distribution of homes of the children in this investigation are probably somewhat skewed toward a superior level. Adoptive homes of even the lowest occupational and economic levels are undoubtedly superior in respect to other traits, since society's control and imposition of standards on this type of home is much greater than on the ordinary home. The educational requirement adhered to in matching our adoptive homes with homes in the general population would tend to raise the environmental and genetic level of the homes of the latter group. This would be particularly true in the lowest occupational groups. In the main, the homes were as variable in essential features as homes of an American urban white population. Clearly they were not as variable as if the homes of southern negroes and poor mountain whites had been included. In consequence, home environment cannot be expected to have as large a proportional effect upon the mental differences of the children studied as though they were being reared in unselected families.

However, attention should also be drawn to the fact that the distribution of inheritable mental capacity of the children in this investigation was probably skewed toward a superior level. No children of the idiot or imbecile grade are included. The true parents of the adopted children were somewhat superior in cultural status to parents of dependent children in general. Hence, heredity cannot be expected to contribute as large a proportional influence to the mental differences of the children as though a greater variation in genetic intelligence was included. Since environment was equally variable in both the experimental and control populations, and since our sample of parents and true offspring (control population) consistently yielded coefficients of resemblance of .50, it is fair to assume that no serious understatement of the general influence of environment exists in our experimental data.

$$\cdots$$

Subjects

SOURCE OF SUBJECTS

Once the decision was made to limit the investigation to children placed in their adoptive homes at a very early age, it was apparent that the records of adopted children deposited in the Children's Bureau of the State Board of Control would be our most complete source for subjects, since the adoption records of the entire state are available there.

Due to the relatively small number of legitimate children that are available for adoption in early infancy, it was deemed better to limit our subjects to illegitimate children. An additional point of significance in favor of illegitimate children was the greater probability of securing a population whose intelligence would be normally distributed. Legitimate children are ordinarily available for adoption only because of serious intellectual and economic inadequacies in their parents or immediate relatives. Illegitimate children, on the other hand, are relinquished for many reasons, namely: the youth of the parents, the social stigma attached to the illegitimacy situation, economic inadequacy of parents, and intellectual incompetency of the parents. The economic inadequacy of unmarried parents is frequently associated with youth, while the economic inadequacy of married parents generally arises from intellectual and personality deficiencies. In general, a population of legitimate dependents appears to come from a narrow socio-economic range, while illegitimate dependents come from a more variable family background.

Our first step, then, in anticipation of our research project was the tabulation of the factual items of family history for the illegitimate children adopted in Minnesota during the period 1918–1928. This period was chosen because it would provide children who would be not less than 5 nor more than 14 years of age at the time of the field investigation, 1932–1933. Records were available for 2449 children. Our transcript included information on the personal history of the child, and true parents and the foster parents.

EXPERIMENTAL GROUP, CRITERIA OF SELECTION

In order that the least possible ambiguity exist in our results, the experimental group was limited to:

1. *Children placed in their adoptive homes at the age of 6 months or younger.* (The mean age of placement was 2.5 months) At this early age precise judgments of mental ability on the basis of test performance, physical development, or overt behavior are highly improbable. Further, this criterion assures from early infancy an environment that is no more or less changing in character than that enjoyed by children in general. Moreover, it definitely avoids the difficulties which would arise in attempting to measure the influence of environment previous to the adoptive one under consideration.

2. *Only those adopted children who were known to be of white race, non-Jewish, north-European extraction.* This prerequisite tends to reduce the possibilities of a fortuitous resemblance between adoptive parent and child on the basis of racial regression. In addition it minimizes the possibility of a spurious heterogeneity arising from uncontrolled factors relating to race. Further, it limits the group to one which is similar in composition to the one on which the Stanford-Binet test was standardized.

3. *Children who were not less than 5 nor more than 14 years of age at the time of investigation.* This age range is conceded to give the most reliable test results.

4. *Children reared in communities of 1000 or more.* In this way we attempted to equalize the influence of such environmental factors as churches, clubs, and schools. No farm children are included. Ninety-five percent of the group have been reared in communities of over 10,000.

5. *Children who were legally adopted by married persons.* Thus we secured a group where the legal relationship and responsibility between parent and child was the same as that of true parent and offspring.

6. *Adoptive parents who were of white race, non-Jewish, north-European extraction.* With this criterion we attempted to reduce the possibility of adventitious resemblance and further reduced the possibility of securing non-English-speaking homes.

By adhering rigidly to the foregoing criteria it is believed that we have controlled the element of selective placement to a point beyond the facilities of earlier investigators and to the highest possible degree that present day child adoption permits. Fitting the child to the home on the basis of coloring, physique, and religious faith, all of which occur, could hardly give rise to mental resemblance. Selective placement upon the basis of cultural status, however, is still possible. But since the preadoptive records did not reveal the facts on this point, we can only infer its existence or nonexistence from an analysis of the relationship of certain indices of cultural status.

In our earliest considerations of a population we conceived a research group which would sample the population of adoptive homes distributed from a socio-economic standpoint as male occupations are distributed in the general population. Because of the limited number of children placed in homes of the laboring class this plan had to be abandoned. In its place we accepted all children available in the two lowest occupational groups and secured at least 40 children at every other level. With these numbers we have not only obtained a fair picture of environmental differences contingent on occupational status, but have also secured a fair sample of the selective placement that may operate on the basis of cultural status. A small number at any level might give a distinctly distorted picture.

CONTROL GROUP, CRITERIA OF SELECTION

With the primary purpose of a control group serving as a check upon the validity of our methods, each *adopted* child was matched with an *own* child as follows:

1. For sex.

2. Within an age range of plus or minus 6 months.

3. Whose fathers' occupations fell in the same group on the Minnesota Occupational Scale.

4. Whose fathers' school attainments agreed within plus or minus one school grade level.

5. Whose mothers' school attainments agreed within plus or minus one school grade level.

6. Whose parents were white race, non-Jewish, north-European extraction.

7. Whose residence has been in communities of 1000 or more.

. . .

In matching cases for occupation and education, we employed the two most objective indices of cultural status that are available. In 12 cases the educational criterion was not adhered to. It was necessary to be content with agreement in education for one parent. In these cases, however, the educational disparity between the other adoptive parent and his control was held within the ordinary school groups of elementary, high school, or college level.

A typical match is illustrated by the following example. A lawyer, in the person of an adoptive father who had completed college and whose wife had finished the eleventh grade in high school, might be matched with an electrical engineer of not less than three or more than five years of college and whose wife had completed at least the tenth, but not more than the twelfth grade in high school, provided the sex and age of their respective children agreed.

If environment is dominant, it would seem that the trend of any trait concerning the children and their environment would be similar in direction and magnitude for both the adopted and control populations. Certainly, our adopted children should clearly reveal the relationship of environment to attributes which are not reciprocally affected by the innate tendencies of the child. For example, the occupation of the adoptive father is obviously not a function of the intelligence of the adopted child, while the number of children's books in the adoptive home and the intelligence of the child are reciprocally dependent. The books may be in the home because intelligent children enjoy books. Or the children may be more responsive and alert because the books are in the home. When the age of our children at the time of the test is considered, it is apparent that there are many factors in the adoptive home whose existence is entirely independent of the child and, therefore, whatever relationship exists between these factors and the child may be regarded as a measure of the influence of environment. The relationship between parent and true offspring, however, is a complex of environment and heredity. Here, for example, the child's intelligence may be not only the result of the quality of the environment that the parents have provided, but also an inherited characteristic from the parents. From the adopted population we should be able to get a measure of the influence of environment; from the control population a measure of the influence of environment reenforced by heredity. Whatever unreliability exists because of imperfections in our measuring instruments will be similarly existent in both populations. Further, whatever the accumulated effect of environment may be, it will be operative in both populations in the same direction since both have enjoyed what might be termed an ordinarily continuous environment.

. . .

Main Results of the Study

The relationship between test intelligence of children and various attributes of their home environment is shown in Table 5.1. Since intelligence and age of child have been demonstrated to be negatively correlated (in these data, age and IQ for adopteds correlated from $-.17$ to $-.19$, for controls from $-.13$ to $-.18$), age has been partialled out and the relationships are expressed in product moment correlations. Because it was not

Table 5.1
Child's IQ correlated with other factors

Correlated factor	Adopted children		Control children	
	r	N	r	N
Father's Otis score	.15	178	.51	175
Mother's Otis score	.20	186	.51	191
Mid-parent Otis score	.18	177	.60	173
Father's S.B. vocabulary	.22	177	.47	168
Mother's S.B. vocabulary	.20	185	.49	190
Mid-parent S.B. vocabulary	.24	174	.56	164
Environmental status score	.19	194	.53	194
Cultural index of home	.21	194	.51	194
Child training index of home	.18	194	.52	194
Economic index of home	.12	194	.37	194
Sociality index of home	.11	194	.42	194
Father's education	.16	193	.48	193
Mother's education	.21	192	.50	194
Mid-parent education	.20	193	.54	194
Father's occupational status	.12	194	.45	194

possible to obtain full information for all the persons participating in the study, the number of cases varies for each correlation.

Although the difference between corresponding correlation coefficients in the Adopted and Control group is consistent and striking, their comparability must be determined before any interpretations are made. The test of comparability is equal variability. A reexamination of the data shows almost perfect agreement in the variability of environmental factors entering our correlational table. Equal variability does not exist for test intelligence, however, in the two sets of data. In the case of the Adopted children it is 12.5, for the Control children, it is 15.4. Although the difference is not large, correction should be made if two equally comparable series of coefficients are desired. Since the nature of the curtailment is known and exists in only one trait, the correction evolved by Pearson may be applied (Kelley, 1923, pp. 225, 316). The corrected correlations are presented in Table 5.2.

Despite the severity of the correction the absolute change in magnitude of our correlations is not great. The greatest single increase is .05; on the average the correlations are increased .038 points. Note that the difference between corresponding coefficients in the Adopted and Control series continues. For the Adopted children they are consistently low, about .20. In the Control group they maintain the level usually found for hereditary physical characteristics, .50. In the case of the latter group heredity and environment are both operative. Hence variance in intelligence is accounted for by variance in heredity and environment combined to the

Table 5.2

Child's IQ correlated with other factors
(r corrected for unequal range in child's IQ)

Correlated factor	Adopted children		Control children	
	r	N	r	N
Father's Otis score	.19	178	.51	175
Mother's Otis score	.24	186	.51	191
Mid-parent Otis score	.21	177	.60	173
Father's S.B. vocabulary	.26	177	.47	168
Mother's S.B. vocabulary	.24	185	.49	190
Mid-parent S.B. vocabulary	.29	174	.56	164
Environmental status score	.23	194	.53	194
Cultural index of home	.26	194	.51	194
Child training index	.22	194	.52	194
Economic index	.15	194	.37	194
Sociality index	.13	194	.42	194
Father's education	.19	193	.48	193
Mother's education	.25	192	.50	194
Mid-parent education	.24	193	.54	194
Father's occupational status	.14	194	.45	194

extent of about 25 percent (square of r .50). In the Adopted group, however, where environment is functioning independently of heredity, variance in intelligence is accounted for by variance in environment only to the extent of about 4 percent (square of r .20). If we neglect whatever artificial heredity selective placement of adopted children may have introduced into the data, these coefficients are clear evidence of maximum variance in intelligence with variance in environment. Apparently environment cannot compensate for the lack of blood relationship in creating mental resemblance between parent and child. Heredity persists.

A second type of analysis of our data appears in Table 5.3, where the mean intelligence quotient of Adopted children in each successive occupation level is compared with the intelligence quotient of Control children similarily classified according to occupation of father. Note the constancy of the IQ of Adopted children, irrespective of occupational level. Its progression is insignificant. When variability in IQ within each occupational group is considered the children in the lowest level almost completely overlap the children in the highest group. The same is true when occupational groups V and I are compared. The difference is entirely effaced between occupational classes III and I. If we ignore the very lowest occupational bracket (VI and VII) in which the number of cases is considerably less than in the other levels, a difference of only one IQ increment exists between the successive occupational classes of Adopted children.

The Control children, on the other hand, advance conspicuously in

Table 5.3

Comparative analysis of intelligence of adopted and control children and environmental status of homes classified according to occupation of father

Occupation of father	Adopted children					Control children				
	N	Intelligence quotient M	S.D.	Environmental status M	S.D.	N	Intelligence quotient M	S.D.	Environmental status M	S.D.
I Professional	43	112.6	11.8	194.6	27.2	40	118.6	12.6	180.4	29.1
II Business manager	38	111.6	10.9	171.3	40.2	42	117.6	15.6	160.7	31.1
III Skilled trades	44	110.6	14.2	133.2	35.2	43	106.9	14.3	106.3	43.4
IV Farmers	—	—	—	—	—	—	—	—	—	—
V Semi-skilled	45	109.4	11.8	94.0	30.3	46	101.1	12.5	77.6	37.4
VI Slightly skilled and	24	107.8	13.6	74.7	28.7	23	102.1	11.0	40.1	26.7
VII Day labor										

mean level of intelligence with fathers' occupation. The difference in IQ between the lowest occupational levels and the middle group (III, skilled workmen, clerks, etc.) is as great as the difference in IQ between the lowest and highest occupational group of the Adopted children. Although the children in the two highest occupational classes (business managerial and professional) are undifferentiated they are widely separated from the children of the middle group (about 12 IQ points). The absolute difference in child's IQ between the extreme occupational levels in the Control group is three times as great as the difference between the extreme levels of Adopted children. The fact that the children of each occupational group are almost identical in age should be borne in mind. If the children in the highest occupational levels were younger than those in the middle and lowest groups, then their superior rating in IQ might be said to be a function of age. It will also be recalled that each Adopted child was matched with a Control child of the same age and whose father's occupation was in agreement with that of the adoptive fathers. Hence, cross-comparisons are entirely valid.

. . .

SUPPLEMENTARY DATA

If environment is dominant we should expect that unrelated children in the same household would agree markedly in ability. The contrary was found as may be seen by the following:

	r	PE	N
IQ of Exper. Adopteds and Own Children	.06	.14	25
IQ of Unrelated Adopteds in Same Household	.12	.22	10
Vocab. of Exper. Adopteds and Own Children	.06	.13	25

Although the number of cases is small the results suggest that the children are widely different in intellectual ability, regardless of their common environment.

In 20 cases of own children of Adoptive parents, IQ of own child and mid-parent Otis correlated .36. This correlation follows the expected familial pattern.

Although our single measure of the emotional stability of the children is probably not sufficiently reliable to permit any conclusions about personality differences, the similarity in the relationship between Woodworth-Mathews' scores and home environment for both groups of children is striking. As indicated below, Woodworth-Mathews' scores correlate:

.10 for Adopteds, .13 for Controls with mid-parent Otis Score

−.04 for Adopteds, .07 for Controls with mid-parent Vocabulary

.06 for Adopteds, .13 for Controls with Cultural index of home

. . .

Conclusions

By methods which allowed the effects of environment to be studied separately from those of heredity in combination with environment, this study attempted to discover the influence of environment and heredity on intellectual variation. As stated in the opening section, the tendencies observed in this study are valid only for populations which are similar to the experimental population in composition. However, the consistency with which a coefficient of .50 was secured for parent and offspring suggests that the restricted range in both the hereditary and environmental variables was reciprocal and hence no serious distortion in our results exists. The main conclusions are as follows:

1. Variation in IQ is accounted for by variation in home environment to the extent of not more than 4 percent; 96 percent of the variation is accounted for by other factors.

2. Measurable environment does not shift the IQ by more than 3 to 5 points above or below the value it would have had under normal environmental conditions.

3. The nature or hereditary component in intelligence causes greater variation than does environment. When nature and nurture are operative, shifts in IQ as great as 20 IQ points are observed with shifts in the cultural level of the home and neighborhood.

4. Variation in the personality traits measured in this study other than that of intelligence appears to be accounted for less by variation in heredity than by variation in environment.

This recent adoption study of intelligence is published here for the first time by the generous consent of Sandra Scarr and Richard A. Weinberg. Like the Leahy (1935) study that precedes it in this volume, these authors demonstrate that variations in intelligence test scores are under substantial genetic control in a middle-class sample. Children biologically related to their parents are more similar to each other than adoptive children and their adoptive parents. Furthermore, Drs. Scarr and Weinberg show that biologically related children resemble each other more closely than unrelated children reared together. The implications of these two studies are profound, for they suggest that within the range of environments represented in the studies, measured socioeconomic factors, when disconnected from biological factors (as they are in the adoptive families) account for relatively little variation in IQ in children. This conclusion is not meant to exclude the possibility (indeed, the likelihood) that if a greater range of environments were included, deleterious environmental effects would be detected.

6

Intellectual Similarities in Adoptive and Biologically Related Families of Adolescents

SANDRA SCARR AND RICHARD A. WEINBERG

As Jencks and Brown (1977) have indicated, there are two basic approaches to estimating the importance of environmental differences for differences in children's outcomes. First, they say, one should begin by offering some meaningful definition of environment. One strategy is to specify the meaning of *measured* environment and study the effects of differences in home background on unrelated children, adopted into the homes. But no such data have been available for adult outcomes. The

Scarr, Sandra, and Weinberg, Richard A. "Intellectual Similarities in Adoptive and Biologically Related Families of Adolescents." 1979. Published here by permission of the authors.

second strategy is to look at only those environmental influences shared by children reared together. These authors state that one can estimate the contribution of such influences to phenotypic inequality by calculating the correlation between the phenotypes of genetically unrelated children reared together (Jencks and Brown, 1977). A study using adoption as a behavior genetic strategy is the subject of this article.

Another strategy to control for genetic differences has been to study sibling and twin differences in outcomes, by regressing differences in one or several outcome variables on another. This strategy reduces, or in the case of MZ (monozygotic, or identical) twins eliminates, the genetic contamination in the prediction of one outcome from another, but it does not speak directly to the matter of measured family background effects. All siblings and twins share a common set of parents and family demographic characteristics.

An elegant way to obtain an estimate of the "true" environmental effects of family background would be with identical twins reared apart in uncorrelated environments. Genetic differences would be controlled, while both within-family and between-family environmental effects would be free to vary. Unfortunately, child development experts have repeatedly warned about the psychological hazards of giving away one of a pair of twins, and there are simply too few cases, too peculiarly sampled, to make these subjects very useful to social science.

Adoptive Families

Adopted children, on the other hand, are almost as useful as the rare identical twins reared apart, and far more available. Adopted children are not genetically related to the family of rearing, so environmental differences between families are not confounded with genetic differences in the children, if the adopted children are randomly placed by adoption agencies. (In practice, the agencies do match natural and adoptive parents' background, but the information they have is sufficiently limited that they cannot bias adoption studies too much.

Theoretically, regressions of adopted child outcomes on adoptive family characteristics will provide genetically unbiased estimates of true environmental effects in the population. Unfortunately, adoptive families are selected by agencies for being above average in many virtues, including socioeconomic status. Thus, they are always an unrepresentative sample of the population to which one would like to generalize. Although it is possible that the adoptive family coefficients on background are good estimates of the population values, it is difficult to know without modeling the way in which the families were selected. An easier corrective for the possible bias of selected adoptive families is to have a comparison sample of biologically related families that are similarly selected. The relative magnitude of coefficients on measured family background variables provides a proportional correction for coefficients in studies of individuals.

Method

SUBJECTS

The 845 subjects in this sample are members of 120 biological and 104 adoptive families in Minnesota. The adoptive sample reported in this article is limited to those 150 of the 194 adopted children whose natural mothers' educational levels were available from the records of the Department of Public Welfare (DPW). Adoptive families were recruited through the DPW, whose director sent letters on behalf of the study to 1620 families who had adopted children between 1953 and 1959. We were particularly interested in families who had adopted at least two children, so that our recruitment concentrated on those volunteers with two available children between the ages of 16 and 21 at the time of testing. Table 6.1 gives the details of adoptive family recruitment.

The biological families were recruited through newspaper articles and advertisements, word of mouth, and the adoptive families. Approximately 153 biological families came from public media and about 41 from recommendations of the adoptive families. Of these, 122 came to the University of Minnesota for the full evaluation. All families who participated in the interview procedure received small payments for their time and transportation and bonuses for recruiting other families. The data were collected from July 1974 to June 1976.

Table 6.1
Recruitment of adoptive and biological families

Adoptive families		Biological families	
Letters sent by DPW	1,620	Eligible to participate	?
Letters returned undelivered	477	Recruited by adoptive families	41
No response	345	Recruited by media	153
Eligible to participate	798	Participated	
Said no	327	By interview	122*
Said yes	471		
Participated			
By mail	164		
By interview	110*		

* The samples reported in this article.

A crucial methodological consideration for any adoption study is the age at which the children are placed with their adopting families. Only early placements can guarantee that potentially confounding early environmental experiences are minimized. All of the children in this study were in their homes before 12 months of age. Exact age of placement was available for 171 of the 194 adopted children. The mean age of placement into the adopted children's present homes was 2.6 months. Of these 171 children, 109 were placed before 2 months of age; 158 were placed at or before 6 months. All but 6 of the 171 were placed by the age of 9 months. All adopted children were genetically unrelated to their adoptive parents and to each other. The biological children were all full siblings and claimed to be the biological offspring of both parents tested.

PROCEDURE

Subjects in the sample were administered a three-hour battery of tests and interviews at the University of Minnesota as part of a behavior genetic study of intellectual, personality, and attitudinal similarities within families. The data reported here are from the Wechsler Adult Intelligence Scale (WAIS),* an individually administered IQ test. Four subtests of the WAIS were administered: vocabulary, arithmetic, block design, and picture arrangement. The combination of these four subtests has been shown to correlate above .90 with the full-scale test score and is generally accepted as a shortened version of the adult test (Doppelt, 1956). The test protocols were scored by an experienced psychometrician who was unaware of the respondents' adoptive status.

Results

SOCIOECONOMIC VARIABLES

The socioeconomic characteristics of the biologically related and adoptive families are shown in Table 6.2. Parental educational levels in both kinds of families are well above the averages of their cohorts in the population. Family income averages $25,000 to $26,000 in both types of families. The variance of the educational, occupational, and income measures is not as restricted as the means might imply. In fact, the standard deviations are roughly comparable to the population figures. Two points should be made, therefore, about the socioeconomic characteristics of these families: first, the adoptive and biological families are fairly comparable, and second, they both represent selected portions of the socioeconomic status

---

* Psychological Corporation, 1949.

Table 6.2

Means, standard deviations, and correlations of adoptive and biological family characteristics (biological children above diagonal; adoptive children below)

Biological children (N = 237)

	Ch IQ	Fa Ed	Mo Ed	Fa Oc	F Inc	B Rnk	F Size	Fa IQ	Mo IQ	N Mo Age	N Mo Ed	N Mo Occ	Mean	S.D.
Child IQ		.26	.24	.10	.22	-.19	-.21	.39	.39				112.82	10.36
Father's Education	.10		.51	.61	.44	.01	-.36	.56	.24				15.63	2.83
Mother's Education	.10	.51		.36	.39	.02	-.36	.43	.46				14.68	2.24
Father's Occupation	.12	.57	.25		.47	.01	-.30	.37	.13				62.47	24.73
Family Income	.06	.50	.40	.46		.00	-.25	.38	.19				24987.34	8770.43
Birth Rank	-.19	.05	.03	.06	.15		.08	-.00	.03				1.62	0.63
Family Size	-.05	.04	.11	-.00	.21	.10		-.30	-.10				3.85	1.48
Father's IQ	.15	.53	.30	.40	.45	.08	.14		.20				118.02	11.66
Mother's IQ	.04	.29	.44	.19	.21	.07	.12	.30					113.41	10.46
Natural Mother's Age	-.10	.04	.03	.12	-.02	-.11	-.04	-.10	.03					
Natural Mother's Education	.21	.33	.24	.29	.43	.09	.14	.20	.10	.07				
Natural Mother's Occupation	.12	-.00	.13	.11	.06	-.06	.11	.11	.15	.28	.33			
Mean	106.19	14.90	13.95	60.30	25935.00	1.43	2.87	116.53	112.43	22.46	11.97	30.44		
S.D.	8.95	3.03	2.06	24.14	10196.78	0.57	1.20	11.36	10.18	5.80	1.66	23.24		

Adopted children (N = 150)

(SES) range in the United States, both regionally and within the region from which they are drawn. It is well known that volunteers in social science research are self-selected for better-than-average characteristics of all kinds, and the sample of biological families is at least as biased in SES characteristics as the adoptive one. This is what we had hoped would happen, without the statistically hazardous procedure of matching individual families.

The adoptive and biological parents are also comparable in mean IQ scores and in the variance of their scores. Compared to the standardization sample for the WAIS, the fathers are more than a standard deviation (S.D.) above the mean and the mothers about three-fourths of an S.D. above. It is not accidental, of course, that samples with above-average income, education, and occupational status also score above the average on a standard IQ test. The standard deviation of the parental IQ scores is only three-fourths of the population standard deviation, a significant restriction. Their scores are significantly restricted in range, with the lowest scores in the mid-90s.

The children of the two types of families are quite comparable in age, the mean being about 18.5 years in both groups. The range of ages is 16 to 22 in both groups (with a few exceptions of ages 15 and 23). The IQ scores of the adopted children are about 6.5 points lower than those of the biological children, however. These results are also shown in Table 6.2. If IQ is heritable to any extent, one should expect the biological offspring of bright parents to have higher IQ scores than unselected people. The adopted children are not a genetically selected group. Their mothers average 12 years of education at an average age of 41 at the present time. The median educational level for women aged 25 to 44 in the Minnesota area is 12.5 years of education. Education is an indirect measure of intellectual ability, but as we have shown in another study, there is good reason to expect that intellectual level of the natural mothers is reasonably well indexed by their educational levels (Scarr and Weinberg, 1976, 1977a, 1977b). Furthermore, there was a large study of unmarried mothers in the state of Minnesota during the years 1948 to 1952, when IQ tests were mandated for all women giving up children for adoption. The average IQ score of 3600 women was 100.00, with a standard deviation of 15.4. Since the mothers were sampled from 1953 to 1959, there is no reason to expect them to differ significantly from the normal population. Fathers, of course, should not be expected to deviate from the average of the population any more than mothers. Thus, the adopted children are genetically an average sample of the population, while the biological children are more selected.

CORRELATIONS AMONG PARENTAL CHARACTERISTICS

The parental educational levels, family income, and father's occupation are similarly correlated in the biological and adoptive families. Despite the above-average means on all of these variables, the correlations are of the same magnitude as those reported from more representative samples by Sewell and Hauser (1975), Jencks (1972), and others. These two facts—the comparability of correlations in the two samples and their comparability with more representative samples—encouraged us to proceed with the regression analyses.

As Table 6.2 shows, mothers and fathers in the adoptive and biologically related families are assortatively mated for educational level with a correlation of about .50. Sewell and Hauser (1975, p. 72) reported .52. Fathers' education correlated with their occupational status (NORC scale) about .57. Sewell and Hauser reported .43 (Duncan SEI). Fathers' occupational status correlated with family income about .46, the same figure obtained by Sewell and Hauser. Mothers' education is correlated with fathers' occupational prestige somewhat more in biological than in adoptive families (.35 versus .25); Sewell and Hauser reported .29. In these samples, mothers' education correlated more highly with family income (.40) than in Sewell and Hauser's study (.24), perhaps because our mostly urban mothers may be more likely to be contributing to that income.

From an examination of the means, variances, and correlations of family demographic characteristics, we concluded that there were no important differences between the adoptive and biological families in the study. The correlational patterns were sufficiently similar to those for more representative samples that the regression analyses were probably more directly generalizable to the general population than we had feared from the selected characteristics of the families.

PARENTAL IQ CORRELATIONS

Fathers' and mothers' IQ scores were moderately correlated with the family demographic characteristics, as might be expected. In both the adoptive and biological families, the father's IQ was more highly correlated with his educational attainment than the mother's was with hers. We suppose this says something about selection for advanced education for women in the cohort that is now 45 to 55 years of age. Adoptive fathers' correlation of IQ score with occupational prestige is a bit lower than the biological fathers' (.39 versus .51). Adoptive parents' IQ scores correlated .30, and biological parents, .20, a moderate difference in assortative mating for IQ. There are no other striking differences in the correlations by family type.

FAMILY SIZE AND BIRTH RANK

The adoptive families have on the average fewer children than the biological families (2.9 versus 3.9). The average birth rank of those children who were of appropriate age to participate in the study, however, did not differ much in the two types of families. In both cases, the participants were between first and second borns, on the average (1.4 and 1.6 in the adoptive and biological families, respectively). This means that the participants in the biological families have a larger number of younger siblings than the adopted children.

Parental characteristics are surprisingly correlated with family size in the biological families. Although it has often been reported in the general population that family size is negatively correlated with parental IQ, occupational status, education, and income, we did not expect to find such relationships in an above-average sample. Yet number of children is significantly negatively correlated with all of the family demographic characteristics and with the father's IQ in the biological families. As we did expect, adoptive families with more children (the range of family size was from 1 to 6 children) were slightly more advantaged than those with fewer children, presumably because adoptive agencies exercise selection of parents who can afford to rear more children.

CORRELATIONS WITH CHILDREN'S IQ SCORES

It is clear from Table 6.2 that parental education, family income, family size, and parental IQ are more highly correlated with biological than adopted adolescents' IQ scores. (Father's occupation and birth rank are not.) The greater resemblance between adolescents' IQ scores and their parents' characteristics in biological families presumably results largely from the genetic resemblance, since both types of families share the home environment. The slight correlation between adopted child IQ and family demographic characteristics is confounded by the selective placement of children of better educated (probably more intelligent) natural mothers in the adoptive families with higher levels of parental education, income, and occupational status. Since the natural mother's educational level (as a very imperfect index of her intellectual level) is moderately correlated with the adopted child's IQ, the correlations between adoptive family demographics and child IQ are inflated by the natural mother-child resemblance and selective placement.

Family size is unrelated to child IQ in adoptive families but negatively correlated in biological families, probably through the negative correlation between family size and parental characteristics in the biological families. Family size per se, however, is not a detriment to IQ in the range of adoptive family sizes represented in this study and at the socioeconomic levels of these families. Birth rank, on the other hand, is clearly related to IQ in both the adoptive and biological families. Later born or adopted children are at a slight disadvantage in IQ.

SELECTIVE PLACEMENT

Adoption agencies are not blind. They have information about the natural mothers' educational levels, occupational prestige, and age, and they use it to match the children of the natural mothers to adoptive families. As shown in Table 6.2, there are substantial correlations between natural mothers' educational levels and the adoptive families' demographic characteristics, particularly family income and fathers' education. Fortunately for the study, the agencies do not have information on the IQ levels of the adoptive parents or the natural mothers, so their effective matching for IQ is quite poor. The correlations of adoptive parents' IQ and natural mothers' education are only .20 and .10 for mother and father, respectively. If the correlation between natural mothers' educational and IQ levels is .70, as Jencks (1972) believes, then the correlation in natural and adoptive parent IQ levels is only $(.15)(.70) = .105$. Since the agencies have little or no information about the natural fathers, the correlation between the IQ's of natural and adoptive parents is undoubtedly lower than .10. This creates a small bias in the genetic variance between adoptive families, accounting for less than one percent of the genetic variance in the population, compared to biologically related families who share half of the genetic variance.

FAMILY CORRELATIONS

For the second approach to deciphering the meaning of the term *family background* we used all of the subjects for whom IQ data were available, regardless of what other information might be missing. Thus, the samples of both adoptive and biological family members are considerably larger, as shown in the middle of Table 6.3.

By calculating the correlations for related and unrelated family members, we hoped to get an estimate of the degree to which similarity in intellectual outcome is conditioned by similarity in the rearing environment. This entails a comparison of biological and adoptive families and a comparison of parent-child with sibling correlations. Parents and children do not share the same rearing environment, whereas siblings do, regardless of their genetic relatedness.

In an earlier study of young adopted and biologically related children, we found that parent-child correlations were much greater for the biologically related pairs (yielding "heritability" estimates in the range of .4 to .7), but the sibling correlations were quite similarly high for both related and unrelated pairs (Scarr and Weinberg, 1977a, 1977b). We speculated that similarities among these young children were greatly influenced by their families' common rearing environments.

Table 6.3

Correlations among family members in adoptive and biologically
related families (Pearson coefficients on standardized scores
by family member and family type) for intelligence test scales

Child score	Biological				Adoptive			
	MO	FA	CH	MP	MO	FA	CH	MP
WAIS IQ	.41	.40	.35	.52	.09	.16	−.03	.14
Arithmetic	.24	.30	.24	.36	−.03	.07	−.03	−.01
Vocabulary	.33	.39	.22	.43	.23	.24	.11	.26
Block Design	.29	.32	.25	.40	.13	.02	.09	.14
Picture Arrangement	.19	.06	.16	.11	−.01	−.04	.04	−.03

___ = bio > adopt. correlation, $p < .05$

	Sample sizes							
	Biological				Adoptive			
	MO	FA	CH	MP	MO	FA	CH	MP
Child Tests	270	270	168	268	184	175	84	168

	Assortative mating	
	Biological FA-MO	Adoptive FA-MO
WAIS IQ	.24	.31
Arithmetic	.19	−.04
Vocabulary	.32	.42
Block Design	.19	.15
Picture Arrangement	.12	.22
Sample Size	120	103

In this sample of late adolescents, we were able to check on the degree
of family environmental influence at the end of the child rearing period.
The results for the parent-child pairs are quite similar to the earlier study,
whereas those for the siblings are very different. The adopted siblings at
the average age of 18.5 years hardly resemble each other.

The evidence for genetic effects in striking in all comparisons of correlations among members of the adoptive and biological families. Even
though the scores of both biological and adoptive family members have
restricted variance, the coefficients for the biological family pairs usually
exceed those of the adoptive family members by a statistically significant
amount. As Table 6.3 shows, in total IQ the biological parent-child pairs,
the midparent-child and the child-child pairs are significantly more similar than the adoptive family members. Only in vocabulary are the adoptive family members similar at a level different from zero. It is no accident
that vocabulary differences are most amenable to social environmental

influence. Language is the mode of social exchange among human beings, genetically related or not, so that people who live together develop more similar verbal skills than random members of the population. Other skills are not notably similar among people who live together, unless they are genetically related. It is also not surprising that the skill most amenable to mate selection is vocabulary. Evidently, courting couples spend some time talking to each other, but are not as concerned with other intellectual skills!

From these family correlations one can calculate the differences between the adoptive and biological correlations and, depending upon the model, the "heritabilities." Genetically related persons in ordinary families share about half of their genes. Unrelated people share none of their genes, except through the selective placement of adopted children for IQ, of which there is only a slight bias in this study, as explained previously. Even though they have always lived together, the correlations of adoptive fathers' and mothers' IQ with adopted children's IQ scores are .15 and .04, respectively, so that there is little evidence for either selective placement or social environmental influence on IQ differences.

Table 6.4 gives the difference between the IQ correlations of biological and adoptive relatives and the "heritabilities," based on a simple-minded model: doubling the difference between the correlations of biologically related and unrelated pairs. This naive model throws the genotype-environment (GE) covariance (if any) into the genetic term, because only biologically related parents transmit both genes and environments to their offspring. The environments that the parents provide are correlated with their own genes and with the genes they transmit to the offspring. The "heritability" terms calculated here are really additive genetic variance plus GE covariance in the parent-child comparisons and broad heritability (including some dominance) in the sibling comparisons. The inexactitude of the measures, however, makes this distinction academic, in all probability.

The differences between biological and adoptive family correlations

Table 6.4

Differences between the correlations of genetically related and unrelated family members and "heritabilities"

Child score	Related-unrelated				Heritability*		
	MO	FA	CH	MP	MO	FA	CH
WAIS IQ	.31	.24	.38	.38	.62	.48	.76
Arithmetic	.27	.23	.27	.37	.54	.46	.54
Vocabulary	.10	.15	.11	.17	.20	.30	.22
Block Design	.16	.30	.16	.26	.32	.60	.32
Picture Arrangement	.20	.10	.12	.14	.40	.20	.24

* $2(r_{np-c} - r_{ap-c})$

range from .10 to .38, with a median difference of .23. Doubling this difference, then, we find that the median value for the combination of genetic variance and GE covariance is .46. Although this "heritability" is a far cry from .80, it is substantially different from zero.

In the simplest-minded genetic model that assumes no environmental transmission or genotype-environment covariation, the regression of offspring value on midparent value is an esimate of narrow heritability or the proportion of additive genetic variance in the total variance (Falconer, 1960). The median value of the midparent regression coefficients is .43, as shown in Table 6.3. By a more sensible model for behavioral traits, one that allows for environmental transmission, the regression of adopted offspring on adoptive midparent values is subtracted from the biological midparent-child regression. The resulting median value of the midparent heritability estimates is .26.

Hereditarian critics of this study will demand that we focus on the total IQ score, for several good reasons. First, the other tests are parts of this larger whole. Second, the subtests are far less reliable than the total score. And, last, the meaning of the whole is greater than the parts taken singly. It is also clear that total IQ has the highest heritability as estimated from the parent-child correlations (.55 is the average of mother-child and father-child comparisons) and from the sibling comparison (.76). These results lead to the same conclusion reached earlier from the regression of child IQ on the family background and parent IQ data; namely, that half or more of the contribution that parents make to differences in their offsprings' intellectual level is genetic. Taking assortative mating into account makes little difference in this conclusion.

So far we have resisted, from ignorance and fear of some formidable critics, the temptation to analyze our data in more sophisticated ways. We cannot defend all of the assumptions that must be made to justify elaborate models, and therefore have hesitated to throw ourselves into an inevitable fray. Nonetheless, it seems evident to us that the study of adoptive and biological families provides extensive support for the idea that half or more of the long-term effects of "family background" on children's intellectual attainments depend upon genetic, not environmental, transmission. Furthermore, in the range of environments sampled in this study, there is little evidence for any measured environmental effects in "family (SES) background." Birth order is the only variable with substantial effects in the adoptive families, and that accounts for about 4 percent of the IQ variation among the adolescent children.

Discussion

Accidents of birth do leave us at the genetic mercy of our parents, it seems. Different people have different responses to the same environment, and the effects of differences in environments within the range we sampled are very small. The comparison of the coefficients of child IQ on family background would lead one to conclude that in unrelated families the effects of measured demographic variables are nearly nil. Even adding a direct measure of social parental IQ does not substantially increase the explained variance for adopted children's IQ differences.

One could argue that the range of environments sampled here is not sufficiently great to bear the weight of any conclusions about the effects of environmental variation in the population. Our counterargument is threefold. First, the comparison with similarly sampled biological families reduces the force of the argument. Second, the coefficients of the biological families are much like those in other studies with more representative samples. And third, the two methods of analysis—regressions of child IQ on measured family variables and the family correlations for IQ—lead to the same conclusion.

Even if differences in measured family environments do not contribute much to differences in offsprings' IQ scores, however, one must not conclude that the levels of environments in general make no difference for the development of intelligence. Obviously, the average performance level of the adopted children depends on the average value of their environments. In this sample, the average level of the environments is above average, and so is the average IQ level of the unrelated children. Presumably, if they had been reared in below-average homes, their average IQ levels would also be below average. The only conclusion that is justified in this regard is that the adopted group were all reared in average to above average family environments and that individual differences among the children depend very little on differences among those environments.

Thus, in some ways we need not be upset about the unequal outcomes for children from different family backgrounds, since little of these lingering effects result from unequal family environments. Perhaps others will be concerned that genetic differences among and within families have large, long-term effects on intellectual functioning. Our view is that democratic principles never promised biological equality, nor by any known democratic method can we assure it. For many other reasons we can and should assure greater environmental equality, but we cannot and should not try to deny that unequal outcomes are also shaped by our individual, genetic differences. Equality of opportunity, yes; equality of outcome, no.

IV

INTELLIGENCE
AND
ENVIRONMENT

This article by Myron Winick, Knarig Meyer, and Ruth Harris is a demonstration of how improved nutrition can result in large increases on certain outcome measures while still preserving initial differences among groups. The findings demonstrate that there is no essential contradiction between views that hereditary or early experimental differences can have lasting effects and demonstrations of large improvements in performance as a result of enrichment.

7

Malnutrition
and Environmental Enrichment
by Early Adoption

MYRON WINICK, KNARIG KATCHADURIAN MEYER,
AND RUTH C. HARRIS

Numerous studies conducted in several different countries have demonstrated that malnutrition during the first two years of life, when coupled with all the other socioeconomic deprivations that generally accompany it, is associated with retarded brain growth and mental development which persist into adult life (Stoch and Smythe, 1963; Birch, 1972; Cravioto, 1966; Hertzig et al., 1972). What is not clear is the contribution of the malnutrition relative to that of the other social and cultural deprivations. When malnutrition has occurred in human populations not deprived in other ways the effects on mental development have been much less marked. Animal experiments have shown that early isolation results in the same type of persistent behavioral abnormalities as does early malnutrition (Levine, 1969). A stimulatory environment has been shown to counteract the untoward behavioral effects of early malnutrition

Winick, M., Meyer, K. K., and Harris, R. C. "Malnutrition and Environmental Enrichment by Early Adoption." *Science*, 1975, Vol. 190, pp. 1173–1175. Copyright © 1975 by the American Association for the Advancement of Science and reprinted by permission.

in rats (Levitsky and Barnes, 1972). These observations have led to the hypothesis that malnutrition and environmental deprivation act synergistically to isolate the infant from the normal stimulatory inputs necessary for normal development (Levitsky and Barnes, 1972). In addition, they suggest that enriching the environment of previously malnourished children might result in improved development. To test this hypothesis, we have examined the current status of a group of Korean orphans who were adopted during early life by U.S. parents and who had thereby undergone a total change in environment.

Experimental Sample

The sample was drawn from records of children who had been admitted to the Holt Adoption Service in Korea between 1958 and 1967. The following criteria were established for inclusion in the sample:

1. The child must be female. This was decided in order to eliminate sex differences; and because many more female than male infants were brought to the agency they provided a larger adoptive sample to choose from.

2. Date of birth and results of physical examination at the time of admission to Holt care, including height and weight, must be available on the records.

3. The child must have been less than two years old when first admitted to Holt care and less than three years old when adopted.

4. The child must have been reported to be full term at birth.

5. The physician's examination at time of initial contact must have revealed no physical defect or chronic illness.

6. The child must have been followed by the adoption service for at least six years and must be currently in elementary school (grades 1 to 8).

7. The child must have a current mailing address in the United States.

From 908 records chosen at random 229 children were found who met all these criteria. We divided these 229 into three groups, as follows, on the basis of how their height and weight at time of admission to Holt related to a reference standard of normal Korean children of the same age (Hong, 1970): group 1, designated "malnourished"—below the 3rd percentile for both height and weight; group 2, "moderately nourished"—from the 3rd through the 24th percentile for both height and weight; group 3, "well-nourished" or control—at or above the 25th percentile for both height and weight.

There were 24 children, randomly distributed through the three groups, whose height and weight were not in the same percentile grouping. These were eliminated from the sample. The remaining 205 consisted of 59 children in group 1, 76 in group 2, and 70 in group 3.

Table 7.1

Number of cases in each group

		Number measured for			
Group	Total number	Current height	Current weight	IQ	School achievement
1	42	41	41	36	40
2	52	50	51	38	38
3	47	47	47	37	37

A letter was sent by the Holt Adoption Service to the parents describing the general objectives of the study and asking their cooperation. It was followed by a letter from us explaining the study in more detail and asking for permission to request information about the child from the school. Where possible, the parents were called by telephone so that any questions they had about the study could be answered. For various reasons, 64 children could not be followed—17 in group 1, 24 in group 2, and 23 in group 3. Most of this loss resulted from inability to reach the parents, from an inadequate response, or from parental refusal. The final sample thus consisted of 141 children—42 in group 1, 52 in group 2, and 47 in group 3.

Information on health, growth and nutrition, and family socioeconomic background was obtained from the families of these 141 children by means of a checklist questionnaire. Information about scores on standardized tests of intelligence and school performance for the years 1971 to 1973 was requested from the schools on a mailed form constructed for this purpose.

The outcome data presented here consist of current height, which was obtainable for 138 children; current weight, obtainable for 139; current IQ, for 111; and current achievement scores, for 115. Table 7.1 shows the number of children in each group about whom these data were obtained.

Results

As may be seen in Tables 7.2 and 7.3, all three groups have surpassed the expected mean (50th percentile) for Korean children in both height and weight. There is a tendency for the children in groups 1 and 2 to be smaller and lighter than in group 3, but the differences are statistically significant only between the mean heights of children in groups 1 and 3 (Table 7.2). Although all three groups are heavier and taller than would be expected if they had remained in Korea, their means all fall below the 50th percentile of an American standard.

Table 7.2

Current height (percentiles, Korean reference standard): comparison of the three nutrition groups. F prob. is the probability that the calculated F ratio would occur by chance.

Group	N	Mean percentile	S.D.	F prob.	Contrast groups	t-test	
						t	P
1	41	71.32	24.98	0.068	1 vs. 2	−1.25	0.264
2	50	76.86	21.25		1 vs. 3	−2.22	0.029*
3	47	82.81	23.36		2 vs. 3	−1.31	0.194
Total sample	138	77.24	23.41				

* Statistically significant.

The mean IQ of group 1 is 102; of group 2, 106; and of group 3, 112 (Figure 7.1). Only the difference between groups 1 and 3 is statistically significant ($P \leq .005$). All the groups have reached or exceeded mean values of American children. When the data are converted to stanines (Table 7.4) the results are the same as with the IQ scores.

Results for achievement scores (Table 7.5) are similar to those for IQ's. All the groups have achieved at least to stanine 5 (the mean for U.S. school children of the same age). There is a highly statistically significant difference between group 1 and group 3 ($P \leq .001$). Differences in achievement between groups 1 and 2 just reach the level of statistical significance. All the groups are doing at least as well as would be expected from an average U.S. population.

Discussion

In the studies referred to earlier which showed persistent retardation in children malnourished during the first two years of life (Stoch and Smythe, 1963; Birch, 1972; Cravioto, 1966; Hertzig et al., 1972) after

Table 7.3

Current weight (percentiles, Korean reference standard): comparison of the three nutrition groups. F prob. is the probability that the calculated F ratio would occur by chance.

Group	N	Mean percentile	S.D.	F prob.	Contrast groups	t-test	
						t	P
1	41	73.95	24.60	0.223	1 vs. 2	−1.24	0.218
2	51	79.94	20.78		1 vs. 3	−1.61	0.111
3	47	82.11	22.66		2 vs. 3	−0.49	0.624
Total sample	139	78.91	22.68				

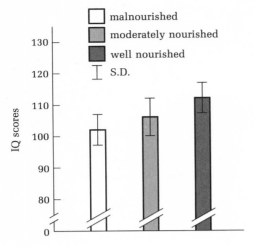

Figure 7.1

The IQ's of the three nutrition groups—means and standard deviations (S.D.).

successful nutritional rehabilitation the children were sent back to the environment from which they came. Even by comparison with nonmalnourished siblings or other children from similar socioeconomic environments their growth and development were retarded (Hertzig et al., 1972). Thus severe malnutrition itself during the first two years of life appears to exacerbate the developmental retardation that occurs under poor socioeconomic conditions. What happens to the child from a high socioeconomic background who becomes malnourished early in life? In the few such cases that have been studied (children with cystic fibrosis or pyloric stenosis) the children have shown a much smaller degree of retardation in growth and development and have tended to catch up with time. What has not been determined yet and what is a much more important practical problem is the fate of a malnourished child from a poor socioeconomic background who is subsequently reared in the relatively "enriched" environment of a higher socioeconomic stratum.

Table 7.4

IQ stanines: comparison of the three nutrition groups. F prob. is the probability that the calculated F ratio would occur by chance.

Group	N	Mean percentile	S.D.	F prob.	Contrast groups	t-test t	t-test P
1	37	5.25	1.32	0.005	1 vs. 2	−1.42	0.160
2	38	5.74	1.62		1 vs. 3	−3.45	0.001*
3	37	6.46	1.66		2 vs. 3	−1.91	0.061
Total sample	112	5.82	1.61				

* Statistically significant.

Table 7.5

Achievement stanines: comparison of the three nutrition groups. F prob. is the probability that the calculated F ratio would occur by chance.

Group	N	Mean percentile	S.D.	F prob.	Contrast groups	t-test t	t-test P
1	40	5.07	1.51	0.002	1 vs. 2	−2.12	0.038*
2	38	5.79	1.47		1 vs. 3	−3.60	0.001*
3	37	6.48	1.89		2 vs. 3	−1.80	0.080
Total sample	115	5.76	1.72				

* Statistically significant.

In a few instances attempts have been made to modify the subsequent environment either by keeping the child longer in the hospital in a program of environmental stimulation or by sending the child home but enrolling him or her in a special preschool program designed to provide a variety of enriching experiences. Improvement in development has been noted with both these approaches but there have been reversals as soon as the special program was discontinued. The data suggest that if a severely malnourished child is subsequently to develop adequately, any program of environmental enrichment must be of long duration. In the present study, severely malnourished children were compared with moderately malnourished and well-nourished children after all had undergone a radical and permanent change in their environments by being adopted into primarily middle-class American homes. (The adoptive parents had no knowledge of the previous nutritional state of the child, and the distribution of these children into their adoptive homes was entirely random.) The results are in striking contrast to those obtained from similar groups of children returned to the environments from which they came (Stoch and Smythe, 1963; Birch, 1972; Cravioto, 1966). Even the severely malnourished adopted Korean children have surpassed Korean norms of height and weight. Moreover, the marked initial size differences between the malnourished and the well-nourished infants have almost entirely disappeared, leaving only a small difference in height. None of the groups reach mean values for American children of the same age. This may reflect either genetic size differences between Korean and American children or the effects of chronic undernutrition extending for several generations in developing countries such as South Korea.

Perhaps even more striking and less in accord with previously reported experience is the fact that the mean IQ of the severely malnourished children is 102 and slightly skewed to the right. It is about 40 points higher than that reported in similar populations that were returned to their early home environments (Stoch and Smythe, 1963; Birch, 1972; Hertzig et al.,

1972). In addition, achievement in school for the severely malnourished group is equal to that expected of normal U.S. children. However, the stigmata of malnutrition had not entirely disappeared by the time these children were studied. There are statistically significant differences between the previously malnourished and well-nourished children in IQ and achievement scores. Whether these are permanent differences it may be too soon to judge. It should be noted, however, that the initially well-nourished children attained a mean IQ and achievement score higher than that of middle-class American children. It may be that these attainments (and those of the other two groups as well) reflect the select character of adoptive parents and of the environment they provide to their adopted children.

In this study all the children came to their U.S. homes before the age of three—the mean age was 18 months. Thus they spent a major portion of their early developmental years in their adoptive homes. It would be important both theoretically and practically to determine whether adoption at later ages produces similar results. Such studies are being planned.

This article by Arthur Jensen is probably the most definitive report demonstrating that a depriving environment can have a cumulatively depressing effect over time on intelligence test scores of very deprived black children. The power of this design is that Jensen controls for average genetic effects by using siblings and comparing the younger to the older child in the family.

8

Cumulative Deficit in IQ of Blacks in the Rural South

ARTHUR R. JENSEN

The cumulative deficit hypothesis is intended to explain the increasing decrement in mental test scores, relative to population norms, as a function of age in groups considered environmentally deprived. According to the hypothesis, the decrement is a result of the cumulative effects of environmental disadvantages on mental development.

The history of the cumulative deficit hypothesis and its theoretical and methodological problems have been reviewed by Jensen (1974a). It was concluded that most of the studies of the phenomenon are seriously flawed by methodological deficiencies. The majority of studies have found no evidence of an age-related IQ decrement in blacks.

Jensen (1974a) proposed investigating IQ decrement by the sibling method; that is, using the difference in standardized test scores between younger and older siblings within the same family as an indicator of IQ decrement. If there is a true IQ decrement, older siblings should obtain lower test scores than their younger siblings, and there should be a positive correlation between sibling age difference and IQ difference. Jensen applied the sibling method to large samples of whites and blacks of ages 5

Jensen, A. R. "Cumulative Deficit in IQ of Blacks in the Rural South." *Developmental Psychology*, 1977, Vol. 13, pp. 184–191. Copyright © 1977 by the American Psychological Association and reprinted by permission.

to 12 in a California school district and found a slight but significant age decrement in verbal IQ in the black sample, but no evidence whatever of a decrement in nonverbal IQ, although the black sample scored equally far below (about one standard deviation) the white sample in nonverbal as in verbal IQ.

Jensen suggested, however, that the sibling method might reveal an age decrement in the IQ of blacks in other regions of the country where blacks have experienced greater environmental disadvantages. Age decrement in verbal and scholastic abilities in Southern blacks was suggested in the Coleman report, (Coleman, Cambell, Hobson, McPartland, Mood, Weinfeld, and York, 1966, p. 274) but is not proven by the cross-sectional IQ × Age data which could reflect selective migration of abler pupils out of the rural South, causing an increasing accumulation of poorer students in the higher grades in school.

Although the cumulative deficit hypothesis applies to scholastic achievement as well as to IQ, it is clear from the literature on this topic that the core hypothesis concerns measured intelligence (Jensen, 1974a). The author has argued elsewhere that standardized IQ tests measure essentially the same general factor of mental ability equally well in both whites and blacks. Although IQ tests are culturally loaded in varying degrees, there is virtually no evidence, in terms of a number of statistical and psychometric criteria (e.g., predictive validity, reliability, item analysis, Race × Items interaction, factor structure, etc.) that the tests are culture biased with respect to the present white and black populations in the United States (Jensen, 1974b, 1976). The black IQ deficit, whatever its causes, appears to be a quite general cognitive deficit rather than narrowly culture specific.

If a cumulative deficit in mental development as indexed by IQ actually exists at all in any segment of the United States population, it should probably be expected most in blacks of the rural South. Their environmental circumstances would seem much more likely to contribute to the cumulative deficit effect than would the relatively good environmental conditions of the California school sample involved in Jensen's first sibling study. The aim of the present study, therefore, is to apply the sibling method to the investigation of IQ decrement in samples of whites and blacks in the rural South. The sampled populations, particularly the black group, are not intended to be representative of the total white and black populations in the United States. Blacks in the locality under study are probably as severely disadvantaged, educationally and economically, as can be found anywhere in the United States today. If an age decrement does not exist in this group, it would seem most doubtful that it could be found in any subpopulation within our borders. Unlike the California study, in which children from kindergarten through sixth grade were used, the present study includes children from kindergarten through twelfth grade, thereby increasing the chances of detecting IQ decrement by the method of differences between younger and older siblings.

Method

The subjects in this study were all of the white and black children enrolled in the public schools of a small rural town in the southeastern part of Georgia.* The population is mostly rural–agricultural, with a very low median family income compared to the national average. The black group as a whole would be classified as very low socioeconomic status (SES) on any index of SES. The white population is predominantly low and lower-middle SES. Some 1,300 school children, approximately 49% whites and 51% blacks, were tested.

TESTS

Subjects were tested on the California Test of Mental Maturity (1963 Revision), a standardized test of general intelligence, which yields deviation IQs for verbal and nonverbal abilities at every grade level from kindergarten through Grade 12 (see Buros, 1972, pp. 631–636). The California Test of Mental Maturity is factorially very comparable to other standardized group tests of verbal and nonverbal IQ such as the Lorge-Thorndike Intelligence Tests, which Jensen (1974a) used in the California study. (The California Test of Mental Maturity was used instead of the Lorge-Thorndike in the Georgia study, since the testing was done as part of the school's state-mandated testing program, which required the California Test of Mental Maturity.) The California Test of Mental Maturity IQs are standardized scores ($M = 100, SD = 15$) based on large samples of school children from 49 states.

Results and Discussion

SAMPLE STATISTICS ON AGE AND IQ

The total white sample ($N = 653$) has a mean age of 12 years 4 months, $SD = 3$ years 7 months. The mean age of the total black sample ($N = 826$) is 11 years 8 months, $SD = 3$ years 3 months. The white mean total IQ is 102, $SD = 16.7$; the black mean total IQ is 71, $SD = 15.1$.

---

* I am indebted to R. T. Osborne for securing these data.

Table 8.1

Mean IQ and age differences of siblings as a function of family size and birth order

Family size	Sibling pair[a]	N B	N W	Total IQ difference (Y − O) Black M[b]	Black SD	White M	White SD	B − W difference t[c]	Verbal Black M[b]	SD
2	A,B	73	121	3.08	16.86	.74	17.48	<1	2.99	15.9
3	A,B	61	44	3.46*	13.23	2.64	13.90	<1	3.89*	13.9
3	B,C	62	48	3.58	17.78	−3.25	16.22	2.10*	3.50*	15.2
4	A,B	39	9	.28	11.90	4.33	15.05	<1	.08	12.2
4	B,C	38	10	8.13**	16.63	−3.30	19.06	1.73*	6.97*	15.3
4	C,D	39	9	2.36	16.38	−3.33	28.36	<1	2.72	15.4
5	A,B	20	3	2.25	20.93	−6.33	3.40	1.69	.05	19.6
5	B,C	19	4	−1.11	16.20	13.75	17.56	−1.56	.47	14.2
5	C,D	20	2	9.95*	17.55	1.50	9.50	1.09	9.40**	14.1
5	D,E	18	4	−.33	16.61	−8.50	18.50	<1	−1.83	15.2

Note: Y − O = Younger − Older; O − Y = Older − Younger; B − W = Black − White.
[a] Birth order goes from oldest sibling (labeled A) to youngest (B, C, etc.).
[b] Asterisks indicate mean is significantly greater than zero by a one-tailed t-test for positive difference,
*$p < .05$, **$p < .01$.
[c] Two-tailed test, *$p < .05$, **$p < .01$.

SIBLING ANALYSES

All of the analyses are based on siblings from families with two or more children who are in school and who have been tested. (The mean number of children per family with two or more children is: white = 2.42, black = 3.29.)

An age decrement in IQ should be indicated by a positive difference between younger and older siblings (i.e., Y − O).

Younger–Older Sibling IQ Difference. If IQ declines with age, there should be a positive mean difference between the IQs of younger minus older siblings (i.e., Y − O). Table 8.1 shows the mean Y − O sibling IQ differences for all sibling pairs of the same birth order within each family of a given size. This method thus does not confound the mean sibling difference with family size as would be the case if we simply averaged all possible sibling differences within each family. Doing the latter tends to exaggerate the magnitude of Y − O sibling differences, should they exist, in whichever group (in this case the black) that has the larger number of siblings per family. Families with more than five siblings were excluded from the analysis, since the Ns are too small to permit reliable statistical treatment.

Positive Y − O sibling differences which are significantly greater than zero are indicated by asterisks. One-tailed t tests are used since only posi-

ence (Y − O)			Nonverbal IQ difference (Y − O)					Age (months) difference (O − Y)				
White		B − W differ-ence	Black		White		B − W differ-ence	Black		White		B − W differ-ence
	SD	t^c	M^b	SD	M	SD	t^c	M	SD	M	SD	t^c
3	17.59	<1	3.89*	19.16	.57	17.20	1.21	36.91	26.18	46.48	30.35	2.32*
8	12.74	<1	2.61	14.66	2.64	17.58	<1	31.29	16.74	38.02	18.35	1.92
8	16.84	1.61	3.85	20.57	−3.94	18.80	2.07*	29.46	16.81	31.02	16.30	<1
4	15.35	<1	.15	15.30	−4.11	35.42	<1	27.52	16.09	37.33	19.92	1.38
0	19.17	1.55	9.13**	17.71	−2.60	17.28	1.90*	28.42	15.60	35.10	19.43	1.01
8	24.86	<1	3.49	18.74	.33	20.61	<1	29.52	16.40	27.00	8.68	<1
3	15.28	<1	3.50	19.00	−4.33	19.19	<1	22.85	10.42	33.25	8.58	1.90
5	21.16	1.61	−1.58	19.93	5.00	15.95	<1	22.26	11.34	25.50	7.92	<1
0	9.00	2.17*	9.60*	23.07	11.00	10.00	<1	25.50	11.49	27.50	2.50	<1
5	14.82	<1	3.17	18.97	−6.25	20.69	<1	24.20	11.17	25.25	4.92	<1

tive Y − O sibling differences are indicative of an age decrement in IQ. (Negative differences could, of course, also be significant and interesting in their own right, but they would not indicate an age decrement in IQ and so would not be relevant to testing the present hypothesis.)

It is clear from Table 8.1 that there are larger and more significant Y − O sibling IQ differences for blacks than for whites. This holds to about the same degree for both verbal and nonverbal IQ. In contrast, the direction and magnitude of the sibling differences in the white sample are inconsistent and small. This finding is made more impressive by the fact that the white sibling pairs show a significantly ($p < .05$) greater age separation than do the black siblings.

Thus, overall there is a significant age decrement in verbal and nonverbal IQ in the black but not in the white sample. The overall mean pooled Y − O total IQ decrement for blacks is 3.31, $SD = 16.22$, and for whites it is $.12$, $SD = 16.80$. The difference of 3.19 between these means is significant, $t(641) = 2.38$, $p < .02$, when the standard error of the difference is based on the mean variance within groups (i.e., family sizes and sibling pairs).

AGE DIFFERENCE AND IQ DIFFERENCE

Table 8.2 shows the size of the IQ decrement as a function of age separation in the black sample. There is a highly significant linear increase in Y − O sibling difference from 1 year apart through 7 years apart. At 8 years apart, the linear trend clearly breaks down, but since the sample size

Table 8.2

Mean difference in verbal (V), and nonverbal (NV), and total (T) IQ between younger and older black siblings as a function of age and age difference, with F test of linear trend in each column

	1 Year apart				2 Years apart		
Ages	V	NV	T	Ages	V	NV	T
6–7	−3.2	1.4	−1.1	6–8	−5.3	−2.0	−3.3
7–8	−3.4	2.5	.1	7–9	−4.0	−.5	−1.3
8–9	−5.1	6.3	−.3	8–10	5.6	0.9	3.9
9–10	−2.8	−8.2	−5.6	9–11	6.3	−3.3	1.2
10–11	6.1	8.8	6.1	10–12	.1	1.8	.3
11–12	−4.6	1.9	−1.1	11–13	5.4	7.5	7.0
12–13	9.4	10.5	10.3	12–14	3.2	3.5	2.3
13–14	−6.6	−7.9	−8.6	13–15	−2.3	−6.7	−5.6
14–15	7.5	10.6	9.6	14–16	4.2	8.3	6.4
15–16	10.2	11.0	11.5				
Mean[a]	−.03	3.13	1.33		2.23	1.60	1.74
F[b]	6.02	.87	3.43		1.57	1.54	.83
df[c]	116	116	116		186	186	186
$p <$	.02	.35	.07		.21	.22	.36

	5 Years apart				6 Years apart		
6–11	8.2	9.2	9.5	6–12	3.6	4.5	4.8
7–12	3.7	4.5	4.9	7–13	9.3	22.8	17.1
8–13	11.0	7.4	9.4	8–14	14.2	6.3	9.5
9–14	7.1	2.4	3.8	9–15	6.3	.2	2.4
10–15	.1	9.3	2.3	10–16	7.5	3.5	5.5
11–16	6.9	9.1	8.3				
Mean	6.58	6.76	6.45		8.30	7.64	7.97
F	.39	.08	.25		.05	2.73[d]	1.34[e]
df	90	90	90		55	55	55
$p <$	.53	.78	.62		.81	.10	.25

[a] Each value was weighted by N in obtaining the mean of the Y − O differences.
[b] F for linear trend only. Other trend components (quadratic, cubic, quartic), if significant beyond $p < .04$ are indicated in footnotes.
[c] Degrees of freedom for the denominator; the numerator always has $df = 1$.
[d] Cubic trend, $F = 6.85$, $p < .02$.
[e] Cubic trend, $F = 4.91$, $p < .03$.

	3 Years apart				4 Years apart		
Ages	V	NV	T	Ages	V	NV	T
6–9	5.7	12.0	10.4	6–10	10.3	7.3	11.1
7–10	10.2	8.1	11.4	7–11	3.3	5.4	3.9
8–11	7.2	3.4	4.3	8–12	2.4	1.5	.9
9–12	7.6	−.4	4.6	9–13	8.1	12.2	9.7
10–13	5.7	11.0	7.5	10–14	5.5	1.7	2.7
11–14	−.6	6.6	2.6	11–15	2.3	.9	1.1
12–15	.5	.1	−1.0	12–16	10.7	12.1	10.6
13–16	−2.2	−3.8	−4.0				
	4.35	4.77	4.53		6.26	6.36	5.97
	7.16	4.16	9.43		.24	.27	.01
	144	144	144		114	114	114
	.01	.05	.01		.63	.60	.90

	7 Years apart				8 Years apart		
6–13	10.3	9.4	10.8	6–14	6.9	2.1	5.6
7–14	2.8	4.3	2.6	7–15	4.0	13.8	8.4
8–15	11.3	13.2	11.4	8–16	3.3	2.7	.7
9–16	15.7	9.3	12.3				
	10.29	9.52	9.75		4.74	5.27	4.34
	1.53	.12	.24		.29	.00	.27
	55	55	55		17	17	17
	.22	.73	.63		.59	.99	.61

in this group is quite small ($n = 20$) one cannot give much importance to this sharp break in the trend. Over the range of 1 to 7 years apart, the regression coefficient of sibling IQ difference on age differences is 1.62 for verbal IQ, 1.19 for nonverbal IQ, and 1.42 for total IQ. That is to say, for every year's difference in age, over the age range from 6 to 16, verbal IQ decreases on the average 1.62 points per year, nonverbal IQ decreases 1.19 points per year, and total IQ decreases 1.42 points per year. This rate of decline could account for a total cumulative decrement of some 14 to 16 IQ points between the ages of 6 and 16 years.

The ages at which the gradual decrement in IQ begins and ends cannot be determined from the present data, which include only subjects ranging in age from 6 to 16 years. It would be important to know if $Y - O$ sibling IQ differences persist beyond the age where the younger sibling is 18. Since mental growth stabilizes at about age 18, one should expect from the cumulative deficit hypothesis that by age 18 the average deficit of the younger sibling should become equal to that of the older, so that the younger-older sibling IQ difference should disappear after age 18 or so. Information regarding this prediction would seem to be crucial for the viability of the cumulative deficit hypothesis.

. . .

Summary and Conclusions

These sibling comparisons for poor black children in rural Georgia clearly show a significant and substantial decrement in verbal and nonverbal IQ between kindergarten and Grade 12. The IQ decrement is a fairly linear function of age within this range. The phenomenon predicted by the cumulative deficit hypothesis is thus demonstrated at a high level of significance.

According to the cumulative deficit hypothesis, the age decrement in IQ is a result of the cumulative effects of environmental disadvantages in factors related to mental development. A counter hypothesis would be that there are genetic differences in the form of the mental growth curves of blacks and whites, with blacks having a more negatively accelerated growth curve, which would result in younger-older sibling differences in black IQ when the IQs are normalized on a predominantly white sample.

The existing data do not permit a definitive rejection of one or the other of these alternative hypotheses. Moreover, these two hypotheses are not mutually exclusive; both genetic and environmental factors could be involved in the progressive decrement phenomenon. However, the present results on Georgia blacks, when viewed in connection with the contrasting results for California blacks, would seem to favor an environmental interpretation of the progressive IQ decrement. If the progressive IQ decrement were a genetic racial effect per se, it should have shown up in the California blacks as well as in the Georgia blacks, even if one granted that

California blacks have a somewhat larger admixture of Caucasian ancestry than do blacks in Georgia (Reed, 1969). But the California blacks showed a slight, though significant, decrement only in verbal IQ, which one might expect to be more susceptible to environmental or cultural effects than nonverbal IQ. The blacks of rural Georgia, whose environmental disadvantages are markedly greater than in the California sample, show considerable decrements in both verbal and nonverbal IQ, but again the decrement is larger for verbal IQ. (Despite this, the verbal IQ still remains slightly higher than nonverbal IQ for the Georgia blacks.) Thus it appears that a cumulative deficit due to poor environment has contributed, at least in part, to the relatively low average IQ in the present sample of blacks in rural Georgia.

V

EDUCATIONAL PROCESSES

In this article Robert McCall correlates IQ test scores obtained during the preschool years and later with adult educational and occupational attainments. The results are provocative, for they demonstrate that there are no substantial improvements in prediction of adult attainments beyond seven or eight years of age. In other words, knowing the IQ's of children at those ages is about as predictive of later educational attainments as knowing the IQ's of those children later. The analyses also show that educational levels of parents play a significant role in predicting adult attainments of their children. In fact, the father's educational level was as good as the child's own IQ in predicting the adult educational attainment of the child.

9

Childhood IQ's as Predictors of Adult Educational and Occupational Status

ROBERT B. McCALL

Many uses of intelligence tests scores (IQ's) are based on the assumption that children's IQ's reveal something of their adult potential for educational and occupational success. But do the tests predict well enough to be used in that way? Jencks and his colleagues (Jencks et al., 1972) recently reviewed the sparse evidence on the predictive validity of IQ tests and found that the correlations between school-age IQ and indices of adult educational and occupational success rarely exceed .60, not high enough for practical purposes requiring long-term prediction. Below we examine evidence on this issue from the Fels Longitudinal Study.

While many of the correlations reviewed by Jencks were based on large samples representing a wide spectrum of socioeconomic classes, often only dichotomous indices of educational or occupational attainment were used (for instance, blue versus white collar), the tests typically had been

McCall, R. B. "Childhood IQ's as Predictors of Adult Educational and Occupational Status." *Science*, 1977, Vol. 197, pp. 482–483. Copyright © by the American Association for the Advancement of Science and reprinted by permission.

given at only one age during childhood, and data were often available only for males. The Fels sample contains families from the top 85 percent of the socioeconomic scale and is somewhat skewed to the right in educational attainment, but it has the advantage that parents and children of both sexes were assessed, over a wide age range, with more accurate procedures than has been typical of many previous reports. An important result of the research reported here is its general consistency with the data reviewed by Jencks.

All Fels subjects who had reached at least 26 years of age, about whom sufficient information was available to determine a Hollingshead scaled score for attained adult education and occupation (Hollingshead, 1957), and who had had at least one IQ determination between 3 and 18 years of age were included in the sample. There were 94 males and 96 females who qualified, and correlations with later attainment could be determined from childhood IQ's at each of 16 ages, based upon 46 to 90 subjects of each sex.

These subjects were born between 1930 and 1943. They scored somewhat above average in IQ (mean of 117, varying somewhat with age) but with average variability (S.D. = 15.9). Of the females, 3 percent had not graduated from high school, 31 percent had gone through high school but not beyond, and 34 percent graduated from college. The comparable figures for males were 1 percent, 22 percent, and 56 percent. Further details of this subject population are given elsewhere (Kagan and Moss, 1962; Sontag, Baker, and Nelson, 1958).

The mental test data available included Pinneau corrected Stanford-Binet IQ (1937) scores at 3, 3½, 4, 4½, 5, 5½, 6, 7, 8, 9, 10, 11, and 12 years (forms L and M were given at alternate ages). Wechsler-Bellevue full-scale IQ at 13 and 16 years, and the total scores from the Primary Mental Abilities (PMA) test at 18 years. Cross-age correlations indicated that the Binet and the Wechsler tests were quite similar to each other but somewhat different from the 18-year PMA, though the PMA is probably as faithful a measure of the general intelligence factor as are the other two. In addition, Hollingshead scaled educational and occupational scores were available from information obtained on the subjects after age 26 years and on their fathers and mothers when the subjects were children. Interrater reliabilities were determined for the six Hollingshead scores on a subset of 26 cases and were acceptable (r's for education were 1.00, .92, and .96; for occupation, .82, .84, and .94).

Figure 9.1 shows the correlations in each sex between individual IQ at various ages in childhood and individual education and occupation ratings in adulthood. Also shown are the correlations between the educational status of the subjects' parents and the subjects' education and occupation ratings as adults. For comparison, Honzik's (1972) correlations between childhood IQ and IQ at age 40 in the Berkeley Child Guidance Study (N's range from 50 to 70 per age group per sex, with a median of 62) are plotted.

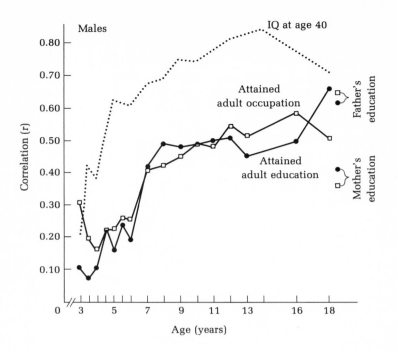

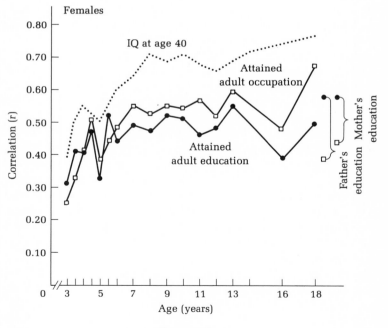

Figure 9.1

Correlations of childhood IQ at various ages with attained adult educational and occupational status (Fels sample) and with IQ at age 40 (Child Guidance sample). Also, correlation of fathers' and mothers' education with offsprings' adult occupational (open square) and adult educational (filled circle) status.

The IQ correlations with attained education and occupation rise until ages 7 to 8, especially for males. Thereafter they remain fairly stable at approximately .50 ($\pm$.10). The r's observed in the Fels sample are quite consistent with the maximum of .60 suggested by Jencks et al. (1972), despite large differences in the size and socioeconomic distribution of the samples and in the precision and frequency of the assessments. They are also consistent with results from a recent large Swedish study (Fägerlind, 1975).

Childhood IQ predicts adult IQ much better than it predicts adult educational and occupational attainment. Whereas the correlations with adult IQ are typically in the range of .70 to .85, those with success criteria are approximately .50 ($\pm$.10). However, this difference must be put into perspective. Consider that the contemporary correlation between adult IQ and adult occupational status approximates .50 (Matarazzo, 1972). If these contemporaneous validity coefficients are taken as maxima, it is remarkable that the correlations of childhood IQ with the adult criteria are approximately at maxima (that is, .50) even before the child has progressed beyond the second grade. But while correlations of .50 may be deemed good on psychometric grounds, especially considering the long prediction interval and the expected maxima for such values, they are probably not sufficiently high to warrant using the IQ's of normal individual children for predictive purposes that might result in limiting their educational opportunities over a substantial period of development. For the Fels sample, 64 to 84 percent of the variability in adult attainment is not reflected in childhood IQ's.

One can only speculate on why these contemporaneous and predictive correlations are modest in value. One of the many possible factors is that bright but disadvantaged children are not able to continue their education, whereas less bright but advantaged children can. If this is true, then there should be a relationship between father's occupation (as a crude index of income, which datum was not available in the Fels study) and offspring's attained education even after childhood IQ has been regressed from the attained education rating. For the ages 12 to 18 these part correlations ranged between .14 and .27 (three of four r's, $.10 > p > .01$, one-tailed) for males and between .26 and .39 for females (all four r's, $.02 > p > .0005$, one-tail). These values suggest that factors associated with father's occupation other than the child's IQ do relate to the child's attained education.

It should be noted in Figure 9.1 that the correlations display greater developmental change for males than for females, with a major surge in predictive power at 6 to 7 years of age for males. Other data indicate that this is a developmental period of considerable transition in mental skills (White, 1965), and inflections in the developmental patterns of IQ are common at these ages (Sontag et al., 1958; McCall et al., 1973). This is also the age at which most of these children began formal schooling.

Note also that mothers' education predicted daughters' educational and occupational attainment better than sons'. Perhaps educated and noneducated mothers differed considerably in their effort to encourage academic and occupational achievement in their daughters at a time when it was not as common for girls to attend college or pursue careers as it was for boys.

Attempts to combine father's and mother's education level to predict child's attained education produced coefficients (for males $R = .62$, for females $R = .63$) not substantially higher than did father's education alone (for males $r = .62$, for females $r = .58$). Nor did combining father's education and child's IQ elevate predictions. For example, these multiple correlations were highest and most consistent between 12 and 18 years, when they averaged .67 for males and .63 for females. Therefore, for sheer predictive purposes father's education level was more accurate than the child's own IQ, which contributed no substantial additional predictive power.

All the relationships depicted in Figure 9.1 were reappraised for the possibility that they might have been influenced by secular changes or by the fact that adult achievement measures were obtained at different ages across the sample. Birth year and the age at which adult information was obtained were not related to IQ, which implies that sampling procedures were relatively constant across the study period. There were modest secular relationships for the educational and occupational ratings (for example, the more recently born obtained more years of schooling than did the early cohorts); but, when the variables were adjusted for differences in birth year and the age at which adult information were obtained, there was essentially no difference between the corrected correlations and those pictured in Figure 9.1. Rarely did a correlation coefficient change by more than ±.03. Therefore, these data are consistent with Jencks's (Jencks et al., 1972) conclusion that educational advances at the time of these studies had not closed the gap in success potential or constituted the "great equalizer" between advantaged and disadvantaged children.

In this article John Fletcher and Richard Atkinson demonstrate the success of a computer-assisted reading instruction program in improving performance of young elementary school children. The article shows that in these early grades children can progress faster with a computer-assisted program than with a traditional program of teaching reading. One must be cautious, however, in generalizing to higher grades and to all courses. Reading, especially before comprehension begins to become more important than the simple decoding of words, and mathematics lend themselves to clear specification regarding the elements to be acquired. Other subjects, especially those in which the necessary prerequisites are harder to specify, might not show such spectacular gains with computer-assisted instruction. Nevertheless, it seems likely that some portions of virtually all courses could be taught using computer-assisted instruction.

10

Evaluation of the Stanford CAI Program in Initial Reading

J. D. FLETCHER AND R. C. ATKINSON

Computer-assisted instruction (CAI) in initial reading (kindergarten through the third grade) has been under development at Stanford University since 1964. Our original goal was to implement a complete CAI curriculum that would present most, if not all, of initial reading instruction under computer control and would depend only minimally on classroom teaching. These early efforts were successful (Atkinson, 1968), but the high cost of the program made it unlikely that it could be implemented on a wide-scale basis in the forseeable future. In addition, our early research indicated that, while some aspects of reading instruction could be handled extremely well and inexpensively under computer control, others

Fletcher, J. D., and Atkinson, R. C. "Evaluation of the Stanford CAI Program in Initial Reading," *Journal of Educational Psychology*, 1972, Vol. 64, pp. 597–602. Copyright © 1972 by the American Psychological Association and reprinted by permission.

were better left to the classroom teacher. This experience led us, during the last 3 years, to design and implement a low-cost CAI curriculum that would serve primarily as a supplement to normal classroom instruction. A student terminal in the current program consists of only a Model 33 tele-typewriter equipped with an audio headset; there is no graphic or photo-graphic capability at the student terminal, and the character set of the teletypewriter is limited to uppercase letters. These are strong constraints from a curriculum viewpoint, but they are partially offset by an extremely flexible audio system. Audio is stored in digitized form on magnetic disks, and the system provides, on a time-shared basis, rapid (30 milliseconds) random access to any one of 6,000 recorded words.

Reading instruction may be divided into two basic tasks variously re-ferred to as decoding and communication. For present purposes, decoding is defined as the rapid, if not automatic, association of phonemes or phoneme groups with their respective graphic representations; communi-cation is defined as reading for meaning, aesthetic enjoyment, emphasis, and the like. The major emphasis of the Stanford CAI program is on decod-ing skills, although work on word and sentence comprehension is also included. Instruction is divided into seven content areas or strands. Strand I, the readiness strand, provides practice with the manual skills required for interaction with the CAI program and instruction on a series of fairly standard "reading readiness" tasks. Strand II, the letter strand, provides practice in copying, recognition, and recall of the letters of the alphabet. The initial pass through the alphabet presents letters singly and in maximally contrasting groups, for example (RTO); later passes through the alphabet present letters in minimally contrasting groups, for example (MNW). Strand III, the word strand, provides for the development of a sight word vocabulary. Seven kindergarten through third-grade reading vocabulary lists were analyzed in developing this strand. Of the words used in Strands III through V, those that do not include regular grapheme-phoneme correspondences are presented only in this strand. Strand IV, the spelling pattern strand, provides for recognition and recall of orthographically regular monosyllabic words arranged in groups which emphasize a single spelling pattern, for example (ran, fan, man) or (fat, fan, fad). Strand V, the phonics strand, provides for direct practice in copying and recognition of the spelling patterns themselves as well as the "construction" of monosyllabic words from given consonant clusters and spelling patterns. Strand VI, the comprehension categories strand, at-tempts to provide practice with the meaning of words by emphasizing the semantic categories of words. Exercises in this strand ask the student to select the word of those displayed that is an animal or that is a color, etc. Strand VII, the comprehension sentences strand, provides practice in read-ing sentences by requiring the student to select a word to fill an empty "slot" in the sentence. On any given day, a student's lesson may involve exercises drawn from one to five different strands. A more complete de-scription of the program as well as the rationale underlying it is presented in Atkinson, Fletcher, Chetin, and Stauffer (1971), and Atkinson and Fletcher (1972); cost considerations are discussed in Jamison, Fletcher, Suppes, and Atkinson (1973).

The CAI program is designed to permit each student to progress at his own rate through a sequence of materials that maximizes his progress. Our approach has been to formulate mathematical models for the acquisition of various decoding skills and use these models to specify optimal procedures. These procedures require that a rapidly accessible response history be maintained for each student. As the student progresses through the curriculum, his history is continually updated and interrogated in order to specify the curriculum items to be presented next. A discussion of optimization procedures developed for the CAI reading program can be found in Atkinson and Paulson (1972).

The first tryout of the program occurred in the 1968–1969 school year with students in kindergarten and Grades 1, 2, and 3. As expected, many problems of curriculum design and system operation were identified and had to be corrected during this period. By the summer of 1969, however, the system and curriculum had stabilized to a satisfactory level of operation, and an evaluation of the program was undertaken during the 1969–1970 school year. The purpose of this article is to summarize briefly some of the more important findings obtained from the evaluation.

Method

The problems of evaluating a new curriculum are many, and it is difficult if not impossible to deal with all of them. The design adopted for this evaluation has its faults, but within the economic and administrative constraints of the situation it appeared to be a reasonable choice. A matched-pairs design was used in which compensation for possible differences between experimental and control groups is achieved by matching on the basis of pretest scores.

Although over 100 students were run for varying periods of time on the CAI reading curriculum, the evaluation was limited to a group of 50 matched pairs. Prior to receiving any exposure to CAI, 25 pairs of first-grade boys and 25 pairs of first-grade girls were matched on the basis of the Metropolitan Readiness Test (MRT). The MRT was administered in October to groups of 10 or less pupils by trained test personnel. The Numbers and Draw-A-Man subtests of the MRT were not administered. Matching was achieved so that the MRT scores for a matched pair of students were no more than two points apart. Moreover, in matching the students an effort was made to insure that both members were drawn from comparable classrooms with teachers of equivalent ability. The mean MRT score for the boys participating in the evaluation was 56.6 and the mean for the girls was 55.1.

The experimental member of each matched pair of students received 8 to 10 minutes of CAI instruction per school day roughly from the first week in January until the second week in June. The control member of each pair received no CAI instruction. Except for the 8- to 10-minute CAI period there is no reason to believe that the activities during the school day were any different for the experimental and control subjects.

Three posttests were administered to all subjects in late May and early June, 1970. Four subtests of the Stanford Achievement Test, Primary I, Form X, were used. These subtests were: word reading, paragraph meaning, vocabulary, and word study. Second, the California Cooperative Primary Reading Test (COOP), Form 12A (Grade 1, spring) was administered. Only the total raw scores were used from this test. Both the Stanford Achievement Test and the COOP were administered to classroom groups by teachers under the supervision of district testing personnel. Finally, a test (DF) developed at Stanford and tailored to the goals of the CAI reading curriculum was administered individually to all subjects. The DF items fell into eight groups yielding the following eight subtests: uppercase letters, lowercase letters, uppercase words, lowercase words, spelling patterns, monosyllabic words comprising these spelling patterns, and nonsense monosyllables comprising these spelling patterns. The words for the subtests were chosen at random from first-grade vocabulary lists. The spelling patterns for the subtests had all been taught in the CAI curriculum, but none of the words or nonsense syllables in the subtests had been taught. In administering the test, an item printed in primary type on a 3 × 5 index card is shown to a subject who then has 10 seconds to read the item aloud.

The CAI subjects were expected to score higher on all subtests of DF than were the non-CAI subjects, since each subtest represented a specific goal of the curriculum.

. . .

Earlier results had shown that boys in CAI initial reading do about as well as girls despite the almost universally expected superior performance of girls in conventional initial reading (Atkinson, 1968). For this reason male and female matched pairs were kept separate to see if this result would hold for the current evaluation.

Results and Discussion

During the course of the school year, an equal number of pairs was lost from the female and male groups; complete data were obtained for 22 pairs of boys and 22 pairs of girls. Means, standard deviations, and t values for differences in Stanford Achievement, COOP, and DF total scores are presented in Table 10.1 for the matched pairs of boys and the matched pairs of girls.

The results of these analyses are heartening. Of the six posttest com-

Table 10.1

Means, standard deviations, and *t* values for the
Stanford Achievement Test, the California Cooperative
Primary Test, and the CAI Reading Project Test

Subjects	Measure	SAT	COOP	DF
		CAI		
Boys	M	109.7	33.2	64.9
	SD	24.1	8.6	7.0
	t	3.60*	4.70*	7.01*
		Non-CAI		
	M	90.2	23.4	53.0
	SD	19.5	8.9	10.4
		CAI		
Girls	M	115.7	33.7	64.1
	SD	26.2	10.4	7.6
	t	2.55*	1.65	3.10*
		Non-CAI		
	M	96.5	28.9	56.6
	SD	30.5	10.8	13.5

* $p < .01$ ($df = 21$).

parisons, only one (COOP for matched pairs of girls) failed to indicate a
significant difference in favor of the CAI reading subjects. These differences are also important from the standpoint of improvement in estimated
grade placement. Table 10.2 displays the mean grade placement of the

Table 10.2

Average grade placement on the
Stanford Achievement Test and the
California Cooperative Primary Test

Subjects	SAT	COOP
Boys		
CAI	2.2	2.5
non-CAI	1.8	1.8
Girls		
CAI	2.4	2.6
non-CAI	2.0	2.2

Table 10.3

Correlations of the number of CAI reading items completed per unit time with the Standard Achievement Test, the California Cooperative Primary Test, and the CAI Reading Project Test

Subjects	SAT	COOP	DF
Boys	.74	.68	.48
Girls	.84	.77	.49

four groups on the Stanford Achievement test and COOP. The differences between CAI and non-CAI groups in estimated grade placement range from .4 to .7 school years....

It was expected that some measure of performance on the system would correlate fairly highly with the Stanford Achievement, COOP, and DF total scores. These correlations are presented in Table 10.3. The measure of performance on the CAI curriculum used here is the total number of curriculum units brought to criterion by a student divided by the total amount of time accumulated on the system. Note that the correlations are particularly high for the Stanford Achievement and COOP scores. Oddly, the smallest correlations are with the DF scores which were expected to reflect more closely than the Stanford Achievement and COOP the goals of the curriculum.

It is interesting to examine the effect of CAI on the progress of the boys compared to the progress of the girls. The results presented in Table 10.1 seem to corroborate the Atkinson (1968) finding that boys benefit more from CAI instruction than do girls. For both the Stanford Achievement and COOP tests, the girls are superior to the boys, but for the non-CAI group the size of the difference is greater than for the CAI group. On the Stanford Achievement Test, the relative improvement for boys exposed to CAI versus those not exposed to CAI is 22%; the corresponding figure for girls is 20%. On the COOP, the percentage improvement due to CAI is 42 for boys and 17 for girls. Finally, on the DF, the percentage improvement is 32 for boys and 13 for girls. Overall, these data suggest that both boys and girls benefit from CAI instruction in reading, but that relatively CAI is more effective for boys. Explanations of this difference are discussed in Atkinson (1968).

Conclusion

The daily, 8- to 10-minute CAI sessions in initial reading yielded improvements on posttest performances that were significant from both a statistical and practical standpoint. These improvements were not limited to the specific, phonics-oriented goals of the CAI curriculum, but include improvements in more general reading skills related to sentence and paragraph comprehension.

In evaluating these results it should be kept in mind that the experimental group received CAI for only 5½ months. The fact that the observed differences are so substantial suggests that the CAI treatment administered over several years could well have dramatic results. Although we have no systematic data on students who have been on the program for several years, the size of the effects observed in this short-term study are in accord with our impressions of the improvements achieved by students with more extended experience.

Other analyses of data have been run but will not be reported here. Our main purpose in this article is to briefly report a few of the more important results from the evaluation, but not to offer any firm conclusions or interpretations. We recognize that some readers will not be happy with our multiple use of paired t tests. They are presented not as definitive measures of statistical significance but rather as rough indexes of the influence of CAI on the various dependent measures.

This influential article by John B. Carroll tries to identify the factors contributing to variations in school achievement using time as a basic ingredient for as many of the relevant parameters as possible. In essence, the degree of learning will be a function of the time actually spent on the task and the time needed to really learn it. Those with more aptitude may need less time, but if they lack the perseverance, they still may not learn. It is also important to distinguish between the time actually spent working and the elapsed time. A common observation is that some individuals are much more efficient in using the time available than others, and measures of elapsed study time may indicate little about these differences. One important consequence of the ideas expressed in this article is that many of the components of differences in scholastic attainment can be brought under empirical observation and that we need not be content with passively accepting these differences, but rather, we may be able to do something about maximizing the learning and performance of all individuals.

11

A Model of School Learning

The primary job of the educational psychologist is to develop and apply knowledge concerning why pupils succeed or fail in their learning at school, and to assist in the prevention and remediation of learning difficulties.

This job is inherently difficult because behavior is complex and has a multiplicity of causes. To deal with it, educational psychologists have evolved a number of concepts which they find useful in classifying the phenomena of behavior. Textbooks in the field are commonly organized around such concepts as maturation, individual differences, learning, thinking, motivation, and social development. These are useful categories, but because they overlap or refer to different levels of organization in the subject matter, it is difficult to build them into an integrated account of the process of school learning. What is needed is a schematic design or con-

Carroll, John B. "A Model of School Learning." *Teachers College Record*, 1963, Vol. 64, pp. 723–733. Reprinted by permission.

ceptual model of factors affecting success in school learning and of the way they interact. Such a model should use a very small number of simplifying concepts, conceptually independent of one another and referring to phenomena at the same level of discourse. It should suggest new and interesting research questions and aid in the solution of practical educational problems. With the aid of such a framework, the often conflicting results of different research studies might be seen to fall into a unified pattern.

Many such formulations, perhaps, are possible. A conceptual model will be presented here that seems to have the advantage of comprehensiveness combined with relative simplicity. The model is amenable to elaboration, but for our immediate purposes, we will leave aside any such elaborations.

Scope of the Model

We need first to define *learning task*. The learner's task of going from ignorance of some specified fact or concept to knowledge or understanding of it, or of proceeding from incapability of performing some specified act to capability of performing it, is a learning task. To call it a task does not necessarily imply that the learner must be aware *that* he is supposed to learn or be aware of *what* he is supposed to learn, although in most cases it happens that such awarenesses on the part of the learner are desirable.

Most, but not all, goals of the school can be expressed in the form of learning tasks or a series of such tasks. Teaching the child to read, for example, means to teach him to perform certain acts in response to written or printed language. Examples of other learning tasks taught in the schools can be multiplied at will: learning to spell all the words in common use, learning to perform certain operations with numbers, learning to explain or otherwise demonstrate an understanding of the subject matter of biology, learning to speak a foreign language, learning to perform in competitive sports, and learning to carry out certain responsibilities of a citizen. Some of these tasks are very broadly defined, such as learning to read printed English, but we can also consider narrowly defined tasks like mastering the content of Lesson 20 in a certain textbook of French, or even mastering a certain grammatical construction covered in that lesson. The model presented here is intended to apply equally well to all such tasks, no matter how broad or narrow. It is required, however, that the task can be unequivocally described and that means can be found for making a valid judgment as to when the learner has accomplished the learning task—that is, has achieved the learning goal which has been set for him.

It will be seen that as many as possible of the basic concepts in the model are defined so that they can be measured in terms of *time* in order to capitablize on the advantages of a scale with a meaningful zero point and equal units of measurement. An effort is made to provide for a mathematical description of the degree to which a learning task is achieved. Although the model applies only to one learning task at a time, it should be possible in principle to describe the pupil's success in learning a series of tasks (e.g., all the work of the fifth grade) by summating the results of applying the model successively to each component task.

The model is admittedly oversimplified. The assumption that the work of the school can be broken down into a series of learning tasks can be called into question. In actual school practice, the various tasks to be learned are not necessarily treated as separate and distinct, and the process of teaching is often organized (whether rightly so or not) so that learnings will take place "incidentally" and in the course of other activities. Nevertheless, a conceptual model requires certain simplifying assumptions, and the assumption of discrete learning tasks is a useful one to make.

The model can be regarded as applying even to those educational goals ordinarily formulated in terms of "transfer"—that is, the ability to apply in a "new" situation something learned previously. The concept of the learning task is defined to include the attainment of that degree of competence which will make "transfer" essentially as automatic as demonstration of performance in the original setting. "Transfer," correctly viewed, is a term in a metalanguage which states the conditions under which particular learnings occur or manifest themselves. Thus, when we say that "learning which occurred in situation A transfers to situation B," we are really saying that "something learned in stiuation A also manifested itself in situation B, there being sufficient commonality between the two situations to elicit the learned performance in both."

The model is not intended to apply, however, to those goals of the school which do not lend themselves to being considered as learning tasks. Such, for example, are those goals having to do with attitudes and dispositions. Educating a child so that he has tolerance for persons of other races or creeds, respect for parental or legal authority, or attitudes of fair play, is thought to be largely a matter of emotional conditioning or of the acquisition of values and drives. Learning tasks may indeed be involved in the cognitive support of such attitudes (as where the child learns facts about different races or creeds), but the acquisition of attitudes is postulated to follow a different paradigm from that involved in learning tasks. Perhaps the distinctions made by Skinner (1953) are of use in this connection: We could say that whereas learning tasks typically involve "operants," the attitudinal goals of education typically involve "respondents."

Overview of the Model

Briefly, our model says that the learner will succeed in learning a given task to the extent that he spends the amount of time that he needs to learn the task. The terms of this statement, however, require special definition,

explication, and interpretation if the statement is to be properly understood.

First, it should be understood that "spending time" means *actually*
spending time on the act of learning. "Time" is therefore not "elapsed
time" but the time during which the person is oriented to the learning task
and actively engaged in learning. In common parlance, it is the time
during which he is "paying attention" and "trying to learn."

Second, there are certain factors which determine how much time the
learner *spends* actively engaged in learning.

Third, there are certain factors which determine how much time a
person *needs to spend* in order to learn the task. These factors may or may
not be the same as, or associated with, those which influence how much
time he spends in learning.

The major part of this article is devoted to a presentation of the factors
conceived as determining the times needed or actually spent in the course
of a learning task and the way in which these factors interact to result in
various degrees of success in learning. Four of these factors are convenient
intervening variables or constructs which may, in turn, be regarded as
functions of still other factors or variables; one, however, is in principle a
directly manipulable and measurable factor ("opportunity").

This model on school learning should not be confused with what is
ordinarily called "learning theory," that is, with the exact scientific
analysis of the essential conditions of learning and the development of
systematic theory about this process. Rather, the model may be thought of
as a description of the "economics" of the school learning process; it takes
he fact of learning for granted.

The five factors or variables in the model will be presented under two
headings: (1) determinants of time needed for learning, and (2) determinants of time spent in learning.

Time Needed in Learning

APTITUDE

Suppose that a randomly selected group of children is taught a certain
learning task by a teacher (or teaching device) with the best possible
teaching techniques. Suppose further that each child is willing to stick
attentively with the learning task for the number of minutes, hours, or
days required for him to learn it to the specified criterion of success, and
that each child is in fact given the opportunity to do this. Common experience, as well as abundant research evidence, suggests that the amounts of
time needed by the children even under these ideal conditions will differ
widely. Let us think, then, of the amount of time the pupil will need to
learn the task under these conditions as the primary measure of a variable
which we shall call his *aptitude for learning this task*. In ordinary par-

lance, learners who need only a small amount of time are said to have high aptitude; learners who need a large amount of time are said to have low aptitude. Some learners, it may be, will never learn even under these optimal conditions; we may say that these learners would need an indefinitely large (or an infinite) amount of time to learn the task.

It will be noted that this variable is measured in the opposite direction from the usual way of measuring aptitude—the shorter the time needed for learning, the higher the aptitude.

Furthermore, it will be noted that the measure of aptitude is specific to the task under consideration. Aptitude may be regarded as a function of numerous other variables. For one thing, it may depend upon the amount of prior learning which may be relevant to the task under consideration. A learner who has already progressed far towards the mastery of a task may not need much time to complete his learning. On the other hand, aptitude may also depend upon a series of traits or characteristics of the learner which enter into a wide variety of tasks; whether these traits can be accounted for solely on the basis of generalized prior learnings, or whether they reflect genetically determined individual characteristics, is of no immediate concern here. It may be useful, however, to conceive that a learner's estimated needed time, α_t, for learning a given task, t, may be written as a mathematical function of a series of basic aptitudes, symbolized with Greek letters and subscripts, minus the amount of time, s_t, saved by virtue of prior learnings relevant to the task. Thus:

$$\alpha_t = f(\alpha_1, \alpha_2, \ldots, \alpha_n) - s_t$$

The exact form of this formula would vary for different tasks. Presumably the basic aptitudes α_1, $\alpha_2, \ldots$, α_n could be measured with considerable exactitude by appropriate tests.

ABILITY TO UNDERSTAND INSTRUCTION

We find it useful to postulate as a variable separate from those we consider under "aptitude" the ability to understand instruction, since this variable (in contrast to pure aptitude variables) is thought of as interacting with the method of instruction in a special and interesting way. The ability to understand instruction could be measured, one would suppose, as some combination of "general intelligence" and "verbal ability"; the former of these two would come into play in instructional situations where the learner is left to infer for himself the concepts and relationships inherent in the material to be learned, rather than having them carefully spelled out for him, while the latter would come into play whenever the instruction utilized language beyond the grasp of the learner. The way in which ability to understand instruction is postulated to interact with the type of instruction will be explained after we introduce a third variable affecting time needed for learning, the *quality of instruction*.

QUALITY OF INSTRUCTION

One job of the teacher (or any person who prepares the materials of instruction) is to organize and present the task to be learned in such a way that the learner can learn it as rapidly and as efficiently as he is able. This means, first, that the learner must be told, in words that he can understand, what he is to learn and how he is to learn it. It means that the learner must be put into adequate sensory contact with the material to be learned (for example, one must insure that the learner will adequately see or hear the materials of instruction). It also means that the various aspects of the learning task must be presented in such an order and with such detail that, as far as possible, every step of the learning is adequately prepared for by a previous step. It may also mean that the instruction must be adapted for the special needs and characteristics of the learner, including his stage of learning. All these things may be summarized in what we call *quality of instruction*. This variable applies not only to the performance of a teacher but also to the characteristics of textbooks, workbooks, films, teaching-machine programs, etc.

Now, if the quality of instruction is anything less than optimal, it is possible that the learner will need more time to learn the task than he would otherwise need. Some learners will be more handicapped by poor instruction than others. The extent of this handicap is conceived to be a function of the learner's *ability to understand instruction*. Learners with high ability in this respect will be able to figure out for themselves what the learning task is and how they can go about learning it; they will be able to overcome the difficulties presented by poor quality of instruction by perceiving concepts and relationships in the teaching materials which will not be grasped by those with lesser ability.

For the purposes of this conceptual model, we shall say that the amount of time actually needed by a person to learn a given task satisfactorily is a function not only of aptitude (as defined previously), but also of the quality of instruction in so far as it is less than optimal. And the amount of additional time he will need is an inverse function of his ability to understand instruction.

We could, of course, apply Occam's razor and get rid of both of the two preceding variables by conceiving that a change in the quality of instruction causes an essential change in the learning task itself. In this case, we would deal only with a learner's aptitude for learning a given task, subscripted with the quality of instruction attached to it. Such a modification of our model seems undesirable, however, for one would tend to lose sight of instructional quality as one of the important manipulable variables in educational psychology.

Time Spent in Learning

TIME ALLOWED FOR LEARNING ("OPPORTUNITY")

It may come as a surprise to some to be told that the schools may allow less than adequate time for learning any task, but second thought will make one realize that this is very often the case. It is partly a consequence of the very large amount of material that the schools are expected to teach; the available time must somehow be distributed among many things. And it is partly a consequence of the very great variation that exists in the amounts of time that children need for learning, even under a good quality of instruction, and particularly when the instructional quality is such that many children of lower ability to understand instruction require much more time than they might otherwise need.

The school responds to differences in learning rates (for that is what differences in aptitude are) in many ways. Sometimes the policy of the school is, in effect, to ignore these differences; a certain amount of time is provided for everybody to learn, and no more. (For example, at some military academics, study time is prescribed and scheduled uniformly for all cadets.) At the opposite extreme is the case where each student is allowed to proceed exactly at his own rate; private instruction in music or foreign languages and self-instruction by teaching machine or other means are approximations to this case. The middle position is occupied by learning situations in which there is some kind of "ability grouping": Pupils are assigned to different groups, classes, or curricula on the basis of estimated learning rates.

Even when there is some constraint upon the amount of time "officially" provided for learning, teachers and instructional programs vary in the amount of time they allow for learning. Some programs present material at such a rapid pace that most students are kept under continual pressure; only the apter students can keep up with this instruction, while the others fall back or out, sometimes never to get caught up. In other programs, the instruction is paced for the benefit of the slower student. The faster student is fortunate if the teacher takes appropriate steps to "enrich" his instructional content; but this will not always happen, and it is undoubtedly the case that many fast learners lose some of their motivation for learning when they feel that their time is being wasted or when they are not kept at the edge of challenge.

Perseverance

Obviously, failure to allow enough time for learning produces incomplete learning. If a person needs two hours to learn something and is allowed only one hour, and if we assume that learning proceeds linearly with time, the degree of learning is only 50 percent. Probably one of the most aversive things which a school can do is not to allow sufficient time for a well-motivated child to master a given learning task before the next is taken up. Children meet such frustrations by indifference or the more extreme avoidance reactions and are, in any case, handicapped in undertaking the next task.

THE TIME THE LEARNER IS WILLING TO SPEND IN LEARNING ("PERSEVERANCE")

The term *perseverance* is used here, rather than persistence, because of the somewhat pejorative connotations of the latter. Nevertheless, the concept is similar to what Paul Brandwein describes in the following passage:

> The characteristics grouped under the Predisposing Factor . . . include a spectrum of traits which the writer places under the head of *Persistence*. This is defined as consisting of three attitudes. (1) A marked willingness to spend time, beyond the ordinary schedule, in a given task (this includes the willingness to set one's own time schedules, to labor beyond a prescribed time, such as nine to five). (2) A willingness to withstand discomfort. This includes adjusting to shortened lunch hours, or no lunch hours, working without holidays, etc. It includes withstanding fatigue and strain and working even through minor illness, such as a cold or a headache. (3) A willingness to face failure. With this comes a realization that patient work may lead to successful termination of the task at hand (Brandwein, 1955, pp. 9–10).

But the variable of perseverance applies not only in the case of the "gifted student" and not only in the case of long durations of effort, but also to all other learners and also to learning tasks which require only short times for mastery. That is, in the general case, a learner who (in view of his aptitude, the quality of the instruction, and his ability to understand the instruction) needs a certain amount of time to learn a task may or may not be willing to persevere for that amount of time in trying to learn. It is not a matter of his predicting how long he will be willing to learn: we simply postulate that there is a certain time over and above which he will not continue active learning of a task, and this time may lie anywhere on the scale from zero to infinity. The learner may not be motivated to learn at all, or he may regard the task as something too difficult for him to learn; in either case, he may spend no time at all in trying to learn. He may start to learn and later become distracted or bored, or he may lose confidence in his ability. He may go far toward mastery and then overestimate his achievement, thus prematurely terminating his efforts to learn. He may, of course, be so highly motivated that he would be willing to spend more time than he needs in order to reach a specified criterion of mastery. Nevertheless, for the purposes of our conceptual model, it will be assumed that the learner will never actually spend more time than he needs to master the task as defined, that is, that he will stop learning as soon as he has mastered the learning task. (In this way we avoid, for the present, the necessity of incorporating a concept of "overlearning" in the model.)

This variable, which may be called *perseverance-in-learning-to-criterion,* is thus measured in terms of time, and if it is not sufficiently great to allow the learner to attain mastery, it operates in our conceptual model to reduce the degree of learning. Assume, as before, that learning proceeds as a linear function of time. Then if a child needs two hours to learn something, is allowed one hour, but will persevere only thirty minutes, the degree of learning is only 25 percent. Perseverance-in-learning is measured only in terms of the amount of time the child is actively engaged in learning; a child who is actively engaged in learning for various periods totaling only thirty minutes during an hour is presumably not paying attention to learning for the other thirty minutes, and this time is not counted.

Perseverance-in-learning is itself a function of many other variables which will not be separately treated in this conceptual model. It is a function partly of what is ordinarily called "motivation" or desire to learn. But there are many reasons for desiring to learn a given thing: To please the teacher, to please one's parents or friends, to get good grades or other external rewards, to achieve self-confidence in one's learning ability, to feed one's self-esteem, to avoid disapproval—all these can operate *in place of* or *in addition to* any incentives for learning which may derive from the intrinsic interest or perceived utility of the thing being learned. And there are probably just as many reasons which one may adopt (consciously or unconsciously) for *not* learning: to avoid the responsibilities which learning brings, to avoid the exertion of learning, to behave consistently with one's image of oneself as a nonlearner, or to avoid wasting time on learning tasks of no perceived importance.

Perseverance-in-learning may also be a function of what are ordinarily called emotional variables. One may desire to learn but be unable to endure frustrations caused by difficulties in the learning task or distractions from external circumstances. It may also interact with the quality of instruction; poor quality of instruction may reduce perseverance-in-learning even beyond the toll it takes in wasted minutes or even weeks.

The Complete Model

It will be noticed that the model involves five elements—three residing in the individual and two stemming from external conditions. Factors in the individual are (1) aptitude—the amount of time needed to learn the task under optimal instructional conditions, (2) ability to understand instruction, and (3) perseverance—the amount of time the learner is willing to engage actively in learning. Factors in external conditions are (4) opportunity—time allowed for learning, and (5) the quality of instruction—a measure of the degree to which instruction is presented so that it will not require additional time for mastery beyond that required in view of aptitude.

Three of the factors are expressed purely in terms of time. If ability to understand instruction corresponds to a combination of general and verbal intelligence, it can be assessed in relative terms by currently available measuring devices. The most elusive quantity in this model is that called *quality of instruction*, but both it and the ability to understand instruction are interconnected with temporally measurable variables in such a way that by appropriate experimental manipulations, they could eventually be indexed in terms of time. Temporarily, let us put quality of instruction on a scale from 0 (poor) to 1 (optimal), and ability to understand instruction on a standard score scale with mean = 0 and $\sigma = 1$.

The five factors can be worked into a tentative formula which expresses the degree of learning, for the ith individual and the tth task, as a function of the ratio of the amount of time the learner actually spends on the learning task to the total amount he needs. Thus:

$$\text{Degree of learning} = f\left(\frac{\text{time actually spent}}{\text{time needed}}\right)$$

The numerator of this fraction will be equal to the *smallest* of the following three quantities: (1) opportunity—the time allowed for learning, (2) perseverance—the amount of time the learner is willing to engage actively in learning, and (3) aptitude—the amount of time needed to learn, increased by whatever amount necessary in view of poor quality of instruction and lack of ability to understand less than optimal instruction. This last quantity (time needed to learn after adjustment for quality of instruction and ability to understand instruction) is also the denominator of the fraction. It is not necessary or worthwhile here, however, to pursue the detailed mathematical formulation, which has been given elsewhere (Carroll, 1962).

As an illustration of the usefulness of this model in clarifying other educational concepts, let us see how it provides a framework for interpreting the notion of "underachievement" as criticized by Henry Dyer (1960). While we are at it, let us also look at the notion of "overachievement." It is our contention that these terms are useful and salvageable if properly defined.

Underachievement and overachievement, like underweight and overweight, are ordinarily taken with reference to some norm or baseline of expectation. The underachiever does poorer than we expect him to, and the overachiever does better than we expect him to. The issue is this:

Upon what do we base our expectation? The approved manner of doing this is to make predictions from those tests or other measurements which in fact yield the best predictions of success, and statistical theory tells us how to make best use of these predictors (i.e., by making our predictions along a regression line). There is, however, a paradox here. Suppose our predictions were perfect: Then there would be no "underachievers" and no "overachievers." An unlikely eventuality to be sure! Nevertheless, our intuitive rejection of the case of perfect prediction lends credence to the following analysis of what we mean by "underachievement"; Underachievement is a situation in which there is a discrepancy between actual achievement and that expected on the basis of a certain *kind* of evidence—evidence concerning the "capacity" or "aptitude" of the individual to achieve in a particular context. Such evidence is recognized as being quite distinct from evidence concerning other factors in achievement, e.g., "motivation," "opportunity for learning," etc., and these latter factors would not figure in forming our expectations. Instead, we would hope to gather as much evidence as possible concerning the "capacity" or "aptitude" of the individual, defined as his learning rate when all other factors are optimal.

Achievement and Expectancy

With reference to the conceptual model presented earlier, our expectation of an individual's achievement in a given learning task would in the strictest sense be that which he would attain when he spends all the time he needs—that is, when the ratio of the time spent to the time needed is unity. Anything less than this is, to some degree, underachievement. From this point of view, *all* learners are underachievers unless they are superhuman beings in an ideal world. Perseverance sometimes flags; the quality of instruction is seldom optimal, and time allowed for learning is not always sufficient.

Let us, therefore, strike some sort of average for perseverance, instructional quality, and opportunity for learning. Our expectation of the degree of learning will be somewhat less than unity because, on the average, individuals will spend less time in learning than they need. And we may gauge underachievement and overachievement with reference to this expectation. In effect, this is what we do by the customary regression techniques based on aptitude measures, although in a less precise way than might be done if we were able to measure each of the components of achievement as stated by the model. In the framework of the model, however, underachievement is now seen to be a state of affairs which results whenever perseverance is less than some "reasonable value," whenever the quality of instruction is poor, whenever time allowed for learning has not been sufficient, or whenever some combination of these conditions has occurred. "Overachievement," contrariwise, may occur when there is an especially favorable combination of attendant events: high perseverance, instruction of high quality, or ample opportunity for learning.

We have a feeling about the relative amenability of different factors in achievement to manipulation or treatment: "Aptitude" is regarded as relatively resistant to change, whereas it is the hope of the psychologist that he can readily intervene to modify "perseverance," "quality of instruction," or "opportunity for learning." To some extent, this feeling is justified not only by logic but also by research findings—by the research on the apparent constancy of the IQ, on the effect of various instructional variables, etc. On the other hand, if aptitude is largely a matter of prior learnings, it may be more modifiable than we think, whereas, conversely, some kinds of clinical findings suggest that motivational characteristics of the individual may be much harder to change than one might think. These considerations, however, need not detract from the basic utility of the concepts of underachievement and overachievement. The concept of "underachievement" does not automatically imply the possibility of remediation any more than the concept of illness does. Some patients never get well, and some underachievers remain underachievers.

Babies and Bathwater

Henry Dyer (1960) has drawn attention to possible dangers in the concept of underachievement—for example, the dangers of making predictions from unreliable or invalid predictors, of assuming that ability is innate or fixed, of making unwarranted inferences from school marks, and of overlooking determinants of school performance which are external to the pupil. Nevertheless, in suggesting that we kill the notion of underachievement, it would seem that he wants to throw out the proverbial baby with the bathwater. The concepts of underachievement and of overachievement are meaningful from both a statistical and a clinical point of view, as shown by the many fruitful studies of "underachieving" groups of students (e.g., Goldberg et al., 1959). Careful attention to the elements of the conceptual model presented here will afford a safeguard against misuse of the concepts: Aptitude must be estimated by relevant and reliable measures (in actuality, all of them measures of past performance); the degree of learning must be accurately appraised, and the possible role of instructional variables must be considered. Above all, the variable which we have called *perseverance* must be validly assessed; the most direct evidence concerning it, our model would suggest, would come from observations of the amount of time the pupil actively engages in learning.

Before leaving this topic, let us consider another way in which the term "overachievement" is sometimes used. When a person is designated as an overachiever, it is often implied that his achievements derive more from his perseverance than from his aptitude or his intelligence. In terms of our model, this can occur when the learning task can be broken down into a series of subtasks of varying difficulty with difficulty roughly gauged in terms of average learning time. Because of his great perseverance, the overachiever masters to a criterion more of the *easy* tasks—tasks which are within the compass of his aptitude—than the student of average perseverance. While he may fail to learn some of the more difficult tasks, the net result may be a high score on an achievement test—a score considerably higher than predicted from aptitude measures. This concept of overachievement is distinctly different from the concept of overachievement suggested previously; responsible users of the term must clearly state which of these meanings they intend.

Future Research

Our conceptual model could lead, it would seem, to almost endless possibilities for research. It should provoke renewed effort to develop measures of each of the basic variables included in the model. The measurement of *aptitudes* is a fairly well advanced art, although the exact ways in which these aptitudes are relevant to school learning tasks remain to be worked out. The same remark may be made about the measurement of *ability to understand instruction*. But measurements of *perseverance* and of *instructional quality* are practically nonexistent. It should be intriguing to attempt to provide a general way of measuring *opportunity to learn*, that is, the actual time available to individual students to learn in view of the pacing of instruction; for it is our hypothesis that variations in the pacing of instruction have remained largely unrecognized in pedagogical discussions.

Research is also needed on the interactions of the several variables in the model. Is the model correctly put together? To what extent are the variables interdependent? For example, how does instructional quality affect perseverance? In what way is the degree of learning a function of the ratio of the amount of time spent in learning to the amount of time needed? Are we correct in postulating an interaction between instructional quality and ability to understand instruction such that pupils low in the latter ability suffer most from poor instructional quality?

One of the most exciting possibilities suggested by the model is that of being able to state parameters for different types of learning by learners of varying characteristics under stated instructional conditions. Perhaps ultimately such parameters could be tied back to the data of pure learning theory. One of the bolder hypotheses implicit in the model is that the degree of learning, other things being equal, is a simple function of the amount of time during which the pupil engages actively in learning. Psychologists have paid little attention to this variable of pure time in human learning. A recent experiment by Bugelski (1962) is one of the few to consider time factors in the field of paired-associate learning; and interestingly enough, it supports the hypothesis that more parsimonious descriptions of learning may be obtained by use of time as a variable rather than, say, number of trials.

What is important to emphasize is that this conceptual model probably contains, at least at a superordinate level, every element required to account for an individual's success or failure in school learning (at least in the learning tasks to which the model applies). The explication and refinement of these factors and the exploration of their interactions constitute a major task of educational psychology. Its other major task is to account for those types of school learning (e.g., attitudinal and emotional conditioning) to which the present model is not intended to apply and for which a separate model might well be constructed.

VI

PERSONALITY

Daryl Bem and Andrea Allen deal with an issue that plagues investigators in personality, namely, the question of cross-situational consistency. Bem and Allen propose that on any trait some individuals are cross-situationally consistent while others are inconsistent. Only the behavior of the consistent group will be explicitly predictable. The authors assume that different people may be consistent or inconsistent on different traits. Further research is required to determine whether consistency-inconsistency is a general characteristic or specific to a different set of traits for each person.

12

On Predicting Some of the People Some of the Time: The Search for Cross-Situational Consistencies in Behavior

DARYL J. BEM AND ANDREA ALLEN

Our persistent belief in personality traits, the stubborn assumption that there are pervasive cross-situational consistencies in an individual's behavior, is, quite literally, one of our most ancient convictions:

> Penuriousness is economy carried beyond all measure. A Penurious Man is one who goes to a debtor to ask for his half-obol interest before the end of the month. At a dinner where expenses are shared, he counts the number of cups each person drinks, and he makes a smaller libation to Artemis than anyone. ...If his wife drops a copper, he moves furniture, beds, chests and hunts in the curtains....[P]enurious men have hair cut short and do not put on their shoes until midday; and when they take their cloak to the fuller they urge him to use plenty of earth so that it will not be spotted so soon [Theophrastus (372–287 B.C.), quoted in Allport, 1937, p. 57].

Bem, D. J., and Allen, A. "On Predicting Some of the People Some of the Time: The Search for Cross-Situational Consistencies in Behavior." *Psychological Review*, 1974, Vol. 81, pp. 506–520. Copyright © 1974 by the American Psychological Association and used by permission.

If this bit of historical personality theorizing has a contemporary ring, it is, in part, because the same underlying assumption of cross-situational consistency is still with us. It is most explicit in trait and type theories of personality, but some variant of it can be discerned in nearly all contemporary formulations. Even psychodynamic theories, which are uniquely competent in dealing with phenotypic inconsistencies in behavior, do so precisely by postulating an underlying genotypic consistency in the personality which rationalizes the apparent contradictions. Our intuitions are even more persuaded. For them the assumption of cross-situational consistency is virtually synonymous with the concept of personality itself. There are few other beliefs about human behavior which are as compellingly self-evident.

But like many other assumptions, the consistency assumption did not fare well during the depression years, when three separate studies with very similar methodologies began to raise serious doubts about its validity. The earliest and best known challenge issued from the extensive multivolume *Studies in the Nature of Character* by Hartshorne and May (1928, 1929; Hartshorne, May and Shuttleworth, 1930), who found so little consistency among diverse measures of "moral character" in a group of children that they concluded that such traits as deception, helpfulness, cooperativeness, persistence, and self-control are "groups of specific habits rather than general traits." Foreshadowing findings which emerged from hundreds of later studies on scores of personality traits, Hartshorne and May reported that the average intercorrelation of the 23 tests used to construct a "total character score" was a modest +.30.

During the same years as the Hartshorne-May inquiry, a less well known but equally troublesome study on extroversion–introversion was published by Theodore Newcomb (1929), who explicitly set out to test the consistency assumption. He kept daily behavioral records on 51 boys at a summer camp for several weeks, recording behaviors in 30 different situations. The behaviors were conceptually organized into 10 separate traits (e.g., volubility versus taciturnity, ascendancy versus submission, etc.) which in turn collectively defined the two personality types of extrovert and introvert.

At the level of specific behaviors, Newcomb found little or no consistency from one situation to another. At the level of trait consistency, the intercorrelations among behaviors composing a given trait averaged only .14, almost identical to the figure obtained from a randomly selected set of behaviors. And finally, there was only a slight tendency for traits to be related to one another as expected by their extrovert–introvert classification.

The third study is in some ways the most damaging of all since it investigated punctuality, a trait one would expect to be much more homogeneous than "moral character" or extroversion–introversion. In this study, Dudycha (1936) made 15,360 observations on over 300 college students, recording each student's time of arrival at 8:00 a.m. classes, commons, appointments, extracurricular activities, vesper services, and entertainments. The mean cross-situational correlation turned out to be +.19, with the highest correlation—between punctuality at entertainments and at commons—reaching .44.

. . .

At the same time that the belief in cross-situational consistency was suffering these empirical blows, stimulus-response behaviorism was providing the theoretical argument for the counter belief in the situational specificity of behavior. And with psychologists like Gordon Allport (1937) and Ross Stagner (1937) willing to defend modified trait conceptions of personality against this onslaught, the controversy was a lively one for nearly a decade before receding into the background just prior to World War II (Sanford, 1970).

All of this leads one to appreciate the sense of déjà vu that must currently be affecting psychology's elder statesmen now that the "consistency problem" has suddenly been rediscovered (e.g., Alker, 1972; Allport, 1966; Argyle and Little, 1972; Averill, 1973; D. Bem, 1972; Bowers, 1973; Campus, 1974; Endler, 1973a, 1973b; Endler and Hunt, 1968; Harré and Secord, 1972; Mischel, 1968, 1969, 1973a, 1973b; Moos, 1969; Peterson, 1968; Stagner, 1973; Vale and Vale, 1969; Vernon, 1964; Wachtel, 1973; Wallach and Leggett, 1972).

The major figure in this current round of debate appears to be Walter Mischel (1968), who, after reviewing both past and current research, concludes that the predictive utility of a trait-based approach to personality still remains undemonstrated and that situational specificity of behavior appears to be the rule rather than the exception. Although other contemporary authors have drawn similar conclusions (e.g., Peterson, 1968; Vernon, 1964), it is Mischel who has provoked the most controversy by arguing that the commonly observed +.30 ceiling on cross-situational correlation coefficients probably reflects true behavioral variability rather than imperfect methodology. Since this constitutes a fundamental conceptual challenge, the controversy is once again filling journal pages after a 30-year intermission.

And the stubborn dilemma which sustains this conflict and accounts for its durability still remains unresolved: The sharp discrepancy between our intuitions, which tell us that individuals do in fact display pervasive cross-situational consistencies in their behavior, and the vast empirical literature, which tells us that they do not. Intuitions or research? One of them must be wrong.

... We believe that there is a basic error in drawing inferences about cross-situational consistency from the traditional research literature in personality, an error which was identified nearly 40 years ago by Gordon Allport (1937). The fallacy resides in the fact that this entire research tradition is predicated upon nomothetic rather than idiographic assumptions about the nature of individual differences. Thus nearly all of the research is based on some variant of the nomothetic assumption that a particular trait dimension or set of trait dimensions is universally applicable to all persons and that individual differences are to be identified with different locations on those dimensions. For example, the Hartshorne–May study (1928) assumed that an honesty–dishonesty dimension could be used to characterize all of the children in the sample and that the differences among the children could be specified in terms of their *degree* of honesty. A more elaborate version of the same nomothetic assumption can be found in factor-analytic formulations which assume that there is a universal factor structure of personality and that individual differences are to be specified by different points in the factor n-space.

In contrast, Allport's idiographic view emphasized that individuals differ not only in the ways in which traits are related to one another in each person but that they differ also in terms of which traits are even relevant. Thus in commenting upon the fact that Hartshorne and May found lying and cheating to be essentially uncorrelated ($r = .13$), Allport noted that one child may lie because he is afraid of hurting the feelings of the teacher, whereas another may steal pennies in order to buy social acceptance from his peers. For neither of these two children do the behaviors of lying and cheating constitute items on a scale called "honesty," a concept which exists in the head of the investigator, not in the behavior of the children. Accordingly, the low correlations "prove only that children are not consistent *in the same way*, not that they are inconsistent with *themselves*" (1937, p. 250). To put the same objection in slightly different terms, the research will yield the conclusion that a sample of individuals is inconsistent to the degree that their behaviors do not sort into the equivalence class which the investigator imposes by his choice of behaviors and situations to sample.

But there is more. Even if an entire sample of individuals does share the investigator's partitioning of behaviors into the same equivalence class, there is a still more stringent requirement of consistency imposed by the traditional research paradigm: scalability.* That is, the sample of individuals must all rank order the "difficulty levels" of the behaviors in the same way.

. . .

Reconsider the traditional research study in which a sample of individuals is assessed on some trait across two or more situations. To the extent that individuals in the sample scale the behaviors differently from one another ... their rankings relative to one another will change from one situation to another....Under such circumstances, the cross-situational correlation coefficients will plummet toward zero. Only to the extent that all of the individuals in the sample scale the behaviors in the same way will the cross-situational correlations be high.

---

* We are indebted to Stanford colleague Lee Ross for bringing this point to our attention.

In summary, then, the traditional trait-based research study will yield evidence of cross-situational consistency only if the individuals in the research sample agree with the investigator's a priori claim that the sampled behaviors and situations belong in a common equivalence class and only if the individuals agree among themselves on how to scale those behaviors and situations. The fallacy to which Gordon Allport originally called attention thus becomes clear. The traditional verdict of inconsistency is in no way an inference about individuals; it is a statement about a disagreement between an investigator and a group of individuals and/or a disagreement among the individuals within the group. This fallacy is a direct consequence of the traditional nomothetic assumptions about individual differences.

. . .

We are not here denying the well-documented biases and illusions which plague our intuitions, nor do we claim that the more formalized idiographic procedures used by clinicians have a better track record in terms of predictive utility than nomothetic ones; they do not (Mischel, 1968). But in terms of the underlying logic and fidelity to reality, we believe that our intuitions are right; the research, wrong.

Idiographic Assessment and Nomothetic Science

The problem with concluding that an idiographic approach represents the path to truth, however, has always been that one is never sure what to do next. To the extent that one accepts psychology's goal as the construction of general nomothetic principles, the idiographic approach appears a scientific dead end....

But the impasse is not insurmountable. The use of idiographic assessment procedures did not appear to deter Freud from formulating nomothetic principles of personality organization. Similarly, albeit more modestly, Mischel (1973b) has recently proposed a set of nonmothetic principles within the idiographic assumptions of social behavior theory. A third example is provided by George Kelly's (1955) psychology of personal constructs and its associated idiographic assessment procedure, the Role Repertory Test. In fact, it is Kelly's approach which best exemplifies the spirit behind the present arguments. Thus Kelly permits the individual to generate his own traitlike descriptors ("constructs") for characterizing himself and his social world and to determine which behaviors and situations are to be embraced by those descriptors, that is, to determine what Kelly has termed the individual's "range of convenience" for the construct. Note that such an approach could reveal, for example, that an individual who regards himself as extremely conscientious might not consider his casual attitude toward personal hygiene as pertinent to that trait. The fact that the investigator's concept or equivalence class of conscientiousness might include personal hygiene within it is not relevant.

The basic point here is simply that there is no inherent conflict between an idiographic approach to assessment and a nomothetic science of personality, whether one opts for a psychoanalytic orientation, a social learning viewpoint, or a systematization of everyman's trait theory.

It should be clear, however, that idiographic assessment only permits one to predict certain behaviors across certain situations for certain people but not beyond that. Consequently, a conflict does arise if an investigator refuses to relinquish the power to decide which behaviors of which people are to be studied in which situations; the logic of idiographic assessment requires that the individual himself must be given this power, whereas the particular concerns of the investigator may require these decisions to be fixed parameters.

Consider, for example, the researcher who wishes to study, say, need for achievement in a particular setting in a particular population. No matter how persuasive he finds our arguments for the merits of idiographic assessment, he is simply not interested in studying a different set of personality variables in each individual. But, on the other hand, our arguments imply that need for achievement may not even be a trait dimension which usefully characterizes many of the individuals in the sample. As his low validity coefficients will attest, those individuals will contribute only noise to his investigation. The dilemma is real. If our arguments here are sound, one simply cannot, in principle, ever do any better than predicting some of the people some of the time. It is an idiographic fact of life.

Our advice to such an investigator, then, follows directly: Find those people. Separate those individuals who are cross-situationally consistent on the trait dimension and throw the others out, for by definition, only the behavior of consistent individuals can be meaningfully characterized by the investigator's construct; only their behaviors can be partitioned into the equivalence class under investigation. Perhaps a statistical metaphor will make this proposal seem less illegitimate: Unless an individual's variance on a particular trait dimension is small, it makes no sense to attach psychological significance to his mean on that dimension.

We submit that even this token gesture toward more idiographic assessment has its rewards. First of all, one may obtain valuable knowledge about the trait dimension itself; it could be useful (as well as humbling) to discover why, which, and how many individuals fail to share the investigator's partitioning of the world into his favorite equivalence class. But perhaps even better, we believe that the rewards for this small idiographic commitment can even be paid in the sacred coin of the realm: bigger correlation coefficients! The following demonstration illustrates the point.

A Priori Assessment of Cross-Situational Consistency

Our purpose in this study was to test whether or not individuals can be divided on the basis of self-report into those who are cross-situationally consistent on a particular trait and those who are not. Our hypothesis is straightforward: Individuals who identify themselves as consistent on a particular trait dimension will in fact be more consistent cross-situationally than those who identify themselves as highly variable. In population terms, the cross-situational correlation coefficients of the self-identified low-variability group should be significantly higher than the coefficients of the high-variability group....

METHOD

As part of a questionnaire entitled the Cross-Situation Behavior Survey (CSBS), all students in Stanford's introductory psychology course were asked to assess themselves on several trait dimensions, including friendliness ... On each dimension, the individual was asked to rate both his overall level and his variability. For example, on the friendliness dimension, he was asked, "In general, how friendly and outgoing are you?" and "How much do you vary from one situation to another in how friendly and outgoing you are?" ... Responses were obtained on a seven-point scale which ranged from "not at all" to "extremely." It will be noted that these questions thus permit the individual to employ his own concept of the trait dimension, to average across the situations he sees as pertinent and to ignore situations he sees as irrelevant. Accordingly, these global self-ratings will be successful in predicting behavior only to the extent that the individual's definition of a trait dimension coincides with the definition we will necessarily be imposing by our selection of situations to sample.

Using the same seven-point response scale, we also obtained each individual's self-ratings on specific behavior-situation items for each trait. For example, the CSBS included a 24-item scale which assessed the trait of friendliness in specific situations (e.g., "When in a store, how likely are you to strike up a conversation with a sales clerk?") ... Thus if the global self-ratings can be seen as reflecting the individual's own definitions of the trait dimensions, then these CSBS scales can be viewed as reflecting the investigators' conception of these dimensions....

Cross-Situational Assessment. From the introductory psychology course, 32 male and 32 female students were recruited as subjects. In addition to the initial testing session in which all students participated, the subjects were seen on three separate occasions, and they also signed release forms giving us permission to obtain ratings on them from their parents and one of their close peers, usually a roommate. From these various sessions, the following six friendliness variables ... were derived.

Friendliness: (1) *Self-Report;* (2) *Mother's Report;* (3) *Father's Report;* (4) *Peer's Reports.* Each of these four judges provided us with an independent assessment of the individual's friendliness by rating him on the global friendliness item and the 24-item CSBS friendliness scale. For each judge, these two measures were combined into a single score. (5) *Group Discussion:* Each individual was observed as he participated in a group discussion with three other subjects of the same sex. A measure of each individual's friendliness in the group was derived from the frequency and duration of his vocalizations and the group's postdiscussion rating of his friendliness. (6) *Spontaneous Friendliness:* Each individual was observed as he waited in a waiting room with an experimental confederate, and a measure of spontaneous friendliness was derived from his "latency" in initiating conversation.

. . .

Finally, it should be noted that experimental assistants and observers were all blind with respect to the individual's scores on the trait dimensions, and no observer made more than one observation for each trait on the same individual.

RESULTS

The first step in the analysis of results was to classify each individual on a priori grounds as a low-variability or a high-variability subject in a way that would not be confounded with his actual position on the trait dimension. Accordingly, for each trait, a subject was first classified into one of seven subgroups on the basis of his response to the question "In general, how friendly and outgoing ... are you?" Then, on the basis of his response to the question "How much do you vary from one situation to another in how friendly and outgoing ... you are?", he was designated as a low-variability or a high-variability subject, respectively, depending upon whether he was below or above the median among the same-sex subjects at the same point on the trait scale. Thus low and high variability were redefined at each of the seven points on the global trait scale in order to partial out any relationship between an individual's self-rated variability and his self-rated position on the trait dimension.

In order to assess each individual's cross-situational consistency ... we converted each of the ... variables to a standard T score with a mean of 50 and a standard deviation of 10 across the 64 subjects. We then calculated each individual's standard deviation across the six friendliness variables. ... The larger the standard deviation, the more variable he is across situations.

With respect to the friendliness dimension, our hypothesis was confirmed. Individuals who indicate that they do not vary much from one situation to another do, in fact, display significantly less variability across

Table 12.1

Intercorrelations among the six friendliness variables for low- and high-variability subjects

Low \ High	Self-report	Mother's report	Father's report	Peer's report	Group discussion	Spontaneous friendliness	All variables
1. Self-Report							
2. Mother's Report	.61 / .52						
3. Father's Report	.48 / .24	.75 / .28					
4. Peer's Report	.62 / .56	.71 / .40	.50 / .34				
5. Group Discussion	.52 / .59	.34 / .41	.50 / .13	.45 / .39			
6. Spontaneous Friendliness	.61 / −.06	.46 / −.18	.69 / −.20	.39 / .09	.73 / .30		
Mean correlations	.57 / .39	.59 / .30	.60 / .16	.54 / .37	.52 / .37	.59 / .01	.57 / .27

situations than do those who say they do vary (6.42 versus 7.90; $t = 2.34$, $p < .02$, one-tailed test). Moreover, an individual's self-rated friendliness per se is not related to his cross-situational variability; in particular, individuals in the lowest, middle, and highest thirds of the distribution on the self-rated friendliness scale did not differ from one another in their cross-situational variability, $F(2, 61) = 1.10$, ns.

Table 12.1 shows how the differential cross-situational consistency of low- and high-variability individuals translates into cross-situational predictability in correlational terms. The intercorrelations of the six variables for the 32 low-variability subjects are shown above the diagonal; intercorrelations for the 32 high variability subjects, below the diagonal. The bottom row of Table 12.1 serves to summarize the matrix by showing the mean correlation between the column variable and the remaining five variables for the two groups separately.

As Table 12.1 shows, 13 of the 15 intercorrelations are higher for low-variability subjects than they are for high-variability subjects, six of them significantly so ($p < .05$, one-tailed test). The mean intercorrelation among all the variables is $+.57$ for the low-variability group and $+.27$ for the high-variability group. Note also that the predicted effect is quite general across different pairs of situations. For example, Mother's Report and Father's Report, two measurements that one would expect to be highly similar and "contaminated" by one another, show a correlation of $+.75$ for the low-variability group but only $+.28$ for the high-variability group ($p < .005$, one tailed test); similarly, Group Discussion and Spontaneous Friendliness, the two methodologically independent behavioral observations, show a correlation of $+.73$ for the low-variability group but only $+.30$ for the high-variability group ($p < .009$, one-tailed test). Thus, not only have our expectations been confirmed, but the magic $+.30$ barrier appears to have been penetrated.

It will be noted that the "moderating variable" in this analysis, the variable which separates the population into groups which are differentially predictable, is the individual's response to the single question "How much do you vary from one situation to another in how friendly and outgoing you are?" ...

Predictive Utility of Traits and Situations

We have argued in this article that it is not possible, in principle, to do any better than predicting some of the people some of the time. Furthermore, our arguments would seem to imply that an investigator must simply abandon the highly variable individual since the trait under investigation has no predictive utility for him. But this is not always true. As Mischel (1968, 1973b) has persuasively argued, variability is not synonymous with either capriciousness or unpredictability. Indeed, an individual's cross-situational variability may well be the mark of a highly refined "discriminative facility" (Mischel, 1973b), the ability to respond appropriately to subtle changes in situational contingencies. Although such an individual cannot be predicted from a knowledge of his standing on a personality trait, he may be precisely the individual who is most predictable from a knowledge of the situation. In short, if some of the people can be predicted some of the time from personality traits, then some of the people can be predicted some of the time from situational variables.

. . .

It should be clear from this discussion that the position we have argued in this article cannot be characterized as opposing either side of the debate between those who believe that behavior is consistent across situations and those who believe that behavior is situationally specific. The shift to idiographic assumptions about the nature of individual differences dissolves this false dichotomy and permits one to believe in both propositions. As noted early in this article, the actual cleavage is between nomothetic and idiographic criteria for consistency and inconsistency.

. . .

The failure of traditional assessment procedures and the belief that person–situation interactions will account for most of the psychologically interesting variance in behavior have led several recent writers to emphasize that personality assessment must begin to attend seriously to situations. We agree. We have merely chosen to emphasize the perfectly symmetric, but perhaps more subtle, point that personality assessment must also begin to attend seriously to persons.

This article proposes two procedures for increasing the size of correlations between self-reports and subsequent behavior. The first is to have subjects report what they are maximally capable of doing in trait-relevant situations rather than what they typically do. This procedure eliminates subjects' having to estimate a weighted average of their behavior across time in trait-relevant situations. The second procedure is to identify those subjects who are sufficiently self-reflective to know what they are capable of doing in any situation. Their self-reports should be more predictively valid than those of people who are not habitually self-reflective. Dr. Turner provides data showing increases in self-report–laboratory behavior correlations when these two procedures are incorporated.

13

Consistency, Self-Consciousness, and the Predictive Validity of Typical and Maximal Personality Measures

ROBERT G. TURNER

Many of the responses to Mischel's (1968) attack on the efficacy of personality traits in predicting criterion behaviors can be sorted into three broad categories. The first emphasizes that it is the interaction between traits and situations, not traits or situations singly, that accounts for the largest percentage of explained variability in analysis of variance designs (Bowers, 1973; Ekehammar, 1974). Studies in the second category have suggested that self-reported trait measures may have predictive validity for only a subset of individuals (Alker, 1972; Bem and Allen, 1974; Fenigstein, Scheier, and Buss, 1975). The third category of responses has been con-

Turner, R. G. "Consistency, Self-Consciousness, and the Predictive Validity of Typical and Maximal Personality Measures." *Journal of Research in Personality*, 1978, Vol. 12, pp. 117–132. Copyright 1978 by Academic Press, Inc., and reprinted by permission.

cerned with assessment procedures and criterion validity issues (Fishbein and Ajzen, 1974; Jaccard, 1974; Wachtel, 1973; Willerman, Turner and Peterson, 1976).

The results of the Willerman et al. (1976) study suggested that personality measures based on a maximal performance format might be superior to those based on the traditional typical performance format in predicting criterion behaviors. Typical performance items are by nature ambiguous in that they require the person to arrive at a rather subjectively weighted average of relevant behaviors. Averaging errors and response biases both contribute to reducing the validity of the typical item. However, maximal personality measures require that the person focus on only one extreme of the relevant trait domain and determine what he can do (Wallace, 1966; Cronbach, 1970, p. 612; Mischel, 1973).

. . .

The fact that ability tests as measures of maximal performance predict with reasonable validity a variety of typical and maximal performance criteria suggested to Willerman et al. (1976) the possibility of constructing maximal performance tests of personality to be validated against both typical and maximal criteria. Accordingly, they compared typical and maximal performance paper-and-pencil tests of anger and elation with typical and maximal performance laboratory behavioral tests of these emotions. The prediction that for both anger and elation the maximal performance paper-and-pencil measures would correlate higher than the typical performance paper-and-pencil measures in both typical and maximal performance in the laboratory was clearly supported for anger and partially supported for elation. The self-report of subjects' maximal expression of anger correlated .48 with their typical expression of angry behavior and .59 with their maximal expression of anger in the laboratory. The corresponding correlations for subjects' report of their typical expression of anger were .32 and −.03. Thus the viability of an ability format for the assessment of expressive behavior was supported.

The initial purpose of the present study was to investigate the predictive utility of employing a maximal format in the assessment of a more cognitively mediated trait such as dominance. As with Willerman et al. (1976) the prediction was that the maximal performance paper-and-pencil measure would correlate higher than the typical performance paper-and-pencil measure with both typical and maximal performance in the laboratory.

An additional purpose was to incorporate this maximal assessment approach toward increasing the predictive validity of self-reports with the procedures suggested by Fenigstein et al. (1975)....

According to Fenigstein et al. (1975) there are two aspects of self-consciousness: private and public. Private self-consciousness focuses on awareness of one's thoughts, feelings, and motives. Public self-consciousness is concerned with awareness of oneself as a social object.

Taking a dispositional approach, they have developed a scale measuring these two components of self-consciousness and reported a correlation of .24 between them for 2000 subjects (Fenigstein et al., 1975).

Because of habitual examination of their beliefs and feelings, the self-reports of high private self-conscious persons are theorized to have greater predictive validity than the reports of those low in private self-consciousness (Fenigstein et al., 1975). Public self-consciousness is theorized to be related to the veridicality of self-reports only to the extent that the self-report measure is susceptible to a social desirability response set. A person high in public self-consciousness, by definition, attends to how he appears to others. He should, therefore, be more concerned with social approval and attempt to present himself as favorably as possible. The result should be lower predictive validity for his self-reports in comparison to that of a person not so concerned with what is "proper" (the low public self-conscious individual).

These conceptualizations were generally supported in a reanalysis of the Willerman et al. (1976) data in which subjects were grouped first according to their scores for private self-consciousness and then by their public self-consciousness scores (Turner and Peterson, 1977). The average predictor-criterion correlation for the low public self-conscious group was .50 while the average for the high public self-consciousness group was .24. The average correlations for the groups high and low on private self-consciousness were .44 and .42, respectively.

Results showing larger self-report-criterion correlations for those relatively unconcerned about the opinions others hold about them (the low public self-conscious group) and those who are habitually self-reflective (the high private self-conscious group) were also expected in the present investigation. In addition, it was expected that within these two groups the predictive superiority of self-reports of maximal performance in comparison to self-reports of typical performance would be maintained.

Method

SUBJECTS

Sixty-two students (26 males and 36 females) from the pool of introductory social science students served as subjects. Each student received course credit for participation in the experiment.

PROCEDURE

At the second class meeting of the trimester, all students taking Introduction to Social Science completed the Self-Consciousness Inventory (Fenigstein et al., 1975).... The Self-Consciousness Inventory (entitled

The California Inventory when it was administered) contains 23 descriptive statements to which subjects responded by circling a number on a one-to-five scale anchored by "extremely uncharacteristic" (1) and "extremely characteristic" (5). The private self-consciousness scale contains items such as, "I reflect about myself a lot." An exemplary item from the public self-consciousness scale is "I'm concerned about what other people think of me."

                                        . . .

One week later subjects who signed up to participate in the present experiment were brought into a testing room in groups of 10–15 to write stories about their typical and maximal dominance behavior. The requests for the two stories were on separate sheets and read as follows:

Typical story request:

Imagine that you are taking a college course in which the professor divides the class into groups of 6 students per group. He then gives each group a problem or project related to the content of the course for the group to discuss. Each group is to report their conclusions back to the total class at the end of the period. Write a description of what you typically do in such situations.

Maximal story request:

Imagine that you are taking a college course in which the professor divides the class into groups of 6 students per group. He then gives each group a problem or project related to the content of the course for the group to discuss. Each group is to report their conclusions back to the total class at the end of the period. Write a description of what you would do in such a situation if you were acting as *dominant* and *assertive* as you can act.

The instructions for both stories were read aloud at the beginning of the session. It was emphasized that one story was to be how dominant they typically acted; the other was to be how dominant they were capable of acting. Subjects were given as long as they needed to complete the stories. The story sheets were stapled together and their order counterbalanced over the whole group.

After completing their stories, subjects signed up for a time to return for the laboratory procedures. The interval between this paper-and-pencil assessment and the laboratory session was from 6 to 28 days.

As subjects appeared for their laboratory session they were greeted by a male experimenter who explained as he led them to the research room that the other students participating in the research were already present. The other students were a male and female confederate. For each subject the same-sexed confederate was waiting in the hall by the research room while the opposite-sexed confederate was already in the room so that he or she could turn on a concealed tape recorder.

The experimenter led the subject and the confederate into the experimental room, introduced everyone by their first names, and had them all sit around a desk-sized table. He then read the following:

> This research is concerned with problem solving. The kinds of problems that we are interested in are often abstract and seem to have no clear-cut answer. However, we are interested in what people's conclusions concerning these problems are and how they arrived at them. I will read the problem to you and then give you 10 min to come up with your conclusions as a group. You may have seen problems similar to this before.
>
> The school district in a small community is in financial difficulty. The school board must dismiss four faculty members in addition to other cutbacks in order to have enough money to complete the school year. A decision has already been made that the four faculty members would be specialists in various areas, not teachers of basic subject areas. Which four would you choose to be dismissed?
>
> 1. Reading specialist
> 2. Counselor
> 3. Assistant football coach
> 4. Special education teacher in math
> 5. Assistant band director
> 6. Drama teacher
> 7. Diagnostician of learning disabilities
> 8. Teacher of accelerated English classes
> 9. Teacher of accelerated math and science classes
> 10. Baseball coach
> 11. Work-study supervisor

The experimenter than placed the description of the problem in the middle of the table along with a pencil and a "group conclusion form" on which someone in the group was to write down the four persons of the group's choice. After reminding the group of the 10-min time limit and pointing out the clock in the room, the experimenter left.

. . .

After 10 min the experimenter returned. If the group had not completed the task, he waited for an additional 1 min at the end of which time all groups managed to finish. He talked briefly about the problem and collected the "group conclusion form." He then told the group he would like to get their individual reactions to the group process and asked the two confederates to separately wait for him in the two rooms adjacent to the experimental room. He said that he would get their reactions after receiving the opinions of the subject. The subject then completed an "evaluation of group members" form on which he rated the leadership ability and passiveness/dominance of each confederate on a one (poor leader or very passive) to six (good leader or very dominant) scale. Finally subjects rated on a one to six scale how dominant and assertive they were during the problem-solving session.

Subjects were then read the following statement:

For the second part of the research you will be with another group of people solving a problem similar to the one you worked on here. In this group I want you to be the leader. I want you to be as dominant and assertive as you can be. This is an ability test. We will tape record this session so that we can see how well you do. Remember, this is a dominance-ability test. You are to see that your group comes up with satisfactory answers to the problem.

The experimenter stated that the students to be in this part of the experiment were ready to begin. As he led the subject to the second experimental room, the experimenter emphasized the ability nature of the assessment.

The maximal laboratory situation was set up similar to the typical situation. The same-sexed confederate was waiting in the hall while the opposite-sexed confederate waited in the experimental room. After following the same introductory procedures as were enacted in the typical situation, the experimenter read the following problem:

Imagine that our country is under threat of imminent nuclear attack. A man approaches you and asks you to make an independent decision: There is a fallout shelter nearby that can accommodate 4 people, but there are 12 people vying to get in. Which 4 do you choose to put in the shelter? Here's all the information we have about the 12 people:

1. A 40-year-old male violinist who is a suspected narcotics pusher.

2. A 34-year-old male architect who is thought to be a homosexual.

3. A 26-year-old lawyer.

4. The lawyer's 24-year-old wife who has just gotten out of a mental institution. They both want to go in together or stay out together.

5. A 75-year-old priest.

6. A 34-year-old retired prostitute who was so successful that she's been living off her annuities for 5 years.

7. A 20-year-old Black militant.

8. A 23-year-old female graduate student who speaks publicly on the virtues of chastity.

9. A 28-year-old male physicist who will only come into the shelter if he can bring his gun with him.

10. A 12-year-old girl who has a low IQ.

11. A 30-year-old female MD who is an avowed bigot.

12. A high school student.

Following the same procedure as before, the experimenter placed a copy of the problem, the "group conclusion form," and a pencil in the middle of the table and left the room after reminding the group of the 10-min limitation.

After 10 min, the same procedure as outlined above was again followed, leading to the subject completing another "evaluation of group members" form. Subjects were then debriefed and asked not to discuss the experiment with anyone until the date the experiment was to be completed.

MEASURES

The typical and maximal predictor stories were rated by two independent judges on the following one-to-five scale.

1. Feels that the group would not want him/her to be the leader or that he/she would not be successful as a leader. Person might express his opinions, but prefers to listen and stay in the background. Person might wait for someone to assign him a topic.

2. Will lead only if group permits or desires it. Wants everyone to get a chance to have their say. Wants to do something in the group that he/she would be interested in.

3. Primarily an organizer to see that the group gets finished on time and the work gets done. Leadership not forceful and less complete.

4. Assumes leadership of group. Directs group communications; not just an organizer but wants his/her opinions incorporated into the group's conclusions. May make the report to the class. (Often uses the word "probably" in describing what he/she would do.)

5. Complete usurption of leadership of group from the outset; gets the discussion going; insists upon having a major impact upon the group's conclusions; gives the report; assumes success in doing so.

The ordering of the categories was determined rationally by five students and the experimenter. The ratings of the two independent raters were summed for each of the two stories and these sums served as the predictors in the study. Thus the range of possible scores for these predictors was from two to ten. Interrater reliabilities were .77 for the typical stories and .92 for the maximal stories.

A criterion measure was desired that would account for what seemed to be the major two ways that dominance might be expressed. The most obvious method of expressing dominance in this kind of situation would seem to be by the content of what one says; i.e., forceful, assertive statements. The second method of dominating situations like these is by simply monopolizing conversation. A measure of the former was obtained from ratings by the confederates. As soon as the confederates left the experimental room, they rated the subject's performance on the following rationally constructed scale:

1. No dominance statements or actions—totally passive.

2. Statements of a general nature; no strong opinions voiced.

3. One or two opinions offered with little conviction or involvement; no disagreement with others expressed.

4. Opinions offered but no attempt to lead group; disagreements subtle and nondirect.

5. Opinions offered with attempts to get some agreement from others; persuasive efforts toward other members. Statements solicitous to support, such as "don't you think."

6. Strong attempts to persuade others and open disagreement with others. Emphatic statements: "I think that." May take a while to warm up, but takes over eventually.

7. Complete usurpation of leadership of group with insistence upon influencing conclusions of group. Usurpation of leadership from the beginning.

Confederates' ratings in both the typical and maximal situations were summed together. The interrater reliability for the typical laboratory situation was .77 while the reliability for the maximal laboratory situation was .79.

A measure of the extent to which the subjects monopolized the conversation was obtained from the tapes of the laboratory situations. The proportion of the time the subject talked during the problem-solving periods was determined for each subject. Since not all groups took the full 10 min to arrive at their conclusions while others took 11 min, the problem-solving period was defined as the time between the exit of the experimenter and the group's agreement upon the last of the four choices required by both the typical and maximal laboratory situations.

The sum of the confederates' ratings in the typical situation correlated .50 with percentage of time talking in the typical laboratory. In the maximal situation, the corresponding correlation was .56.

Both the sums of the confederates' ratings and the proportions of time each subject talked were converted to their z score equivalents and summed to form composite dependent variables from both laboratory situations.

Results

The means of the ratings of the typical and maximal stories, the composite laboratory measures, and subjects' ratings of their laboratory dominance are presented in Table 13.1 for the total sample and each sex. The mean dominance ratings of the maximal stories were significantly larger than the ratings of the typical stories for the total sample and each sex. In addition, subjects reported that they were significantly more dominant in the maximal laboratory situation than in the typical situation. Further-

Table 13.1

Means and standard deviations (in parentheses) for typical and maximal stories, composite laboratory measures, and self-reports of laboratory dominance

Measure	Sample	N	Typical	Maximal
Story	Total	62	3.98 (1.63)	7.15 (1.42)**
	Males	26	4.31 (1.87)	6.92 (1.23)**
	Females	36	3.75 (1.42)	7.31 (1.55)**
Laboratory	Total	62	.03 (1.71)	.00 (1.76)
	Males	26	.27 (2.27)	.17 (1.92)
	Females	36	−.15 (1.16)	−.12 (1.65)
Self-report	Total	62	4.42 (.76)	4.97 (.85)**
	Males	26	4.46 (.95)	5.12 (.91)*
	Females	36	4.39 (.60)	4.86 (.80)*

$*\ p < .01.$
$**\ p < .001.$

more, the means of the males and females did not significantly differ on either the stories or the laboratory measures. However, the variability of females' responses was less in each assessment except the maximal story.

Correlations between the predictors and laboratory measures are presented in Table 13.2 for the total sample and each sex. The large correlation between the typical and maximal laboratory situations (.72) suggests

Table 13.2

Intercorrelations of predictor and laboratory measures for total sample and by sex

Sample	Maximal story	Typical laboratory	Maximal laboratory
Total (N = 62)			
Typical story	.31*	.20	.27*
Maximal story		.44**	.47**
Typical laboratory			.72**
Males (N = 26)			
Typical story	.25	.26	.46*
Maximal story		.58**	.52**
Typical laboratory			.81**
Females (N = 36)			
Typical story	.43**	.04	.05
Maximal story		.42**	.47**
Typical laboratory			.62**

$*\ p < .05.$
$**\ p < .01.$

that, relative to their peers, subjects expressed themselves in the typical laboratory session in much the same way as they did after being told to be dominant. The general trend in each instance is for the maximal stories to correlate higher than the typical stories with both typical and maximal laboratory behavior. As predicted, in the total sample the maximal story is superior to the typical story in predicting typical dominance behavior $[t(59) = 1.72, p < .05$, one-tailed test] and marginally superior in predicting maximal dominance behavior $[t(59) = 1.50, p < .10$, one-tailed test]. For men, although the correlations of the maximal story with the laboratory behaviors are larger than those for the typical story, the advantage is marginal in predicting typical laboratory behavior $[t(23) = 1.56, p < .10$, one-tailed test] and negligible for the maximal laboratory behavior. However, for women the maximal story is clearly superior in predicting both typical behavior $[t(33) = 2.29, p < .02$, one-tailed test] and maximal behavior $[t(33) = 2.61, p < .01$, one-tailed test]. The reports of females of their typical dominance behavior is, for all practical purposes, independent of their laboratory expression of dominance behavior.

SELF-CONSCIOUSNESS

The mean private self-consciousness score of the total sample was 35.7 $(SD = 5.52)$ while the mean score on the public self-consciousness scale was 26.7 $(SD = 4.51)$. On the private self-consciousness scale, 31 subjects scored above the mean (high private self-consciousness group) and 31 scored below the mean (low private self-consciousness group). The correlations of the typical and maximal predictors with the laboratory measures are presented for the private self-consciousness group in the upper half of Table 13.3. The upper and lower triangles of correlations are for the high and low private self-consciousness groups, respectively. The average of the four predictor-criterion correlations for the high private self-consciousness group is .47 while that of the low group is .24. In addition, within the high private self-consciousness group the maximal story is significantly superior to the typical self-report in predicting subjects' maximal expression of dominance behavior $[t(28) = 1.86, p < .05$, one-tailed test] and marginally superior in predicting their typical behavior $[t(28) = 1.57, p < .10$, one-tailed test].

The lower half of Table 13.3 contains the corresponding predictor-criterion correlations resulting from dividing the subjects into high and low public self-consciousness groups. The correlations of those scoring above the mean $(N = 35)$ are in the upper triangle of the matrix, while the lower triangle of the matrix consists of the correlations of the low public self-consciousness group $(N = 27)$. The average of the predictor-criterion correlations for the low public self-consciousness group was .46, while that of the high public self-consciousness group was .28. Within the low public self-consciousness group, the maximal story was superior to the

Table 13.3
Intercorrelations of predictor and laboratory measures for self-consciousness groups

Self-consciousness group	Typical story	Maximal story	Typical laboratory	Maximal laboratory
Private[a]				
Typical story		.35	.27	.38*
Maximal story	.27		.55**	.67**
Typical laboratory	.13	.32		.63**
Maximal laboratory	.19	.33	.83**	
Public[b]				
Typical story		.43	.29	.22
Maximal story	.16		.30	.30
Typical laboratory	.09	.66**		.69**
Maximal laboratory	.37	.71**	.77**	

[a] High private self-consciousness ($N = 31$) correlations in upper triangle; low private self-consciousness ($N = 31$) correlations in lower triangle.
[b] High public self-consciousness ($N = 35$) correlations in upper triangle; low public self-consciousness ($N = 27$) correlations in lower triangle.
* $p < .05$.
** $p < .01$.

typical story in predicting both typical laboratory behavior [$t(24) = 3.64$, $p < .001$, one-tailed test] and maximal laboratory behavior [$t(24) = 2.23$, $p < .02$, one-tailed test].

The direction of the differences in the mean correlations of the high and low private self-consciousness groups and the high and low public self-consciousness groups is consistent with the theorizing of Fenigstein et al. (1975). In addition, in all eight instances the correlations of the maximal story with the laboratory behaviors are larger than the correlations of the typical story with these criteria, in four instances significantly so.

After obtaining these results it was decided to investigate the validity of the self-reports of subjects within the four groups resulting from all combinations of the two levels of both private and public self-consciousness (i.e., high public–high private, high public–low private, low public–high private, and low public–low private). From the previous results and from Fenigstein et al. (1975), the low public–high private self-consciousness group should have the most predictively valid self-reports and the high public–low private self-consciousness group should have the least predictively valid self-reports. The correlations of the typical and maximal stories with the typical and maximal laboratory measures are presented for all four groups in Table 13.4. The varying number of subjects in each group reflects the .56 correlation between the public and private self-consciousness scales in this sample.*

* Since Fenigstein et al. (1975) report a correlation of .24 between these two scales for 2000 subjects, the size of the present correlation may be the result of sampling error.

Table 13.4

Intercorrelations of predictor and laboratory measures for groups
of different levels of private and public self-consciousness

		Public self-consciousness			
		Low		High	
Private self-consciousness		Typical laboratory	Maximal laboratory	Typical laboratory	Maximal laboratory
High	Typical Story	−.48	.31	.37	.42*
	Maximal Story	.66	.88*	.54**	.65**
	N		7	24	
Low	Typical Story	.19	.40	.13	−.10
	Maximal Story	.67**	.71**	−.36	−.34
	N		20	11	

* $p < .05$.
** $p < .01$.

The correlations for the high public–low private self-consciousness group show that the self-reports of the eleven subjects in this group (seven females and four males) are indeed predictively invalid. However, the predictor-criterion correlations of each of the other three groups are sizeable and very similar. Thus it appears that in the present data, more valid self-reports are insured by the subject being either low public self-conscious or high private self-conscious. In addition, within each of these three groups, the maximal stories show higher correlations than the typical stories with the criteria.

. . .

Discussion

Consistent with the findings of Willerman et al. (1976), the results of this investigation suggest that a personality measure of dominance based upon a maximal performance format is superior to one based upon a typical performance format in predicting dominance behavior in the laboratory. Several factors would seem to be contributing to this superiority.

Self-reports of typical behavior are by nature ambiguous and require that the person arrive at some average of behaviors from the entire range of the trait-relevant behaviors of which he is capable (Mischel, 1973). The rather low correlation ($r = .31$) between subjects' typical and maximal stories suggests that the result of this averaging process is only modestly related to what the person reports he is capable of performing.

In the Willerman et al. (1976) study, the correlation between subjects' stories of their typical and maximal expression of anger was only .27. In addition, in both studies the interrater reliabilities for the maximal stories were higher than the reliabilities for the typical stories: .92 compared to .77 in the present study and .85 compared to .76 in Willerman et al. (1976). Thus there would seem to be at least two rather compatible explanations for the superiority of the maximal stories. First, subjects more validly report what they are capable of doing in a situation than what they typically do. In the present study this seems especially true for women. Along with the averaging required by typical reports, females were also confronted with the sex role stereotype against women being dominant. As a result, their self-reports of typical dominance behavior were of no predictive value (see Table 13.2). However, their report of what they were capable of doing was significantly related to their behavior.

Second, the maximal self-reports may be predictively superior because of their increased reliability: i.e., the behaviors at the upper end of the dominance and anger dimensions were easier for subjects to reliably report and scorers to reliably rate. The future development of more objectively scored, psychometrically adequate instruments will hopefully eliminate differences in scorer reliability.

. . .

Most of the predictions relating to private and public self-consciousness were supported. The expectation of greater predictive validity for the self-reports of the high private self-conscious group and the low public self-conscious group was fulfilled. The almost total lack of positive correspondence between the self-reports and behavior of the eleven subjects who were both low private self-conscious and high public self-conscious is consistent with the theorizing of Fenigstein et al. (1975). This result suggests the futility of trying to predict from a self-report measure the behavior of a person who rarely reflects upon his behavior and who is very concerned about his appearance to others. The presentation of results with this group excluded would seem to be a viable alternative. The size of the maximal story-criteria correlations presented certainly reinforces this procedure. It is interesting that while response styles have been extensively investigated (Cronbach, 1970, pp. 495–504; Edwards, 1970), the effect of varying levels of habitual self-reflection on the predictive validity of self-reports has not received much attention.

The value of maximal measures in predicting both typical and maximal laboratory behavior has now been demonstrated for an expressive behavior (anger) and a more cognitively mediated behavior (dominance). The susceptibility of other traits to assessment via a maximal performance format is currently being investigated. Two additional directions to be followed involve developing more objectively scored instruments and extending the criteria to behavior outside the laboratory.

VII

PSYCHOPATHOLOGY

This article by Seymour Kety, David Rosenthal, Paul Wender, and Fini Schulsinger gives results from a remarkable adoption study nearing completion in Denmark. The biological and adopted families of adopted individuals who became schizophrenic were compared with the corresponding families of other adopted individuals who did not turn out to be schizophrenic. The results indicated that for some forms of schizophrenia, genetics seemed to be playing a strong role. In addition, the article contains an important response by the authors to critics who questioned their interpretations. Much, though not all, of this response is retained in this edited version of the article to show that even scientists of good will can have strong differences of opinion. The reader is invited to consult the journal in which the article originally appeared to examine the critics' views of the original research.

14

Studies Based on a Total Sample of Adopted Individuals and Their Relatives: Why They Were Necessary, What They Demonstrated and Failed to Demonstrate

SEYMOUR S. KETY, DAVID ROSENTHAL, PAUL H. WENDER,
AND FINI SCHULSINGER

Studies of adopted individuals and their biological and adoptive families offer a means of disentangling the genetic and environmental contributions to a disorder such as schizophrenia and permit an examination of the effects of one type of influence while the other is randomized or controlled. Using this strategy in a series of studies, we have obtained results pertinent to genetic and family-interaction theories of etiology subject in a

Kety, S. S., Rosenthal, D., Wender, P. H., and Schulsinger, F. "Studies Based on a Total Sample of Adopted Individuals and Their Relatives: Why They Were Necessary, What They Demonstrated and Failed to Demonstrate." *Schizophrenia Bulletin*, 1976, Vol. 2, pp. 413–428. Reprinted by permission of the authors.

considerably lesser degree to the confounding of these influences that have flawed previous studies in both fields. There is every reason that these studies should be presented and criticized in an issue of the *Schizophrenia Bulletin* devoted to genetics, just as another strategy—high risk studies—was previously examined.

The masterful review by Garmezy (Garmezy with Streitman, 1974, and Garmezy, 1974) on individuals at high risk for schizophrenia, published in the *Schizophrenia Bulletin*, presented the hypotheses, research design, results obtained, and conclusions permissible in that area, as reported by the various investigators. The reader could readily judge the pertinence and validity of the reviewer's critique. In contrast, the reviews of the adoption studies to be found in the critical essays by Gottesman and Shields (1976) and by Lidz (1976) suffer from a selective and incomplete presentation of the data obtained in the studies under examination, the omission of important conclusions, and the paraphrasing of others; it is difficult, as a result, to evaluate the validity of much of the two critiques and their relevance to the important issues. For that reason, we have requested and received this opportunity to respond.

A View of Adoption Studies from the Twin Study Vantage Point—The Critique by Gottesman and Shields

Gottesman and Shields have reason to be proud of the Maudsley twin study (Gottesman and Shields, 1972), which successfully minimized many of the methodological biases (Kety, 1959, and Rosenthal, 1962) of earlier studies and laid to rest the notion that the syndrome of schizophrenia was a myth. On the other hand, it shared with the earlier twin studies an inability to control environmental factors, permitting one to conclude only that the results were compatible with the operation of genetic factors in the transmission of schizophrenia. Strömgren (1975), in a survey of genetic research in schizophrenia, stated:

> Although family studies and twin-studies tended to show the importance of genetic factors, the only quite unquestionable result of genetic studies, especially the twin-studies, was that environmental factors contribute extensively to the etiology of schizophrenia.
>
> Not until large scale studies of adoptees were performed was it possible to demonstrate with certainty the great importance also of genetic factors. [p. 17]

The series of adoption studies that we have been carrying out for the past 15 years (Kety et al., 1968, and 1975; Rosenthal et al., 1968; Wender, Rosenthal, and Kety, 1968; and Wender et al., 1973 and 1974) came about because of our independently arrived at dissatisfaction with existing evidence and our recognition that adopted individuals offered a means of disentangling genetic and environmental variables. Kety (1959) expressed it as follows:

> Another possible means of better controlling the environmental variables would be to make a careful study of schizophrenia in adopted children, with comparison of the incidence in blood relatives and in foster relatives. Perhaps only a survey on a national scale would provide the requisite numbers of cases for any of these studies. [p. 1594]

Individual and joint efforts by three of us to compile appropriate samples in Maryland and the District of Columbia caused us to realize that it would be difficult in the United States to achieve our goal of surveying a total population of adopted individuals, in which the appearance of schizophrenia in the adoptee and the biological relatives occurred after the time of adoption and was not a basis for the transfer, and where the presence of mental illness in the relatives and the adoptees would be largely unknown to each other. In 1962, our collaboration with Schulsinger took place with the realization that the remarkable records that existed in Denmark would make it possible to reduce to a minimum many types of selective, ascertainment, and diagnostic biases.

Our sample of 5,483 children, now adults, containing all those legally adopted in the city and county of Copenhagen by individuals not biologically related to them was used as the basis of the studies reported to date. Since that time, the sample has been extended to all of Denmark, although the first report of the larger study has not yet been published. The two initial studies were begun simultaneously. One involved blind psychiatric diagnoses from hospital records, and eventually from interviews, of the biological and adoptive relatives of 33 adoptees who had become schizophrenic and their matched adoptee controls (Kety et al., 1968). The other examined, by means of extensive interviews, adoptees whose biological mother or father had eventually become schizophrenic, along with suitable, matched control adoptees (Rosenthal et al., 1968).

Recognizing the subjectivity of and variance in the diagnosis of schizophrenia, the studies in Denmark took great precaution to minimize the operation of subjective bias, and considerable thought was given to defining the concept of schizophrenia for the purpose of these studies. Danish psychiatrists follow the European tradition and use the term in the narrow classical sense, which emphasizes chronicity and severity of cardinal features. American psychiatrists, however, have broadened the concept to include two additional syndromes "latent" or "borderline" schizophrenia and "acute schizophrenic reaction" on the assumption that these are variants of the original concept. In the hope that ultimately we might be able to examine the genetic relatedness of these three syndromes, we decided to use them (grouped under "definite schizophrenia") in the selection of index cases and the diagnosis of relatives. We quickly realized, as had others before us, that many individuals who cannot correctly be diagnosed as schizophrenic have some of the characteristics of schizophrenia. We decided to test the hypothesis that there was an even wider "schizophrenia spectrum" that would include "uncertain schizophrenia" and "schizoid or inadequate personality." The characteristics of chronic, borderline, and acute schizophrenia and of schizoid and inadequate personality, taken largely from the American Psychiatric Association's (1968) *Diagnostic and Statistical Manual (DSM II)*, were spelled out in our first papers (Table 14.1). Uncertain schizophrenia was of necessity a vague category used when the features of schizophrenia were too few, too mild, or not sufficiently typical.

In what we call the "family studies," 33 adoptees were found in the Greater Copenhagen sample in whom four raters could agree on a diagnosis of definite schizophrenia. A group of control adoptees was selected, matched with them for age, sex, socioeconomic class of the adopting family, and length of time spent with a biological parent. The biological and adoptive parents and full and half siblings of index and control adoptees were then identified. On the basis of institutional records (Kety et al., 1968) or transcripts of psychiatric interviews (Kety et al., 1975) edited to remove any indication of the relationship of a relative to a proband, independent and consensus diagnoses were arrived at for the various relatives. A more complete presentation of the published results than Gottesman and Shields cite will be found in Tables 14.2 and 14.3. Our conclusions read (Kety et al., 1975):

> These results, based now on psychiatric interviews on relatives outside of psychiatric institutions confirm results previously obtained only from institutional records. The greater yield of psychiatric diagnoses made possible by the interview, however, permits a greater resolution into more specific diagnostic categories within what was designated as the "schizophrenia spectrum" in the earlier study. Not only is there a highly significant concentration of diagnoses over that spectrum in the biological relatives of adoptees who became schizophrenic, but diagnoses of chronic, latent, and uncertain schizophrenia are also significantly concentrated in that population and randomly distributed in the other three populations of relatives ... none of whom are genetically related to the schizophrenic index cases. This is strongly suggestive of the operation of genetic factors, a conclusion which is confirmed by the concentration of schizophrenia in the biological paternal half-siblings of the schizophrenic index cases with whom they did not share *in utero* or neonatal experiences but only a certain amount of genetic overlap. [p. 163]

Since they represent a separation of genetic from environmental influences unattained by any other approach, the findings in the biological paternal half siblings constitute very compelling evidence for the operation of genetic factors in the etiology of schizophrenia.

Gottesman and Shields do, however, comment on the "muddling" we appear to introduce by giving equal weight to half siblings as to first-

Table 14.1

Diagnostic classification system employed*

A. Definitely not schizophrenia (specify diagnosis†).

B. Chronic schizophrenia (chronic undifferentiated schizophrenia, true schizophrenia, process schizophrenia).

Characteristics: (1) Poor prepsychotic adjustment; introverted; schizoid; shut-in; few peer contacts; few heterosexual contacts; usually unmarried; poor occupational adjustment. (2) Onset: gradual and without clear-cut psychological precipitant. (3) Presenting picture: presence of primary Bleulerian characteristics; presence of clear rather than confused sensorium. (4) Posthospital course: failure to reach previous level of adjustment. (5) Tendency to chronicity.

B2. Acute schizophrenic reaction (acute undifferentiated schizophrenic reaction, schizoaffective psychosis, possible schizophreniform psychosis, [acute] paranoid reaction, homosexual panic).

Characteristics: (1) Relatively good premorbid adjustment. (2) Relatively rapid onset of illness with clear-cut psychological precipitant. (3) Presenting picture: presence of secondary symptoms and comparatively lesser evidence of primary ones; presence of affect (manic-depressive symptoms, feelings of guilt); cloudy rather than clear sensorium. (4) Posthospital course good. (5) Tendency to relatively brief episode(s) responding to drugs, electroshock therapy, etc.

B3. Borderline state (pseudoneurotic schizophrenia, borderline, ambulatory schizophrenia, questionable simple schizophrenia, "psychotic character," severe schizoid individual).

Characteristics: (1) Thinking: strange or atypical mentation; thought shows tendency to ignore reality, logic, and experience (to an excessive degree) resulting in poor adaptation to life experience (despite the presence of a normal IQ); fuzzy, murky, vague speech. (2) Experience: brief episodes of cognitive distortion (the patient can, and does, snap back, but during the episode the idea has more the character of a delusion than an ego-alien obsessive thought); feelings of depersonalization, of strangeness, or of unfamiliarity with or toward the familiar; microphychosis. (3) Affective: anhedonia—never experiences intense pleasure—never happy; no deep or intense involvement with anyone or anybody. (4) Interpersonal behavior: may appear poised, but lacking in depth ("as if" personality); sexual adjustment—chaotic fluctuation, mixture of heterosexuality and homosexuality. (5) Psychopathology: multiple neurotic manifestations that shift frequently (obsessive concerns, phobias, conversion, psychosomatic symptoms, etc.); severe widespread anxiety.

C. Inadequate personality.

Characteristics: A somewhat heterogeneous group consisting of individuals who would be classified as either inadequate or schizoid by the APA (1968) *Diagnostic Manual.* Persons so classified often had many of the characteristics of the B3 category, but to a considerably milder degree.

D1, 2, or 3. Uncertain B1, 2, or 3 either because information is lacking or because even if enough information is available, the case does not fit clearly into an appropriate B category.

---

* From Kety et al. (1968).

† See note to table 4 on p. 356 of Kety et al. (1968) for diagnoses used.

Study	N	Definite schizophrenia		Uncertain schizophrenia		Schizoid or inadequate personality		Total spectrum	
		N	Per-cent	N	Per-cent	N	Per-cent	N	Per-cent
Early study:*									
Biological relatives of schizophrenic adoptees	150	7	4.7	4	2.7	2	1.3	13	8.7
Biological relatives of control adoptees	156	2	1.3	1	0.6	0	0.0	3	1.9
p†			.077		NS		NS		.007
Most recent study:‡									
Biological relatives of schizophrenic adoptees	173	11	6.4	13	7.5	13	7.5	37	21.4
Biological relatives of control adoptees	174	3	1.7	3	1.7	13	7.5	19	10.9
p			.026		.009		NS		.006
Biological half siblings of schizophrenic adoptees	104	10	9.6	10	9.6	6	5.8	26	25.0
Biological half siblings of control adoptees	104	1	1.0	2	1.9	11	10.6	14	13.5
p			.005		.017		NS		.026
Biological paternal half siblings of schizophrenic adoptees	63	8	12.7	6	9.5	4	6.3	18	28.5
Biological paternal half siblings of control adoptees	64	1	1.6	1	1.6	9	14.1	11	17.2
p			.015		.055		NS		.094
Biological families of index adoptees§	33	14	42.4	17	51.5			23	69.6
Biological families of control adoptees	34	3	8.8	5	14.7			16	47.0
p			.002		.001		NS		NS

* Based on hospital records (Kety et al., 1968).
† Fisher's one tailed exact probability. NS (not significant) is listed for p values greater than .10.
‡ Based on interviews (Kety et al., 1975).
§ Tabulating number of probands whose biological parents, siblings, or half-siblings include at least one diagnosis of definite uncertain, or spectrum, cumulatively.
Note: See note to table 14.3.

Table 14.3

Schizophrenia spectrum diagnoses in the adoptive families of schizophrenic and control adoptees

Study	N	Definite schizophrenia		Uncertain schizophrenia		Schizoid or inadequate personality		Total spectrum	
		N	Percent	N	Percent	N	Percent	N	Percent
Early study:*									
Adoptive relatives of schizophrenic adoptees	74	0	0.0	1	1.4	1	1.4	2	2.7
Adoptive relatives of control adoptees	83	2	2.4	1	1.2	1	0.0	3	3.6
p†			NS		NS		NS		NS
Most recent study:‡									
Adoptive relatives of schizophrenic adoptees	74	1	1.4	1	1.4	2	2.7	4	5.4
Adoptive relatives of control adoptees	91	2	2.2	3	3.3	2	2.2	7	7.7
p			NS		NS		NS		NS
Adoptive families of index adoptees	33	1	3.0	3	9.0			5	15.2
Adoptive families of control adoptees	34	3	8.8	5	14.7			7	20.6
p			NS		NS		NS		NS

* Based on hospital records (Kety et al., 1968).

† Fisher's one tailed exact probability. NS (not significant) is listed for p values greater than .10.

‡ Based on interviews (Kety et al., 1975).

Note: Uncorrected prevalence of these diagnoses in the general population can be estimated using all adoptive relatives and biological control relatives. The individual subsamples do not differ significantly from each other. For definite schizophrenia (from hospital records) = 4/313 or 1.3 percent; for definite schizophrenia (from interview survey of the population) = 6/339 or 1.8 percent; for uncertain schizophrenia (from hospital records) = 3/313 or 1.0 percent; for uncertain schizophrenia (from interview survey of the population) = 7/313 or 2.2 percent.

degree relatives in analyzing the results. We toyed with the idea of giving them half the weight as soon as we realized how many were being identified but rejected it as being too pretentious. We decided to treat them together as relatives as long as we made clear what we were doing and tabulated them separately in all of our publications—and that we have done. For the hypothesis that genetic factors play a significant role in the transmission of schizophrenia (which is the hypothesis we tested), it seems perfectly appropriate to compare the two groups—biological relatives of schizophrenia adoptees with biological relatives of control adoptees since the only criterion on which they differ is their genetic relatedness to a schizophrenic proband, while the number of first- and second-degree relatives, their age, sex, and other variables are comparable. Perhaps a more conservative way to analyze our results would be by the biological families of schizophrenic and control adoptees. Since the composition of the average family is the same for both groups, the half siblings would not pose a problem. We have done that (Tables 14.2 and 14.3), and the differences remain highly significant.

In what we call the "adoptees" studies, index adoptees whose biological mother or father eventually became schizophrenic are selected and compared with a matched group of adoptees whose biological parents have never been admitted to a mental hospital. Both groups of adoptees have been extensively interviewed and tested by psychiatrists and psychologists who were unaware of the mental status of their biological parents. Independent and consensus diagnoses are being made by three raters from the extensive transcripts of these interviews and will eventually be reported. Diagnostic evaluations made by the psychiatric interviewer and global psychopathology ratings have been used in the reports thus far (Rosenthal et al., 1968, and Wender et al., 1974). Comparisons using these ratings have also been made between adoptees whose adoptive parents were normal and those in which the adoptive mother or father had been psychotic (the cross-fostered group). The conclusions reached have been modest. Adoptees reared with a psychotic foster parent show no more psychopathology than those not so reared, while adoptees, one of whose biological parents eventually became psychotic, show more psychopathology even though they are reared by normal individuals.

Curiously enough Gottesman and Shields do not cite our conclusions from these studies; they draw other conclusions that are quite invalid: "... the major accomplishment of the adoption studies was to determine that numerous alleged environmental factors were neither necessary nor sufficient for the occurrence of schizophrenia ..." (p. 366). And again: "The principal conclusion that can be reached at this stage from the adoption work is that it disconfirms the widely held hypothesis that the high schizophrenia rate observed in the children of schizophrenics was due to an interaction between schizophrenogenic rearing and genetic predisposition ..." (p. 367).

We have been careful to point out that our data do not permit such conclusions (Kety et al., 1975):

> The data analyzed thus far do not pertain to possible environmental factors which may operate in the development of schizophrenia, although it is clear from these results that one of them—schizophrenic illness in the rearing family—is not necessary. [p. 163]

And in the case of the cross-fostering study (Wender et al., 1974):

> Does this study, therefore, document the fact that environmental factors play no role in the genetics of the schizophrenias? No. First, it may be maintained that "schizophrenogenicity" in a parent is different from a parent's being schizophrenic....
>
> A second, and important, group of environmental factors are not illuminated by this study. Obviously, this study sheds no light on the role of extrafamilial environmental factors in the genetics of the schizophrenias. It leaves open the contributions of nongenetic biological factors (such as fetal development, birth and neonatal histories, the role of putative schizophrenogenic viruses, etc), as well as the role of extrafamilial psychosocial factors such as peer relationships and school experiences. [p. 127]

Although ignoring the findings we report and the conclusions we draw that are based on appropriate tests of statistical significance in carefully matched groups, they take us to task for presumed differences in some of our data from their expectation, even though these differences are not valid or are based on inappropriate comparisons. Having presented our data in their way, they then begin to make the point that they belabor over the next several pages to the effect that the prevalence of schizophrenia we find in our populations is surprisingly and suspiciously high. In order to do this, however, they have combined our diagnoses of "definite" and "uncertain" schizophrenia, which inflates the prevalence of definite schizophrenia to twice its magnitude. Our criteria for definite schizophrenia are broader than those used by European epidemiologists. The frequency with which we made that diagnosis in populations not known to be related biologically to a schizophrenic adoptee were (Tables 14.2 and 14.3) 1.7, 1.4, 2.2, and 1.8 percent, a far cry from the 6.3 percent that they derive by lumping definite and uncertain together. Our "uncertain schizophrenia" is what the designation implies, and we have not attempted to be explicit about our individual or collective degrees of uncertainty. We find it interesting that this highly subjective and as yet nonexplicit category is very significantly concentrated in the biological relatives of schizophrenics, not only on the basis of our blind consensus diagnoses but also in the independent diagnoses of the individual raters. Having found that this vague and subjective category, which hardly qualifies as schizophrenia according to our own or other criteria, may be genetically related to classical schizophrenia, we felt that it merited better definition. Over the past year, Wender, in collaboration with Spitzer, has been making a detailed, computer-based analysis of these interviews from which a more explicit characterization, we hope, will emerge.

Another type of inappropriate comparison that some have made is that between adoptive and biological relatives. Thus, Tables 14.2 and 14.3 indicate that nearly 8 percent of the biological relatives of control adoptees were diagnosed by us as schizoid or inadequate personality compared with 2 percent of the adoptive relatives. That difference even approaches statistical significance; yet it would not permit the obvious conclusion that there is more of that type of psychopathology in biological relatives of adoptees than the general population. Adoptive relatives are older, more have died or become senile, and fewer have been interviewed so that the opportunities for ascertainment of nonhospitalized character disorders is greater in biological relatives. In addition, they differ in respect of other demographic variables. For similar reasons one cannot conclude from existing evidence that there is a high rate of psychopathology in adoptees generally. That is one of the reasons that led us to compile our matched sample of nearly 5,500 nonadopted persons in Greater Copenhagen. When the analysis of that sample is completed, we hope to be able to throw some light on the question.

We have attempted conscientiously to anticipate and control the nongenetic variables that might have affected our results and to rule out alternative explanations for them. We feel that our findings permit the conclusion that genetic factors play an important etiological role in the majority of patients suffering from schizophrenia. Our studies do not indicate that schizophrenia is a homogeneous syndrome, nor have they yet contributed to the mode or modes of genetic transmission. Neither have they cast doubt on the importance of environmental factors, although they indicate that one type of environmental influence—schizophrenia or severe psychopathology in the rearing family—is not necessary for the development of schizophrenia.

A View of Adoption Studies Through the Holes of a "Tightly Knit Theory" of Parental Deviance—The Critique by Lidz

In his critique of our adoption studies, Lidz (1976) exercises enough license in his inaccurate attribution to us of motives and biases as to make it necessary for us to explain why we applied an adoption strategy to his hypothesis. This may displease him even more than have our findings. While we were pointing out some of the flaws in the evidence bearing on genetic hypotheses of schizophrenia, we became aware of Lidz' hypothesis and were disappointed with the observations and logic on which it was based (Lidz et al., 1957a and 1957b); in comparison, the genetic studies we were criticizing were models of rigor. We were not alone in that dissatisfaction, and a number of competent critics, including Clausen (1959),

Kohn (1968), Mishler and Waxler (1968), Howells (1972), Hirsch and Leff (1975), Wing (1975), and Maher (1976)—none of whom can be accused of an antienvironmental bias—have pointed out the various flaws. The observations on the parents of schizophrenics were neither blind nor controlled, a deficiency that was emphasized in 1961 by Renaud and Estess, who reported in a considerably less intensive survey of the childhood histories of 100 men selected for normality that these

> were laden with events of a kind ordinarily considered productive of later mental conflict. Included in abundance were overt parental discord as seen in divorce or separation; covert parental discord as manifest in lengthy periods of withdrawal, seclusiveness or lack of mutuality....In short, these data abound with material such as we are accustomed to encounter in the histories of psychiatric patients. [p. 795]

Alanen (1968) avoided this deficit by including comparison groups of parents of normals and of neurotic individuals along with the parents of schizophrenics, although he did not attempt to keep himself blind. His observations, which Lidz cites in support of his theory, revealed significant differences between the three types of parents on a scale of psychopathology from healthy or slightly neurotic to manifestly psychotic. Wynne (1968) began his studies with Singer on parental Rorschachs, which included both blind ratings and comparison with controls, and found a significant increase in a substantial number of categories of communication defects and deviances in the parents of schizophrenics.

But there were still four hypotheses that could account for this observations:

- That the transmission of irrationality was from parents to child in the rearing process
- That the psychopathology and communication deviance found in the parents were a reflection of genetic factors they shared with the children
- That these psychological changes in the parents resulted from the rearing of a schizophrenic child
- That the findings were artifacts produced by the test situations to which parents who had reared a schizophrenic responded differently from those who had not.

Recognizing that an adoption strategy would permit an examination of the second hypothesis, Wender, Rosenthal, and Kety (1968) conducted a study of three groups of parents: couples who had adopted a child who became schizophrenic, couples who had reared a child of their own who became schizophrenic, and a control group of adoptive parents of normal individuals. These were American families studied at the Clinical Center of the National Institute of Mental Health and were not part of the national Danish sample. Questions of selective and subjective bias are fully discussed in the paper, requiring no great insight on the part of the reviewer.

The study did not replicate Lidz' design in that a control group was included and came closer to Alanen's (1966) study, except that a blind rater was included for the psychopathology scores along with the interviewer who was not blind. A summary of the ratings for psychopathology for the three types of parents is compared in Table 14.4 with Alanen's ratings in the natural parents of schizophrenics and neurotics.

The average severity of psychopathology among the biological parents of schizophrenics is virtually identical in the two studies. Likewise, the severity of psychopathology among the adoptive parents of schizophrenics in our study was practically the same as that found by Alanen in the natural parents of neurotics.

> The inference to be drawn from the comparability of these data depends on how Alanen's data are interpreted; but under the psychological transmission hypothesis the adoptive parents in this sample should not have been capable of generating more than neurotic dysfunction in their offspring. Thus one may conclude that psychopathology in the parents is not a sufficient cause of schizophrenia. [Wender, Rosenthal, and Kety 1968, p. 248]

Whether influenced by this study or not, Lidz does not emphasize psychopathology as an indication of parental deviance but rather the parents' interactive and communicative defects. Although he certainly reports (Lidz, 1972) considerable suggestions of psychopathology in the parents he studied ("mothers highly unstable," "fathers equally disturbed," "families strange and even bizarre," "fathers suspicious and often paranoid," "60 percent of the patients had at least one parent who

Table 14.4

A comparison of the data of Alanen (1966) and the adoptive parents study of Wender, Rosenthal, and Kety (1968)*

Alanen		Adoptive parents study	
Group	Mean severity of psycho-pathology	Group	Mean severity of psycho-pathology
Fathers of schizophrenics	4.8	Fathers of schizophrenics	4.2
Mothers of schizophrenics	4.8	Mothers of schizophrenics	4.9
Parents of schizophrenics	4.8	Parents of schizophrenics	4.6
Fathers of neurotics	3.2	Adoptive fathers of schizophrenics	3.2
Mothers of neurotics	3.4	Adoptive mothers of schizophrenics	3.5
Parents of neurotics	3.3	Adoptive parents of schizophrenics	3.4
		Adoptive fathers of normals	2.6
		Adoptive mothers of normals	3.0
		Adoptive parents of normals	2.8

* From Wender, Rosenthal, and Kety (1968).

was psychotic"), he also emphasizes communication defects now presumed to be the rearing factor of etiological significance.

The Wender, Rosenthal, and Kety (1968) study also made us aware of an important confound that critics of intrafamily hypotheses have repeatedly mentioned (Clausen, 1959; Hirsch and Leff, 1975; Maher, 1976; Mishler and Waxler, 1968; and Schopler and Loftin, 1969) but to which Lidz has remained oblivious. Had he quoted the entire paragraph below rather than merely the sentence in brackets, this problem would have become more obvious:

> It must be mentioned in passing that the evaluation of psychopathology in the adoptive parents of the schizophrenics was complicated by the fact that some of their psychopathology appeared to the raters to be reactive to pathology in their children. [Many of these parents presented a picture of depression, apathy, social withdrawal, preoccupation, anxiety, and feelings of futility and guilt.] In about one-half of the couples these symptoms seem clearly related to the onset of severe problems in their offspring. It was impossible for the raters to make allowances for these reactive symptoms and interpersonal difficulties, which seem to have led to an attribution of more severe psychopathology than would have been made if these parents had not been faced with and reacting to such a stress. [Wender et al., 1971, p. 1016]

Nevertheless, we concluded that the slightly higher level of psychopathology in the adoptive parents of schizophrenics versus the adoptive parents of normals did not permit us to assert that experiential factors play no role in the development of the illness.

The Word Association Test yielded a significant increase in original and deviant responses among the biological as compared to the adoptive parents of the schizophrenics, suggesting a genetic component in that observation. On the other hand, results of the Object Sorting Test, analyzed either by Wender's group or by Lidz' group, failed completely to show more deviance in the parents, natural or adoptive, of schizophrenics than in controls.*

That entire study has now been replicated (Wender 1975): The adopting and biological parents of schizophrenics were compared with a third group, the natural parents of nongenetic retardates. Interviews were performed with a standard format using the Current and Past Psychopathology Scales (CAPPS), which was scored by a DIAGNO-II program. The clinical interviews as well as the Minnesota Multiphasic Personality Inventories of the parents showed that the adopting parents of schizophrenics and the biological parents of retardates did not differ from each other,

---

* Lidz asked for and was sent the test protocols that Cynthia Wild rated blindly. The groups overlapped completely, and no difference at all emerged. It is curious that the Yale group did not complain about the inadequacy of the protocols until after they learned of their negative results. Singer was sent the Rorschach protocols and did successfully discriminate the parents of schizophrenics from those of normals....

while both differed greatly from the biological parents of schizophrenics. The Rorschach protocols of these three sets of parents have now been blindly evaluated, producing results different from those obtained in the first study: The adoptive parents of schizophrenics did not differ from the biological parents of retardates, while both groups manifested less psychopathology than the biological parents of schizophrenics.

. . .

Lidz' perceptive and imaginative theory has not been destroyed; the only threat to it is that it is being tested. Our findings thus far have failed to support it, but those of Wynne, Singer, and Toohey are compatible with the hypothesis of parental communication deviance. We do not doubt their finding that parents, natural or adoptive, who have reared a child who became schizophrenic respond differently in a Rorschach test situation from those whose child turned out normally. Whether this has important etiologic significance remains to be demonstrated. It is possible that Wynne and Singer will do so, or it may be that the ingenious strategy that Kinney and Jacobsen (1976) are applying to our adoption data may also do so. But it would be unfortunate if we permitted the design, results, and credibility of studies in this field or in the area of genetic factors to be judged by whether or not they support Lidz' theory.

We believe that the design, logic, and results of the adoption studies have closed important gaps in the evidence for substantial genetic influences in schizophrenia that the twin studies were unable to close. No plausible alternative explanation consistent with the data has been proposed. Much remains to be done to determine what is genetically transmitted and to determine the modes of transmission and expression.

The evidence that environmental factors are necessary for the development of schizophrenia is equally compelling, and here, too, there is a need for further research to identify the relevant factors among the many psychosocial, physical, chemical, and infectious influences that affect the developing individual, and to examine how they interact with hereditary vulnerabilities to produce or prevent the syndrome we call schizophrenia.

Fini Schulsinger's article uses an adoption methodology for untangling genetic and environmental influences on psychopathy. This psychiatric disorder, associated with chronic criminality or callous and shallow interpersonal relationships, has been regarded as a kind of "moral" insanity. Schulsinger provides evidence that hereditary factors are playing a significant role. To be sure, psychopathy itself is not inherited, since lawlessness is dependent on cultural norms, which vary from time to time and society to society. What is inherited is some biological processes that make it more difficult for affected individuals to adhere to the laws and mores of the society to which they belong.

15

Psychopathy:
Heredity and Environment

FINI SCHULSINGER

Nothing indicates that the disease or condition we today call "psychopathy" has not been prevalent as far back in the history of mankind as have psychosis, mental retardation, and neurosis.* Once psychosis and mental deficiency had been delimited, psychiatrists became interested in describing and classifying those conditions that could not be ascribed to either psychosis, mental deficiency, or gross neurological damage.

. . .

Schulsinger, F. "Psychopathy: Heredity and Environment." *International Journal of Mental Health*, 1972, Vol. 1, pp. 190–206. Copyright © by International Arts and Sciences Press, Inc., and abridged version reprinted by permission of M. E. Sharpe, Inc.

* The author...wishes to emphasize that the analyses of the data collected in the study described in this paper are still in a very preliminary stage and that some of the findings reported here may be altered with more detailed analysis. Nevertheless, because there is a great deal of current interest in questions about etiology in relation to psychopathy and because the research uses a unique sample in which genetic and environmental variables can be separated more satisfactorily than has previously been possible, it was considered important to publish this provisional report.

Kraepelin (1915) conceived of the psychopathic conditions as circumscribed infantilism or circumscribed development inhibitions. He described and subclassified the psychopathic conditions into seven groups and presented their sex distribution and prevalence on the basis of a hospital population.

Kahn (1931) and Kretschmer (cited in Schneider, 1934) both tried to correlate psychopathy with other aspects of personality. Kahn described 16 types of psychopathy, which he then assigned to either a drive, a temperament, or a characterological aspect of the personality. But these aspects of the personality were further elaborated, which again had the sad effect of enabling very few patients to be assigned more easily to one of Kahn's subclasses than to several of the others. Kretschmer's typology was more dynamic: it was based on four psychological stages: "the uptake," "the retention," "the working through," and "the release." A person's way of experiencing something could vary from sthenic to asthenic, which made three forms of reaction possible: the primitive reaction, the expansive reaction, and the sensitive reaction. Each of these three forms of reaction were characterized by a different constellation of the above-mentioned four psychological stages.

Obviously, the classification of psychopathy is an intricate problem. Inasmuch as we have been unable to classify psychopathic disorders according to well-known etiologies, the most useful compromise has been to classify them purely on the basis of clinical description. This is what Kraeplin did, and it is what Schneider (1934) called a "system-free typology." Schneider improved Kraepelin's typology to some extent because he added to Kraepelin's mainly transgressive psychopaths some groups of personality deviations that did not necessarily lead to antisocial behavior. Schneider aimed at a concept and classification free of moral values. He conceived of psychopaths as deviants from average norms. The deviations caused the affected individual and/or his environment to suffer. Since the only behavioral norms clearly outlined are those that can be deducted from the penal code, it is difficult to imagine how Schneider could settle on norms without making a choice based on his own moralistic equipment (Vanggaard, 1968). Apart from this philosophical weakness, Schneider's typology has been relatively easy to apply: and it has, to a large extent, pervaded European and other schools of psychiatry.

Up until 1939, British psychiatry favored a concept of psychopathy mainly as a moral disease. Since then, Henderson (1939), Curran & Mallinson (1944), and Craft (1966) have made classifications of psychopathy on a purely descriptive basis, but in a much less elaborate way than their German colleagues. None of the British authors specified more than three classes....

In the United States, Benjamin Rush (cited in Craft, 1966) wrote:

> There are many instances of persons with sound understanding and some of uncommon talent who are affected with this disease in the world. It differs

from exculpative, fraudulent and malicious lying in being influenced by none of the motives of any of them. Persons with this disease cannot speak the truth on any subject.

Rush thought of psychopaths as having an originally defective organization "in those parts of the body which are occupied by the moral faculties of the mind." He called the condition "moral derangement," and he considered in a valid entity for treatment by physicians.

In the twentieth century, American interest in psychopathy has taken a course that differs in some ways from the European traditions. First, the application of research methods has been more common, perhaps because psychologists and sociologists have had greater academic prestige in the United States than is common in Europe. Second, psychoanalytic theory and practice were integrated into mental health practice much earlier in the United States than in Europe, where it was delayed partly as a consequence of the opposition of the German Nazis to psychoanalysis. The result has been a vast body of more or less sociologically oriented surveys in America on large populations of delinquents and criminals many of whom were psychopaths. Another result has been several very different attempts at unifying psychoanalytic and descriptive principles in relation to the concept of psychopathy (Greenacre, 1945; Karpman, 1947; and others). Partridge (1930) proposed the term "sociopathic personality," which has become the official American term for psychopathy, a term possibly adopted for operational reasons, but with an unavoidable moralistic content, which does not make it easier for modern criminologists to fight the spirit of retaliation in the penal systems.

Alexander (1930) supplied a comprehensive description and explanation of the "neurotic character," which was the old-time analysts' term for psychopathy. His psychodynamic interpretations of case records are not easy to evaluate from a scientific viewpoint, but his clinical descriptions add much to the otherwise usable, system-free, descriptive classifications of Kraepelin and Schneider. Alexander's description of the "neurotic character" makes the concept of psychopathy a coherent one. Its focus is on personality traits that are also common, to a large extent, to Kraepelin's and Schneider's subgroups, which then become more meaningful. The essence of Alexander's description is that "neurotic characters" show a consistent pattern of acting out and that this acting-out is mainly of an alloplastic nature (except, perhaps, for some alcoholics and a few others).

This very sketchy and condensed review of such a huge topic as the concept of psychopathy does not pretend to do justice to all facets of the subject and all the authors who have written about it. I find a relatively simple, descriptively based concept of psychopathy the most useful tool in research; and, as will be evident later, Alexander's description has proved most tempting and also operationally useful to me.

Etiology

GENETICS

The very special eugenic ideas of the Third Reich involved some German psychiatric geneticists in the classical type of family studies on relatives of psychopathic probands (Berlit, 1931; Riedel, 1937; Stumpfl, 1939). Their work was carried out in the same neat way as other, respectably intended, genetic work from the famous Munich school. The results of these studies unanimously indicated that heredity plays a role in the etiology of psychopathy.

The nature-nurture problem has always been particularly pronounced with regard to psychopathy, because therapists of all kinds have always been struck by the terrible environments to which many of their delinquent and/or psychopathic patients have been exposed. Newkirk (1957) stated "As adopted delinquents permit research on the constitutional separate from the environmental element, thorough statistics on adoption and adopted persons including their ancestry should be devised and collected" (p. 54). Reiter (1930) tried to utilize this technique in a prospective design; but, for unknown reasons, nothing but a first presentation of the study has been published. Perhaps he feared German eugenics of the 1930s!

BRAIN PATHOLOGY

A number of electroencephalographic (EEG) studies on psychopaths, in different countries, have shown an excess of abnormal EEGs in psychopaths compared with the general population. The more violent or impulsive the psychopaths are, the greater is the number of their EEG abnormalities. The deviations have been shown to be of an unspecific nature, neither focal nor epileptic. Generally, these mild dysrhythmias are viewed as signs of immaturity. Otherwise it is difficult to interpret certain findings. How much of the abnormality is inherited, and how much comes from insufficient obstetrical care, or from series of minor cerebral concussions among the wildest of boys? This physiological correlate of psychopathy cannot yet, in any case, be ruled out as a possible etiological factor.

CYTOGENETICS

Among tall, violent lawbreakers, the prevalence of the XYY syndrome is greater than among other offenders and the general population (Court Brown, 1968; Nielsen, Stürup, Tsuboi, & Romano, 1969). Such findings are fascinating and encouraging. However, as only about 1% of severe criminal psychopaths in two psychopathic prisons showed this chromosome abnormality, a cytogenetic solution to the etiology of psychopathy is not to be expected in the near future.

DEPRIVATION IN INFANCY

Broken homes, loss of parents, hospitalization, lack of proper physical and emotional care, and institutionalization are all factors believed by many psychologists and psychiatrists to be of etiological significance in psychopathy, retardation of development, and other mental abnormalities occurring in childhood and later. This belief, or conviction, has been utilized in many countries to convince politicians and administrators of the value of humane and well-staffed children's institutions. Unfortunately, it is often difficult to provide proper care for children simply because they deserve it.

Writers such as Spitz (1945) and Bowlby (1951) have been influential in a positive way. From a scientific viewpoint, however, most of the classics on early experience and its later effects are more dubious, as has been shown in the more recent works of Clarke (1968), Heston (1966), and Pinneau (1955). A basic methodological error in the classical studies of institutionalization effects was that they were performed without proper genetic control. Heston's study has shown with reasonable certainty that the genetic variable is far more important than institution versus family rearing with regard to the later development of psychosis, personality deviations, and other manifest mental disturbances.

Current Investigations in Denmark

Inasmuch as any pathological condition is a result of an interaction between genetic and environmental factors, the ideal research should aim at clarification of this interaction. The greater the knowledge about one of the two factors, the greater are the possibilities of planning investigations on the impact of the other factor.

The usual genealogical studies in psychiatry show that the closer the relationship between a family member and a mentally ill proband, the greater is the risk of mental illness for the family member. As already indicated, the relatives in the usual studies share with the probands not only genes but also environment. A realistic way to "isolate" the genetic factor is to conduct studies of probands who have been reared apart from their biological relatives and to analyze the prevalence of mental disorders among their biological and their foster relatives. This idea is not new, but the practical implications of this technique have generally discouraged possible investigators from making serious attempts.

In an investigation initiated by Kety, Rosenthal, Wender, & Schulsinger (1968) seven years ago, we explored the possibilities in Denmark of conducting such a study on schizophrenia. It turned out that studies of the desired nature were feasible in Denmark, for the following reasons:

1. Denmark has a central register of all adoptions, under the supervision of the State Department of Justice. This department, understanding and appreciating our scientific goals, gave us permission to use its registers. (Of course, permission was granted only subject to several discretionary conditions.)

2. Denmark has a central register of psychiatric hospital admissions meant for research purposes. This register goes back to 1916.

3. Denmark has maintained, since 1924, municipal population registers that make it possible to trace a person if one address from 1924 or later is known. By use of old census lists, it is possible even to trace people farther back—in some instances, as far back as the year 1800. In addition, the Danish population is relatively homogeneous, and there are few emigrants.

The schizophrenic probands in the first adoption study were found among 507 adoptees with psychiatric hospital records from a total pool of 5,483 adoptees, encompassing all the nonfamily adoptions in the city and county of Copenhagen between 1924 and 1947. All the case record material for these 507 adoptees with a record of mental illness was screened and reviewed by two Danish psychiatrists, the writer being one.

During this work I was amazed to find a relatively large number of adoptees who had been in contact with psychiatrists because of personality disturbances. Therefore, I planned to do a family study of psychopathy using this adoptive sample, for which it was possible to separate hereditary from environmental factors. The study began in June 1967, and the collection of data ended in September 1969.

PROCEDURES

The first step was to establish an operational and reliable definition of psychopathy. The following criteria were subjected to reliability testing:

1. A consistent pattern, lasting a reasonable period beyond adolescence, of impulse-ridden or acting-out behavior must be evident. This behavior can be (a) mainly active, expansive, or manipulating, or (b) mainly passive-asthenic. (Alcohol and/or drug abuse can be an expression of either a or b).

2. The abreactions are inadequate in relation to the precipitating factors (of course, on the basis of very vaguely defined Danish behavioral norms).

3. The abreactions are frequently of an alloplastic nature.

These criteria are all positive. The negative criteria are the following:

4. Character neurosis must be excluded, i.e., a consistent pattern of neurotic restriction of activity and gratification.

5. Borderline psychosis must be excluded.

6. Cases in which acting-out is found in an otherwise psychotic person are excluded.

I think most psychiatrists would consider this definition of psychopathy adequate for most cases.

Twenty cases were picked from the 507 mentally ill adoptees whom I had originally given a diagnosis of psychopathy in 1964, before the present study was planned and before the above definition of psychopathy was formulated. Twenty other cases with other diagnoses, but with the same amount of case record material and of the same sex and age as the 20 psychopaths, were selected from the same pool.

All the available sets of records for the two groups were then mixed into a common group and evaluated again blindly by two other experienced psychiatrists and me, following a discussion of the criteria. Each of the criteria was rated on a four-point rating scale. I now found 21 persons of the 40 who could be classified as psychopaths. The other psychiatrists considered 17 and 16 of these 21 cases, respectively, to be psychopathic. In 14 cases all three of us agreed upon the diagnosis of psychopathy; and as the raters had classified, respectively, 21, 22, and 20 persons as psychopaths, the over-all agreement among the three raters was 67%. However, one of the criteria, i.e., that the acting-out behavior should have lasted a reasonable time beyond adolescence, was applied differently by the three raters. An exclusion of the cases below 20 years of age from the screening raised the over-all agreement to 74% among the three raters. If agreement about absence of psychopathy were included, the over-all agreement would increase to 82%.

It turned out that the scoring system discriminated very well between psychopaths and character neurotics. Eight of the 40 persons were characterized by one or two raters as possibly borderline psychotics. The total scores of these eight persons were rather varied with regard to psychopathy, but none of them was high. As a result of the reliability testing procedure, the original definition was changed on one point: it was now required that the psychopathic symptoms should have lasted beyond the age of 19.

On the basis of the definition thus established, it was possible to select 57 psychopathic probands from the 507 adoptees with known mental disorders. Then, from the pool of nearly 5,000 adoptees who were not mentally ill, a control was selected for each of the 57 index probands. For every adoptee in this pool there was a form in the central register showing sex, age, and age at first transfer to the adoptive family; names and birthdates of the adoptive parents; occupation of the adoptive father, his stated annual income and financial status, and his address at the time of the

Table 15.1

Descriptive statistics of index probands and control groups

	Index probands	Controls
Number of females	17	17
Average age of females	35.8 years	35.8 years
Number of males	40	40
Average age of males	36.7 years	35.8 years
Number of environmental shifts	1.18	1.21
Months of institutionalization	5.63	5.62

adoption; and the names, birthdates, occupations, and addresses of the biological parents. Starting with the form on the index proband, an alternating forward and backward search was made until four possible controls had been found. A control had to be of the same sex and born during the same period, to avoid the different influences of changing society. They were also matched for the age at transfer to the adoptive home and for the social class of the adoptive parents, on the basis of a Danish classification by Svalastoga (1959).

A pretransfer history was prepared for every index proband and his or her four possible controls that is, a report of how long, with whom, and where each stayed until the transfer to the adoptive parents. In almost every one of the 57 cases it was possible to find a perfect control, with exactly the same age, social background, length of institutionalization, length of stay with biological relatives, and number of environmental shifts before the transfer. It was easy to match for social class, and in many cases to match even for the same section of the city of Copenhagen. The comparability of the two groups is evident in Tables 15.1 and 15.2.

Table 15.2

Total number of biological and adoptive relatives
of index proband and control groups

Relationship	Index probands*		Controls*	
	Biological	Adoptive	Biological	Adoptive
Half-sibs	169	12	156	8
Full sibs	25	8	16	11
Fathers	54	54	56	57
Mothers	57	57	57	57
Totals	305	131	285	133

* Three biological fathers of index probands and one biological father of a control could not be identified. Three adoptive mothers of probands were unmarried at the time of adoption. Adoptive full sibs are offspring of both adoptive parents, adoptive half-sibs are offspring of only one of the adoptive parents.

The total number of biological and adoptive relatives age 20 or above was 854. Their distribution in terms of relationship was fairly similar for the two groups, as Table 15.2 indicates.

FINDINGS

Mental illness among the relatives was found through a search for the names of all 854 relatives in the archives of all the psychiatric institutions in Denmark. A research assistant traveled throughout the country and spent several days at each institution searching the files (with greatly appreciated assistance from the local secretaries). I reviewed and sum-marized all the available case record material and did a diagnostic clas-sification blindly, i.e., without knowing whether the person was related biologically or by adoption to an index proband or to a control. The find-ings on mental illness in the various categories of relatives are sum-marized in the table.

The distribution of mental illnesses of all types was as follows (total number of ill relatives, 129):

	Biological	*Adoptive*
Index	$\frac{58}{305} = 19.0 \pm 2.3\%$	$\frac{18}{131} = 13.7 \pm 3.0\%$
Control	$\frac{37}{285} = 13.0 \pm 2.0\%$	$\frac{16}{133} = 12.0 \pm 2.8\%$

It may be noted that the rates of illness are approximately the same in both groups of adoptive relatives and in the biological relatives of the controls. The over-all rate of illness for the biological relatives of the index pro-bands, however, is considerably higher than the rates for the other three subgroups of relatives.

The quality of the case record material, of course, varied according to the institution, the tradition of the time, and, especially, the length of institutionalization. It therefore seemed most useful to operate with a *spectrum* ... of personality disorders, in which psychopathy was the "nu-clear" disease. In some cases a diagnosis of psychopathy was rather likely, but the case record material did not permit application of all the criteria from the definition of psychopathy. These cases were classified as "obser-vation for psychopathy" (probable psychopathy). Some cases were too mild or too inconsistent to be classified psychopathic according to the definition, and they were just classified as "character deviations." If the case record material was relatively sparse in such cases, they were clas-sified as "observation for character deviation." A number of cases had to be classified as evidencing either criminality, alcoholism, or drug abuse, with no other clarifying diagnosis. (In my view, they probably belong to the spectrum of personality disorders more or less related to psychopathy.) A few cases had to be diagnosed as hysterical character deviation (but not conversion hysteria). These cases were counted within the psychopathy spectrum. A single case of an obsessive-compulsive character was not included in the psychopathy spectrum: nor were cases of completed suicide for whom there was no psychiatric information.

The figures that follow show the distribution of psychopathic spectrum disorders among the relatives:

	Biological	Adoptive
Index	$\frac{44}{305} = 14.4 \pm 2.0\%$	$\frac{10}{133} = 7.6 \pm 2.3\%$
Control	$\frac{19}{285} = 6.7 \pm 1.5\%$	$\frac{7}{133} = 5.3 \pm 1.9\%$

It is immediately evident that there is a great surplus of such disorders among the biological relatives of the index probands, more than 14% of whom have a psychopathic spectrum disorder compared with 5–8% among the other three relative groups. Among the biological relatives of the index probands, 76% of "mental illnesses of all types" belong to the psychopathy spectrum, compared with 44–56% in the other relative groups. The differences between the biological relatives of the index probands and the other relative groups would have been even greater if the diagnosis of hysterical character deviation had been omitted from the psychopathy spectrum.

Base rate figures for the expectancy of psychopathic spectrum disorders as classified here are not available for the Danish population. It may be seen, however, that the rates of disorder are again about the same in all of the relative groups except the biological relatives of the index probands.

The prevalence of the core disease, psychopathy, among the relatives is shown below:

	Relatives	
	Biological	Adoptive
Index	$\frac{12}{305} = 3.9 \pm 1.1\%$	$\frac{1}{131} = 0.8 \pm 0.8\%$
Control	$\frac{4}{285} = 1.4 \pm 0.7\%$	$\frac{2}{133} = 1.5 \pm 1.0\%$

Psychopathy is certainly overrepresented among the biological relatives of the index probands.

This difference is even more marked when the distribution of psychopathy is compared in the four parent group only.

Parents only

	Biological	*Adoptive*
Index	$\frac{5}{111} = 4.5 \pm 2.0\%$	$\frac{1}{111} = 0.9 \pm 0.9\%$
Control	$\frac{1}{113} = 0.9 \pm 0.9\%$	$\frac{0}{114} = 0\%$

In fact, as none of the mothers in any group received the diagnosis of core psychopathy, the comparisons may be confined to the fathers only. Psychopathy occurs more than five times as frequently among the index probands biological fathers as among their adoptive fathers or the biological fathers of the controls, as may be seen here:

Fathers

	Biological	*Adoptive*
Index	$\frac{5}{54} = 9.3 \pm 4.0\%$	$\frac{1}{54} = 1.9 \pm 1.9\%$
Control	$\frac{1}{56} = 1.8 \pm 1.8\%$	$\frac{0}{57} = 0\%$

Referring back to the table, it will be noted that there is an over-all tendency for the psychopathic spectrum disorders, and for core psychopathy in particular, to appear more frequently among the male than among the female relatives. The sex differences, however, are not as marked and consistent in the sibling and half-sibling subgroups as in the parent subgroups. The table also shows that the differences between the biological relatives of the index probands and the controls do not increase consistently as one moves from the comparisons of rates of mental illness in toto to rates of psychopathic spectrum disorders to core psychopathy. The differences between the index and control relatives increase substantially, for example, as one goes from the psychopathic spectrum disorders to core psychopathy in the biological fathers, while in the biological mothers the increase occurs between the all-mental-disorders category and the spectrum-disorders category. It is not entirely clear from these preliminary analyses, therefore, whether the psychopathic spectrum as classified here is meaningfully related to the definition of core psychopathy. The difference in the patterns of the mothers and fathers may reflect the genetically agreed upon fact that males are more likely than females to be classified as core psychopaths in Denmark. The symptomatology involved in the author's definition of psychopathy is more easily recognized in males who have to go to a hospital.

Assuming, however, that the psychopathy spectrum *is* appropriately classified, it is of further interest to examine the distribution of spectrum disorders on a family basis. The figures in Table 15.3 indicate the distribution of the psychopathic spectrum disorders in the affected families, the

Table 15.3

Total number of biological and adoptive relatives
of index proband and control groups

| | Number of families | | |
	Index	Control	Total
Group 1: biological +, adoptive −	27	11	38
Group 2: biological −, adoptive −	22	39	61
Group 3: biological +, adoptive +	5	4	9
Group 4: biological −, adoptive +	3	3	6
Totals	57	57	114

presence of such a disorder in a biological or adoptive family being indicated by +, and its absence by −. A chi-square test for this distribution (with groups 2 and 3 combined) results in $P < 0.005$.

Discussion

The conclusion to be drawn from these findings is that genetic factors play an important role in the etiology of psychopathy. The definition of psychopathy that we used is purely descriptive, and, applied to case record material, it requires only a minimum of interpretation of the data. The definition has proven reliable, and it probably has face validity as well.

The selection of controls was made with due respect to possible etiological factors. Social background in the adoptive homes was matched, as was the period of birth. Even the possibility of deprivation during infancy was partially taken into consideration, as the controls and the index probands had been subject to the same number of environmental shifts, had spent the same amount of time in institutions, and had been with their biological relatives the same length of time before placement in their adoptive homes.

. . .

Although the design of this study aims especially at demonstrating possible genetic factors in the etiology of psychopathy, this does not at all mean that the findings exclude environmental factors. However, the figures indicate that the frequency of psychopathy and related disorders in the adoptive families can be excluded as an important etiological factor in this sample. Only three of the index probands had a unilateral prevalence on the adoptive side, and three of the controls also had this environmental load. Only five index probands and four controls had a bilateral load of psychopathic spectrum disorders.

Another possible environmental factor is deprivation during early infancy, as expressed in number of environmental shifts and lengths of institutionalization in early childhood. If this factor were to be tested in the study, it would have to be a test of, for example, the hypothesis that psychopathic spectrum disorders would be less frequent among the biological relatives of the index probands who were transferred late to their adoptive homes than among those transferred at an early age.

One of the possible etiological factors in psychopathy is brain damage. The case record material available for the relatives does not permit an evaluation of this factor, which would require a personal examination of all the relatives. However, a relevant factor could be pregnancy and birth complications. A search for the official midwife reports about the childbirths of the 114 probands and controls yielded 107 reports. Information on the births of 50 matched pairs of probands and controls was thus available.

The content of older Danish midwife reports is difficult to evaluate. There is some agreement in Denmark that not every complication is registered in these reports. On the other hand, if something is registered, one can feel sure that it really happened. In other words, the midwife reports yield minimum information. Every midwife report was rated according to a five-point rating scale devised in collaboration with Professor F. Fuchs, Chairman of Gynecology and Obstetrics at Cornell Medical School, New York. This scale, based on the relatively primitive type of information in the midwife reports, ranged from 0 (no complications) to 4 points (for severe complications): the total score could be 5 or more points.

The figures in Table 15.4 compare the pregnancy/birth complications of the index probands and the controls.

Table 15.4

Number of pregnancy/birth complications of index probands and controls

	Index probands	Controls
Number with birth records	53	54
Total scores	94	105
Average score	1.8	1.9
Number with birth records for both groups	50	50
Total scores	80	97
Average score	1.6	1.9
Number with score of 0	24	19
Number with 1–4 points	21	19
Number with 5+ points	5	9
Number with single scores of 3 and/or 4	8	5
Number with single scores of 4	6	3

This analysis does not establish a brain damage etiology of psychopathy, at least insofar as brain damage from birth complications is concerned. If there were such brain damage etiology, we could expect the index probands without obstetrical complications to have a more severe genetic load of psychopathic spectrum abnormalities than the index probands with complications. Twenty-four index probands had not suffered any pregnancy/birth complications (score 0), and 14 had a total score of 3 or above. To obtain a score of 3+, they had to have experienced one or more serious complications, or a combination of minor complications. Comparing the biological family scores for psychopathic spectrum disorders for the two groups, using the t test, we found no significant difference in the genetic load in the two groups (P > 0.20). Therefore, this analysis, too, failed to yield support for an etiological role of pregnancy/birth complications in psychopathy per se.

Summary

In summary, this study of the 854 biological and adoptive relatives of 57 psychopathic adoptees and their 57 matched controls shows the frequency of mental disorders to be higher in the biological relatives of the psychopathic probands than among their adoptive relatives or than among either group of relatives of the controls. The difference is even greater when only psychopathic spectrum disorders are considered. The study supports a hypothesis of heredity as an etiological factor in psychopathic spectrum disorders. Deprivation during infancy and brain damage caused by pregnancy birth complications were not found to be etiologically significant, at least as measured by the somewhat crude indices utilized in this investigation.

VIII

MENTAL RETARDATION AND OTHER HANDICAPS

In this article Edward Zigler distinguishes between mild and severe mental retardation, pointing out that the severely retarded often have diagnosed organic pathology while the mildly retarded do not. He suggests, then, that the causes of the two types of retardation are different. Additionally, Zigler points out that the experience of being retarded often exaggerates difficulties in solving problems because of a tendency to crave social interaction more than trying to get the problem right.

16

Familial Mental Retardation: A Continuing Dilemma

EDWARD ZIGLER

The past decade has witnessed renewed interest in the problem of mental retardation. The interest has resulted in vigorous research activity and the construction of a number of theories which attempt an explanation of attenuated intellectual functioning. However, much of the research and many of the theoretical efforts in the area appear to be hampered by a variety of conceptual ambiguities. Much of this ambiguity is due to the very heterogeneity of phenomena included within the rubric of intellectual retardation. A portion of this ambiguity also appears to be the product of many workers' general conceptual orientation to the area of mental retardation.

The typical textbook pictures the distribution of intelligence as normal or Gaussian in nature, with approximately the lowest 3 percent of the distribution encompassing the mentally retarded (see Figure 16.1a). A homogeneous class of persons is thus constructed, a class defined by intelligence-test performance which results in a score between 0 and 70. This schema has misled many laymen and students, and has subtly influ-

Zigler, E. "Familial Mental Retardation: A Continuing Dilemma." *Science*, 1967, Vol. 155, pp. 292–298. Copyright © by the American Association for the Advancement of Science and reprinted by permission.

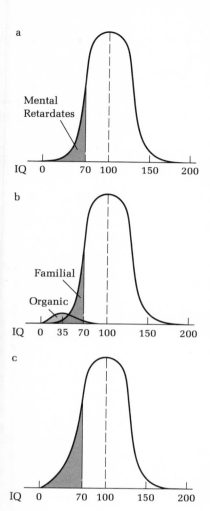

Figure 16.1

(a) Conventional representation of the distribution of intelligence; (b) distribution of intelligence as represented in the two-group approach; (c) actual distribution of intelligence (after Penrose, 1963).

enced the approach of experienced workers in the area. For if one fails to appreciate the arbitrary nature of the 70-IQ cutoff point, it is but a short step to the formulation that all persons falling below this point compose a homogeneous class of "subnormals," qualitatively different from persons having a higher IQ. The view that mental retardates comprise a homogeneous group is seen in numerous research studies in which comparisons are made between retardates and normal individuals with the two groups defined solely on the basis of an IQ classification.

This practice gives rise to a "difference," or "defect," orientation to mental retardation. Such an approach historically included the notion of moral defect and had many origins, ranging from the belief that retardates were possessed by a variety of devils to the empirical evidence of the higher incidence among them of socially unacceptable behaviors, such as crime and illegitimacy. More recently, the notion of defect has referred to defects in either physical or cognitive structures. This defect approach has one unquestionably valid component. There is a sizable group of retardates who suffer from any of a variety of known physical defects. For example, mental retardation may be due to a dominant gene, as in epiloia; to a single recessive gene, as in gargoylism, phenylketonuria, and amaurotic idiocy; to infections, such as congenital syphilis, encephalitis, or rubella in the mother; to chromosomal defects, as in mongolism; to toxic agents, as in retardation caused by radiation in utero, lead poisoning, or Rh incompatibility; and to cerebral trauma.

The diverse etiologies noted above have one factor in common; in every instance, examination reveals an abnormal physiological process. Persons who are retarded as a result of an abnormal physiological process *are* abnormal in the orthodox sense, since they suffer from a known physiological defect. However, in addition to this group, which forms a minority of all retardates, there is the group labeled "familial"—or, more recently, "cultural-familial"—which compromises approximately 75 percent of all retardates. This group presents the greatest mystery and has been the object of the most heated disputes in the area of mental retardation. The diagnosis of familial retardation is made when an examination reveals none of the physiological manifestations noted above, and when retardation of this same type exists among parents, siblings, or other relatives. Several writers have extended the defect notion to this type of retardation as well, although they differ as to what they propose as the specific nature of the defect. On the basis of differences in performance between retardates and normals on some experimental task rather than on the basis of physiological evidence, they have advanced the view that all retardates suffer from some specifiable defect over and above their general intellectual retardation.

Some order can be brought to the area of mental retardation if a distinction is maintained between physiologically defective retardates, with retardation of known etiology, and familial retardates, with retardation of unknown etiology. For the most part work with physiologically defective retardates involves investigation into the exact nature of the underlying physiological processes, with prevention or amelioration of the physical and intellectual symptoms as the goal. Jervis (1959) has suggested that such "pathological" mental deficiency is primarily in the domain of the medical sciences whereas familial retardation represents a problem to be solved by behavioral scientists, including educators and behavioral geneticists. Diagnostic and incidence studies of these two types of retardates have disclosed certain striking differences. The retardate having an extremely low IQ (below 40) is almost invariably of the physiological defective type. Familial retardates, the other hand, are almost invariably mildly retarded, usually with IQ's above 50. This difference in the general intellectual level of the two groups of retardates is an important empirical phenomenon that supports the two group approach to mental retardation, the approach supported in this article.

A Two-Group Approach

Hirsch (1963) has asserted that we will not make much headway in understanding individual differences in intelligence and in many other traits, unless we recognize that, to a large degree such differences reflect the inherent physiological properties of man. We can all agree that no genotype spells itself out in a vacuum, and that the phenotypic expression is finally the result of environment interacting with the genotype. However, an appreciation of the importance of genetic differences allows us to bring considerable order to the area of mental retardation.

We need simply to accept the generally recognized fact that the gene pool of any population is such that there will always be variations in the behavioral or phenotypic expression of virtually every measurable trait or characteristic of man. From the polygenic model advanced by geneticists, we deduce that the distribution of intelligence is characterized by a bisymmetrical bell-shaped curve, which is characteristic of such a large number of distributions that we have come to refer to it as the normal curve.

With the qualification noted below, this theoretical distribution is a fairly good approximation of the observed distribution of intelligence. In the polygenic model of intelligence (see Hirsh, 1963; Gottesman, 1963; Penrose, 1963), the genetic foundation of intelligence is not viewed as dependent upon a single gene. Rather, intelligence is viewed as the result of a number of discrete genetic units. (This is not to assert, however, that single gene effects are never encountered in mental retardation. As noted above, certain relatively rare types of mental retardation are the product of such simple genetic effects.)

Various specific polygenic models have been advanced which generate theoretical distributions of intelligence that are in keeping with observed distributions (Gottesman, 1963; Burt and Howard, 1956, 1957). An aspect of polygenic models of special importance for the two-group approach is the fact that they generate IQ distributions of approximately 50 to 150. Since an IQ of approximately 50 appears to be the lower limit for familial retardates, it has been concluded (Penrose, 1963; Burt and Howard, 1956; Allen, 1958) that the etiology of this form of retardation reflects the same factors that determine "normal" intelligence. With this approach, the familial retardate may be viewed as normal, where "normal" is defined as meaning an integral part of the distribution of intelligence that we would expect from the normal manifestations of the genetic pool in our population. Within such a framework it is possible to refer to the familial retardate as less intelligent than other normal manifestations of the genetic pool, but he is just as integral a part of the normal distribution as are the 3 percent of the population whom we view as superior, or the more numerous group of individuals whom we consider to be average (McClearn, 1962).

The two-group approach to mental retardation calls attention to the fact that the second group of retardates, those who have known physiological defects, represents a distribution of intelligence with a mean which is considerably lower than that of the familial retardates. Such children, for the most part, fall outside the range of normal intelligence—that is, below IQ of 50—although there are certain exceptions. Considerable clarity could be brought to the area of mental retardation through doing away with the practice of conceptualizing the intelligence distribution as a single, continuous, normal curve. Perhaps a more appropriate representation of the empirical distribution of intelligence would involve two curves, as Figure 16.1b illustrates. The intelligence of the bulk of the population, including the familial retardate, would be depicted as a normal distribution having a mean of 100, with lower and upper limits of approximately 50 and 150, respectively. Superimposed on this curve would be a second, somewhat normal distribution having a mean of approximately 35 and a range from 0 to 70. (That the population encompassed by the second curve in Figure 16.1b extends beyond the 70-IQ cutoff point is due to the fact that a very small number of individuals with known defects—for example, brain damage—may be found throughout the IQ continuum.) The first curve would represent the polygenic distribution of intelligence; the second would represent all those individuals whose intellectual functioning reflects factors other than the normal polygenic expression—that is, those retardates having an identifiable physiological defect....

Limitations of space prevent consideration here of the controversy concerning the role of environmental factors in the etiology of familial retardation. Although such factors cannot be ignored by the serious student of mental retardation, the general dispute, discussed below, between adherents of the defect theory and of the general developmental theory can be examined somewhat independently of the environmental issue. That there will always be a distribution of a particular shape is a conclusion inherent in the polygenic argument, but the absolute amounts of intelligence represented by the various points on the distribution would still depend in large part on environmental factors.

Developmental Versus Defect Orientation

Once one adopts the position that the familial mental retardate is not defective or pathological but is essentially a normal individual of low intelligence, then the familial retardate no longer represents a mystery but, rather, is viewed as a particular manifestation of the general developmental process. According to this approach, the familial retardate's cognitive development differs from that of the normal individual only in respect to its rate and the upper limit achieved. Such a view generates the expectation that, when rate of development is controlled, as is grossly the case when groups of retardates and normals are matched with respect to mental age, there should be no difference in formal cognitive processes related to IQ. Stated somewhat differently, this means that the familial retardate with a chronological age of 10, an IQ of 70, and thus a mental age of 7, would be viewed as being at the same developmental level intellectually as a child with a chronological age of 7 and an IQ of 100.

In contrast, according to the defect orientation, all retardates suffer from a specific physiological or cognitive defect over and above their slower general rate of cognitive development. This view generates the expectation that, even when the rate of cognitive development is controlled, as in the situation where mental ages are matched, differences in intellectual functioning which are related to IQ will be found. On their face, the repeated findings of differences in performance between groups of normals and retardates matched as to mental age have lent credence to the defect theory and have cast doubt on the validity of the developmental theory.

The developmental theorist's response to these frequently reported differences has been to point out that performance on any experimental task is not inexorably the product of the subject's cognitive structure alone but reflects a variety of emotional and motivational factors as well. To the developmentalist, then, it seems more reasonable to attribute differences in performance between normals and retardates of the same mental age to motivational differences which do not inhere in mental retardation but are, rather, the result of the particular histories of the retarded subjects.

It should be noted that most theories in the area of mental retardation are basically defect theories. These differ among themselves, however. A major difference involves the theoretician's effort to relate the postulated defect to some specific physiological structure....

Where the hypothesized defect is an explicitly physiological one, it would appear to be a simple matter to obtain direct evidence that the defect does or does not exist. Such evidence would come from biochemical and physiological analyses as well as from pathological studies of familial retardates. A number of such studies have, of course, been carried out. Although there is an occasional report of some physical anomaly, the bulk of the evidence has indicated that the familial retardate does not suffer from any gross physiological defects. Indeed, if such evidence were readily available the defect theorist would cease relying on the more ambiguous data provided by studies of molar behavior. Failure to find direct evidence of a physiological defect in familial retardates has not deterred, and should not deter theorists from postulating such defects.

In spite of the negative physiological evidence, workers such as Spitz

(1963) maintain that all retardates, including familial retardates, are physically defective, and that our failure to discover defects in familial retardates is due to the relatively primitive nature of our diagnostic techniques. This view is bolstered by Masland (1959), who has also noted the inadequacies of such techniques. It is perfectly legitimate for the defect theorist to assert that, although not at present observable, the physical defect that causes familial retardates to behave differently from normals of the same mental age will someday be seen. These theorists operate very much as the physicists of a not-too-distant era did when they asserted that the electron existed even though it was not directly observable. Analogously, defect theorists in the area of mental retardation undertake to validate the existence of a defect by first asserting that it should manifest itself in particular phenomena—that is, in particular behaviors of the retarded—and then devising experiments in which, if the predicted behavior is observed, the existence of the hypothesized defect is confirmed. Not only is this approach legitimate but, as noted above, it has become increasingly popular as well.... In the following paragraphs I briefly summarize the major defect positions.

An influential defect position is that of the Russian investigator A. R. Luria (1963), whose work has now also influenced investigators in England and the United States. In the Soviet Union no distinction is made between retardates having known organic impairment and that larger group whose retardation is of unknown etiology, nor are genetic or cultural factors considered to be determinants of mental retardation. All grades of mental retardation are attributed to central-nervous-system damage believed to have occurred initially during the intrauterine period or during early childhood. Thus the diagnosis of mental retardation necessarily involves specification of a defect in some neurophysiological system; in fact, in the Soviet Union, professionals who work with the mentally retarded are called "defectologists."

Luria's interest in defective functioning appears to be an outgrowth of his more basic concern with the development of the higher cognitive processes in man. The influence of both Vygotsky and Pavlov may be seen in his work, which has been primarily concerned with the highly intricate development of the role of speech and language in regulating the child's behavior. In his comparisons between normal and retarded children, Luria has demonstrated that the behavior of retardates resembles that of chronologically younger normal children in that verbal instructions do not result in smooth regulation of motor behavior. Luria has found that retarded subjects have considerable difficulty with tasks requiring verbal mediation. Thus, Luria has inferred that the major defect in the retarded child involves an underdevelopment or a general "inertness" of the verbal system, and a dissociation of this system from the motor or action system. This dissociation is vaguely conceptualized as resulting from a disturbance in normal cortical activity.

The view that the behavior of a retardate resembles that of a chronologically younger child is, of course, consistent with the general developmental position. However, several English and American investigators (see, for example, O'Connor and Hermelin, 1959; Milgram and Furth, 1963) have demonstrated that, even with mental age level controlled, retardates have more difficulty on tasks requiring verbal mediation than normal subjects have. On the other hand, other such investigations have failed to provide support for Luria's position (Ball and Zigler, 1964). To date, findings related to this position can best be described as equivocal.

Another major defect position is that of Herman Spitz (1963), who has extended the Köhler-Wallach (1900) cortical satiation theory to the area of mental retardation. According to Spitz, all retardates suffer from inadequate neural or cortical functioning; the inadequacy is best characterized by a certain sluggishness, or less-than-normal modifiability, in the functioning of cortical cells. Thus, Spitz believes that in retardates it takes longer to induce temporary, as well as permanent, electrical, chemical, and physical changes in stimulated cortical cells, and furthermore, that once such a change is produced, it is less readily modified than in the case of normal persons.

Spitz's evidence in support of his theory has come primarily from comparisons of the performance of retardates and normals of the same chronological age on a variety of perceptual tasks—for example, figural aftereffects and Necker-cube reversals. The heuristic value of Spitz's position may be seen in his recent efforts to extend his postulates beyond the visual perception area and employ them to generate specific predictions concerning the phenomena of learning, transposition, generalization, and problem solving. The evidence in favor of Spitz's position is far from clear-cut, however. Spivack (1963) has pointed out that Spitz's findings are in marked contrast to those of other investigators. The very nature of many of Spitz's measures—for example, a verbal report—raises the troublesome issue of how well they reflect the perceptual responses being investigated. It should be noted that, in respect to this point as well as to other criticisms, Spitz himself has become one of the most cogent critics of his own efforts.

. . .

Ellis (1963) has also advanced the view that the retardate is basically different from the normal individual and that this difference is a result of central-nervous-system pathology from which all retardates suffer. Ellis views this central-nervous-system pathology as producing a short-term memory deficit which, in turn, underlies the inadequacy of much of the retardate's behavior. The theoretical model presented by Ellis includes two major constructs, stimulus trace and neural integrity.

The stimulus trace, the mechanism underlying short-term memory functions, is conceptualized as a neural event or response which varies with the intensity, duration, and meaning of the stimulus situation confronting the subject. The stimulus-trace construct is thus anchored to stimulus characteristics on the one hand and to the subject's responses to these characteristics on the other. The neural-integrity construct is conceptualized as the determinant of the nature of stimulus-trace activity, and is defined by "measures of behavioral adequacy." The typical measure of neural integrity employed by Ellis is the IQ. Thus, a person of low IQ is said to suffer from a lack of neural integrity. This lack, in turn, delimits or restricts stimulus-trace activity, and such restriction results in a variety of inadequate behaviors.

· · ·

Perhaps the oldest of the more influential defect positions is the Lewin-Kounin (1941a, 1941b) formulation that familial retardates are inherently more "rigid" than normal individuals of the same mental age. This position differs from the others discussed above in that the defect is conceptualized as inhering in a hypothesized cognitive structure without reference or reduction to any specific physiological entities. By the term *rigidity*, Lewin and Kounin were referring not to behaviors, as such, but rather to characteristics of the cognitive structure. These theorists felt that the essential defect, in retardation, was the lowered capacity for dynamic rearrangement in the "psychical system." This "stiffness" in cognitive functioning was conceptualized as being due to the relative impermeability of the boundaries between cells or regions of the cognitive structure. *Rigidity*, then, referred primarily to the nature of these boundaries, and to the resulting degree of communication or fluidity between regions.

· · ·

Lewin and Kounin appear to be the only defect theorists who have dealt adequately with the problem of etiology, which becomes a crucial issue in the controversy over the two theories. Their formulation was limited to familial retardates, and only such retardates were employed in Kounin's experiments. The other defect theorists have tended to argue that the distinction between familial and organic retardates is misleading, and, as a result, they have used groups of retardates of both types in their experiments. This presents an almost insurmountable problem when one attempts to evaluate the degree to which any uncovered differences in behavior support the major theoretical premise which underlies most defect approaches. This premise, clearly seen in the work of Luria, Spitz, and Ellis, is that all retardates, familials and organics alike, suffer from some specifiable defect. However, until the etiological issue is attended to in the research design, there is no way of assessing how much of the revealed difference between normals and retardates of the same mental age is a product of the gross organic pathology known to exist in the organic retardates included in the retarded group and how much is a product of the defect thought by the defect theorists to exist in all retardates.

The general developmental approach is applicable only to the familial retardate, and this approach does not speak to the issue of differences discovered between normal children and organic retardates. The developmental theorist also believes that, even when a difference in behavior is found between normals and familial retardates of the same mental age, it need not be attributed to any defect which inheres in familial mental retardation. Such differences are viewed as the possible outcome of differences in a variety of motivational factors which exist between the two groups. A sampling of the literature which lends credence to this view follows.

Motivational and Emotional Factors

The view of those of us who believe that many of the reported differences between retardates and normals of the same mental age are a result of motivational and emotional differences which reflect differences in environmental histories does not imply that we ignore the importance of the lower intelligence per se. In some instances the personality characteristics of the retarded individual will reflect environmental factors that have little or nothing to do with intellectual endowment. For example, many of the effects of institutionalization may be constant, regardless of the person's intelligence level. In other instances we must think in terms of an interaction; that is, a person with low intellectual ability will have certain experiences and develop certain behavior patterns differing from those of a person with greater intellectual endowment. An obvious example of this is the greater amount of failure which the retardate typically experiences. What must be emphasized is the fact that the behavior pattern developed by the retardate as a result of such a history of failure may not differ in kind or ontogenesis from patterns developed by an individual of normal intellect who, because of some environmental circumstance, also experiences an inordinate amount of failure. By the same token, if the retardate can somehow be guaranteed a history of greater success, we would expect his behavior to be more normal regardless of his intellectual level. Within this framework, I now discuss several of the personality factors which have been known to influence the performance of the retarded.

It has become increasingly clear that our understanding of the performance of the institutionalized familial retardate will be enhanced if we consider that inordinate amount of social deprivation these individuals have experienced before being placed in institutions (Clarke and Clarke, 1954; Zigler, 1961). A series of recent studies has indicated that one result of such early deprivation is a heightened motivation to interact with a supportive adult. These studies suggest that, given this heightened motivation, retardates exhibit considerable compliance with instructions when the effect of such compliance is to increase or maintain the social interaction with the adult. These findings would appear to be consistent with the often-made observation that the retarded seek attention and desire affection (Hirsh, 1959).

. . .

Although there is considerable evidence that social deprivation results in a heightened motivation to interact with a supportive adult, it appears to have other effects as well. The nature of these effects is suggested in observations of fearfulness, wariness, or avoidance of strangers on the part of retardates, or of suspicion and mistrust (Hirsh, 1959; Woodward, 1960). The experimental work done by Zigler and his associates on the behavior of institutionalized retarded individuals has indicated that social deprivation results in both a heightened motivation to interact with supportive adults (a positive-reaction tendency) and a wariness of doing so (a negative-reaction tendency). The construct of a negative-reaction tendency has been employed to explain certain differences between retardates and normals reported by Kounin, differences that have heretofore been attributed to the greater cognitive rigidity of retarded individuals. For instance, it has been demonstrated that, once the institutionalized familial retardate's wariness has been allayed, he becomes much more responsive than the normal individual to social reinforcement....

. . .

Another factor frequently mentioned as a determinant in the performance of the retarded is their high expectancy of failure. This failure expectancy has been viewed as an outgrowth of a lifetime characterized by confrontations with tasks with which they are intellectually ill-equipped to deal. The work of Cromwell and his colleagues (1963) has lent support to the general proposition that retardates have a higher expectancy of failure than normals have, and that this results in a style of problem-solving in which the retardate is much more highly motivated to avoid failure than to achieve success. However, the results of experimental work with retardates to investigate the success-failure dimension are still somewhat inconsistent, suggesting that even such a relatively simple proposition as this one is in need of further refinement.

Recent studies have indicated that the many failures experienced by retardates generate a cognitive style of problem-solving characterized by outer-directedness. That is, the retarded child comes to distrust his own solutions to problems and therefore seeks guides to action in the immediate environment. This outer-directedness may explain the great suggestibility so frequently observed in the retarded child. Evidence has now been presented indicating that, relative to normals of the same mental age, the retarded child is more sensitive to verbal cues from an adult, is more imitative of the behavior of adults and of his peers, and does more visual scanning. Furthermore, certain findings suggest that the non-institutionalized retardate is more outer-directed in his problem solving than the institutionalized retardate is. This makes considerable sense if one remembers that the noninstitutionalized retardate lives in an environment that is not adjusted to his intellectual shortcomings and, therefore, probably experiences more failure than the institutionalized retardate.

Another nonintellective factor important in understanding the behavior of the retarded is the retardate's motivation to obtain various types of reinforcement. The social-deprivation work discussed indicates that retardates have an extremely strong desire for attention, praise, and encouragement. Several investigators (Cromwell, 1963; Beller, 1955) have suggested that, in normal development, the effectiveness of attention and praise as reinforcers diminishes with maturity and is replaced by the reinforcement inherent in the awareness that one is correct. This latter type of reinforcer appears to serve primarily as a cue for self-reinforcement.

Zigler and his associates have argued that various experiences in the lives of the retarded cause them to care less about being correct simply for the sake of correctness than normals of the same mental age. In other words, these investigators have argued that the position of various reinforcers in the reinforcer hierarchies of normal and of retarded children of the same mental age differ.

Clearest support for the view that the retardate cares much less about being correct than the middle-class child of normal intellect does is contained in a study by Zigler and deLabry (1962). These investigators found, as Kounin (1941) did, that when the only reinforcement was the information that the child was correct, retardates were poorer on a concept-switching task than middle-class normal children of the same mental age. However, when Zigler and deLabry added another condition, reward with a toy of the child's choice for concept-switching, they found that the retardates performed as well as the middle-class normal children. Since the satisfaction of giving the correct response is the incentive typically used in experimental studies, one wonders how many of the differences in performance found between retardates and normals are actually attributable to differences in capacity rather than to differences in the values such incentives may have for the two types of subjects.

Much of this work on motivational and emotional factors in the performance of the retarded is very recent. The research on several of the factors discussed is more suggestive than definitive. It is clear, however, that these factors are extremely important in determining the retardate's level of functioning. This is not to assert that these motivational factors cause familial mental retardation but to say, rather, that they lead to the retardate's behaving in a manner less effective than that dictated by his intellectual capacity. An increase in knowledge concerning motivational and emotional factors and their ontogenesis and manipulation would hold considerable promise for alleviating much of the social ineffectiveness displayed by that rather sizable group of persons who must function at a relatively low intellectual level.

In this article B. M. Byrne, L. Willerman, and L. L. Ashmore support the view that there are at least two broad classes of language impairment and that these classes are similar to those hypothesized for mental retardation. Severe handicaps are more likely associated with rare genetic events or major environmental trauma. The milder forms seem to represent the lower end of the normal distribution for the trait.

17

Severe and Moderate Language Impairment: Evidence for Distinctive Etiologies

BRIAN M. BYRNE, LEE WILLERMAN, AND LEAR L. ASHMORE

Introduction

MENTAL DEFICIENCY: NATURAL VARIATIONS VS. PATHOLOGY

Researchers in the area of mental retardation have established the existence of two generally distinct forms of intellectual deficiency. The types have been variously labeled as "high-grade" vs. "low-grade" defectives, "familial-cultural" retardates vs. "major gene defects," and "normal" vs. "pathological," among others. To facilitate discussion of a number of studies which use some or all of these terms interchangeably, this paper will make use of the more general terms "moderate" and "severe."

Though the essential ingredients of the hypothesis concerning the different forms of deficiency were evident early in the twentieth century (Pearson and Jaederholm, 1913–1914), the complete proposal was most clearly advanced by Roberts in a lecture to the British Eugenics Society.

Byrne, B. M., Willerman, L., and Ashmore, L. L. "Severe and Moderate Language Impairment: Evidence for Distinctive Etiologies." *Behavior Genetics*, 1974, Vol. 4, pp. 331–345. Copyright © 1974 by Plenum Publishing Corporation and reprinted by permission.

Summarizing the results of his investigations in the area, Roberts concluded

> that the higher-grade defectives, roughly the feebleminded, are the lowest part of the ordinary distribution of intelligence in the population, no more abnormal than the geniuses and near-geniuses at the other end of the scale. Below that come the pathological variants, roughly the idiots and imbeciles, owing their mental state to some major accident of heredity or environment. (Roberts, 1952, p. 72)

An alternate phrasing advanced by other authors (Penrose, 1963; Burt and Howard, 1956, Allen, 1958) is that the same factors that determine average and superior intelligence can also account for moderate retardation, while individuals with IQs below 50 apparently constitute a separate distribution based on pathology.

The classic studies in this area which permitted formulation of the above conclusions are essentially of two types. The first involves predictions from the normal curve concerning the number of cases in the general population that should fall into any given IQ score interval assuming the normal distribution of intelligence.

In analyzing data gathered on the school children of Stockholm (Pearson and Jaederholm, 1913–1914; Pearson, 1930–1931), it was discovered that the fit of the normal curve to actual population intelligence figures was three times closer if children from "help classes" (equivalent to moderate retardation) were included. Inclusion of the severely retarded, however, created a surplus at the lower end of the distribution. In Roberts' (1952) study of 3361 Bath School children, expected frequencies as predicted by the normal curve were compared with the number of cases actually occurring in designated IQ intervals. The expected frequencies and actual incidence figures did not differ significantly for IQ above 45. For IQs of 45 and below, the actual number of cases was found to be 18 times greater than expected. Both the above studies revealed a higher incidence of severe retardation than could be predicted from the normal curve, while the number of moderately deficient individuals coincided closely with expectations.

A second type of research strategy involved the calculation of regression coefficients. Knowledge of the proportion of total genes shared by index cases and their different-degree relations (0.5 for first-degree, 0.25 for second-degree, and 0.125 for third-degree relatives) allows prediction of the average resemblance which should exist between the groups on a polygenically determined trait. Assuming absolute polygenic determination of a trait, the predicted correlations for measures of that trait would be identical to the proportion of gene overlap (Jensen, 1969; Erlenmeyer-Kimling and Jarvik, 1963). A regression analysis performed on data gathered by Roberts (1940) revealed an IQ correlation between moderately retarded individuals and their sibs of 0.53, while the correlation for the

severely retarded and their sibs was not significantly different from 0. A
similar study carried out by Penrose (1939) produced parallel findings,
through the correlation of the moderate retardates with their sibs was
slightly lower (0.42). In plainer terms, both studies confirmed that the
average resemblance between the moderate-grade retardate and his sibs
was of the order predicted by the polygenic model. These studies have
generally neglected the possibility that the resemblance between the
moderately affected and their relatives can be interpreted from either a
genetic or an environmental perspective, and it should be said that the
data to be presented can shed no light on the comparative merits of either
position.

THE PRESENT STUDY: POSSIBLE DISTINCTIONS
WITHIN THE LANGUAGE-IMPAIRED

As in the case of mental deficiency, the application of summary labels
such as "language-impaired" or "speech problems" may encourage conceptions of uniformity with respect to a potentially diverse population.
Admittedly, the diagnosis terminology employed in the speech clinic
(e.g., "receptive/expressive aphasia," "auditory/vocal channel deficit,"
"automatic/representational level") allows finer descriptive distinctions
than the label of "mental retardation." Still there exists the possibility that
functionally equivalent impairments may differ with respect to etiology.
The present question is whether or not individuals whose disabilities are
strictly language-related may be resolved into subgroups analogous to
those discovered in the area of mental deficiency.
    The data on which the present study is based are taken from the case
histories of children enrolled in remedial therapy at the University speech
clinic. More specifically, the sample is restricted to cases diagnosed as
"delayed speech." As the related studies in the area of intelligence dealt
with general rather than specific intellectual deficiencies, so does "delayed speech" refer to impairment in the overall level of language functioning. The delay-speech cases were divided into "severely" and
"moderately" subnormal groups according to the extent of their impairment on a measure of linguistic abilities. It is expected that the "severely"
impaired do not represent instances of normal variation in linguistic ability, but rather a separate distribution rooted in physical damage or major
genetic defect. Conversely, it is proposed that "moderate" language impairment derives from the same distribution of factors (genetic and environmental) which determine average and even superior linguistic ability. The present investigation differs essentially from prior studies in terms
of its target population, strictly language-impaired as opposed to intellectually deficient individuals.
    Since the present data are compiled from past case histories on file in

the University clinic, it was necessary to construct meaningful hypotheses around the information available. A first prediction which allowed test is that the parents of the "severe" group should possess greater mean language abilities than the parents of the "moderate" group. From the available data, years of education and occupational status were selected as measures which might reflect the differential language abilities in the parental groups. In view of the demand placed on verbal skills in traditional classroom methods (Jensen, 1969, p. 7) and the relationship between education and occupational attainment (Duncan et al., 1968), these measures would seem appropriate indicators of parental language capabilities. The initial hypothesis is that

1. The parents of "severely" affected children will on the average be better educated and enjoy higher occupational status than the parents of the "moderately" handicapped children.

Information provided by a questionnaire completed by the parents at the time of their child's acceptance into therapy, extensive case histories prepared by clinic personnel, and attached medical reports permitted the formulation of three additional hypothesis.

2. Speech- and language-related disabilities should be reported with greater frequency in the relatives of "moderately" affected children as compared with those of their "severely" affected counterparts.

3. The incidence of physiological abnormality and/or physical defect should be substantially greater in "severe" as compared with "moderate" cases.

While the evidence from prior studies convincingly demonstrated that "severe" mental deficiency is not a reflection of natural variation, it did not allow a determination of the proportion of critical "accidents" which are genetic or environmental in origin. As noted by Vernon during discussion of Roberts' 1952 lecture, the researcher's opinion that one-half to two-thirds were genetic in origin lacks substantiating data. For this reason, an attempt is made to compare the number of potential environmental risks which befell the "severe" and "moderate" group children. Should the results indicate that the groups are in fact distinct, the relative incidences of potential risks should provide at least an indication of the importance of environmental stresses in the etiology of severe deficiency. Should environmental stresses constitute a significant proportion of "accidents" related to marked deficiency, it would be expected that

4. The case histories of the "severely" affected children should contain poorer pregnancy period ratings and more frequent reports of prenatal, perinatal, and childhood stresses.

Procedure

SUBJECTS

The cases for the present study were drawn from the current and inactive files of The University of Texas Speech and Hearing Clinic for the period January 1962 to March 1973. The sample was restricted to white children who had received the diagnosis of "delayed speech." All cases in which either possible or actual mental retardation formed part of the clinician's diagnosis were excluded. Additionally, children from bilingual and minority group backgrounds as well as those exhibiting severe emotional complications were not included, as assessment of their language abilities based on standardized tests could not be guaranteed as valid. In the event that more than one child per family satisfied all other requirements, only the first child appearing alphabetically was chosen in order to maintain the independent nature of the data.

Each case history was subsequently reviewed to determine the completeness of required information. The cases were required to have on file an Illinois Test of Psycholinguistic Abilities (ITPA), a profile report form to allow determination of the extent of impairment (three cases in which the ITPA administration was incomplete but supplemented by specific "moderate" diagnoses were allowed), a reasonably complete Preliminary Case History Questionnaire submitted by the child's natural parents, and a case history or summary completed by the clinic personnel.

Of the 42 cases which met these specifications, 22 were classified as instances of "severe" language impairment (ITPA 85 and below), while 20 were classified as "moderate" (ITPA above 85). The cutoff score of 85 was decided on after a preliminary examination of the range of scores. The distribution appeared bimodal, with one group clustering near a score of 70, another in the low 90s. The intermediate score of 85 was chosen as a reasonable point for separation.

At this point, it was decided to scrutinize each "severe" case more closely and decide on a uniform criterion to insure against the inclusion of mentally deficient individuals. The criterion which appeared meaningful while not reducing the sample size too greatly was twofold. The first requirement was a specific and decided statement by the clinician that the child's level of general intellectual function was at least "dull normal." Second, the clinician's assessment had to be supplemented by supporting test data in the form of a performance IQ of 90 or better. Due to handling by clinicians with varying preferences and changes in clinic policy, the actual performance IQ measures available were unavoidably disparate. They included among others the Merrill-Palmer Performance Scale, the Leiter International Performance Scale, and the WISC and WPPSI performance scales. The mean performance IQs of the "severe" and "moderate" groups computed on the measures available in each case were 102.1 and 100.5, respectively. The final sample consisted of 19 "severe" (mean ITPA

72.8) and 20 "moderate" cases (mean ITPA 93.9). The "severely" affected children ranged in age from 3 years 4 months to 8 years 8 months (mean age 5 years 6 months), while the "moderately" affected children ranged in age from 3 years 9 months to 7 years 1 month (mean age 5 years 7 months) on enrollment with the clinic.

DATA COLLECTION

Educational Level and Occupational Status of Parents.   The Preliminary Case History Questionnaire submitted by the children's parents served as the source of the data on parental educational level and occupational status. Educational level was analyzed in terms of the number of years of education successfully completed. The fathers' occupations were assigned ratings from 1 (highest) to 7 (lowest) according to the scale developed by McGuire specifically for the Texas population (McGuire and White, 1952), and is a revision of Warner's scale (Warner et al., 1949). Due to the large number of mothers in both parental groups listed as housewives, for which no particular rating appeared justifiable, ratings were not assigned to the mothers' occupations.

Language-Related Disabilities in Relatives.   Information concerning the incidence of language-related disabilities in the child's relatives was also obtained from the above questionnaire. A space was provided to indicate the existence of relatives known to suffer speech, hearing, or other language-related disabilities, the nature of their problem, and their relation to the child. Relatives with essentially hearing problems were excluded, as present interest is restricted to language impairment.

Pregnancy Ratings: Prenatal, Perinatal, and Childhood "Potential Risks." Pregnancy ratings assigned by the children's mothers were also contained in the intake questionnaire. A space was provided to check either "good," "fair," or "poor" in response to the question "How would you rate your pregnancy overall?." The questionnaire additionally requested extensive information concerning the occurrence of complications, accidents, or illnesses during pregnancy, birth, and early childhood. The information provided by the questionnaire on the child's prenatal, perinatal, and general medical history was supplemented by a review of attached physicians' reports and the case histories prepared by the clinic personnel. The term "potential risk," borrowed from Walker (1966), is used to indicate the occurrence of a condition or event which may have had physically damaging consequences for the child. Due to the varied forms of complications, accidents, and illnesses and the lack of definitive knowledge on many conditions, Walker's list of "potential risks" was used as a general guide for the pre- and perinatal periods. Length and severity of childhood illnesses were among the factors determining their inclusion.

Results

EDUCATIONAL AND OCCUPATIONAL STATUS

Table 17.1 gives educational and occupational data for the parents of the affected children. The range of educational level in the fathers of "severely" affected children extended from less than a high school education to graduate and professional degrees, with the modal category for "severe" group fathers being a college degree. The range of education levels for our "moderate" cases extended only to the college degree, with no father holding a graduate or professional degree. The modal category for the "moderate" fathers is the high school diploma, with more than three-quarters of their number falling in or below this level. The analysis of years of education confirms that the fathers of "severely" affected children on the average attained a significantly higher level of education than their "moderate" group counterparts ($t = 4.93$, $p < 0.001$).

Table 17.1

Educational and occupational attainments of "severe" and "moderate" group fathers and mothers

Rating	"Severe" group	"Moderate" group
Educational level (fathers)		
Less than high school diploma	1	3
High school diploma	2	12
Some college	3	3
Bachelor's degree	7	1
Graduate or professional degree	6	—
Mean years education	15.63	12.00
Educational level (mothers)		
Less than high school diploma	1	4
High school diploma	6	12
Some college	8	2
Bachelor's degree	3	2
Graduate or professional degree	1	—
Mean years education	13.84	12.10
Occupational rating		
1 (highest)	6	—
2	3	2
3	5	3
4	2	1
5	2	8
6	1	3
7 (lowest)	—	1
Mean occupational ratings	2.74	4.55

The education of the mothers of "severely" affected children ranged from less than a high school diploma to graduate and professional degrees. The modal category was "some college," with more than half attaining this level or better. The education of the "moderate" group mothers extended from less than high school to the college degree. Again, the modal category was a high school degree, with three-fourths at or below this level. No mother in this group fell into the graduate or professional degree category.

The t-test for the differences in mean number of years of education for the mothers of the "severe" and "moderate" groups reveals that the mothers of "severely" affected children attained a significantly higher level of education ($t = 2.75$, $p < 0.01$). The lower level of significance for the mothers' results compared to the fathers' perhaps indicates differential societal pressures on the sexes to achieve the highest level of education of which they are capable.

The occupational ratings for the fathers are presented in the lowest portion of Table 17.1. As the variety of occupational fields which cut across each level is considerable, no attempt is made to attach labels to the numerical ratings. The reader may refer to McGuire's scale on which the ratings are based. The t-test for the difference in mean occupational ratings reveals that the fathers of "severely" affected children on the average enjoyed significantly higher status ($t = 3.72$, $p < 0.001$).

The significantly greater educational attainments and higher occupational status of the "severe" group parents serve to confirm the first prediction, namely that parents of severely impaired children on the average possess language abilities superior to the parents of the moderately deficient.

RELATIVES

Table 17.2 gives the percentages of case histories reporting language-related disabilities in relatives for the "severe" and "moderate" groups (16.67% and 55.00%, respectively, $p < 0.05$). Rather than attempting to

Table 17.2

Differences in the percentage of "severe" and "moderate" cases reporting relatives with language-related disabilities

Group	N	No. cases reporting affected relatives	Percentage	t ratio
"Severe"	18	3	16.67	2.46*
"Moderate"	20	11	55.00	—

* Significant at the 0.05 level of confidence.

assess actual incidence figures, the analysis was performed solely on the percentage of cases in each group reporting language-disabled relatives. Calculation of true incidence figures was not feasible as the number of actual relatives was indeterminable. The significantly higher percentage of "moderate" case histories referring to language-impaired relatives conforms to predictions.

PHYSIOLOGICAL ABNORMALITIES AND PHYSICAL DEFECTS

The percentages of "severe" and "moderate" cases in which physical abnormalities were noted are 79.00% and 15.00%, respectively. The t-test for the difference in percentages between the two groups is presented in Table 17.3. As expected, a significantly higher percentage of the "severe" cases contained evidence of physical impairments.

For descriptive purposes, an attempt was made to group these impairments into categories according to the affected system. Of the 18 cases reported abnormalities, one case specified three different impairments, while four cases specified two, resulting in a total of 24 specific abnormalities. The abnormalities occurring by system in the "severe" group are as follows: voluntary muscle: eye (1), tongue (1); central nervous system: seizures/convulsions (5), minimal brain injury (2), EGG (2); skeletal malformations: inner ear (2), palate (1), cranium (1), spinal cord (1). Single instances of hyperthyroidism, congenital cataracts, and hydrocephaly also were present. The impairments in the "moderate" group included single cases of malformation of the inner ear, eye muscle impairment, convulsions, and minimal brain injury.

PREGNANCY RATINGS AND POTENTIAL RISK SITUATIONS

Overall pregnancy ratings assigned by the children's mothers were available for 17 of the 19 "severe" cases and 15 of the 20 "moderate" cases. The percentage of pregnancies rated as "fair"/"poor" as opposed to "good"

Table 17.3

Differences in the percentage of "severe" and "moderate" group children with physiological abnormalities or physical defects

Group	No. cases reporting abnormality or defect	Percent	t ratio
"Severe" ($N = 19$)	15	79	3.99*
"Moderate" ($N = 20$)	3	15	—

* Significant at the 0.05 level of confidence.

Table 17.4

Differences in the percentage of "severe" and "moderate"
group pregnancies rated as "fair" or "poor"

Group	Number of Pregnancies Rated "Fair"/"Poor"	Percentage	t ratio
"Severe" ($N = 17$)	7	41.17	2.15*
"Moderate" ($N = 15$)	1	6.67	—

* Significant at the 0.05 level of confidence.

were 41.17% for the "severe" and 6.67% for the "moderate" groups. The
t-test for the difference in percentages of pregnancies rated "fair" or
"poor" in the two groups is presented in Table 17.4. The results indicated
that a significantly higher percentage of "severe" group mothers considered their pregnancies as less than optimal, which coincides with
predictions.

The number of cases and percentage in the "severe" and "moderate"
groups whose histories contain at least one instance of "potential risk"
during pregnancy, birth, or via childhood illness are presented in Table
17.5, with the results of the appropriate t-tests for differences. As expected, the incidence of "potential risks" was higher for the "severe"
group children at each point in their development.

To avoid possible ambiguity concerning the present use of the term
"potential risk," the conditions considered sufficiently serious to warrant
their inclusion are presented in Table 17.6 for pregnancy, birth, and childhood illness, respectively.

Table 17.5

Differences in the percentage of "severe" and "moderate" cases
experiencing "potential risk" during pregnancy, birth, and childhood

Potential risk periods	"Severe" ($N = 19$)		"Moderate" ($N = 20$)		t ratio
	Number	Percentage	Number	Percentage	
Pregnancy	9	47	3	15	2.28*
Birth	9	47	2	10	2.96*
Childhood illness	16	84	6	30	3.38*

* Significant at the 0.05 level of confidence.

Table 17.6

List of "potential risks" in "severe" and "moderate" groups

Period of occurrence	No. reported instances in "severe" group*	No. reported instances in "moderate" group*
Pregnancy		
Automobile accident	1	—
Falls	2	—
Viral infection	2	2
Protracted pregnancy (10 months or longer)	2	1
Premature delivery (less than 8 months)	1	—
Intrauterine bleeding	2	—
Attempted abortion	1	—
Rubella	1	—
Drug overdose	1	—
Birth		
Protracted labor (12 hr or longer)	3	1
Use of forceps	1	1
Cord tangle	1	—
Asphyxia at birth	2	—
Rh complication	2	—
Ruptured membrane	1	—
Caesarian section	—	1
Multiple birth	2	—
Childhood illness		
Various undiagnosed fevers/viral infections (temperature of 105° for 24 hr or more)	9	5
Chicken pox	3	1
Mumps	1	1
Kidney infection	2	—
Leukemia	2	—
Respiratory illness	1	1
Ear infection	1	1
Pneumonia	2	—
Mononucleosis	1	—

* The number of reported conditions exceeds the number of children "at risk," as several children experienced more than one risk condition.

Discussion

The present strategy involved the division of the language-impaired into groups differing with respect to the extent of their disability. To substantiate the distinctiveness of these groups, a number of comparative analyses were performed. In accordance with expectations, the parents of "severely" affected children were found to have experienced relatively greater success within the educational system and in terms of occupational status, an indication of higher mean verbal abilities than their "moderate" group counterparts. A significantly greater proportion of the "moderate" cases reported relatives suffering language-related disabilities, while physical abnormalities and the occurrence of "potential risks" were far more common in the histories of the "severe" group. As was the case with mentally subnormal populations, it appears possible to apply the yardstick of severity to the language-impaired and distinguish contrasting groups. The present study not only provides evidence of heterogeneity within the population of individuals with subnormal language skills but additionally implicates differences in etiology parallel to those underlying the established forms of mental deficiency as one point of distinction.

Moderate language impairment appears to represent "natural" variation drawn from the lower end of the distribution of linguistic abilities while the severely impaired appear to be individuals who, barring misfortune, would have possessed language skills spanning the spectrum of ability. Although severe deficiency in both the areas of general intelligence and language skills appears to represent "accidental" damage rather than normal variation, it seems unwise to assume as did Roberts that the majority of these misfortunes are genetic in origin. In view of the lesser nature of the physical abnormalities found in the present "severe" cases, as compared to those found among severe mental defectives (Jensen, 1969; Kushlick, 1966), combined with the present "severe" group's high rate of "potential risks," a strong argument could be made for involvement of environmental-stress factors in severe impairment. Similarly, though the evidence indicates that moderately deficient individuals are members of the same distribution as persons with average or even superior skills, the factors underlying this distribution of normal variation cannot be assumed to be exclusively genetic. The research strategies past and present do not permit consideration of the separate contributions of genetic and cultural-familial factors. Thus while the present data support the "normal variation" vs. "pathology" distinction in the etiologies of moderate and severe language impairment, contrary to Roberts' claims the environment could conceivably play as dominant a role as heredity in both normal variation and pathology.

One possible criticism is that in the present sample cases the parents are not entirely representative of the general population. Persons residing in and around a university area, with knowledge of and access to a university clinic, may differ from the population at large. Perhaps they may be on the average more linguistically gifted, better educated, and more gainfully employed. Even though this may in fact be the case, if the "severe" and "moderate" distinctions were meaningless, parental abilities, education, and occupations would have been randomly distributed between the two groups and significant group differences would have then failed to appear. It is likely, however, that the magnitude of the differences in the parental groups' educational and occupational status is exaggerated by their selection from a university clinic. A selection bias may account for some of this difference since it is likely that lower SES children with severe speech defects might be classified as mentally retarded as well and thereby be excluded from the sample used in this study.

Another possible objection concerns the higher incidence of "potential risks" reported in the "severe" cases. It might be argued that the mothers of these children, due to higher socioeconomic status, received closer medical attention which, combined with their better educations, made them more likely to notice, recall, and report such occurrences than "moderate" group mothers. In the general population, however, more favorable social conditions have actually been associated with a lower incidence of "potential risk" (Graves et al., 1968). It is, of course, still possible to contend that this discrepancy is due to the difference between actual and reported occurrences. That is, although "potential risk" situations occur less frequently in higher socioeconomic groups, they have a greater tendency to be noticed and reported. The findings on abnormality and defect do not appear to be open to the same criticism. Their detection was not solely dependent on the mothers' observations but also on diagnosis by appropriate specialists. In response to the above objection, it can then be said that the higher incidence of abnormality and defect in the "severe" cases favors an interpretation in terms of true, rather than merely reported, "potential risk" differences.

It would be well advised to consider the practical applications of the study. It appears that standard test scores for language disability offer not only quantitative specifications of the extent of disability but also a clue to the underlying etiology of the condition. A worthwhile consideration for the clinician may be whether a child's score reflects impairment which could reasonably represent natural variation or is so severe that critical genetic or accidental damage appears more plausible. At this stage, it is not clear that differential treatments would follow on such etiological judgments, but therapies in the future may depend more than now on proper etiological diagnoses.

XI

GENIUS
AND
CREATIVITY

This article by Robert Albert is a major reformulation of the nature and definition of genius. Albert advances the view that people do not have genius, but rather that label is assigned by experts to those who have prodigiously produced works of lasting importance—works that often require a complete revamping of the field under investigation. There can be no geniuses who have never produced great works, and genius is not equivalent to high IQ. The latter represents only a potential for great work, not necessarily its realization.

18

Toward a Behavioral Definition of Genius

ROBERT S. ALBERT

This article discusses some of the troublesome issues involved in the concept of genius. An operational definition of genius is proposed; some of the implications for research on high achievement are presented; and supporting evidence is offered to indicate that it is possible to operationalize such an apparently global concept if one restricts its use to the behavioral, rather than to the sometimes superficially dramatic, components of high achievement. Because genius is typified by behavior that is exceptional, often unpredictable, and influential to many, it is not surprising to find genius a topic of concern for many eminent psychologists and social philosophers, for example, Freud, Galton, William James, Kretschmer, and Terman (Annin, Boring, and Watson, 1968).

For the most part, Western views of extraordinary creative behavior have been variations of two early Greek views of genius (Klineberg, 1931; Nahm, 1957) in which genius was equated with demigods, with madness, or with both. As an act of demigods, genius came from inspiration; the source of this inspiration was the gods and to be inspired was to per-

Albert, R. S. "Toward a Behavioral Definition of Genius." *American Psychologist*, 1975, Vol. 30, pp. 140–151. Copyright © 1975 by the American Psychological Association and reprinted by permission.

sonify a mystical power. Socrates described this power as a 'daemon,'' heard it "murmuring in his ears like the sound of the flute in the ears of the mystic." Centuries later, Goethe expressed much the same point when he spoke of poets as "plain children of God" and stated that his poems "made me, not I them." At other points in Western history, the Greek daemon has been spoken of as "divine spark," "divine fire." In the late Renaissance, Michelangelo was called "divino," and it is not uncommon for artists of all types and from all eras to be described as "divine" in many circles. Such a view of creativeness as inspiration places the creative person within an implicit mythology, attributing his creative (inspired) moments to the intervention or the guidance of gods. Viewed this way, the major source of an individual's creative behavior lies less within him and more outside him in the realm of the supernatural or preternatural.

The second early Western view ascribes madness to extraordinary creativity, which resembles what we now speak of as severe psychopathology.* For Aristotle "there is no great genius without madness." Coupled with "madness" was "possession," for example, Plato's view of poetic inspiration as a madness "taking hold of a delicate and virgin soul, and there inspiring frenzy, awakens lyrical and all other numbers." In both of these accounts, we see a relationship presumed among human creation, personal or poetic madness, and demonic inspiration or possession. This view is not limited to the early Greeks; Dryden's seventeenth-century axiom has come down to us as a basic belief of many: "great wits are sure to madness near allied, and thin partitions do their bounds divide." To the extent that one subscribes to such views, there are several serious implications. Extraordinary creative behavior is severely removed from scientific exploration as well as from the capacities of most persons; it is not under the control of "sane" or purposeful men.

Through the centuries, genius has been modeled after everything from demigods, heroes, prophets, martyrs, social activists, and supermen— "capable of re-creating the human cosmos, or part of it, in a way that was significant and not comparable to any previous recreation [Eissler, 1963, p. 1353],"—to the more mundane models such as children with very high IQ scores or persons with some inordinate "luck." Encompassing such a variety of specimens over so long a history, the idea of genius is basically an intriguing idea with a sad and overgenerous past. Most of the work on genius, or exceptional creative behavior, has been a confusion of two classes of variables: factors of motivation (the "why" questions) and

---

* This led a few of Freud's contemporaries to attack the early psychoanalytic positions if not always for the best of reasons or with a light touch:

> Nerve doctors who ruin genius for us by calling it pathological should have their skulls bashed in by the genius' collected work.... One should grind one's heel into the faces of all rationalistic helpers of "normal humanity" who give reassurance to people unable to appreciate works of wit and fantasy [Karl Kraus, quoted in Janik and Toulmin, 1972, p. 77].

statements of consequences (the "effects" questions). The common behavioral denominators to this confusion have been rarity and social, as well as intellectual, consequences that are far out of proportion to, and of greater unpredictability than, most human endeavors. Because of such characteristics, theories of genius, like theories of history, have been used frequently as a means of selective bidding for a particular model of human nature (cf. Plumb, 1969). Seen from these vantage points, creative people are heroic, mysterious, and inexplicable. But they are also not the stuff of science or, often, of this world.

Galton and Freud

The study of eminence and creative behavior needed the work of both Galton and Freud to get past many of the earlier, prohibitive attitudes and presumptions that bound thinking about creative behavior in such motley bundles of whole cloth.

Galton and Freud shared much of the nineteenth century's interest in biological and developmental processes; they agreed in more than principle that genius and creative behavior are primarily biological phenomena. Out of this shared perspective emerges what has become a contemporary focus on genius and creative behavior—emphasis on an individual's family as biological inheritance and as social-psychological influence. For Galton, the family was a genetic pool of talents that its progeny inherit, in different degrees, depending primarily on their biological distance from the center of the pool. For Freud, the family is a psychological reality in which conflicting, motivating processes are instigated and defensive patterns are shaped and interlocked. Out of the interrelationships between inherited talents and conflicts incited and shaped by the family, a person's capacity for creative behavior emerges. Just as important, by viewing both development and capacity as matters of degree, Galton and Freud made a monumental break from earlier views of genius that ascribed to each person distinct states of inspiration, of possession, of enthrallment, or of complete lack of genius.

Needless to say, how one defines genius is critical to how one will study it. It is the basic step. Galton's very effort to operationalize genius was itself extraordinary. Prior definitions had been remarkably varied, unanchored to observables, and almost always post hoc. Despite years of study, there had been a paucity of efforts toward agreement on what, why, or who genius was. Galton's definition was and remains one of the few detailed ones. It rests on five interlocking propositions: that a measure of an individual's genius can be derived from his degree of eminence; that on this rests a man's reputation; that this reputation, although based on contemporary critical opinion, is long term in character; that critical opinion is focused on a real, extensively acknowledged achievement; and that such achievement is the product of natural abilities that are made up of a blend of intellect and disposition (or what is now termed *intelligence and personality*). The following excerpt from Galton makes this clear:

> Let it be clearly borne in mind, what I mean by reputation and ability. By reputation, I mean the opinion of contemporaries, revised by posterity ... the favourable result of a critical analysis of each man's character, by many biographers. I do not mean high social or official position, nor such as is implied by being the mere lion of a London season; but I speak of the reputation of a leader of opinion, of an originator, of a man to whom the world deliberately acknowledges itself largely indebted [Galton, 1869, p. 33].

It is interesting to note in this statement that genius qua eminence was historically bound and a matter of revision, not a once-for-all-time phenomenon. There are several crucial implications to this definition. It deals in observable influences, not supposed ones or the momentary opinion of one or a few persons. In Galton's view, eminence is an objective attribute: it is known only after something occurs and influences a large number of persons over many years (at least long enough to be "revised by posterity"). An interesting correlate is that a person's genius may vary over the years, although the substrate of natural abilities on which it is based need not vary. As for the nature of the relationship between a person's eminence and those abilities, Galton again was remarkably and refreshingly specific.

> By natural ability, I mean those qualities of intellect and disposition, which urge and qualify a man to perform acts that lead to reputation. I do not mean capacity without zeal, nor zeal without capacity, nor even a combination of both of them, without an adequate power of doing a great deal of very *laborious work*. But I mean a nature which, when left to itself, will, urged by an *inherent stimulus*, climb the path that leads to eminence and has strength to reach the summit—on which, if hindered or thwarted, will fret and strive until the hindrance is overcome, and it is again free to follow its labouring instinct [Galton, 1869, p. 33, italics added].

Seemingly paradoxical for a view that puts so much emphasis on other persons' opinions and external acknowledgement, Galton subscribed heavily to the idea that the necessary condition to genius is intrinsic motivation, "an inherent stimulus" that urges and compels hard work. That one needs abilities to match the compulsion goes almost without saying but should be recognized. Given a combination of strong urges and exceptional natural abilities, Galton thought that the continued interaction *would* establish a noteworthy reputation, that genius "would out."
...

. . .

Galton assumed that a man's genius or his potential for it, though evidenced by the man himself, derived from genetic sources entirely external to him. Even if genius was within the genetic pool of his family, the locus of origin and the locus of control were outside the individual, since no one can choose his family of origin. Thus, Galton's position assigns importance to luck or chance as a determinant of genius. This bears a resemblance to the Greek view that a man of genius is one who, without choice, is touched by, inspired by, or visited by an outside god-spirit or daemon; one who is thereafter compelled or, in Galton's terms, "urged" to perform deeds that gain him a favorable reputation.

On the other hand, in Freud's view of creative behavior, while the locus of origin is external, the locus of control, like the major motives for creative behavior, is within the individual, allied to "madness" though it may be. Out of the meshing of the claims of biology and of society comes art. In Freudian theory, art, or creative behavior, is used in the service of protecting the individual and his primary groups, even if paradoxically it jeopardizes his reputation.* Galton's creative individuals are not the potential enemies of society, that is, the "detonators of change" that Freud's are. Galton's world is more rewarding and accepting, "fairer," and less destructively critical than Freud's. Galton's social environment is Darwinian, judging the adaptive abilities and endurances of species through sheer capacity to survive. In Freud's world, survival is also at issue, but on a much different level.

Although he made a lifelong practice of studying men of genius—Leonardo Da Vinci (Freud, 1910/1953), Dostoevsky (Freud, 1928/1948), Moses (Freud, 1938/1955)—Freud never believed that he understood genius. In a later edition of *Hereditary Genius* Galton wished that he had used the word *ability* instead of *genius* in his title. Thus, Galton and Freud ended their studies of genius dissatisfied with it as an explanation.

Drawing a general conclusion at this point, one must confess that there is little that specifically helps in the understanding of genius or exceptional creative behavior. Pooling the work of Galton and Freud, we see genius as the esteemed *product* of high general abilities and continuous, energetic, highly personal effort over most of a lifetime. Implied in this conclusion are several aspects of interest. One does not have genius, one does genius-level work. High general abilities and prolonged, personal motivations are dispositional conditions to this level of performance. When we say a person has genius it is much like saying they have the flu—at best a descriptive label, superficial and begging questions. Genius is inferred from behavior having protracted influence; equally important, it is behavior that is eventually recognized as influential and esteemed by many of the influenced. We know that such behavior is itself considerably influenced by situational and environmental conditions, conditions which

---

* Freud maintained this view throughout his career:

The artist has also an introverted disposition and has not far to go to become neurotic. He is one who is urged on by the instructional needs which are too clamorous; he longs to attain honour, power, riches, fame, and the love of women; but he lacks the means of achieving these gratifications [Freud, 1933/1969, pp. 327, italics added].

if left unacknowledged and unanalyzed give the appearance of luck or of genius to extraordinary achievement. Yet if one wishes to go beyond this general statement more is called for. Since historical eminence occurs in many different kinds of behavior, we need first to determine if there is a set of discriminating attributes common to this diversity of activities.

Definition of Genius

One should look to persons of recognized eminence for genius, since genius is evidenced in a consensus of peers and is operationalized through the various reward procedures that every society and profession has for acknowledging members' contributions (Cole and Cole, 1973; Zuckerman, 1967a). This statement follows Galton's wish to do away with the word *genius*. Furthermore, we should accept the fact that there is no one criterion, person, or group that can determine who has genius and who does not. Freud and others dealt with the motivational and personality correlates to creative behavior at levels and complexity deeper than Galton's "qualities of intellect and disposition." From them we take the idea that for the attainment of a great, enduring reputation, along with gifted cognitive abilities, there must be deep-seated, strongly persistent personality determinants operating, which are essentially developmental in nature, longitudinal in occurrence (rather than situationally determined and sporadic), and conducive to behavior of influence and consequence. These determinants urge men and women "to perform acts that lead to reputation" or eminence. Influence is a continuous phenomenon in every sense and is comparative and judgmental in part. Eminence is built on influence and is social, as well as individual, in origin and behavioral in nature. For these reasons, eminence is built only on public acts.

Therefore, a person of genius is anyone who, regardless of other characteristics he may possess or have attributed to him, produces, over a long period of time, a large body of work that has a significant influence on many persons for many years; requiring these people, as well as the individual in question, to come to terms with a different set of attitudes, ideas, viewpoints, or techniques before all can have "peace of mind," that is, a sense of resolution and closure.

The work associated with this person must be presented to others, for their use and evaluation; it is a public work and takes other talented men and women years to understand, to implement, and, equally important, to surpass. It is others' *necessary* effort that makes up the basic thrust of this person's impact. Others often spend their own careers working out the implications of this work, for in the end they must come to terms with it. It is this aspect that is so important, whether it is wanted by others or predictable.

Acknowledgement usually occurs through the work being referred to often and being explicitly incorporated in others' work. The individual most responsible for the work receives institutionalized awards, for example, the Nobel prize, and, lastly, he becomes the object of archival interest, first within a profession (*The Excitement and Fascination of Science,* 1965) and, if his influence is extraordinary, eventually among a wider, interested lay public (evidenced in popular and "serious" biographies).

The key ingredient to genius is productivity—large in volume, extraordinary in longevity, more or less unpredictable in content. The impact of the work is dislocation or sudden reorganization constituting a major shift, that is, productions of "originality" rather than of reasonable extension (cf. Ghiselin, 1963; Kuhn, 1962, for an important discussion of this process in the physical sciences). Productivity in any area is a continuous variable. Influential productivity is also continuous, but it is very rare within any field, a point originally made by Galton. Cole and Cole (1967) reported that of the quarter million scientists appearing in the 1961 *The Science Citation Index,* only 1.08% has received 58 or more citations, which is the physics Nobel laureates' average number of citations between 1955 and 1965. Another study (Garfield, 1970) showed that on the basis of number of citations, one can predict the most likely candidates for the Nobel prize in science, and, in fact, did locate both winners in physics. The basis of long-term influence, extraordinary productivity, can be observed for many persons of extraordinary influence in a variety of areas: Bach's 46 volumes of compositions; Binet's 277 publications (Dennis, 1954b); Darwin's 119 (Darwin, 1896); Einstein's 248 (Weil, 1960); Freud's 330 (Tyson and Strachey, 1956); Galton's 227 (Dennis, 1954b); Maslow's 165 (MacKinnon, 1972); and William James, who complained most of his life of work inhibition, produced 307 publications (Dennis, 1954a). Zuckerman (1967b) noted that laureates in science publish earlier, more, and longer than do matched scientists drawn from *American Men of Science.* The former have a median of 3.9 papers per year to the latters' 1.4 papers. Zuckerman noted even more prolific eminent mathematicians— Poincaré's 500 papers and 30 books over 34 years and the 995 papers of Arthur Cayley (who published a paper every two or three weeks).

Influential persons' productive longevity is also clearly observed: For example, Freud produced his psychoanalytic work over a 45-year span after shifting from neuropsychiatry in his late 30s; Picasso worked for over 75 years; Darwin and Einstein produced their work over periods of 51 years and 53 years, respectively. Raskin (1936) studied groups of eminent nineteenth-century scientists and writers and found that their periods of productivity averaged 34 years and 30 years, respectively (see also Lehman, 1953).

· · ·

Taking influential, long-term productivity as the basis and hallmark of eminence, we can now put into sharper perspective several of the attributes that are often attached to genius. So-called "works of genius" may be the individual parts in a prolonged series of efforts made public over time. When examined closely, one finds that this voluminous series comprises a set of intricately linked core problems and an exceptionally large number of ideas about them (Merton, 1961), which, over time, lead to innovation.... To call a major segment of a science or art Darwinian biology, Einsteinian physics, Freudian psychology, or Newtonian, Pavlovian, Picasso-like, Chagal-like, etc., is to state for the record that a discernible historical development has occurred, that major periods of change are traceable and identifiable rather than random, fated, and more or less unattributable....

So far we have spent a good deal of time discussing influence as one of the critical independent variables in the achievement of eminence. Yet, it would be misleading to suggest that the attainment of great influence, or impact, is what extraordinary creative behavior is all about, the aim of it all. It is not; it is the need to work on problems considered significant and troublesome by the individual. Influence is a highly personal, varied, and unpredictable adjunct to a man's work; man's specific aim for influence is erratic and its attainment out of his control....

Consequences of the Definition

The above definition, therefore, helps to clear up several misconceptions linked to the extraordinary influences which in the past have attracted somewhat romantic and even heroic explanation. "Undiscovered genius" is one common misconception. If our definition is valid, then one knows of persons of extraordinary abilities by the use of these abilities and by the subsequent influence they have. The proposed definition does not attempt in any way to second-guess history, for clearly there are no "might-have-beens," no undiscovered geniuses, no potential geniuses cruelly snuffed out or mysteriously prohibited (usually by an equally ill-defined fate). As we have seen, genius is, at best, a judgment placed on the degree of influence of a person's work and cannot be meaningfully placed on the origins or the style of that work, regardless of its appeal. Nor are there particular political, religious, social-economic groups, nationalities, races, or sexes with more genius than others, as others tried to demonstrate. Various groups of people may have more facilities, more opportunities, and even more motivation, predisposing them to concern themselves with certain phenomena, but none has intrinsically more genius per se, for there is no such thing. Areas of interest and the preferred means by which they work are a function of the resources and traditions available (Lehman, 1947), not of any inherent qualities to members of the groups. As Clark (1969) reminded us, "although circumstances and opportunities may vary, human intelligence seems to remain fairly constant ... [p. 17]." Who has more "genius," the first men to harness fire or those who split the atom, those who developed the alphabet or those who used it to produce

Oedipus Rex, Hamlet, or *War and Peace?* These are unanswerable questions that may call out preferences and prejudices but not meaningful answers. Nor can we put the tag of "genius" on work that is interesting to us or strikes us as unusual in some manner. This type of work obviously does not warrant the claim of genius unless such performances show the essentials of extraordinary creative behavior by being highly productive, influential, and generative over many years.

Some works are spoken of as being "ahead of their time"—a natural enough but not conclusive attribute to *potentially* significant work. This is not only post hoc but begs the question of what the merits are and for whom. Less dramatically stated, to call work "ahead of its time" means it was produced before it was well understood, as in the case of Mendel; before it could be technically confirmed, as in the case of Einstein; or before it could be appreciated and accommodated, as in the case of some major composers. If anything, these examples point to another facet of the generative capacity of influential work. Since it is simply not possible for a work to be done and, on that basis alone, to be judged accurately for its importance and/or the presence of genius, we turn to another index of extraordinary work of impact. It must be not only of large volume but it must be taken up, responded to (for and against), examined, and put to use by others. Its degree of "fit" with the field around it can only be determined empirically; this is one of the essential tests of its impact. Its endurance is another test, and this quality of work grows from and feeds into its generative capacity.

. . .

Such terms as *unique* and *de novo* are not only oversimplifications but grossly misleading. They make a very complicated and often contentious historical process appear ahistorical, split off from the rest of life, and, ironically, they belittle the very achievement they attempt to credit by conveying the false impression that the works in question occur in a relatively unchallenged field with few or no other persons working in the same area or even on the same problems. All that we know of important persons, work of influence, and eminence suggests just the opposite conditions hold true. That is why, in part, the works in question are significantly influential. If the issues involved are serious to begin with, so are the competitors and the resistances (cf. Ellenberger, 1970; Kuhn, 1962; Shakow and Rapaport, 1968, especially chapters 1 and 2 for very detailed discussions; Watson, 1968).

More Contemporary Issues and Evidence

Until now we have discussed the problems involved in defining genius. Within our concern for a proper definition has been a more basic, if implicit, concern: Can one predict who might become an eminent person?

The importance of this question cannot be underestimated; related to its answer is our understanding of what the major facilitative variables and experiences are that contribute to the works that are underlying in the achievement of eminence. The essential issue is not eminence per se but the clues that indicate how we might increase the type of behavior that eminence results from.

Research on eminent persons has been conducted off and on over the many years since Freud's and Galton's pioneer efforts. The bulk of this research shows that persons who do achieve extraordinary eminence generally begin their productive careers significantly earlier than their less productive peers (Albert, 1971; Cox, 1926; Lehman, 1953; Raskin, 1936; Roe, 1952). More recent evidence on productive careers suggests that early starts are a solid index by which to estimate a person's productive ability. In several studies of University of Chicago PhDs, eight years after their receiving their degrees, Bloom (1963) showed that those more creative than matched controls had significantly more publications. In fact, the large majority of publications came from less than 10% of the subjects, which is consistent with Dennis' (1954a) earlier finding regarding eminent psychologists. Bloom concluded that "while productivity is clearly not synonymous with creativity, it seems quite likely that unless there is some minimum or *threshold of productivity* there is little probability or likelihood that the individual is creative [p. 256, italics added]."...

We know that genius is not a function of differences in measured intelligence: Many researchers have found that once the IQ is higher than 120, other variables become increasingly important (Barron, 1969; Bloom, 1963; Cox, 1926; Harmon, 1963; Helson and Crutchfield, 1970; MacKinnon, 1962, 1968; Oden, 1968; Roe, 1952; Terman, 1954), although it would be absurd to argue that more "intelligence" would make no difference!

There are also interesting data pertaining to the "age of ascent" in productive careers. A number of studies have independently reported almost identical ages of "creative" subjects' first productions. Raskin (1936) noted 25.2 years and 24.2 years for her select groups of nineteenth-century subjects: Helson and Crutchfield (1970) noted 24.8 years for their subjects. Like Bloom's (1963) and Harmon's (1963) creative subjects, Helson and Crutchfield's creative subjects published more, as well as earlier, than their controls. Even more telling was the fact that Raskin was able to determine that as far back as 1735 the average age for first publication was 25 years. When she separated her samples into the 25 highest ranking scientists and the 25 highest ranking men of letters (lists included Darwin, Faraday, Gauss, Maxwell, and Pasteur; Balzac, Coleridge, Goethe, Poe, Tolstoi, and Wordsworth), the average age for first productions was reduced only to 22 years. The present study shows that Freud was 21 years old at the time of his first professional publication, and Darwin and Einstein each were 22 years old at the time of their first papers, ages almost identical to Raskin's most eminent samples. Across a variety of fields and a two-century time span, there is a stable age at which eminent persons begin to be actively and publicly influential.

Additional data are closer at hand. Examination of the publication careers of 48 psychologists who, up to 1971, were awarded The Distinguished Scientific Contribution Award (DSC) by the American Psychological Association shows that, diverse as their special interests are, they are not too far from the performances described above for other fields. Recipients first published at the average of 25.3—almost identical to Raskin's (1936) and Helson and Crutchfield's (1970) subjects. Raskin also found that the productive careers of scientists and men of letters in her study averaged 34.2 years and 29.8 years, respectively. (We noted earlier that Darwin produced important work for over 51 years, Einstein for 53 years, and Freud for almost 55 years.) Recipients of the award have long productive careers before being honored—averaging almost 31 years of publishing up to the time of their recognition, although a few were in their forties and fifties when so awarded. Assuming that there might be a difference between the careers of those who received the DSC when it was instituted in 1956 and those more recently awarded, we analyzed data for the first and last 12 recipients. The median number of years between first publication and time of award was 25.5 and 26.5 years, respectively. With few exceptions, long productive careers precede psychology's highest acknowledgement of influential work.

This median number of years has been consistent, for over two centuries, for persons working in various sciences and different forms of literature. What factors are behind its stability? Although education, formal and otherwise, has changed tremendously over the past 200 years, the average age of first publications for young creative scientists and a variety of highly eminent people remains much the same. This fact leads one to speculate that the basis for the type of creative behavior leading to very high eminence requires a particular combination of cognitive and personality development and early family experiences, both of which begin early in childhood.

. . .

The above evidence provides strong support for the basic contention in this article: Long-term creative behavior, as evidenced in influential productivity, is the "carrier" of genius qua eminence. The earlier a person starts and the more he does, the more likely will his impact on others be significant and, eventually, the higher his eminence will be. This does not say what, if any, special cognitive, cultural, personality, racial, religious, or social attributes are necessary or involved in such behavior. For the time being, we can say that injecting additional words like *genius* or *unique* into our thoughts on the matter does not appear at all necessary or helpful.

Final Observations

One aspect needs further consideration; in many respects it may be the most important; it is certainly the least understood. For creative behavior, or any behavior, to continue, there must be close congruence between some of the processes a person uses and some of the characteristics of the phenomenon dealt with. It would be difficult, if not impossible, at present to characterize such a "fit" as antecedent or consequence. What begins as a vague correspondence between process and phenomenon becomes progressively closer the more intensively and the longer a person does his work. Artists and scientists alike often speak of a dimly conceived, intuited, "reality" to their early efforts, one that appears early in life and seems to guide much of their behavior as a concerted effort to apprehend, to symbolize, and to control such a reality. Polanyi (1967) and Holton (1971) discussed such a consequence in Einstein's career.* A similar case can be made for Freud by going into his early family life and the cultural events surrounding him (Albert, 1973). Hollingsworth (1942) has shown that the interests and questions of the exceptionally gifted child are remarkably accelerated and border on the profound very early in childhood. With the "precocious" questioning and interest often comes an intense involvement with selected materials, problems, and cognitive processes that are consonant with later-discovered adult professions and life work. If one identifies his interests and special capacities early in life and discovers the existence of such possible enterprises, it follows that he is on his way earlier than most other persons (see Cox, 1926; Ellmann, 1959; Meschkowski, 1964; Roe, 1952; Schilpp, 1949).

The "realities" that make up the content of long-term creative behavior occur noticeably early and more or less independently. These parallels are not explicit and are far from exact; they require lifelong efforts to tease them out, not unique intelligence or aptitude.

---

* Einstein's early years present a picture remarkable for its suggestiveness on this point. In a number of biographies and in Einstein's own autobiography, he appears at age 12 to have already worked free from what he termed:

the chains of the "merely personal," from an existence which is dominated by wishes, hopes, and primitive feelings. Out yonder there was this huge world, which exists independently of us human beings and which stands before us like a great, eternal riddle, at least partially accessible to our inspection and thinking [Schilpp, 1949, p. 5].

We are told by Einstein that his early development of relativity came

After ten years reflection ... from a paradox upon which I had already hit at the *age of sixteen* ... [furthermore] *From the very beginning it appeared to me intuitively clear* ... [Polanyi, 1955, p. 59, italics added].

Conclusion

The above arguments suggest that genius is not a blessing, a danger, or a fortuitous occurrence; it is not a trait, an event, or a thing. Rather, it is, and always has been, a judgment overlaid with shifting values. What genius has often been based on is far more solid—behavior. What it must be based on is creative behavior, which, although highly personalized, is made public and is eventually influential over many years and often in unpredictable ways. By being both productive and influential, this behavior can be measured, its influence traced, and the factors and events underlying it better understood. Of all the qualities attributed to persons of genius the most remarkable, along with perceptiveness, are continuity, endurance, productivity, and influence. Men and women with such attributes are usually esteemed and often honored. They are almost always eminent in comparison to others. But they do not have genius.

This selection by Ann Dell Warren Duncan is interesting because of the novel idea of using rate measures of performance to differentiate gifted and regular classroom children. She shows that these measures of performance rates correlate substantially with traditional measures of intellectual performance. It is worth comparing the results of this study with the studies of Hunt et al. and Carroll, which appear earlier in this book. The findings in these three studies bear more than a superficial resemblance to each other.

19

Behavior Rates of Gifted and Regular Elementary School Children

ANN DELL WARREN DUNCAN

Rate as the Measure

Rate as a basic datum has been used since the first half of the century (Skinner, 1938). It is one of the most sensitive measuring procedures used to quantify behavioral phenomena. Sensitivity is characterized by the rapid, efficient, and economical differentiation between variables; rate has sensitivity as its cornerstone (Lindsley, 1964).

All precise educators use some type of measuring device to assay their particular area. The natural sciences have predicated their measurement on time and space dimensions (Hanson, 1958; Lindsley, 1966b). It is by combining precise, functional dimension points of time and space that man is able to bring order out of seeming chaos.

This marks the potential contribution of rate in precision teaching.

It is incomplete simply to know, note, or mark that a given event has occurred—nor is it sufficient to record its force, amplitude, latency, or duration. These behavioral parameters are limited in precision of record-

Duncan, A. D. W. "Behavior Rates of Gifted and Regular Elementary School Children." *Monograph of The National Association for Creative Children and Adults*, 1969. Reprinted by permission.

ing and frequently are more indicative of the observer's decisions than of the subject's behavior (Skinner, 1961). In addition, traditional behavior measures of force, amplitude, duration, or latency are not directly relevant to the majority of educational problems. Education is not concerned with amount of force a child uses in a temper tantrum but rather his rate of outbursts.

Skinner (1966) notes five germane points about rate of responding as a datum. First of all, rate of responding is important because it is especially relevant to the principal task of a scientific analysis. The drama of behavior should not obscure the search for *why;* the *"whys"* become clear when rate records are kept. The second point declares that rate of responding is an important step in the direction of prediction and control of behavior—which calls for an evaluation of the probability that a response will be emitted.

The third point is of particular relevance to education:

> Rate of responding is one of those aspects of a subject matter which do not attract attention for their own sake and which undergo intensive study only when their usefulness as a dependent variable has been discovered. Other sciences have passed through comparable stages ... the mere weight of a given quantity of a substance is of little interest in its own right. Yet it was only when the weights of substances entering into reactions were found to obey certain laws that chemistry moved into its modern phase. Combining weight became important because of what could be done with it. Rate of responding has emerged as a basic datum in a science of behavior for similar reasons (p. 16).

The fourth point Skinner makes, "rate of responding differs from the measures derived from earlier devices ... such as the time required to complete a task or the effort expended or the number of errors made in doing so (p. 16)," has direct implications for education. Teachers vary in their criterion of what the "effort is for a given task" or the precise definition of an error. Rate puts the responsibility of behavior where it belongs: with the child.

This is related to the fifth point, which suggests that "changes in rate of responding are directly observed, they have dimensions appropriate to a scientific formulation, and under skillful experimental control they show the uniformity expected of biological processes in general (p. 17)."

Method

CHILDREN

The author obtained behavior rates from 46 gifted and 30 regular children in grades four, five, and six. Table 19.1 separates the distribution of pupils by grades.

Table 19.1

Frequency breakdown for gifted and regular
pupils in grades four, five, and six

Categories	Grades			Total
	4	5	6	
Gifted (IQ 130 or above)	9	13	24	46
Regular	10	10	10	30
Total	19	23	34	76

Two schools from a large metropolitan area contributed to this study:
19 gifted pupils participated from accelerated special classes in a suburban school; 27 gifted pupils participated from a private urban school for
young men.

Each teacher selected the children in her class whom she considered
gifted, and then defined what the term meant to her. The author selected
pupils with intelligence-test scores of 130 or above (41 boys and five girls)
from this group. A comparison group of 30 regular children (18 boys and
12 girls) was randomly selected from other classrooms in the suburban
school. No pupils had auditory, motor, or uncorrected visual deficits.

The school records provided California Test of Mental Maturity scores
for all children. For the regular pupils, scores ranged from 93 to 120, with
a median of 110. For the gifted, scores ranged from 130 to 166 with a
median of 138.

BEHAVIORS

The five behaviors whose rates were measured included tapping, walking,
reading, answering, and calculating. The child tapped the table 100 times
with his index finger. He then walked in place for 100 times; each foot
touching the ground counted as one. The child then read aloud two paragraphs from the eighth-grade level of the *Diagnostic Reading Scales*
(Spache, 1963). Reading rate correct was computed by dividing total
words correct by total time required. For the answer rate, the child responded to a question for one minute. The number of words he spoke was
tallied. For calculation rate correct, the child worked a page of arithmetic
problems from the *Wide Range Achievement Test* (Jastak and Jastak,
1965). The number of successful operations required to complete each
problem, per unit of time, determined the calculation rate correct.

Rate or rate correct served as the measure for each behavior; that is,
number of responses divided by time. In four of the rates (tap, walk, read,

and calculate), number was held constant and time varied. For the answe
rate, time (one minute) was held constant and number varied.

School records provided the pupils' scores on the *Stanford Achieve
ment Test* (1953). Selected scores included: total battery median, arithme
tic computation section, word meaning section for grades four and five
and paragraph meaning section for grade six. Since the pupils were in
three different grades, a direct comparison of scores would be unfair to the
younger pupils, who possibly had minimal exposure to the test material
Thus the author computed a difference score, based on grade level, for
each pupil. In other words, if the pupil took the test in the eighth month o
his fourth school year and obtained a total battery-median score of six
years and two months, a difference score of one year and four month.
(based on the achievement test's 10-month year) would result. Achieve
ment comparisons were made on the basis of these difference scores.

EQUIPMENT AND SETTING

The only equipment required for the rate sample was paper, pencil, stop
watch, and wrist counter (Lindsley, 1966a). Any available room in the
school served as the setting. Each child was seen individually for the
duration of the sampling. Median time required to complete sampling o
four behaviors (tap, walk, read, answer) was 11 minutes. Median time
required to complete the calculation sample was 10 minutes.

Research

In general, the results of this study show that: (1) gifted pupils' perfor
mance rates *overlap* with those of regular children; (2) on the average
gifted pupils perform significantly faster than regular pupils on both
academic and non-academic behaviors; (3) significant differences exist
between the grades; and (4) correlations between the academic rates and
achievement scores, non-academic rates, and intelligence-test scores are
all beyond the .005 level of significance.

RATE OVERLAP DESCRIPTION

As graphically demonstrated in Figure 19.1, rate distributions of regular
(R) and gifted (G) children overlapped. The vertical axis, a six-cycle
logarithmic scale, represents movements per minute (rate). The loga
rithmic scale allows calculation rate correct and tapping to appear on the
same graph without distorting the proportional differences between the

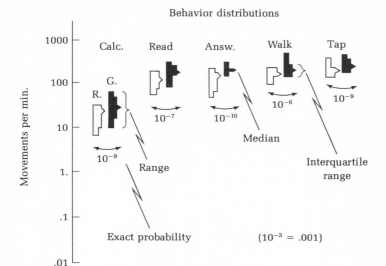

Figure 19.1

Behavior-rate distributions overlap between the performance of regular (R) and gifted (G) pupils plotted on a six-cycle logarithmic scale. The exact probability levels indicate gifted performed significantly faster than regular pupils on all measures.

two behaviors. In other words, on a logarithmic scale, the distance from one to two calculating operations correct per minute is as important as the distance from 100 to 200 taps per minutes. An arithmetic scale would graphically compress these differences. All children tapped much faster than they calculated; calculation rate correct was the slowest behavior sampled. Similarities existed in the upper limit of the reading and answering ranges; however, both gifted and regular children answered (medians) faster than they read (medians). Median rates of gifted children on all five behaviors were faster than those of regular pupils.

STATISTICAL ANALYSIS

Percentages of rate overlap between gifted and regular pupils' behavior distributions included: tapping, 20 percent; walking, 24 percent; reading, 16 percent; answering, 20 percent; and calculating, 24 percent.

Pearson product-moment correlations were computed between each measure and all others. Table 19.2 presents all the correlations—some of which will be discussed in subsequent sections. All correlations were significant beyond the .005 level....

Table 19.2

Correlations* of variables with gifted and regular children

Compared	Measures							
	Walk	Answer	Read	Calculate	Tot. Md.	Read	Arith.	IQ
Tap	.80	.42	.44	.37	.47	.43	.36	.40
Walk		.32	.41	.37	.45	.43	.36	.41
Answer			.50	.33	.46	.47	.32	.40
Read				.66	.79	.75	.58	.65
Calculate					.63	.56	.72	.53
Tot. Md.						.91	.75	.82
Read							.63	.76
Arith.								.61

* Pearson product-moment correlations for the five behavioral rates, three achievement-test scores, and the intelligence-test scores were all significant beyond the .005 level.

Summary

From this study, eight possible conclusions may be drawn. The rate sample showed: (1) Behavior rates of gifted and regular pupils overlapped. (2) On the average, rates of gifted were significantly faster than regular pupils. (3) The sample successfully discriminated gifted from regular pupils as well as grade levels. (4) The differences between gifted and regular pupils increased with grade level, but not as a function of grade level.

Achievement-test scores showed: (5) Gifted performed significantly higher than regular pupils. (6) The sixth-grade gifted pupils did better on all three achievement scores, and were significantly different from the regular pupils.

Correlations between measures indicated: (7) The highest and most significant correlations were intelligence-test scores with total battery-median scores and tapping with walking. (8) All correlations were beyond the .005 level of significance, indicating there was a relationship between each measure examined in this study. Therefore, it is meaningful to talk about fast and slow people—they exist.

The major demonstration of this study is that rate is a sensitive, accurate measure which can differentiate between individual children as well as groups such as gifted and regular pupils. Furthermore, the differences between these children increase as the children get older. Hence, it appears vital that intermittent rate samples as well as continuous rate records be kept for each child. When the records indicate there is a deceleration in rate, appropriate steps may be taken by the child, his teacher, and parents before academic retardation becomes pervasive and difficult to remedy.

Since these data were not taken directly from the classroom, one must be cautious about extrapolating to classroom behavior rates. By using discrete rate measures, this study suffers from the inadequacies of all "one-shot" measurements. However, further exploration is definitely indicated. For example, one way of determining how much of the variance in the data is due to a child's giftedness would be to take a non-gifted child (by some definition, whether intelligence-test score, self opinion, teacher opinion, standardized achievement-test score or whatever) and accelerate his various behavior rates by means of contingent consequences and appropriate programming. Then, using standardized measuring devices, determine whether or not the child now fits into the appropriate category of giftedness.

If production of high rates leads to membership in the category of giftedness, then we as educators have a singular opportunity to provide the world with highly productive citizens. We no longer need to be content with simply honing the rough edges of behavior and imparting currently popular curricula. We may be in a position to produce giftedness.

Investigation of such a challenge would seem to be imperative.

This article by David Harrington deals with the measurement of creativity. He points out that virtually all creativity measures are given under instructional conditions which do not maximize creative performances. When instructions are altered in such a way that the subject knows what is meant by a creative response, substantial correlations between creativity and personality traits emerge. The importance of this article is that it forces a reevaluation of much of the earlier creativity research, which had found fairly low correlations with personality measures.

20

Effects of Explicit Instructions to "Be Creative" on the Psychological Meaning of Divergent Thinking Test Scores

DAVID M. HARRINGTON

Divergent thinking tests have been viewed for nearly three-quarters of a century as a possible means of measuring certain components of problem-solving and creative thinking abilities (e.g., Binet and Henri, 1896; Burt, 1962; Dearborn, 1898 and Whipple, 1915). Because they require subjects to produce a variety of possible solutions to open-ended problems, divergent thinking tests are presumably able to measure important idea-generating abilities far more directly than tests which call only for the selection or production of a single correct answer. For reasons cited below, however, it is entirely possible that the potential inherent in the divergent thinking test format never has been fully realized.

In the first place, divergent thinking tests are most often scored solely in terms of the number or novelty of the solutions proposed, although problem-solving proficiency in the real world is probably a function of the

Harrington, D. M. "Effects of Explicit Instructions to 'Be Creative' on the Psychological Meaning of Divergent Thinking Test Scores." *Journal of Personality*, 1975, Vol. 43, pp. 434–454. Copyright © 1975 by the Duke University Press and reprinted by permission.

number and qualitative excellence of initially generated approaches and ideas.

In the second place, divergent thinking test instructions rarely provide subjects with unequivocal information regarding qualitative scoring criteria in those cases where they are applied. For example, subjects are not instructed to produce particularly clever responses to the Plot Titles Test (Sheridan Supply Co., 1962) although responses are subsequently scored for cleverness. Similarly, responses to the Consequences Test (Christensen, Merrifield and Guilford, 1958) are evaluated in terms of a remoteness-obviousness dimension which is not mentioned in the instructions. In other cases (e.g., Torrance, 1966) subjects are asked to pursue several different test goals simultaneously (e.g., produce as many solutions as possible, produce "interesting" solutions, produce "clever" solutions) and are therefore forced to either scatter their test-taking efforts or to pursue one performance criterion at the expense of others. Because accurate estimates of ability must be based upon maximum performances (Cronbach, 1960), because subjects must know where to direct their test-taking efforts in order to achieve maximum performances, and because subjects certainly cannot be expected to fall uniformly short of their maximum levels of performance when poorly directed, inadequately informative instructions fail to create conditions necessary for either the accurate assessment of divergent thinking abilities or for the meaningful evaluation of qualitatively-oriented scoring procedures.

Surprisingly little attention has been focused directly upon the coordination of test instructions with qualitatively-oriented scoring criteria as a means of influencing the degree to which divergent thinking tests assess components of creative-thinking abilities. Although several investigators have examined the effects of administering divergent thinking tests under more or less relaxed conditions (see Kogan, 1973; Vernon, 1971; Wallach, 1971 for useful reviews), these studies have not involved rigorous application of qualitatively-oriented scoring procedures nor have they systematically manipulated the informativeness of the instructions. Like several other studies which indicate that simple instructional manipulations can increase overall levels of performance (reviewed in Harrington, 1972, pp. 326–327; Vernon, 1971; Wallach, 1971), these studies of testing atmosphere are clearly related to the issue of how to elicit maximum performances, but are only tangentially relevant to the issue of coordinating test instructions with qualitatively-oriented scoring procedures. In the one study which has addressed this latter issue directly, however, the results were encouraging. In an investigation reported by Datta over a decade ago (Datta, 1963), on-the-job creativity ratings of 16 research scientists correlated strongly ($rho = +.71$) with scores based upon the number and quality of their responses to a battery of three tests (including two divergent thinking tests) which had been administered using instructions which described the qualitative scoring criteria. On the other hand, Datta reported a somewhat negative relationship ($rho = -.17$) between on-the-job creativity ratings and scores based on the same tests which had been administered to 15 other research scientists in the same laboratory using instructions which did not mention the qualitative scoring criteria.

If the arguments presented here are valid and if the Datta finding is representative of what might be found with other tasks and other samples, it should be possible to substantially improve the capacity of many divergent thinking tests to measure abilities associated with real-life problem-solving proficiency and creative achievement by embodying realistic standards of excellence in the scoring procedures and by constructing test instructions which inform subjects of those criteria.

To test the efficacy of these ideas, divergent thinking tests were administered to one set of subjects using special instructions to "be creative" (these subjects were instructed to produce responses which were simultaneously novel and worthwhile or important) and to another set of comparable subjects using the standard instructions which say nothing about qualitative criteria. Efforts were then made to rate the responses reliably in terms of their creativity and to derive satisfactorily reliable summary indices. The psychometric and psychological properties of adequately reliable scores generated under the two instructional conditions were then analyzed and compared.

Method

SUBJECTS

The subjects consisted of 105 undergraduate males who signed up for the experiment in partial fulfillment of psychology course requirements.

Intact sign-up groups were assigned to one experimental condition or the other by a procedure which kept the two conditions balanced with respect to the point in the academic quarter when the subjects volunteered. Fifty subjects were assigned to the creativity condition and 55 to the standard condition.

Subsequent analyses of Scholastic Aptitude Test data, available for approximately 88 percent of the subjects, revealed that the final groups were well matched in terms of both Verbal Aptitude scores (standard condition $M = 561$; creativity condition $M = 578$; $t = .86$) and Mathematical Aptitude scores (standard condition $M = 640$, creativity condition $M = 627$; $t = -.68$). The two groups also produced an equal number of responses to the similarities test, a divergent thinking measure which was administered to all subjects using standard instructions (standard condition $M = 20.6$; creativity condition $M = 20.8$; $t = .12$), and were comparable in terms of a broad spectrum of personality characteristics (see Harrington, 1972, for details).

ASSESSMENT PROCEDURES

The psychological instruments and questionnaires were administered by the author to all subjects in the following order: A brief biographical information sheet; a dittoed form of the Adjective Check List (ACL) (Gough, 1952) in which the adjective "creative" had been inserted; a 164-item psychological inventory (the Berkeley Self-Report Personality Inventory) which included items from the Dominance and Self-Control Scales of the California Psychological Inventory (CPI) (Gough, 1956) and items from the Berkeley Psychological Inventory (Block, undated); a three-part, six-minute version of the Similarities Test (after Wallach and Wing, 1969); Form A of the Alternate Uses Test (Christensen, Guilford, Merrifield and Wilson, 1960)....

DIVERGENT THINKING TEST INSTRUCTIONS

Because the test instructions were a central issue of this study, they are described here in full for the two tests upon which subsequent analyses were focused.

All subjects received the following instructions for the Similarities Test:

> On each of the next three pages will appear the names of two objects. You are to write down all the different ways you can think of in which the two objects are alike. You will have two minutes to work on each page and will be told when to start and when to stop.
>
> Remember, your task is to write down all the ways you can think of in which the two objects are similar. You need not use complete sentences.

Subjects in the creativity condition were handed dittoed booklets labeled "Creative Thinking Tests (Forms 1, 2, and 3)" and standard condition subjects were given similar booklets labelled "Open-ended Tests (Forms 1, 2, and 3)." Each booklet contained a cover sheet of general instructions and a copy of the Alternate Uses Test, the Consequences Test and the Brick Uses Test.

Phrases printed in brackets below appeared on the covers of the standard condition booklets only, phrases printed in parentheses appeared only on the creativity condition booklets and non-bounded phrases appeared on both.

> The three tests of [intellectual abilities] (creative thinking) contained in this booklet are probably quite different from tests you are familiar with and may very possibly be of a kind which you have never before encountered.
>
> Unlike most tests which ask you to produce or identify one correct answer to a question or problem, the tests in this booklet will [present you]

(give you an opportunity to think creatively by presenting you) with problems or questions for which you will be able to think of many possible solutions. It will be your task to produce as many (creative) solutions which meet the conditions of the problem as you can think of within the allotted time.

(Not only will these tests give you the opportunity to be creative, but the instructions to the individual tests will urge you to be creative and will tell you what general conditions an answer should meet in order to be considered creative.) Because the instructions for each of the three tests differ somewhat from one another, you will probably find it helpful to read and listen rather carefully to the instructions for each of the tests.

Subjects in the creativity condition received the following instructions to the Alternate Uses Test:

The following is a test of your ability to think creatively about uses for some common objects. Each of the objects you will be asked to think about has a common use which will be stated. Your task is to list up to six other *creative* uses for which the object or parts of the object could serve. A creative use is one which is both *unusual* (a use which other people would be unlikely to think of) and *worthwhile*.

In trying to be creative, therefore, you should try to list uses which are both *unusual* and *worthwhile* at the same time.

(By the way, uncreative uses do not count against you, they just do not count for you.)

Consider an example: (the standard example was presented at this point).

While these uses are not of particularly high creative quality, notice that all of the uses listed are different from each other and different from the primary use of a newspaper. Each use should be different from others and from the common use, of course.

Do not spend too much time on any one item. Write down those creative uses that occur to you and go on to the others in the same part. You may return to the incomplete items in a part if time for the part permits.

There are three parts to this test, with three items per part. You will have four minutes for each part.

Try to be creative.

If you have any questions, ask them now.

Instructions at the beginning of each part reminded subjects to: List as many as six unusual and worthwhile uses for each of the following objects. BE CREATIVE.

Subjects in the standard condition received normal alternate uses instructions, the format of which closely resembled those used in the creativity condition. Standard instructions simply asked subjects to produce up to six different uses for each object and made no mention of creativity or of qualitative scoring criteria.

Instructions developed for the Consequences and Brick Uses Tests are available elsewhere (Harrington, 1972) and can be obtained from the author.

METHODS OF SCORING THE DIVERGENT THINKING TESTS

Similarities.   Similarities Fluency scores were based upon the number of different similarities listed. The estimated internal reliability (coefficient *alpha*) of the Similarities Fluency score was .80 in the standard condition and .72 in the creativity condition.

Alternate Uses.   In an attempt to assess directly and reliably the relative creativity of each Alternate Uses response, three advanced graduate students in psychology were given nine decks of cards, each of which contained every distinct use proposed for each of the nine target objects. Each judge then independently rated the creativity of the uses proposed for a given object by assigning each response to one of five categories of a prescribed flattened-normal distribution. This process was repeated for each of the nine objects; uses for one object were therefore never compared with the uses proposed for any other object. A composite was formed of the ratings of the three judges.

In order to transform the final creativity ratings into overall indices of performance, each of the nine distributions of creativity ratings was split at the median. Subjects were then assigned scores based on the number of uses falling above the medians (creative uses) or below the medians (uncreative uses) of these nine rating distributions. The estimated internal reliability (coefficient *alpha*) of the creativity uses score was .64 in the standard condition and .82 in the creativity condition. Corresponding reliability estimates for uncreative uses scores were .77 and .60.

Subjects were also assigned a total uses score, the estimated internal reliability of which was .86 in the standard condition and .87 in the creativity condition.

It should be noted that the creative and uncreative uses scores were essentially uncorrelated in both instructionl conditions ($r = +.14$ in the standard condition and $-.03$ in the creativity condition).

. . .

SCORING THE PERSONALITY INSTRUMENTS

The Berkeley Self Report Personality Inventory was scored in terms of the CPI Dominance and Self-Control Scales (Gough, 1957 and 1968).

The ACL was scored with respect to its 24 standard scales (Gough and Heilbrun, 1965) and in terms of two scales developed specifically for this study: the ACL Creative Personality Scale and the ACL Creative Abilities Scale. The ACL Creative Personality Scale consists of 42 adjectives which have significantly discriminated between creative and uncreative individuals in at least two of five previous investigations (Domino, 1970; MacKinnon, 1962 and 1966; Smith and Schaefer, 1969; Taft and Gilchrist, 1970 and Van Zelst and Kerr, 1954). An individual's score was based upon the degree to which he applied these adjectives to himself, appropriately corrected for his general propensity to check adjectives. The ACL Creative Abilities Scale consists of 16 adjectives (artistic, clever, creative, curious, foresighted, humorous, imaginative, ingenious, insightful, intelligent, inventive, original, quick, resourceful, sharp-witted and versatile) each of which presumably refers to some facet or manifestation of a creative thinking ability. Again, scale scores were corrected for general tendency to check adjectives.

Results

EVIDENCE THAT THE CREATIVITY INSTRUCTIONS AND SCORING CRITERIA WERE WELL COORDINATED: TWO MANIPULATION CHECKS

Subjects in the creativity condition produced significantly more creative uses ($p < .05$) and fewer uncreative uses ($p < .00005$) than did subjects in the standard condition, as can be seen in Table 20.1.

After completing the divergent thinking tests, all subjects used a six-point rating scale to compare their performances to that of a hypothetical average undergraduate Berkeley male. Among creativity condition subjects these posttest evaluations of performance were strongly correlated ($r = +.58, p < .001$) with the number of creative uses produced and were essentially uncorrelated ($r = -.02$) with the number of uncreative uses produced. These two correlations differed significantly beyond the .002

Table 20.1

Alternate uses test performance as a function of test instructions

Alternate Uses Test scores	Instructional condition				Indices of between-group differences	
	Standard instructions		Creativity instructions			
	M	SD	M	SD	t	p*
Creative uses	13.51	5.18	16.12	6.50	2.29	.05
Uncreative uses	17.29	6.51	12.24	4.85	−4.47	.00005
Total uses	30.80	8.85	28.36	7.99	−1.48	NS

Note: Standard condition $N = 55$; creativity condition $N = 50$.
* Two-tailed tests.

level, suggesting that subjects in the creativity condition judged the excellence of their performances in terms of the creativity of their responses. Among standard condition subjects, however, posttest evaluations of performance were correlated significantly with both the number of creative and uncreative uses produced ($r = +.30$, $p < .05$ and $r = +.38$, $p < .01$, respectively) and were correlated most strongly with the number of total uses produced ($r = +.45$, $p < .001$), suggesting that these subjects ignored the creativity of their responses and judged excellence solely in terms of raw fluency.

The mean differences in Table 20.1 and the correlational differences involving posttest evaluations of performance both indicate that the subjects in the creativity condition were more closely attuned to the qualitative scoring criteria than were standard condition subjects. These results also indicate that the demarcation line separating creative from uncreative uses was drawn in a manner which captured the change associated with the instructional modification. In short, these data suggest that the test instructions and scoring criteria were well coordinated in the creativity condition and were poorly coordinated in the standard condition, as intended.

EVIDENCE THAT THE COORDINATION CHANGED AND SHARPENED THE PSYCHOLOGICAL MEANING OF ALTERNATE USES SCORES

Patterns of correlations involving standard personality scales and Alternate Uses Test scores in the two conditions reveal that the coordination of instructions and scoring criteria significantly changed and sharpened the psychological meaning of Alternate Uses Test scores.

As can be seen in Table 20.2, only three of the 26 standard personality scales correlated significantly with the production of creative uses in the standard condition, only six correlated significantly with the number of total uses produced and none of these scales yielded a correlation with an absolute value exceeding .40. This pattern of low to moderate correlations is typical of previous findings (e.g., Gough and Heilbrun, 1965, p. 18; Guilford, Christensen, Frick and Merrifield, 1957; Jones, 1964 and White, 1968). In the creativity condition, on the other hand, 16 of the standard personality scales were significantly associated with the production of creative uses and 13 of these scales yielded correlations with absolute values exceeding .40. Furthermore, the correlations in the creativity condition were psychologically plausible. On the basis of interpretations provided for the eight scales yielding absolute correlations with creative uses in excess of .50, it can be inferred that the production of creative uses in the creativity condition was associated with self-confidence, intellectual competence and ambition (Gough and Heilbrun, 1965 and Gough, 1968).

. . .

Table 20.2

Correlations between alternate uses scores and personality scales and the significance of between-group correlational and regression-slope differences

Personality Scales Standard ACL Scales	Standard condition		Creativity condition	p^a of Between-group correlational and regression-slope differences	
	r with creative uses	r with total uses	r with creative uses	Creative uses vs. creative uses[b]	Total uses vs. creative uses[c]
Total	+.05	+.09	+.17	NS	NS
Defensiveness	−.28*	−.17	+.29*	.005	.05
Favorable	−.18	−.04	+.46***	.001	.02
Unfavorable	+.23	+.16	−.23	.025	.10
Self-confidence	+.17	+.21	+.53***	.05	NS
Self-control	−.20	−.12	+.03	NS	NS
Lability	+.05	+.13	+.17	NS	NS
Personal adjustment	−.30*	−.24	+.18	.025	.05
Achievement	−.08	+.02	+.54***	.0025	.01
Dominance	+.07	+.20	+.62***	.005	.05
Endurance	−.17	−.08	+.44***	.001	.01
Order	−.10	−.04	+.43**	.005	.02
Intraception	−.11	−.02	+.38**	.01	.05
Nurturance	−.29*	−.24	+.02	NS	NS
Affiliation	−.24	−.12	+.05	NS	NS
Heterosexuality	−.13	−.08	+.13	NS	NS
Exhibition	+.21	+30*	+.41**	NS	NS
Autonomy	+.16	+.30*	+.48**	.10	NS
Aggression	+.16	+.19	+.14	NS	NS
Change	+.07	+.26*	+.29*	NS	NS
Succorance	−.09	−.12	−.68***	.001	.002
Abasement	−.18	−.32*	−.62***	.005	.10
Deference	−.24	−.39**	−.54***	.10	NS
Counseling readiness	−.16	−.26	−.51***	.05	NS
CPI scales:					
Dominance	+.14	+.29*	+.67***	.025	NS
Self-control	−.13	−.02	+.23	.10	NS
Special ACL scales:					
Creative personality	+.20	+.26*	+.69***	.01	.05
Creative abilities	+.16	+.22	+.64***	.05	.05

Note: Standard condition $N = 55$; creativity condition $N = 50$.

[a] All significance levels are for two-tailed tests.

[b] Between-group differences involving relationships between creative uses scores and personality scales were evaluated by comparing regression slopes (McNemar, 1969, p. 161).

[c] Where personality scale variances were larger in the creativity condition, r's in both groups were adjusted to what they would have been had the personality scale variances in both groups equalled the variance of the pooled sample and these range-equated r's were then compared using the r to z transformation (McNemar, 1969, pp. 157–162). These adjustments generally decreased the significance of between-group correlational differences and therefore worked against the hypothesis of an instructional effect. In the few cases where they increased the significance of the differences, the probabilities associated with the raw differences are reported.

* $p < .05$.

** $p < .01$.

*** $p < .001$.

Similar results were also obtained when creativity condition correlations involving creative uses scores and the standard personality scales were compared to corresponding creativity condition correlations involving Similarities Fluency scores. (For example, the creative uses × ACL Succorance r of −.68 in the creativity condition was compared to the Similarities Fluency × ACL Succorance r of −.20 in the creativity condition.) Of the fourteen scales which had yielded significant between-group regression-slope differences involving creative uses scores, eleven exhibited significant correlational differences within the creativity condition and one yielded a marginally significant difference ($p < .10$, two-tailed). By way of contrast, none of the corresponding correlational differences in the standard condition was even marginally significant (all p's $> .10$). Clearly, these within-group analyses, in which the Similarities Test functioned as a standard-condition, quasi-parallel form of the Alternate Uses Test, lend substantial support to the conclusion that the observed between-group correlational differences involving creative uses scores were due to the instructional modification rather than to intrinsic between-group differences.

RELATIONSHIPS INVOLVING THE CREATIVE PERSONALITY AND CREATIVE ABILITIES SCALES

As can be seen in Table 20.2 the ACL Creative Personality and Creative Abilities Scales were more strongly related to the production of creative uses in the creativity condition than they were to the production of creative or total uses in the standard condition (all p's $< .05$, two-tailed). Both scales also yielded significant within-group correlational differences involving creative uses r's vs. Similarities Fluency r's in the creativity condition but yielded totally insignificant within-group correlational differences in the standard condition. As expected in the creativity condition, the ACL Creative Ability Scale also correlated more strongly with creative uses scores ($r = +.64$) than with uncreative uses scores ($r = −.03$, $p_{diff} < .001$, one-tailed) or with total uses scores ($r = +.50$, $p_{diff} < .03$, one-tailed) and the ACL Creative Personality Scale also correlated more strongly with creative uses scores ($r = +.69$) than with uncreative uses scores ($r = −.02$, $p_{diff} < .001$, one-tailed) or with total uses scores ($r = +.55$, $p_{diff} < .03$, one-tailed). (The comparisons of correlations involving creative uses and total uses scores appropriately incorporated the fact that creative uses and total uses scores were strongly correlated ($r = +.795$) in the creativity condition.) (McNemar, 1969, p. 158) To the extent that these ACL scales reflected accurate self-assessments of creative thinking abilities, these results support the hypothesis that the coordination of properly designed instructions and qualitative scoring procedures can improve the degree to which a divergent thinking test measures components of creative thinking abilities.

It should be carefully noted that the substantial correlations between the creative personality and creative abilities scales and creative uses production in the creativity condition were not a function of variance shared with the SAT Verbal Aptitude scores. As in previous studies involving young adults and similar tests (Cropley, 1968; Cropley and Maslany, 1969 and Wallach and Wing, 1969), raw fluency was insignificantly related to verbal aptitude in both the standard and creativity conditions (r's = +.14 and +.16, respectively). Verbal aptitude was, however, positively related to creative uses score in both the standard and creativity conditions (r's = +.41 and +.43, respectively; both p's < .01) and was negatively related to uncreative uses scores in the two conditions (r's = −.13 and −.34), significantly so (p < .05) in the creativity condition.

The verbal aptitude index, however, accounted for a very small proportion of the variance shared by the Creative Personality Scale and the creative uses score in the creativity condition and accounted for none of the variance shared by the ACL Creative Ability Scale and the creative uses score. Partialling Verbal Aptitude from the creative uses × ACL Creative Personality relationship among the 44 subjects for whom SAT scores were available reduced that correlation only slightly, from +.69 to +.68. Partialling Verbal Aptitude from the creative uses × ACL Creative Ability relationship left that correlation unchanged (r = +.65). It is clear from these figures that the creative uses score reflected an important dimension to which the SAT Verbal Aptitude score was comparatively insensitive.

THE ROLE OF ACHIEVEMENT MOTIVATION

Though the instructional manipulation did increase the degree to which test performance reflected achievement motivation (as measured by the ACL Achievement Scale), achievement motivation cannot explain away or account for the substantial correlation between creative uses production and the ACL Creative Abilities Scale. While the correlation between creative uses production and the ACL Achievement Scale was very strong in the creativity condition (r = +.54), the correlation between the ACL Creative Abilities Scale and creative uses score, with ACL achievement partialled out, was equally strong (r = +.54, p < .0001).

DIRECTION OF INSTRUCTIONAL EFFECT AS A FUNCTION
OF PERSONALITY CHARACTERISTICS

In the study conducted by Datta (1963), instructions to "be creative" apparently improved the performance of these research scientists who were placed in the upper one-third of their supervisors' creativity ratings and apparently depressed the performance of those scientists who fell in the bottom one-third of the creativity ratings. In an attempt to replicate this aspect of Datta's work, the distribution of ACL Creative Personality Scale scores was trichotomized (on the assumption that this scale was the closest approximation to Datta's on-the-job creativity ratings) and the instructional impact was then analyzed with respect to the three levels of Creative Personality Scale scores. The results were congruent with those reported by Datta. Subjects in the upper third of the Creative Personality Scale performed much better if placed in the creativity condition (an average difference of 5.96 creative uses, $p < .001$), subjects in the middle third of the scale performed somewhat better in the creativity condition (an average difference of 2.64 creative uses, $p < .10$) and, as predicted from Datta's results, subjects in the lower third of the scale performed somewhat less well in the creativity condition (an average decrement of 3.45 creative uses, $p < .03$) (all one-tailed tests). Similarly, subjects in the upper third of the ACL Creative Abilities Scale performed significantly better in the creativity condition ($p < .001$), subjects in the middle third of the scale performed insignificantly better and subjects in the lower third performed insignificantly worse in the creativity condition.

· · ·

Discussion

The correlations involving the ACL Creative Abilities and Creative Personality Scales, like the results reported by Datta (1963), support the hypothesis that properly designed and coordinated test instructions and qualitative scoring criteria can increase the degree to which a divergent thinking test measures components of creative thinking abilities. Furthermore, the correlations involving ACL Achievement Scale and SAT Verbal Aptitude scores indicate that the substantial relationships observed between the ACL Creative Abilities Scale and creative uses production in the creativity condition cannot be accounted for in terms of achievement motivation or traditional measures of verbal aptitude.

While these correlations do suggest that the creativity instructions and qualitatively-oriented scoring procedures functioned better than the standard instructions and the purely quantitatively-oriented scoring procedures, there is also evidence that the creativity instructions need improvement. The analyses which indicated that the creativity instructions depressed the performance of subjects who lacked intellectual self-confidence and who were particularly susceptible to anxiety suggest the operation of an anxiety-arousing component in the creativity instructions. Because optimal test instructions should elicit maximum performances from all subjects, and because anxiety was almost surely depressing the performance of some subjects and may well have been adversely affecting the performance of all subjects to some degree, new instructions should be devised which convey information about the scoring criteria in a non-threatening and possibly encouraging manner. Efforts should then be made to determine whether removing the anxiety-arousing component from informative instructions influences the degree to which subsequently elicited performances reflect creative thinking abilities.

. . .

Obviously, there can be no assurance that the results obtained here with the Alternate Uses Test will be replicated easily or exactly using other divergent thinking tests or other samples. Indeed, the kinds of problems encountered in attempting to develop and coordinate informative test instructions and reliable scoring procedures for the Consequences Test may arise repeatedly in other contexts. The development of optimal instructions and qualitative scoring procedures will certainly have to be undertaken on a test-by-test basis which considers the characteristics of the task, the individuals to be tested and possibly the circumstances and purposes of their assessment. However, because there are good a priori reasons to believe that properly designed and coordinated test instructions and qualitative scoring procedures can increase the degree to which divergent thinking tests measure components of creative thinking abilities, and because those beliefs are now supported by two empirical studies which employed different tests, different instructions, different scoring procedures and different indices of creative thinking abilities, a certain degree of optimism seems warranted.

Summary

The Alternate Uses Test was administered to 50 undergraduate males instructed to produce creative (i.e., novel and worthwhile) uses and to 55 comparable subjects simply instructed to produce as many uses as possible. All uses were rated for creativity. An index of self-assessed creative thinking ability correlated significantly more strongly ($p < .05$) with the number of creative uses produced in the qualitatively-oriented condition than with the number of creative or total uses produced in the standard, quantitatively-oriented condition. The correlation between self-rated creative ability and creative uses production in the qualitatively-oriented condition remained significant ($p < .001$) after indices of achievement motivation and general verbal aptitude were partialled out. The results were interpreted as demonstrating the value of coordinating informative divergent thinking test instructions with qualitative scoring criteria.

X

SEX
DIFFERENCES

This article by Rae Carlson documents differences in men and women in the way they experience and attend to various aspects of their environments. She points out that men and women differ in the kinds of experiences that appear important to them and discusses a theory that can help put the different experiental styles into a coherent framework.

21

Sex Differences in Ego Functioning: Exploratory Studies of Agency and Communion

RAE CARLSON

Contemporary personality research confronts an embarrassment of riches in the extensive evidence of sex differences in personality. How is this knowledge to be assimilated? How is psychosexuality to be understood? The voluminous literature documenting psychological sex differences (Garai and Scheinfeld, 1968; Maccoby, 1966) is far beyond the scope of any single review. However, much of the current status of the field may be summarized by a few assertions which seem to have implications for how sex differences are studied in psychology:

1. Overlapping distributions of males and females are typically found for all dimensions studied (including masculinity–femininity); mean differences occur rather regularly, along with more important sex differences in patterns of relationships. The implications seem to be that strictly dimensional approaches fail to reflect adequately the nature of psychosexuality, and that qualitative, typological approaches are required for the understanding of the nature of sex differences.

Carlson, R. "Sex Differences in Ego Functioning: Exploratory Studies of Agency and Communion." *Journal of Consulting and Clinical Psychology,* 1971, Vol. 37, pp. 267–277. Copyright © 1971 by the American Psychological Association and reprinted by permission.

2. More interrelationships among variables are typically found for males across the widest variety of personality studies. Moreover, the personality research literature, taken as a whole, reflects a serious imbalance in sex composition of S samples, and a neglect of attention to sex differences in personality (Carlson, 1971; Carlson and Carlson, 1960). These observations suggest that the problems, methods, and strategies of research may reflect unintended masculine bias embedded in the conventions of psychological inquiry.

3. Current approaches in personality theory are not capable of dealing with the mounting evidence of biological bases of psychological sex differences (Broverman, Klaiber, Kobayashi, and Vogel, 1968; Hamburg and Lunde, 1966; Zigler and Child, 1968). Psychoanalytic theory notes the anatomical difference between the sexes, but proceeds with a universalistic account of personality in terms of drives, defenses, and structures, while within psychoanalytic literature those formulations potentially capable of illumining problems of psychosexuality (Deutsch, 1944; Erikson, 1950) have not been influential in guiding inquiry. Social learning theories (Mischel, 1966) "explain" sex differences by positing different reinforcement histories for sex-typed response classes, while variations of this approach in social role theories "explain" sex differences by positing different role prescriptions for males and females. Cognitive-developmental approaches (Kohlberg, 1966) appear to have come closest to confronting the basic problem, but workers in this tradition appear to be struggling to account for evidences of constitutional factors and qualitative patterning which intrude upon their investigations rather than pursuing the intrinsic problem.

What seems urgently needed is an approach to sex differences in personality as a focal problem. This, in turn, requires a conceptual framework to guide such inquiry—a conceptualization capable of representing qualitative patterning, of giving a psychological account of constitutional aspects of psychosexuality, and of going beyond a mere restatement of the facts of sex differences to suggest some potential integration of these phenomena in a coherent picture of total human functioning.

Within the past few years, two theoretical formulations have appeared that offer some promise of integrating existing knowledge and directing focused inquiry in this area: Gutmann's (1965) paper on women and the conception of ego strength, and Bakan's (1966) formulation of agency and communion in human sexuality. The present investigation was designed to develop implications of these formulations by testing explicit hypotheses derived from Gutmann's and Bakan's work.

Study I: Sex Differences in Ego Functioning— Gutmann's Formulation

Working within the context of psychoanalytic theory, Gutmann (1965) noted implicit masculine bias in the conception of ego strength, observing that

The ego strength concept ... has more relevance for men than for women, and may even lead to inaccurate judgments of female ego functioning as being regressive and maladaptive. ... Male and female ego functions develop in and are coordinated to significantly different "habitats" ... [p. 229].

Central to Gutmann's formulation is the contrast between two kinds of "maturational milieus" of men and women. Men inhabit an impersonal milieu—whether of business, battlefield, or prairie—a milieu governed by impersonal laws of nature, of economics, of the political order. Women inhabit the personal world of family, neighborhood, community—a milieu governed by familiar forces of feelings, shared expectancies, predictabilities. From such normative sketches of the average expectable environments in which male and female egos develop, Gutmann suggests that different adaptive capacities are relevant to masculine and feminine psychological ecologies.*

Contrasting the phenomenal worlds of males and females in terms of experiences of self and others, space and time, constancy and change, Gutmann examined traditional criteria of ego strength (capacity for delay, future orientation, firm ego boundaries, objectivity) and noted that these criteria are relevant to the masculine world, but essentially irrelevant to the feminine world.

The first study addressed the issues raised by Gutmann by testing four hypotheses derived from this formulation.

SELF AND OTHERS

According to Gutmann's (1965) formulation, in the masculine world "others are a class of objects to be tested and investigated as such. Objectifying others, we also objectify ourselves, and thereby come to experience our own separateness ... ," while in the feminine world "the self derives its definition and its 'names' from the groupings to which it belongs, the distinctions between self and others are blurred over ... [p. 235]," and "we come to know the other and predict the other in terms of [our] wishes ... [p. 237]." Two hypotheses were derived from this formulation:

Hypothesis 1. Males tend to experience and represent the self in individualistic terms; females tend to experience and represent the self in terms of interpersonal relatedness.

---

* Since Gutmann clearly locates the sources of distinctive masculine and feminine styles in cultural rather than constitutional influences ("ego properties we ascribe to women have to do with socialization ... and may owe little to any innate 'femaleness.' ... Male habitués of autocentric enclaves may be as likely as women to display a 'female' ego structure, just as females significantly involved in allocentric concerns may show a 'male' version of ego functioning ... [p. 238]"), the question of possible constitutional bases for cultural arrangements is not addressed.

Hypothesis 2. Males represent others in objective, classifying terms; females represent others in subjective, interpretive terms.

REPRESENTATIONS OF SPACE

Gutmann contrasts male and female experience of the physical environment as follows: In the masculine world "Space tends to be open, a region of channels, pathways, and vistas which do not converge upon the self ... ," while in the feminine world "space is enclosed ... pathways can be experienced as converging toward and radiating from the self ... [p. 234]." Basically, males differentiate self from milieus, while females experience themselves as an intrinsic part of the milieu. This formulation led to the third hypothesis:

Hypothesis 3. Females, more than males, experience and represent the physical environment in "self-centered" terms.

REPRESENTATIONS OF THE FUTURE

Gutmann proposes that the future is differently structured by males and females; in the masculine world "the future is always in doubt ..." and "present security is bolstered by plans ... which represent the future as already mastered . . . ," while in the feminine world "the future can be viewed as a continuation of the present, and change is seen to proceed from one's own personal or shared purposes [p. 236]." This reasoning led to the fourth hypothesis:

Hypothesis 4. Males represent the future in terms of instrumental actions and external change; females represent the future in terms of interpersonal events and inner change.

METHOD

This study was based on a series of investigations conducted over several semesters in the writer's upper-division personality course. Several considerations involved in the use of these data should be noted. The data were not collected with the present hypotheses in mind; while there is some loss of efficiency in the use of such preexisting data, expectancy effects of Ss and E are minimized by this procedure. The nature and setting of the tasks were such as to maximize Ss' motivation, involvement, and candor in responding. The Ss were participating in class projects exploring methods of assessing personality. Tasks were administered in class or as outside assignments; anonymity was guaranteed by a strict coding scheme to enable class use of resulting data in various projects. While students' participation was entirely independent of course grades, virtually all students completed all tasks.

. . .

The Ss included a total of 213 college students and community adults ranging in age from 19 to 55, with considerable diversity in education, socioeconomic, and marital status. The tests of the several hypotheses are based on different subsamples, with Ns ranging from 35 to 82; some overlap of Ss is involved in tests of Hypotheses 3 and 4. When analyses involved qualitative data, Ss' responses were typed on 3 × 5 cars in order to remove possible cues (e.g., handwriting style) to Ss' sex in order to control any rater expectancies. Sex composition of samples, measures, procedures, and results are described in reporting tests of specific hypotheses.

Hypothesis 1

REPRESENTATIONS OF SELF. Self-descriptions on the Carlson Adjective Checklist (Carlson and Levy, 1968) were obtained from 37 males and 39 females. On this instrument an S describes himself by choosing 10 terms from a balanced set of 30 socially desirable adjectives. An S is classified as socially oriented if choices of "social" terms (requiring an implicit social object—e.g., friendly, persuasive, etc.) exceed choices of "personal" terms (which do not require a social object—e.g., ambitious, idealistic, etc.). The prediction that males should describe themselves in individualistic (personal) terms and females in interpersonal (social) terms was evaluated with chi-square comparison. Nineteen of the 37 males, as compared with 32 of the 39 females, described social self-concepts; the chi-square of 6.88 is significant at the .01 level.

. . .

Hypothesis 2

REPRESENTATIONS OF OTHERS. College students (42 males and 40 females) were asked to write "a brief personality sketch of someone you know fairly well." Instructions emphasized that technical terms or concepts were not desired; Ss were asked to use their own spontaneous language in capturing salient aspects of another person.

To test the hypothesis that males represent others in more objective, classifying ways, the first sentence of each personality sketch was scored blindly for the presence or absence of demographic constructs (e.g., "Miss L is a 24-year-old divorcee employed as a stenographer"; "X is a 10-year-old of Japanese ancestry"). Introductory sentences were chosen as the unit of analysis in order to tap salient constructs used by Ss. (Subsequent analyses supported this basic assumption in virtually all cases; if demographic constructs were used at all, they were used in the first sentence.) As predicted, males (22 of 42) were more likely to use demographic constructs in describing another person than were females (7 of 40). The chi-square of 8.1 is significant at the .01 level.

Hypothesis 3

REPRESENTATIONS OF THE PHYSICAL ENVIRONMENT.   The prediction that females should give more "self"-centered representations of space was tested by comparing descriptions of the physical environment of childhood milieus responses to the following item from a six-item Projective Questions instrument: "Describe the physical-geographic environment (community, neighborhood, house, area of country, etc.) where you lived longest during your first ten years."

Discarding responses of seven Ss (4 males and 3 females) who either omitted the question or reported so much moving during early years that no impressions were available, the responses of 23 males and 25 females were categorized as "proximal" or "distal." The nature of the proximal–distal scoring may be best illustrated by typical responses; in order to point up the independence of categorization and sex of respondent, both examples are drawn from responses of male Ss:

Responses were classified as "proximal" if a person-centered representation of space, including personal participant memories of the "insider," was given, as in the following example:

> I lived in a four-story house until it was sold while I was in college. I was born in that house. It was large to me as a child and I haven't seen it very much as an adult. It remains large in my memory. Secret hiding places, large rooms for lots of kids to play and a big yard and a big field behind the house. Trout stream nearby and a huge lake 4 blocks away. Large ravines and tunnels under the streets to play in.

"Distal" responses were descriptions of childhood milieus in terms of environmental features seen from the vantage of the "outsider," as in the following example:

> I lived on the west side of a town which had approximately 300,000 inhabitants. The community was fairly close-knit, and upon occasion there were businessmen's circuses where the local population participated. There were four seasons in this Midwestern city with snow and ice in the winter and a high degree of humidity in the summer. The social range of the neighborhood ran from upper-lower to lower-middle class.

Eight of the 23 males, and 18 of the 25 females gave "proximal" responses; the chi-square of 4.96 is significant at the .05 level.

Hypothesis 4

REPRESENTATIONS OF THE FUTURE.   The prediction that males structure the future in instrumental and external terms, females in expressive, internal terms was tested on data obtained from the same Ss and the same Projective Questions instrument described above. Responses of 27 males and 28 females were obtained to the following item: "What sort of person do you expect to be 15 years from now? What will you be doing? How might you have changed by then?"

Twelve content categories had been previously devised for another purpose, and individual responses scored for presence or absence of each category. The present hypothesis was tested by comparing frequencies of males and females using the instrumental external categories of "work" and "physical change" and the expressive internal categories of "family" and "inner psychological change."

As predicted, the sexes were differentiated in their structuring of the future. Nineteen of 27 males, as compared with 11 of 28 females, used work categories ($\chi^2 = 4.16$, $p < .05$); family was mentioned by 20 of 28 females, but only 9 of 27 males ($\chi^2 = 6.51$, $p < .01$); inner psychological change was mentioned by 19 of 28 females and only 7 of the 27 males ($\chi^2 = 8.05$, $p < .01$). Physical change was mentioned by very small proportions of either sex (6 of 27 males, 3 of 28 females), and the sex difference is not significant.

RESULTS

Overall, the results of Study I clearly supported the qualitative differences in styles and adaptive capacities of males and females proposed by Gutmann. Several samples gave a consistent picture in which males represent experiences of self, others, space, and time in individualistic, objective, and distant ways, while females represent experiences in relatively interpersonal, subjective, immediate ways in responding to a range of common tasks. Thus the data suggest that distinctive masculine and feminine styles, discernible in quite diverse areas, may serve as indicators of different kinds of ego strengths.

While Gutmann's formulation describes important and hitherto neglected patterning of ego functions, at least two aspects of his formulation should be noted as limiting its range: (a) The formulation does not account for the considerable overlap of males and females on different tasks, and (b) the attribution of sex differences to the influence of cultural-ecological factors ignores (and may capitalize upon) innate bases of psychosexuality.

As a basis for further inquiry, a conceptualization is needed which could retain the power of Gutmann's formulation in capturing distinctive qualitative features of masculine and feminine ego functioning while also accounting for the presence of both "male" and "female" qualities within the individual. Further studies attempted exploratory work on such a conceptualization: Bakan's (1966) formulation of agency and communion in human sexuality.

Bakan proposes that a fundamental polarity underlies human existence at all levels from the cellular to the societal—the constructs of agency and communion which Bakan (1966) introduces as follows:

> I have adopted the terms "agency" and "communion" to characterize two fundamental modalities in the existence of living forms, agency for the existence of an organism as an individual, and communion for the participation of the individual in some larger organism of which the individual is a part. Agency manifests itself in self-protection, self-assertion, and self-expansion; communion manifests itself in the sense of being at one with other organisms. Agency manifests itself in the formation of separations; communion in the lack of separations. Agency manifests itself in isolation, alienation, and aloneness; communion in contact, openess, and union. Agency manifests itself in the urge to master; communion in noncontractual cooperation. Agency manifests itself in the repression of thought, feeling, and impulse; communion in the lack and removal of repression.... I conceive of agency and communion at a rather high level of abstraction, as manifested in various ways and in various contexts ... [p. 15].

In Bakan's view, the balance of agency and communion is critical. "Unmitigated agency,"—whether seen in the destructive proliferation of cancer cells, in the isolation and alienation leading the individual to murder or suicide, or in a society's heedless expansion of technology at the expense of human qualities—is the source of evil. Both agency and communion are necessary qualities within any organism; the integration of agency and communion is a developmental task of the individual and a condition for a viable organism or society.

Clearly, the agency-communion conception parallels and derives from such other, more familiar, polarities in psychological thought as those of Freud, Jung, or Angyal. However, the abstractness and comprehensiveness of Bakan's formulation, along with its freedom from a developed theoretical context, lend the agency-communion formulation to focused attempts to translate the polarity into empirical terms.

. . .

Study II: Agency and Communion in Affective Experience

This study sought to test the agency-communion formulation by studying sex differences in representations of affects. Assuming, with Tomkins (1962–1963), that affects are primary motivational constructs and that cognitive-affective dynamics reflect central psychological processes of the person, the operation of agency and communion should be reflected in the qualities of significant emotional experiences remembered by males and females.

The basic hypothesis derived from Bakan's formulation was as follows: Males, as compared with females, express more agentic themes in reporting significant affective arousal; females (on the basis of their presumably greater bisexuality) express more communal and mixed themes in reporting significant affective experiences.

METHOD

As a laboratory assignment in an upper-division personality course, college students reported anonymously critical incidents of seven affects—negative affects of shame, fear, anger, and disgust, and positive affects of joy, excitement, and surprise. Specific instructions to Ss were as follows:

> ... The objective is to get a fairly full description of the one situation in your experience which best exemplifies each of the affective states involved. Record your responses on 8½ × 11 pages with your code number and the affect term which you are reporting at the top of the page.

Affect instances were submitted by 18 males and 23 females; the number of affects reported by individual Ss ranged from 1 to 7, with a mean of 5.9 for males and of 5.5 for females.

Individual affect instances were transferred to cards and each response independently coded as agentic, communal, or mixed. Given the complexity of the theoretical framework, an adequate coding scheme necessarily involved a global, thematic analysis employing raters' judgments. The following instructions and scoring criteria were used:

> Use only one category for each response. Score AGENTIC when the theme concerns achievement, success, risk, intrusion, separateness or aloneness [if welcomed by S], aggression, danger, sexuality as drive or conquest. Score COMMUNAL when the theme concerns social acceptance, togetherness or re-union, receptivity, dependence, altruism, sexuality as belonging. Score MIXED only when both agentic and communal themes are clearly present in a response.

Independent judgments by two professional psychologists agreed in classifying 93% of a sample of 30 affect instances. Completely "blind" judgments were not possible since reports of significant affective experiences necessarily included internal evidence revealing the sex of the S....

RESULTS

A total of 239 affect instances were obtained (109 from males; 130 from females). Overall, 60% of the responses of males were coded agentic, as compared with only 40% of the responses of females. Since different

1umbers of responses were contributed by various Ss, the affect instances :annot be treated as independent events as required for direct statistical est of the predicted sex differences.

However, when the data are collapsed to reflect individuals' scores, a lirect test of the hypothesis is possible. Accordingly, each individual was :lassified as primarily agentic or as communal/mixed as determined by he preponderance of these scores across his own affect responses; four nales and three females with tied scores were omitted from the analysis. ẟmong the remaining Ss, the predicted sex difference emerged clearly. [en of the 14 males were primarily agentic, as compared with only 5 of the ?0 females. The chi-square of 5.44 is significant at the .02 level.

The data further provide suggestive trends in line with other expecta- ions from Bakan's formulation. If "unmitigated agency" represents nox- ous trends in the organism, one would expect agentic themes to be associ- ated with negative affects, and communal themes with positive affects, ·egardless of sex. Of the 133 negative affects reported by the entire sample, ʹ0% were scored agentic, while of the 106 positive affects, 70% were :ommunal/mixed.

Moreover, a Sex × Affective Tone interaction, implicit in Bakan's dis- :ussion, is also suggested by the data. While negative affects are associ- ated with agentic themes overall, this effect appears somewhat stronger in nales: 14 of the 18 males, as compared with only 9 of 22 females, pro- luced agentic themes in reporting negative affects ($\chi^2 = 4.1$, $p < .05$). Conversely, while positive affects are generally associated with communal and mixed themes, this effect is clearer in women: 20 of 22 females, as :ompared with only 11 of 17 males, reported communal and mixed hemes of positive affects. While only one of these additional analyses ʹielded statistically significant findings, both trends are consonant with he formulation.

The results of Study II thus offer clear although modest support for the 1euristic value of Bakan's formulation of psychological sex differences. Iowever, the confirmation of theoretical expectation in the realm of affec- ive experiences provides only a limited test of the range of propositions ¡enerated by the agency-communion formulation, and does not, in itself, ¡upport any conclusions concerning either the comprehensiveness of the :onceptualization or the biological bases of sex differences embedded in he formulation.

...

Discussion

[aken together, the results of ... quite diverse studies—despite their obvi- ɔus limitations of small samples and primitive measures—offer confirma- ion of the basic soundness of Gutmann's and Bakan's conceptualizations.

The findings suggest the possibility of focused inquiry on psychosexuality and the need for serious consideration of issues neglected in current approaches to problems in this area.

The present data offer only limited bases for choosing between the compatible but far from identical formulations of Gutmann and Bakan. Bakan's agency-communion conceptualization could assimilate the predictions and findings of Study I based on Gutmann's formulation. . . While Gutmann's formulation is clearly the better elaborated in portraying the qualities of masculine and feminine ego functioning, Bakan's conceptualization—given more systematic development—seems capable of subsuming it and addressing a wider range of phenomena.

The clear support for the agency-communion formulation provided by the present studies would equally support other theoretical formulations which share its essential features. For example, Erikson's (1950, 1964) discussion of psychosexuality deals conceptually with precisely the issues touched by the present data—the "inside"/"outside" orientations of males and females, and the nature of polarities and their integration through "psychosocial crises," among others—and commands a wealth of clinical and correlational support (cf. Douvan and Adelson, 1966) which needs to be considered in further inquiry.

However, the present study, as an initial empirical test of the agency-communion formulation, encourages further exploration of several other issues posed by Bakan's conceptualization, as well as an examination of its intrinsic problems. Any simple, sovereign theory offers a universal "explanation" of human nature at the risk of eliding critically important differences lying outside its range of convenience. The "agency" of the scientist, the athlete, and the rapist are equivalent only at high levels of abstraction; obviously, much searching inquiry is needed before the nature of agency and communion and the modes of their expression in personality can be fully assessed.

· · ·

SEX DIFFERENCES IN OCCUPATIONAL IDENTITY

Within the realm of work, distinctive masculine and feminine styles of performing comparable roles would be predicted on the grounds that occupations will have quite different meanings when defined in agentic or communal terms. From an extensive literature bearing upon this question, two recent examples may be noted: (a) Masling and Harris' (1969) finding that male clinicians—unlike their female peers—tended to exploit the projective testing situation for (agentic) "voyeuristic" exploration of sexual themes with clients, and (b) Bernard's (1964) demonstration that male and female academicians define their professional identities in different terms, with males using agentic definitions of scholarly prestige and institutional power, and females using more communal definitions in terms of developing students, developing scholarship, and fostering professional goals through institutional service. (As Bernard noted, some of the discrimination against females in academia may stem as much from feminine rejection or disregard of the power-prestige meanings of academic roles as from such factors as economic competition, sexual threat, or differential competence.)

Among the obvious questions for further research stemming from an agency-communion formulation of work roles, several propositions may be advanced:

1. Females should be more effective than males in administrative positions to the extent that feminine definitions of administration (instrumental activity in the service of shared purposes) involve integration of agentic and communal features, while masculine definitions (instrumental activity in the service of order, control, or power) may tend toward "unmitigated agency."

2. Proportions of males and females performing an occupational role should be predictable from the latitude with which the role may be defined in either agentic or communal terms. (For example, the role of physician tends to be predominantly a masculine one in the United States where power, prestige, and income tend to be among its defining characteristics, but a bisexual or even feminine role—as in some European and Asian countries—where "service" connotations are salient.

3. Long-range personal satisfaction and effectiveness in any occupational role should be a function of the opportunities afforded (or used by) the individual for the integration of agentic and communal features. ("Clinical" examples may convey this point: the retired military officer who becomes an educator, the businessman who becomes a minister—among many other relevant examples—suggest such a trend.)

Although further extrapolations of this conceptualization to other problems are obvious, the basic contribution of Bakan's agency-communion theory is clearly heuristic. Considerable work remains to be done in translating the implications of Bakan's theory into explicit hypotheses and operations.

It is clear, however, that an adequate formulation of personality must recognize the existence of stable and well-replicated qualitative differences in personality organization of males and females. An adequate formulation must deal with both the constitutional bases of psychosexuality and with the psychological and social processes involved in integrating the "maleness" and the "femaleness" of the individual in the development of personality structure and in social interactions. The results of the present study suggest that the agency-communion formulation is a promising conceptual framework for such future work.

This article presents more data on the behavioral correlates of masculinity and femininity. Drs. Bem, Martyna, and Watson suggest that males or females who are simultaneously high on measures of masculinity and femininity appear to have the greatest flexibility to respond to either masculine or feminine situations in a positive fashion. There are clear implications here for the view that androgynous individuals (high masculine and high feminine) may be the most mentally healthy.

22

Sex Typing and Androgyny: Further Explorations of the Expressive Domain

SANDRA LIPSITZ BEM, WENDY MARTYNA, AND CAROL WATSON

Both historically and cross-culturally, masculinity and femininity have represented complementary domains of positive traits and behaviors. Different theorists have designated different labels for these domains. According to Parsons (Parsons and Bales, 1955), masculinity has been associated with an "instrumental" orientation, a cognitive focus on getting the job done or the problem solved, whereas femininity has been associated with an "expressive" orientation, an affective concern for the welfare of others and the harmony of the group. Similarly, Bakan (1966) has suggested that masculinity is associated with an "agentic" orientation, a concern for oneself as an individual, whereas femininity is associated with a "communal" orientation, a concern for the relationship between oneself and others.

Bem, S. L., Martyna, W., and Watson, C. "Sex Typing and Androgyny: Further Explorations of the Expressive Domain." *Journal of Personality and Social Psychology*, 1976, Vol. 34, pp. 1016–1023. Copyright © by the American Psychological Association and reprinted by permission.

... The concept of psychological androgyny implies that it is possible for an individual to be both masculine and feminine, both instrumental and expressive, both agentic and communal, depending upon the situational appropriateness of these various modalities; and it further implies that an individual may even blend these complementary modalities into a single act, being able, for example, to fire an employee if the circumstances warrant it, but to do so with sensitivity for the human emotion that such an act inevitably produces.

Empirical research on the concept of androgyny is now beginning to appear in the psychological literature. For example, a more androgynous view of oneself has recently been found to be accompanied by greater maturity in one's moral judgments (Block, 1973) and by a higher level of self-esteem (Spence et al., 1975). In our own laboratory studies, we have found that androgynous individuals not only perform cross-sex behavior with little reluctance or discomfort (Bem and Lenney, 1976) but display both "masculine" independence when under pressure to conform as well as "feminine" nurturance when given the opportunity to interact with a baby kitten (Bem, 1975).

However, for many individuals, traditional sex roles still produce an unnecessary and perhaps even dysfunctional pattern of avoidance, which prevents the possibility of androgyny from ever becoming a reality. For example, in the study by Bem and Lenney (1976), sex-typed individuals not only actively avoided a wide variety of simple, everyday activities (like nailing two boards together or winding a package of yarn into a ball) just because those activities happen to be stereotyped as more appropriate for the other sex, but they also reported discomfort and even some temporary loss of self-esteem when actually required to perform such activities.

Moreover, this pattern of avoidance is not limited to simple, everyday behaviors but appears to constrict the individual's instrumental and expressive functioning as well. Thus, whereas androgynous individuals in the Bem (1975) study displayed high levels of both masculine independence and feminine nurturance, nonandrogynous individuals did not. Rather, masculine males were low in nurturance, and feminine males were low in independence.

Like the nonandrogynous males, the nonandrogynous females were also constricted, but their behavioral patterns were more complicated. As anticipated, masculine females were quite independent, but they were not significantly less nurturant toward the kitten than were androgynous females. Hence, it could not be concluded that the masculine woman was low in her expressive functioning. But it was the behavior of the feminine woman that was the most surprising and the most constricted. Not only was the feminine woman low in independence but she was also low in her nurturance toward the kitten. Of course, it is possible that feminine women might simply find animals unappealing for some reason and that they might therefore display much greater nurturance if they were given the opportunity to interact with another human being rather than with a kitten.

The current investigations represent a further exploration of the expressive domain. In an attempt to give the feminine women a fairer test of their expressive functioning, two additional studies were carried out. Because we wished to clarify whether the feminine woman's low level of nurturance was unique to her interaction with animals, both of these studies were designed to be genuinely interpersonal situations in which the subjects' nurturant sympathies were more likely to be aroused. In addition, because it also seemed possible that feminine women might be insufficiently assertive to act out their nurturant feelings if the situation required that they take responsibility for initiating the interaction, the second study was designed not only to be genuinely interpersonal but also to place the subject into a more passive role that would require very little initiative or improvisation and in which there would be virtually no ambiguity about what a subject ought to do if he or she wished to be nurturant. Accordingly, the first study gave the subject the opportunity to interact with a human baby, and the second required the subject to listen to a fellow student who openly shared some of his or her unhappy emotions.

Experiment 1*

METHOD

Subjects.   Subjects were 84 undergraduates (half males and half females) from Stanford University who participated in the experiment during the winter and spring quarters of 1974. All of the subjects had taken the Bem Sex Role Inventory at the beginning of the quarter, and all had experienced relatively little prior interaction with babies. One third of the subjects had been preselected as masculine, one third as feminine, and one third as androgynous on the basis of the androgyny t ratio, a difference score that measures the extent to which subjects distinguish between masculine and feminine personality characteristics in their self-descriptions. In general, the greater the absolute value of the androgyny t ratio, the more a person is sex typed or sex reversed, with positive scores indicating femininity and negative scores indicating masculinity. The smaller the absolute value of the androgyny t ratio, the more a person is androgynous. An androgynous sex role thus represents the equal endorsement of both masculine and feminine personality characteristics.

---

* Carol Watson was primarily responsible for the design and execution of Experiment 1. She would like to give particular thanks to Fred Bart Astor for his invaluable assistance during all phases of the study. She would also like to express her gratitude to Carol Carpenter, Barbara Finn, Linda Krieger, Lyn Littlefield, Susie Lynn, and Dana McComber for serving long hours as experimenters and coders.

Also participating in the study were 14 babies (10 males and 4 females), each of whom interacted with one representative of each of the six different sex roles. During the experimental sessions, however, each baby was dressed in sex-neutral clothing and was randomly assigned to be introduced to all six subjects either as "David" or as "Lisa." The babies ranged in age from 4½ to 7 months. Naturally, great care was taken to protect the health and well-being of all of the babies who participated.

Dependent Variables.   Subjects were solicited for a study of social responsiveness in infants and were then left alone with a baby for a period of 10 minutes while we observed the interaction from behind a one-way mirror. Specifically, the subject's behavior was time sampled every 10 sec by one of three female coders, all of whom were blind with respect to the subject's sex role and all of whom observed an approximately equal number of masculine, androgynous, and feminine subjects of each sex. For each subject, the coder made 60 3-sec observations. The following six behaviors were coded as present or absent: Was the subject smiling directly at the baby? Was the subject talking to the baby? Was the subject kissing or nuzzling the baby? Was the subject holding the baby chest to chest? Was the subject stimulating the baby in a way that involved touching (e.g., tickling, patting, stretching)? Was the subject stimulating the baby in a way that did not involve touching (e.g., shaking a rattle, squeaking a toy)? These behavioral measures were all highly reliable, with two independent coders agreeing perfectly on over 90% of the observations for each measure. Moreover, because only nonphysical stimulation was negatively correlated with the other behaviors ($r = -.13$), a summary measure of behavioral nurturance was constructed by averaging together the standard score equivalents of the remaining five behaviors. The mean intercorrelation of these behaviors was $+.24$, yielding an internal reliability (coefficient alpha) of $+.62$ (Nunnally, 1967) for the composite.

In order to derive a summary measure of subjects' self-reported feelings of nurturance toward the baby, we also averaged together the subject's ratings on seven written questions asked at the end of the study. These questions asked such things as how positive the subject's feelings were toward the baby and how much the subject wanted to be affectionately responsive to the baby. The mean intercorrelation among these items was $+.32$, yielding an internal reliability of $+.82$ for the composite.

RESULTS

Both the summary measure of behavioral nurturance and the summary measure of subjects' self-reported feelings of nurturance were analyzed by means of a 2 (Sex of Subject) × 3 (Sex Role of Subject) × 2 (Assigned Sex of Baby) analysis of variance, as well as by a series of planned comparisons. The two orthogonal comparisons to be tested were the following: (a) that feminine and androgynous subjects would both be significantly more nurturant to the baby than masculine subjects and (b) that feminine and androgynous subjects would not differ significantly from one another in this regard.

The results of the overall analysis of variance indicated a significant main effect only for the baby's assigned sex, with David receiving more behavioral nurturance than Lisa, $F(1, 72) = 6.32, p < .02$.* Thus, the predicted effect of the subject's sex role did not reach significance in the overall analysis of variance for either of the dependent measures, nor did it reach significance in the planned comparisons. Accordingly, our hypotheses with respect to sex role failed to receive confirmation.

As Spence et al. (1975) have pointed out, however, our use of a difference score to define androgyny serves to obscure a potentially important distinction between those individuals who score high in both masculinity and femininity and those individuals who score low in both. Moreover, they argued that those individuals who score low in both masculinity and femininity should not even be included in the group defined as androgynous. In accordance with this suggestion, the androgynous subjects in this study were subdivided on a post hoc basis into those who were below the Stanford median in both masculinity and femininity, henceforth labeled "undifferentiated," and those who were not. As a supplement to the analyses described earlier, the summary measure of behavioral nurturance was reanalyzed by means of a 2 (Sex of Subject) × 4 (Sex Role of Subject) × 2 (Assigned Sex of Baby) analysis of variance for unequal cell frequencies as well as by the same set of planned comparisons described earlier.

The results of this reanalysis revealed a significant main effect of the subject's sex role, $F(3, 68) = 2.67, p = .05$, with mean scores of $-.19$, $-.15$, $+.18$, and $+.16$ for the undifferentiated, masculine, androgynous, and feminine subjects, respectively. Moreover, planned comparisons indicated that as predicted, masculine subjects were significantly less nurturant toward the baby than feminine or androgynous subjects, $t(68) = 2.12, p < .05$, and furthermore, that feminine and androgynous subjects did not differ significantly from one another, $t(68) < 1$, ns. Finally, there was a trend for androgynous subjects to be more nurturant toward the baby than undifferentiated subjects, $t(68) = 1.73, p < .10$.†

Although these supplementary results can only be seen as suggestive, they do serve to replicate conceptually our earlier finding (Bem, 1975) that feminine and androgynous males were more nurturant toward a kitten

---

* An analysis of the individual behaviors further revealed that David was held chest to chest more than Lisa, $F(1, 72) = 5.81, p < .02$, and that he was also physically stimulated more than Lisa, $F(1, 72) = 4.86, p < .03$. Perhaps college students think that baby girls are too fragile to be manipulated physically.

† All probability levels for the t values in this article are based on two-tailed tests of significance. In addition, because of unequal cell frequencies in some comparisons, all comparisons for the sexes combined are based on individual cell means for males and females considered separately.

than masculine males; they also suggest that the feminine woman's low level of nurturance was situation specific and probably resulted from having her interact with an animal rather than with another human being.

Experiment 2*

The supplementary results of Experiment 1 offer tentative support to the hypothesis that feminine and androgynous subjects of both sexes are more nurturant than masculine subjects. Experiment 2 represents an attempt to test this hypothesis still further. Because it seemed possible that feminine women might be most capable of acting out all of their nurturant feelings in a situation where they did not have to take responsibility for initiating and sustaining the interaction, as they had to do with both the kitten and the baby, the situation in Experiment 2 was designed not only to be genuinely interpersonal but also to place the subject into a more passive or responsive role. Accordingly, Experiment 2 was designed to evoke sympathetic and supportive listening on the part of the subject but, at the same time, did not require the subject to play an active or initiating role in the interaction.

METHOD

Subjects.   Subjects were 84 undergraduates (half males and half females) from Stanford University who participated in the experiment during the spring quarter of 1974. All had taken the Bem Sex Role Inventory at the beginning of the quarter, with one third of each sex preselected as masculine, one third as feminine, and one third as androgynous on the basis of the androgyny t ratio.

Three undergraduate experimenters and four undergraduate confederates also participated in the study. They interacted with subjects of their own sex only, were blind with respect to the subjects' sex roles, and interacted with approximately equal numbers of masculine, androgynous, and feminine subjects.

Procedure.   Two males or two females, one of whom was a subject and one of whom was a confederate, participated together in a study whose alleged purpose was to find out "whether you begin to feel close to another

* Wendy Martyna was primarily responsible for the design and execution of Experiment 2. She would like to give particular thanks to Dorothy Ginsberg, a senior honors student in psychology who collaborated in every phase of the study. She would also like to express her gratitude to the experimenters, Richard Rector, Janet Langston, and Maria Rodriguez, who also coded the subjects' nonverbal behavior and helped in scheduling subjects for the experimental sessions, and to the confederates, Sharon Biagi, Susan Mercure, Fred Behling, and John Mensinger, who also coded the subjects' nonverbal behavior and aided in the debriefing.

person primarily because of the things you learn about the other person, or primarily because of the things you tell that other person about yourself." The two "subjects" drew lots to allegedly determine who would take the role of "talker" and who, the role of "listener," but in fact, the confederate always served as the talker and the subject always served as the listener. The experimenter explained that the talker's role was simply to talk about himself or herself for approximately 10 minutes. The talker was told to begin with some general background information and, at the experimenter's signal, to move on to more personal material. In contrast, the listener's role was primarily to listen. Thus, the listener was allowed to ask questions or make comments but never to shift the focus of the conversation to himself or herself.

After explaining the roles of talker and listener, and after pointing out that he or she would be able to hear the conversation from behind the one-way mirror, the experimenter left the room. At that point, the talker began, somewhat shyly and nervously, to deliver a memorized script. The first half of the script dealt with relatively casual background information (e.g., major, hometown, summer job, new apartment, etc.), whereas the second half was more personal. In general, the talker described himself or herself as a recent and rather lonely transfer student to Stanford University. He or she talked about problems such as missing old friends, the difficulty of making new friends now that cliques had already been established, and having to spend more time alone than he or she would have liked. In short, the talker described feelings common to many new transfer students. He or she did not seem neurotic, just somewhat isolated, and rather pleased to have this opportunity to share some of his or her feelings with another person.

After the talker had finished, the experimenter returned with questionnaires for the two "subjects" to fill out. He or she mentioned that the experiment was now over and that the subjects were no longer expected to play the roles of talker and listener. The subjects were then left alone in the room again while they filled out their questionnaires.

After they had both finished filling out their questionnaires but before the experimenter had returned to the room, the confederate/talker turned to the subject and said, "I really feel better after talking to you. It's too bad we didn't get a chance to talk longer." This statement was designed to provide the subject with his or her only opportunity to be responsive outside of the listener role. Following the subject's response, the experimenter returned to the room and began the debriefing process.

Dependent Variables. As in Experiment 1, a summary measure of behavioral nurturance was developed by averaging together the standard score equivalents of five individual behaviors. The intercorrelations among these behaviors were all positive, with a mean of $+.19$, thereby yielding an internal reliability (coefficient alpha) of $+.54$ for the composite. The five behaviors were as follows:

1, 2. HEAD NODS AND FACIAL REACTIONS (NONVERBAL RESPONSIVENESS). Listeners who nodded their heads or changed their facial expression in response to what the talker was saying seemed, in most instances, to be listening to the talker and to be involved. Accordingly, the experimenter time sampled the subject's behavior every 15 sec and recorded whether or not each of these two behaviors occurred. Both measures were highly reliable, with two independent coders agreeing perfectly on over 93% of the 40 5-sec observations for each behavior.*

3. VERBAL RESPONSIVENESS. Although the listener was instructed to keep the focus of the conversation on the talker, he or she was allowed to ask questions and to make comments. Moreover, if the subject had said nothing during the entire 10 minutes, the interaction would have been very strained and the talker would have been made to feel extremely uncomfortable. Accordingly, the interaction was recorded on audiotape and was later scored for the subject's number of verbalizations. This measure was highly reliable, with a correlation of +.92 between two independent coders.

4. POSITIVE REACTION TO THE TALKER'S IMPLICIT REQUEST FOR FURTHER CONTACT. The subject's response to the statement, "I really feel better after talking to you; it's too bad we didn't get a chance to talk longer," was coded into one of five categories: (1) no response, (2) acknowledgement that the talker had spoken, (3) sympathetic response, (4) interest expressed in getting together again, and (5) specific time offered for getting together again. Independent coding yielded 100% perfect agreement on this measure.

5. DEGREE OF NURTURANCE AS PERCEIVED BY OTHERS. Both the experimenter and the confederate/talker independently rated the subject on a 5-point scale in terms of "how nurturant" he or she had been to the talker. Because they agreed within a single scale point on 96% of the subjects, their ratings were averaged together.

In addition, in order to derive a summary score of subjects' self-reported feelings of nurturance toward the talker, we also averaged together the subject's ratings on four written questions that asked "how close" the subject felt to the talker, "how much of a real identification or empathy" he or she felt with the talker, "how concerned" he or she felt about the talker, and "how eager" he or she would be to talk to the talker "in a real situation (not an experiment)." The scale ranged from 1 (not very much) to 6 (extraordinarily). The mean intercorrelation among these items was +.63, yielding an internal reliability of +.87 for the composite.

---

* We also attempted to code eye contact during the conservation, but because virtually every subject made eye contact during every observation period, this variable was eliminated from further analysis.

RESULTS

The composite measure of behavioral nurturance, the individual nurturant behaviors, and the subjects' self-reported feelings of involvement with the talker were all analyzed by means of a 2 (Sex of Subject) × 3 (Sex Role of Subject) analysis of variance as well as by a series of planned comparisons. The two orthogonal comparisons to be tested were as follows: (a) that feminine and androgynous subjects would both be more nurturantly responsive to the talker than would masculine subjects and (b) that feminine and androgynous subjects would not differ significantly from one another in this regard.*

The first rows of Tables 22.1 and 22.2 present the mean scores on the composite measure of behavioral nurturance for the masculine, androgynous, and feminine males and females, respectively. As the tables suggest, there was a significant main effect of the subject's sex role for this measure, $F(2, 78) = 6.55, p = .003$, with mean nurturance scores of $-.29$, $+.04$, and $+.25$ for the masculine, androgynous, and feminine subjects, respectively. Moreover, planned comparisons indicated that, as predicted, masculine subjects were significantly less nurturant than feminine or androgynous subjects, $t(78) = 3.37$, $p < .002$, and furthermore, that feminine and androgynous subjects did not differ significantly from one another, $t(78) = 1.38$, ns. This pattern of results replicates the supplementary findings of Experiment 1, in which subjects interacted with a baby.

An analysis of the individual measures that were scored during the subject's interaction with the talker provides a close-up of what behaviors most differentiated the three groups of subjects. The lower portions of Tables 22.1 and 22.2 display the means for each of these measures. The overall analyses of variance revealed significant or near-significant main effects of the subject's sex role for head nods, $F(2, 78) = 3.08, p = .05$, for verbalizations, $F(2, 78) = 3.05$, $p = .05$, and for the global rating of nurturance given to the subject by the experimenter and the talker, $F(2, 78) = 2.76$, $p < .07$. In addition, planned comparisons for each of these measures indicated that masculine subjects were significantly less nurturant than feminine or androgynous subjects, $t(78) \geq 2.14$, in each comparison, $p < .05$; and furthermore, that feminine and androgynous subjects did not differ significantly from one another. Finally, with respect to subjects' self-reported feelings of nurturance toward the talker, feminine

---

* In parallel with the data analysis of Experiment 1, the data from Experiment 2 were also reanalyzed with the androgynous subjects subdivided on a post hoc basis into those who were below the masculinity and femininity medians and those who were not. In contrast with Experiment 1, however, no consistent differences emerged between the androgynous and "undifferentiated" subjects in Experiment 2. Perhaps this is because the supportive listening situation did not require the subject to play an active or initiating role in the interaction. In any case, these supplementary analyses are not discussed further.

Table 22.1

Male nurturance toward a lonely fellow student

Measure	Subject		
	Masculine	Androgynous	Feminine
Summary			
Observed nurturance	−.43	−.04	+.05
Self-reported nurturance*	3.45	3.80	3.64
Individual			
Global rating†	2.6	3.0	3.1
Verbalizations	42.1	56.1	60.4
Behavioral offer†	3.1	3.5	3.3
Head nods‡	17.1	18.3	19.9
Facial reactions‡	8.7	10.4	11.4

Note: For all subjects, n = 14.
* Max = 6.
† Max = 5.
‡ Max = 40.

Table 22.2

Female nurturance toward a lonely fellow student

Measure	Subject		
	Masculine	Androgynous	Feminine
Summary			
Observed nurturance	−.16	+.11	+.43
Self-reported nurturance*	3.59	3.45	4.13
Individual			
Global rating†	2.8	3.1	3.3
Verbalizations	51.6	61.8	64.1
Behavioral offer†	2.9	3.1	3.4
Head nods‡	19.6	22.9	27.1
Facial reactions‡	12.5	12.2	15.0

Note: For all subjects, n = 14.
* Max = 6.
† Max = 5.
‡ Max = 40.

women described themselves as feeling significantly more nurturant than androgynous women, $t(78) = 2.18$, $p < .05$, but none of the other planned comparisons approached significance for either sex, nor was there a significant main effect of sex role for this variable.

. . .

General Discussion

INSTRUMENTAL AND EXPRESSIVE FUNCTIONING

As noted in the introduction to this article, the two studies reported here represent an attempt to broaden the empirical base upon which our earlier conclusions about sex typing and androgyny were founded. Although the results that emerged from the reanalysis of the baby study can only be seen as suggestive by themselves, the two studies taken together conceptually replicate the low nurturance of the masculine male, and even more importantly, they demonstrate that the low nurturance of the feminine female does not extend beyond her interaction with animals.

In addition, we would now like to pull together all of our findings on the instrumental and expressive domains in an attempt to reach some tentative conclusions about the effects of sex typing and androgyny. We will begin with the men because their data have been so consistent. Quite simply, only androgynous males were high in both the instrumental and the expressive domains; that is, only androgynous males were found to stand firm in their opinions as well as to cuddle kittens, bounce babies, and offer a sympathetic ear to someone in distress.

In contrast, the feminine male was low in independence, while the masculine male was low in nurturance. Because at least one third of college-age males are classified as masculine, it is noteworthy that masculine males were lower in nurturance than androgynous or feminine males whether they were interacting with a kitten, a baby, or a lonely fellow student. In other words, they were relatively low in nurturance in all of the diverse situations that we designed to evoke their more tender emotions—to tug, if only a little, on their heartstrings.

The results for women are less consistent, but the same general pattern emerges. Only androgynous women were high in both independence and nurturance; feminine women were low in independence; and masculine women were (in two situations) low in nurturance. Thus, for both men and women, sex typing does appear to restrict one's functioning in either the instrumental or the expressive domains. Masculine individuals of both sexes are high in independence but low in nurturance, and feminine individuals of both sexes are high in nurturance but low in independence. In contrast, androgynous individuals of both sexes are capable of being both independent and nurturant, both instrumental and expressive, both masculine and feminine.

This brief article by Margaret Backman deals with differences in ability patterns as a function of sex, socioeconomic status, and ethnicity. The results are remarkable, in that sex differences in patterns of ability are much greater than reported previously, while ethnicity and socioeconomic status account for only a negligible proportion of the variance. Previous studies like this one have usually used younger subjects, where sex differences are not so distinct.

23

Patterns of Mental Abilities of Adolescent Males and Females from Different Ethnic and Socioeconomic Backgrounds

MARGARET E. BACKMAN

Several years ago, Lesser, Fifer, and Clark (1965) and Stodolsky and Lesser (1967) found that first-grade children exhibit patterns of mental abilities characteristic of their ethnic group. For a given ethnic group, the shape of the pattern remained the same regardless of socioeconomic status (SES); children of lower SES, however, tended to have lower scores on all the abilities measured. Lesser et al. also reported that "no marked pattern differences emerged when boys and girls were compared [p. 65]."

Although previous research has shown that by adolescence, males and females do exhibit different patterns of mental abilities, little is known about the relationship of ethnicity and SES to these patterns. Thus, the present study was designed to examine the patterns of mental abilities of adolescent males and females from different ethnic and SES backgrounds.

Backman, M. E. "Patterns of Mental Abilities of Adolescent Males and Females From Different Ethnic and Socioeconomic Backgrounds." *Proceedings, 79th Annual Convention,* 1971.

Method

SUBJECTS

The Ss were twelfth graders from among those who had participated in Project TALENT, a nationwide study conducted in 1960. The present sample was restricted to those who had responded to a follow-up survey 5 yr. after graduation, as Project TALENT had not obtained information on ethnic background until that time. The sample was composed of 1,236 Jewish-whites, 1,051 non-Jewish-whites, 488 Negroes, and 150 Orientals.

The SES Index has a mean of 100 and a standard deviation of 10 for twelfth graders (Shaycoft, 1967, Appendix E). In order to have sufficient numbers of Ss from each ethnic group at each level of SES studied, the sample was restricted to the middle range of the SES scale and divided into two groups: lower-middle SES and upper-middle SES, i.e., 80–99 and 100–119, respectively, on the SES scale.

The index was based on the following information: father's occupation and education, mother's education, family income, value of the home, availability of own room and desk, number of books in the home, and access to specific appliances, such as a television and telephone.

PATTERNS OF MENTAL ABILITIES

Group means on six mental ability factors were examined for the presence of patterns in the specific ethnic, SES, and sex groups. The factors have means of 50 and standard deviations of 10 for high school students (Lohnes, 1966). The factors are (a) verbal knowledges (VKN)—a general factor, but primarily a measure of general information; (b) English language (ENG)—grammar and language usage; (c) mathematics (MAT)—high school mathematics with a minimum of computation; (d) visual reasoning (VIS)—reasoning with spatial forms; (e) perceptual speed and accuracy (PSA)—visual-motor coordination under speeded conditions; (f) memory (MEM)—short-term recall of verbal symbols.

PROCEDURES

The statistical model was an analysis of variance (Block, Levine, and McNemar, 1951). The level of a pattern of mental abilities was computed by averaging a group's mean scores on the six factors; differences among groups in the levels of their patterns were reflected by the main effects of ethnicity, SES, and sex, and their interactions. The shape of a pattern refers to the rank order of a group's mean scores and the extent to which these mean scores differ; differences among groups in the shapes of their patterns were reflected by the interactions of ethnicity, SES, and sex with the mental ability factors.

Estimates of the proportion of the total variance accounted for by the main effects and interactions of the variables (ω^2) were computed (Hays, 1963, pp. 406–407).

Table 23.1

Patterns of mental abilities of ethnic, SES, and sex groups

Group	Mental abilities					
	VKN	ENG	MAT	VIS	PSA	MEM
Ethnicity*						
Jewish-white						
$\overline{X}$	57.1	50.8	58.6	46.0	51.0	47.8
$SE\overline{X}$	.3	.2	.7	.4	.5	.2
Non-Jewish-white						
$\overline{X}$	51.9	51.1	52.1	51.8	49.5	50.9
$SE\overline{X}$	.3	.2	.3	.2	.4	.3
Negro						
$\overline{X}$	46.0	47.5	47.3	45.1	50.9	50.4
$SE\overline{X}$	.7	.6	.6	.4	.8	.6
Oriental						
$\overline{X}$	49.0	52.5	59.1	49.4	50.3	51.6
$SE\overline{X}$	.6	.7	1.2	.9	.7	1.1
SES†						
Upper-middle						
$\overline{X}$	53.0	50.6	56.2	48.9	50.5	50.0
$SE\overline{X}$	.4	.4	.5	.4	.5	.5
Lower-middle						
$\overline{X}$	49.0	50.3	52.4	47.2	50.3	50.3
$SE\overline{X}$	.3	.3	.6	.4	.4	.3
Sex†						
Male						
$\overline{X}$	53.7	40.9	63.9	54.5	49.1	44.3
$SE\overline{X}$	.4	.4	.6	.3	.5	.5
Female						
$\overline{X}$	48.3	60.0	44.6	41.7	51.7	56.0
$SE\overline{X}$	.3	.3	.5	.5	.4	.4

* Data based on 16 replicated samples per group.
† Data based on 32 replicated samples per group.

Replicated sampling was used to obtain equal cell frequencies (Cochran, 1963, pp. 383–385; Hays, 1963, p. 408). According to this procedure, Ss within each of the 16 subgroups (Ethnicity × SES × Sex) were randomly divided into four replicated samples. Group means were computed by summing over replicated samples. Standard errors of the mean (Table 23.1) were derived from pooled estimates of error variance, based on deviations of the means of the four replicated samples from their own means.

Results

Ninety percent of the total variance was accounted for by the main effects and interactions of the variables. Statistical relationships accounting for 2% or less of the total variance were considered too weak to be important.

Differences between the patterns of mental abilities of males and females were more marked than were differences among the patterns of ethnic or SES groups (Table 23.1). Considering differences in shape alone, sex accounted for 69% of the total variance, ethnicity 9%, and SES 1%. Considering differences in level alone, sex accounted for 0% of the total variance, ethnicity 4%, and SES 1%.

Females received their highest mean scores on ENG, PSA, and MEM; males received their highest mean scores on VKN, MAT, and VIS (Table 23.1). The pattern of mental abilities of Jewish-whites was characterized by high mean scores on VKN and MAT, Negroes on PSA and MEM, and Orientals on MAT. As the factor scores had been standardized on a sample that was predominantly non-Jewish-white, there was little variation among the mean scores of that group.

Conclusions

A comparison of the results of the present study with those of Lesser et al. (1965) suggests that differences between the sexes on specific mental abilities become more marked with age.

The twelfth-grade students exhibited patterns of mental abilities characteristic of their sex; these patterns were only slightly modified by ethnic background. Differences in the patterns related to SES—although statistically significant—were judged too small to be important. The weak relationship found between SES and the patterns of mental abilities may have been related to the restricted range of SES studied; twelfth graders—particularly the present sample—are more homogeneous in terms of SES than is the general population.

It should be pointed out that the present study was not designed to answer questions regarding heredity and environment, and there is no way to determine the contributions of heredity and environment to differences among the groups on the mental ability factors.

ACKNOWLEDGMENT   This investigation used the Project TALENT Data Bank, a cooperative effort of the United States Office of Education, the American Institutes for Research, and the University of Pittsburgh. The design and interpretation of the research reported in this article, however, are solely the responsibility of the author.

XI

INTELLIGENCE
AND AGING

This selection provides a comprehensive review of information on the changes in abilities that occur as people age. Dr. Botwinick shows that the first signs of intellectual decline occur much later than previously thought and that some abilities seem to be spared until very late. Additionally, the author unravels the complex methodological problems associated with conducting longitudinal and cross-sectional studies.

24

Intellectual Abilities

JACK BOTWINICK

Does Intelligence Decline in Old Age?

An earlier review of studies on intellectual abilities was introduced with the question: "Does intelligence decline in old age?" It was followed by the statement: "Is the study of aging, no problem has received greater attention than that of intelligence; yet in spite of the abundance of research data gathered, many questions remain" (Botwinick, 1967, p. 1). This statement notwithstanding, the introductory question was largely rhetorical since evidence was mustered that many, but not all, abilities do decline with age. Wechsler (1958, p. 135) was even more emphatic: "nearly all studies ... have shown that most human abilities ... decline progressively after ... ages 18 and 25."

Since then more research data have been added to the already abundant literature, yet the initial question, "Does intelligence decline in old age?" no longer is rhetorical. There is a growing controversy as to the answer, or, at least, to what its emphasis ought to be. For example, Green (1969, p. 618) wrote: "It is surprising that ... (so much evidence) ... has not seri-

Botwinick, J. "Intellectual Abilities." In J. E. Birren and K. W. Schaie (eds.). *Handbook of the Psychology of Aging.* New York: Van Nostrand-Reinhold Company, 1977, pp. 580–605. Copyright © 1977 by Litton Educational Publishing, Inc., and reprinted by permission of Van Nostrand-Reinhold Company.

ously eroded belief in the decline hypothesis. . . . It seems that if belief in the decline hypothesis is to be finally discouraged, Wechsler's work (of decline) will have to be directly attacked." In like manner, several important articles emphasizing little or no decline with age have become prominent; each could be described by the title of one of them—"Aging and IQ: The Myth of the Twilight Years" (Baltes and Schaie, 1974). Others have lined up on the "no decline" side of the controversy; it catches the imagination and seems to please.

Nevertheless, after reviewing the available literature, both recent and old, the conclusion here is that decline in intellectual ability is clearly part of the aging picture. The more recent literature, however, is bringing attention to what has been under-emphasized in the older literature, viz., these declines may start later in life than heretofore thought and they may be smaller in magnitude; they may also include fewer functions.

Controversy as to whether intelligence declines in old age centers around several related factors, which, unfortunately, are often overlooked. Among these factors are inconsistencies regarding (1) what is meant by age or aging, (2) types of tests used, (3) definitions of intelligence, (4) sampling techniques, and (5) research methods and their pitfalls.

AGE AND AGING

Generalizations as to whether intelligence declines with age depend upon where in the age spectrum one chooses to look. Historically, intelligence testing was begun in the early part of this century and was largely directed to assessing the ability of children in order to predict school achievement. The concept of mental age (MA) was evolved as was the concept of IQ that was related to it. These concepts were instrumental in spuriously pointing to a decline in intelligence beginning as early in life as the teens.

It was natural for child psychologists, now called developmental psychologists, to extend their interests to adults. Using different tests and different concepts of IQ, they soon discovered that intellectual decline is not a teenage phenomenon. It is hard now to believe that it was not until the mid-1950s that this was clearly demonstrated (Bayley, 1955). Based on periodic testings of children grown to adulthood, Bayley reported that growth continued to at least age 36; she even developed a "theoretical curve of the growth of intelligence" to demonstrate this (Bayley, 1970). Her studies were most impressive to child psychologists raised in the tradition of MA and the related IQ concept. But psychologists not reared in this tradition seemed less impressed with constancy or even rise in test scores to age 36, or even to age 50 as indicated by later studies. For psychologists interested in the later years—for gerontologists—50 might be a starting point to look for age patterns, not an end point.

It is clear that in what is meant by age and aging, vastly different conclusions will be drawn. Between ages 20 and 40, and between 60 and

80, different age patterns hold. Those who argue for "no decline" in intellectual ability often focus either on the earlier adult years or on "life span" data. Those arguing for "decline" may point to the later years. If ameliorative measures are possible for the elderly, then the later years are where the focus may best be.

TYPES OF TESTS USED

Generalizations as to whether intelligence declines with age also depend upon the types of tests used. It is very clear that however intelligence may be defined, the specific test used is crucial to what inferences and generalizations will or may be drawn: some functions peak early and are maintained well into old age, others may show recession beginning in early adulthood. Clearly, inferences and generalizations regarding intellectual ability would be very different if only tests of the first kind were given, and not the other. Test scores which fall with age often involve perceptual-motor and speed functions; those holding with age tend to involve verbal functions. The reasons for emphasizing one set of functions and not the other relates to the definition of intelligence. Not everyone agrees that perceptual-motor and speed functions are part of what is called intelligence. This will be elucidated later.

DEFINING INTELLIGENCE

Different Views.   Most everyone seems to know what is meant by intelligence, but efforts to provide a formal definition that is both meaningful and useful are elusive. On one extreme, intelligence is an unseen, inferred attribute of a person, part or all of which is genetically given. Experience and biological change modify the basic potentialities, but precisely how and how much is not easily determined. The emphasis is on *capacity*—a theoretical limit when health, educational opportunity, social background, motivation, and other factors do not detract from performance. An alternate definition of intelligence focuses on *ability* rather than capacity. Nothing is said here of potential or biological limit. The emphasis is simply on what a person can do now—at the present time of testing.

Generalizations and inferences of test performances may take forms related to definitions of intelligence. One can make inferences regarding capacity; it is here that controversy and emotionality are most severe. Another type of inference is of ability. Thus, for example, old people doing well on Vocabulary tests and poorly on Digit Symbol tests may suggest that broad, general verbal skills are performed well and perceptual-integrative ones are not. Knowing this, jobs, roles, problems needing aid and improvement are highlighted for meaningful decision. No reference need be made to capacity, or to intellectual potential, or even to biological change; certainly no reference need be made to genetic determination. This emphasis on relative ability should encourage emphasis on ameliorative change and should minimize controversy.

Modifiers. There is no question that the test performances of the elderly are modified or altered by a large number of important factors. What these modifiers mean depends on whether the issue is one of capacity or ability. For example, Furry and Baltes (1973) investigated what they called an "ability-extraneous" variable—in this case, test fatigue. They showed that older people may tire in the course of extended testing and this could impair their performances.

These results indicate that inferences regarding intelligence (capacity) are wrong if reference is not made to the modifying fatigue factor. However, if intellectual performance in the ability sense is stressed, then fatigue is not "ability-extraneous." Older people in their work roles, in retraining programs, must account for their fatigability—it is part of their overall intellectual skill. Roles and functions that do not permit proper rest are to be avoided or minimized if intellectual performance is to be of a high level. Further research questions may then be directed to the issue of fatigability, but efforts to ignore or negate this modifying factor may well be harmful.

There are many other test performance modifiers, among which are education, socioeconomic status, and cohort or cultural-generational factors. They are so important, in fact, that they can be more important than age itself in test performance. Birren and Morrison (1961), for example, reported a higher correlation between intelligence test scores and education level than between these scores and age. Others have also emphasized the role of education (e.g., Granick and Friedman, 1973). Modifiers such as education and fatigue have different meaning when intelligence is viewed in the ability sense than when viewed as capacity.

SAMPLING TECHNIQUES

Just as the specific tests and evaluation of modifiers are crucial in forming generalizations regarding intellectual ability, so are the criteria of subject recruitment for investigation. For example, choosing subjects of specific education levels can alter age relationships drastically.

Green (1969) compared cross-sectional age curves based on subjects who were recruited by stratified random selection to age curves based on subjects matched for education level. The random sample reflected overall age decline, while the matched education sample did not. Which is the more correct?

Again, if intelligence in the sense of capacity is meant, then the matched groups might be given emphasis. If intellectual ability as it is distributed currently in the "real world" is the concern, then the random sample is to be emphasized. Any random sampling of people of different ages would likely result in samples of decreasing education level with increasing age of group. This reality exists now; it may not exist in the future. Now, it has to be said that older people, as they have been educated, tend to be lower in ability as measured by a particular test such as the WAIS.

Sampling problems are present in longitudinal research also. A main one is selective subject dropout (mentioned briefly in the next section and discussed fully later). The specific samples of subjects that are examined and, to an extent, the particular age pattern that is observed, depend on when in the course of time in the longitudinal research one chooses to analyze the data.

RESEARCH METHODS

The problem of subject sampling relates to the issue of method of investigation used in aging research, i.e., cross-sectional or longitudinal. And the method used has a direct bearing on the controversy regarding intelligence and age; the method relates to what the results may be. The cross-sectional method may spuriously magnify age decline, and the longitudinal method may minimize it.

The cross-sectional method may even manufacture age decline because the different age groups have their origins and upbringing in different eras. A cohort born in 1900, for example, may score less well on a test than a cohort born in 1950, not because of being older but because of social and educational experiences less adequate for good test performance. Thus, a presumed age effect may be due to cohort experience. However, this argument in extreme form fails to recognize the obvious fact that cohort and age are inseparable; at best, only approximations to the isolation of the two effects are possible. In the world outside the laboratory where abstractions differentiating between cohort and age do not exist, age and cohort are one. Age is not synonymous with biology, nor is cohort synonymous with sociocultural influences.

Negative age patterns tend to be less apparent in longitudinal research than in cross-sectional research. One reason for this is the selective subject dropout, noted earlier. Not all individuals remain equally available for retest; it is mainly the more able ones who are available, thus providing the investigator with increasingly biased samples for examination as the age of the sample subjects increases (e.g., Riegel, Riegel, and Meyer, 1967). A method of investigation combining cross-sectional and longitudinal research has been developed by Schaie (1965) and modified by Baltes (1968); it is called sequential analysis and holds much promise. A major goal of this method—sequential strategy research—is to disentangle the effects on performance that could be attributed to age and to the different cohort groups (cultural backgrounds). Sequential analysis has the potential for doing much toward the goal of disentangling these effects but the very nature of the entanglements precludes total or absolute solution. In human investigations, at least, some ambiguity in determining the effects of age isolated from cohort must always remain.

Longitudinal Studies

Recent longitudinal age studies have forced a review and re-emphasis of the interpretations of cross-sectional studies. Part of this may be seen in contrasting the views presented just above with those seen in previous reviews of cross-sectional studies where interpretations of decline starting early in adult life were more prominent (as for example, Jones, 1959; Botwinick, 1967; and more obviously, Wechsler, 1958, quoted in the beginning of the present chapter). Thus, the interpretations of the longitudinal data and their analyses which follow are not very different from those of the cross-sectional studies as summarized above. Differences are quantitative: by and large, longitudinal studies show less decline than do cross-sectional ones; they may also show the decline starting later in life. Where maintenance or improvements in function are seen cross-sectionally, they are also seen longitudinally.

SAMPLING BIAS: SELECTIVE DROPOUT

Whereas previous interpretations of cross-sectional data under-emphasized cohort or cultural effects, current interpretations of longitudinal data tend to underemphasize a sampling bias intrinsic to this method of investigation. While this sampling bias is now very well known, having been reported in a variety of contexts (e.g., Jarvik and Falek, 1963; Riegel, Riegel, and Meyer, 1967; Baltes, Schaie, and Nardi, 1971), too few investigators seem to be sufficiently impressed with how great a problem this can be.

A Reversal of Age Difference.   The sampling bias is one of selective dropout in longitudinal research. For different reasons, people who perform poorly tend to be less available for longitudinal retesting than those who perform well. Thus, as a longitudinal study continues over time, superior-performing older people remain and this may make for spurious conclusions. Observe Figure 24.1 of PMA test data collected during three test periods, each 7 years apart. Note a most extreme example of selective dropout in the case of Word Fluency.

In 1956, Schaie (1958) tested 500 subjects representing several age groups; in 1963 he retested them (Schaie and Strother, 1968), but only 302

274

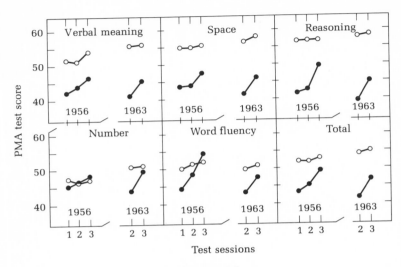

Figure 24.1

An example of selective dropout in longitudinal research (see text for explanation). The original 1956 data were regrouped from Table 5 of Schaie (1959). The data based on the second testing were regrouped from photocopies provided by ASIS National Publication Service, c/o CCM Information Services (Order NAPS Document No. 00160). The third testing data were provided by Schaie in personal communication. His study of selective dropout provides additional information (Schaie, Labouvie, and Barrett, 1973).

of them were available for this retest. In 1970, the subjects were again tested, but this time only 161 were available (Schaie and Labouvie-Vief, 1974). In Figure 24.1, two age groups of the several that were tested are compared—the open circles represent subjects aged approximately 25 years at the time of the first testing in 1956, and the closed circles represent subjects aged approximately 67.

Figure 24.1 may be understood this way: the mean scores made by the subjects within these two groups during the first test session in 1956 are represented on the abscissa by the number 1. When their numbers were reduced in the second testing, 7 years later, *the means of the 1956 scores, but of the remaining subjects only* (N = 302), were higher than those of the total group tested in 1956 (N = 500). This is seen in Figure 24.1 as 1956, number 2. With the third testing in 1970, *the same 1956 scores of the still remaining subjects* (N = 161) were even higher. This may be seen on the abscissa of Figure 24.1 as 1956, number 3. The important thing to remember is that 1, 2, and 3 of 1956 represent the same two age groups at the same time of testing—only the numbers of subjects within the age groups are different.

In Figure 24.1, the 1963 data are interpreted similarly. Those subjects retested in 1963 made scores represented by the number 2 of that year. The retest 7 years later was based on fewer subjects. The 1963 scores of these remaining subjects were higher than the 1963 scores of the total sample tested then. Moreover, this was more so for the 67-year-olds (in 1956) than the 25-year-olds.

Looking at Word Fluency, the 67-year-olds performed less well in 1956 than did the 25-year-olds. When their numbers were reduced in 1963 (second testing), the 1956 scores of those remaining showed cross-sectional age decline, but to a lesser extent. When their numbers were further reduced in the 1970 testing, the remaining 1956 scores were higher for the old than the young! Here we see a reversal in the age difference: the very same cross-sectional data, but based on only those people who did not drop out over the 14-year longitudinal period, show an age pattern different from the original one. Following up only these superior 67-year-olds, and not all those originally tested, can yield longitudinal data from which only very limited generalizations may be made. While these Word Fluency data are extreme in pointing to this, it may be seen that the general pattern of retest availability of superior old subjects holds for each of the 5 PMA abilities and the average or total of these 5.

(Later, it will be seen that the aging patterns of high and low ability people were similar, at least over the first 7-year retest interval. If the aging patterns of the elderly who were retested and those who dropped out of the study were also similar, then the problem of subject attrition might be less severe than indicated above. While there is no sure way to determine this, WAIS data suggest that the subject attrition problem is important. Also, in Figure 24.2, the difference between repeated and independent PMA measurements, especially with Cohorts V and VI, suggests the importance of dropout considerations.)

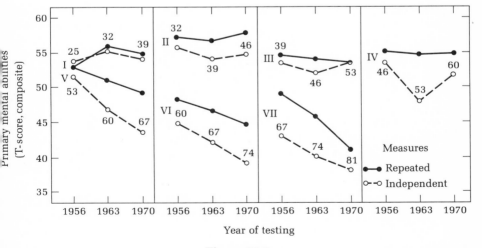

Figure 24.2

Age change analysis: longitudinal (repeated) measures and independent sample measures. Drawn from data provided by Schaie. (Reported in different form in Schaie and Labouvie-Vief, 1974; Schaie, Labouvie, and Buech, 1973.)

Terminal Drop.   Why this relative unavailability for longitudinal retesting of those performing poorly, especially those among the aged? There are several reasons. One may be that those performing poorly, or those who have declined from former levels, tend to die sooner than those maintaining function and performing well. The former are thus not available for retesting later on. Kleemeier (1962) was the first to provide data emphasizing the relationship between test performance and survival.

Using the WB, he tested elderly men on four separate occasions in the course of 12 years. Each of the men showed a decline in score over the 12-year period, but some declined more than others. Kleemeier compared the decline scores between those who later died and those who survived, and found that the decline (terminal drop) scores were greater for the deceased.

Terminal drop is but one sampling factor making the longitudinal method imperfect—there are others, e.g., health and interest in being tested. As already indicated, these sampling biases tend to increase as the study continues, and probably do so more for the old than the young. The expectation, therefore, is that longitudinal studies, while accurately reflecting changes among those people available for retesting, do not accurately reflect changes of more complete populations. This is the reason why it was said earlier that the longitudinal method may minimize age differences, just as the cross-sectional method may exaggerate them.

EARLY LIFE AGE CHANGES

In this and in the next section most of the important longitudinal studies on intellectual ability in adulthood will be presented. It will be seen that there are not many of them.

Childhood to Age 30.   Several of the longitudinal studies on early adult development came from a common data pool begun in 1931 by Terman. In that year, children aged from 2 to 5½ years were tested with the Stanford-Binet intelligence test. Ten years later, in 1941, most of these children were retested. Then, in 1956, 15 years later when the children were grown (about age 30), they were given a third testing. Different forms of the Binet test were used in the course of the three test periods, and, in addition, in 1956 the WAIS was given.

About half of the original 1931 sample was available for all three tests. For this remaining group, no change in the Stanford-Binet IQ was seen in the first 10-year interval (from approximately the ages of 4 to 14 years), and an increase was seen during the next 15-year interval. The Binet IQ scores increased from approximately 113 to 124 (Bradway, Thompson, and Cravens, 1958).

Mid-Life Patterns

TO THE MID-FORTIES.   The above study was continued by Kangas and Brad-way (1971). In 1969 there was a fourth test session, the children approximately 4 years old at the start were now near 42 years old. Their Stanford-Binet IQs were estimated at 130, a growth of another 6 IQ points. Their WAIS scores also increased—the change over the previous 13 years was from 110 to 118. Important to note is that from age 30 to 42, *both* the WAIS Verbal and the WAIS Performance scores increased.

The subjects in these studies were of relatively high IQ. In fact, most of the data of early and middle age development are of intellectually superior subjects, and this limits the generalizations which may be made. The next three studies taken together bear this out.

The first study was that of Nisbet (1957), who reported two testings of graduate students covering a 24-year period (from age 22½ to age 47). The Simplex Group Test was used which essentially is a test of verbal functions. The second study is that of Bayley and Oden (1955) who also used verbal tests in their study of intellectually superior subjects. Their subjects were so superior that they were classed as "gifted"; they had been selected when they had been children by Terman and his associates for the study of "genius" (Terman and Oden, 1947). Their ages in the Bayley-Oden study were from about 29 to 41 years.

Both Nisbet and Bayley and Oden reported that test scores increased with age. Since these two studies were of intellectually superior adults tested for verbal skills, the results might have been anticipated from the literature of cross-sectional studies. What would studies on more average people given nonverbal tests show? The third study, that of Tuddenham, Blumenkrantz, and Wilkin (1968), helps answer this question. Men retiring from the army after 20 years of service were given the Army General Classification Test (AGCT). This test has four parts; three could be classed as verbal and one nonverbal. Over a period of 13 years, from the approximate ages of 30 to 43, each of four parts of the AGCT showed age decline, but only one was statistically significant—the nonverbal one.

During this relatively early part of adult life, studies more varied with respect to subject populations might well point to what was indicated by the cross-sectional literature—relative maintenance of verbal functions and decline of nonverbal ones, especially when speed is involved. Most studies of later life show this.

TO AGE 50 AND BEYOND.   Under a different heading, studies of subjects of advanced age will be reviewed. First, however, two studies which included subjects aged 50 and over will be highlighted separately, because they were the first to draw attention to the fact that even to this relatively late age, decline is not a necessary eventuality.

The gifted subjects in Bayley and Oden's study were tested, on the average, when they were approximately 29 years old and then again when they were 41. Since there was a spread in the ages of these subjects—some were in their early twenties at the first test, and some were in their late forties at the second test—Bayley and Oden were able to divide their samples into 3 or 4 age groups, depending upon the specific analysis. "The impressive thing that comes out of this division into age groups is that all groups show similar and significant tendencies to increase in scores over the twelve-year interval" (p. 104). Bayley and Oden also concluded, "Our material does not ... cover the later ages at which real senescent decrements in intellectual functioning are to be expected. Further, our material is not concerned with speed, either in physical action or in intellectual processes." But, at least during the age period 20 to 50, superior adults improve in "knowledge of symbols and abstractions and in ability to use these in relation to each other" (p. 106).

A second study which made an important impact when first reported was by Owens (1953). In 1919, 363 students entering Iowa State College were given the Army Alpha intelligence test. Thirty years later, Owens was able to locate and retest 127 of them, thus making for a two-point longitudinal study—at the approximate ages of 19 and 49.

The Army Alpha test that Owens used comprised eight subtests, most seemingly more similar to the WAIS Verbal subtests than the Performance, but with speed a more important factor. With one exception (Arithmetical Problems) all of the subtests showed increased scores over the period of 30 years, with four or five of these (depending on criterion) being statistically significant. The overall total score of the eight subtests showed a significant increase as well.

Owens (1966) was able to retest 97 of the 127 some 11 years later, when the subjects were near 61 years of age. He reported that none of the subtest scores changed significantly over this period, thus suggesting a plateau was reached and maintained during the fifties. However, Owens grouped the data in accord with a reported factor analysis by Guilford, and found that of the three factors representing the eight subtests, one showed age decline. A Numerical factor showed a significant, although slight, decline from age 49 to 61, but the factors labeled Verbal and Reasoning did not show decline—in fact, the Verbal score showed nonsignificant improvement.

Owens then carried out an interesting second analysis on these data. He compared the original 1919 scores with those made by students of similar age (19 years) who were tested for the first time in 1961. He found improvement in most of the Army Alpha subtest scores in the newer sample when compared to the 1919 sample, and he labeled this "cultural change." Owens then subtracted these cultural change scores from the longitudinal age difference scores that he obtained with the original group. When he did this he found that while the Verbal factor score showed gain over the period from age 19 to about 61, a small loss was seen in the Numerical factor score and a larger one with the Reasoning. The latter factor score was based more on the speeded test items than the other

actor scores: in this way it was more similar to the WAIS Performance
ubtests than the Verbal.

Cunningham (1974) carried out an almost identical study which he
nodeled after Owens'. College student subjects tested during 1944 were
ocated and tested again 28 years later in 1972. The test used was also the
Army Alpha, but in a somewhat different version. The results of the two
tudies were similar in several important ways. From both, it is possible to
onclude that a type of classical age pattern was seen to hold longitudi-
ially as well as cross-sectionally. In this case, it held from the period of
ate teen-age to mid-life and beyond.

he Primary Mental Abilities Test (PMA).   The best planned and exe-
uted longitudinal investigation concerned the PMA. Beginning with an
nitial testing in 1956, Schaie and collaborators tested those available
gain in 1963, and again in 1970. In addition to a uniform pattern of test
chedules (every 7 years), they tested so many subjects across the whole
dult life span that they were able to categorize these subjects into uni-
orm age groupings. Moreover, their careful planning and their large
umber of subjects permitted sophisticated statistical analyses of data.
Iowever, the unavoidable problem of selective subject dropout, as expli-
ated in Figure 24.1, remained.

Their study includes not only the five PMA test scores and totals of
hese, but also other procedures. However, since the central thesis is not
Itered appreciably if the discussion is confined to the PMA, this will be
lone here for the sake of simplicity.

GE CHANGES.   Figure 24.2 shows the mean scores made by the subjects in
he various age groups with a composite of the five PMA tests. The figure
hould be understood this way: Cohort I was of subjects aged approxi-
nately 25 years when they first took the test in 1956. They were aged 32 in
.963 (the time of the second testing), and 39 in 1970 (third testing). Simi-
arly, Cohort VII was of subjects aged approximately 67, 74 and 81 years
espectively. The closed circles are of traditional longitudinal data, the
ppen circles will be discussed later. These data are the same as part of
hose seen in Figure 24.1 demonstrating the problem of selective dropout.

Schaie and Labouvie-Vief (1974) reported the study in the context of a
:ross-sequential analysis, i.e., a complex statistical solution in which lon-
;itudinal and cross-sectional age patterns are simultaneously examined.
'or now, only the longitudinal aspect of their investigation is reported
Schaie having graciously made the data available for this purpose).

It may be seen in Figure 24.2 (closed circles) that in the course of 14
years, no age decline at all was present in Cohorts I through IV. This is
:ompatible with the data of Owens (1953) and of Bayley and Oden (1955)
liscussed earlier. However, beginning with Cohort V, i.e., beginning in
he fifties, age decline continued progressively. Table 24.1 provides the
ictual mean age changes in the PMA T-scores. From age 53 to 67 (Cohort

Table 24.1

Age decline in composite PMA scores. Values are the difference
in age groups between means of T scores (Mean = 50; SD = 10).*

Cohort	Method	Age (years)		
		25 to 32	32 to 39	25 to 39
I	Longitudinal	−2.81	1.00	−1.81
	Cross-Sectional	−4.80†	−3.39	−2.19†
		32 to 39	39 to 46	32 to 46
II	Longitudinal	0.34	−1.07	−0.73
	Cross-Sectional	−3.39	3.31	−0.08
		39 to 46	46 to 53	39 to 53
III	Longitudinal	0.66	0.38	1.04
	Cross-Sectional	3.31	−1.59	1.72
		46 to 53	53 to 60	46 to 60
IV	Longitudinal	0.37	−0.06	0.31
	Cross-Sectional	−1.59	4.62	3.03
		53 to 60	60 to 67	53 to 67
V	Longitudinal	1.54	1.53	3.07
	Cross-Sectional	4.62	4.41	9.03
		60 to 67	67 to 74	60 to 74
VI	Longitudinal	1.87	1.66	3.53
	Cross-Sectional	4.41	1.41	5.82
		67 to 74	74 to 81	67 to 81
VII	Longitudinal	3.00	5.08	8.08
	Cross-Sectional	1.41	4.07†	8.68†

* We are grateful to K. W. Schaie who made his data available, enabling this analysis. The cross-sectional age sequences, with exceptions noted below, were derived from the means of the three different periods of testing, i.e., 1956, 1963, and 1970. They could have been derived from any single period of the three, rather than the mean of them, with results which might have been different. The present reanalysis is not in terms of statistical tests of significance, only of observed mean differences.

† Cross-sectional age comparisons within a single time of measurement. All others are means of three times of measurement. Scores indicated here as negative indicate increment with age.

V), the mean decline was 3.07; from age 60 to 74, it was 3.53; and from age 67 to 81, the decline was more appreciable—8.08 T-score points. (The size of these declines is best evaluated with the recognition that 10 points equal one standard deviation.) The statistical analyses by Schaie and Labouvie-Vief indicated that the difference in age patterns among the seven cohort groups of Figure 24.2 was statistically significant as was the age change in the two oldest cohorts.

AGE SEQUENCE ANALYSIS.   Do these longitudinal data of Figure 24.2 reflect the same age patterns seen in cross-sectional data?...

Schaie and Labouvie-Vief carried out a cross-sequential analysis and concluded that the cross-sectional age difference was greater than the

ongitudinal age change. Overall, this was so; it might even have been
anticipated since the longitudinal age comparison was 14 years and the
cross-sectional comparison was over 40 years. The basic question, however, was not asked: Do the longitudinal age sequences in Figure 24.2
show greater or lesser decline than do cross-sectional sequences of the
exact same age?

An attempt was made here to answer this question by a reanalysis
of their data. This may be seen in Table 24.1. Up to the mid-forties,
the longitudinal and cross-sectional functions provided similar
information—little or no age decline. The two also provided similar information for the oldest age sequence, 67 to 81 years, showing age declines of between 8 and 9 T-score points. However, during the years represented in Cohorts IV through VI, the cross-sectional method showed
greater age decline than the longitudinal.

The largest difference between cross-sectional and longitudinal age sequences was with Cohort V, between ages 53 and 67. The longitudinal age
decline was 3.07, the cross-sectional was 9.03. It is possible, however, that
this latter decline is unrepresentatively large. The 1956 age difference
covering this period was 3.67, and the comparable age difference in 1970
was 4.11. For some reason the age difference in the 1963 testing was 8.96.
Note that 9.03 is not the mean of these three values—the cross-sectional
age sequence decline scores were derived in the manner indicated in
Table 24.1.)

The main point of Table 24.1 has been suggested several times previously: the difference between longitudinal and cross-sectional age patterns is more quantitative than qualitative.

INDEPENDENT GROUPS.   There is a type of age comparison which appears
analogous to the longitudinal comparison, but actually it is an age comparison which is neither longitudinal nor cross-sectional, but in between.
Schaie, Labouvie and Buech (1973) gave the PMA test to seven cohorts in
1956, to different people of the same cohorts in 1963, and to still different
ones in 1970. Thus, they had independent measures (as opposed to repeated measures in longitudinal research) of subjects of the same cohort
but tested in three different periods of time. It is as if they carried out a
cross-sectional study, measuring the youngest age group in 1956, the next
oldest in 1963, and the oldest in 1970. Schaie, Labouvie, and Buech rea-
soned that this type of analysis should result in the same or similar findings as the longitudinal repeated measures study. In the main, the longitudinal repeated measures and independent measures did show similar
results; the two were similar in the sense that the longitudinal and cross-
sectional age sequences were similar. The independent measures data may
be seen in Figure 24.2 as the open circles.

With Cohorts I through III, no age change was seen over 14 years with
either repeated or independent measures, nor was it seen cross-sectionally
for this age grouping. With Cohorts IV and V, the independent measures

decline scores fell in between the longitudinal and cross-sectional mea
sures of Table 24.1. It was nearly identical to the cross-sectional age de
cline of Cohort VI (5.72 points decline) and less than both the cross
sectional and longitudinal of the oldest Cohort (VII), aged 67 to 81 years
The age decline was 5.75 points. Summarizing all these data, it woulc
seem that where differences are found among the methods of investiga
tion, more often than not they are in the following order in showing age
declines from greater to lesser magnitude: cross-sectional, independen
measures, longitudinal.

It is not surprising that the independent measures method showec
greater age decline than the longitudinal repeated measures method. Ir
the longitudinal investigation, the investigator makes every effort to retes
each and every one of his subjects, but if this cannot be done, it just isn't
In the independent measurement design, if at time 2 (1963 in the case o
Schaie, Labouvie and Buech) or at time 3 (1970) one subject is not avail
able, another one may be selected—just as in cross-sectional studies. Wha
differences were found between both methods of investigation, i.e., be
tween longitudinal and independent measures, might be attributable to
the problem of selective dropout.

DIFFERENTIAL PERFORMANCE.   Each of the five PMA tests reflect their owr
distinctive age pattern, but in the main three show patterns not very dif
ferent from that of the composite of Figure 24.2. The Reasoning, Space anc
Verbal Meaning tests show no age decline until age 53 or perhaps 60, bu
then decline sets in. In fact, the Verbal Meaning test shows a rise in the
performances to this age, before the decline.

The Word Fluency and Number tests reflect different age patterns. Ir
the cross-sectional analysis both these tests showed increased scores unti
the mid-forties. In the longitudinal (repeated measures) study of Schaie
and Labouvie-Vief, Word Fluency scores were mainly downward begin
ning with Cohort II, i.e., age 32 years. This is just the opposite for the firs
half of the adult life span seen in the cross-sectional data. Here, if any
thing, the longitudinal measure showed greater decline than the cross
sectional. The Number test showed no age change at all for any cohort—
neither rise nor decline.

XII

RACE
AND
ETHNICITY

This selection from a book by John Loehlin, Gardner Lindzey, and James Spuhler is rightly regarded as the most comprehensive and balanced view regarding race and ethnic differences in patterns of performance. A careful reading of this selection will reveal how difficult it is to conduct good research in this area.

25

Cross-Group Comparisons
of Intellectual Abilities

JOHN C. LOEHLIN, GARDNER LINDZEY,
AND JAMES N. SPUHLER

In this chapter we will focus on studies that compare different U.S. subpopulations on measures of one or more intellectual abilities. Such subpopulations may be presumed to differ environmentally as well as in gene frequencies and hence any observed behavioral differences are potentially ambiguous. Nevertheless, the magnitude and patterning of the ability differences between groups may shed some light on the causal influences that are operating, and the absence of differences, in the face of environmental or genetic variation, can also be instructive.

We will begin the chapter with an examination of racial-ethnic and social-class differences in general intelligence, and then proceed to a discussion of different patterns or profiles of ability in different U.S. groups.

Race, Social Status, and General Intelligence

Social-class differences in the United States tend to be associated with average differences in level of performance on intelligence tests. So do racial- or ethnic-group differences. Furthermore, ethnic-group member-

Loehlin, J. C., Lindzey, G., and Spuhler, J. N. "Cross-Group Comparisons of Intellectual Abilities." In J. C. Loehlin, G. Lindzey, and J. N. Spuhler. *Race Differences in Intelligence*, Chapter 7. San Francisco: W. H. Freeman and Company, 1975, pp. 164–195. Copyright © 1975 by W. H. Freeman and Company and reprinted by permission.

ship and social status tend to vary together. Inherent in this pattern of facts is the opportunity for disagreement in interpretation.

Let us illustrate with some data derived from the Coleman Report, as reanalyzed by Mayeske et al. (1972). These authors examine the predictability of a composite achievement variable from several other composite variables scored in such a way as to maximize the prediction of achievement. We will be concerned with two of these composites: Socioeconomic Status (SES) and Racial-Ethnic Differences. The first combines data on father's and mother's education, father's occupational level, number of siblings, reading materials in the home, and appliances in the home, to give a single overall index of SES. The second variable scores ethnic-group membership so as best to predict average achievement: white and Oriental American highest in achievement, Mexican American and American Indian intermediate, black and Puerto Rican lowest. The achievement measure includes verbal and nonverbal ability scores, plus reading and mathematics tests. One would expect it to correlate highly, although not perfectly, with a traditional measure of intelligence. The variables and scoring in the various composites differ slightly from grade to grade; we may take the middle level studied, grade 6, as representative.

In grade 6, SES correlated .50 with achievement, Racial-Ethnic differences correlated .49 with achievement, and SES and Racial-Ethnic differences correlated .37 with each other. Table 25.1 shows what this means in terms of the proportions of the total variance in achievement predictable from these variables. Thus in these data we find roughly 25 percent of the total variance in achievement predictable from SES, and nearly the same amount from racial-ethnic group membership. However, slightly more than half of this in either case is overlapping. The joint racial-SES component is inherently ambiguous. As far as these data go, it is correct to say that 25 percent of the variance in achievement is predictable from SES, with an additional 11 percent predictable from racial-group membership.

Table 25.1

Proportions of the variance in children's intellectual achievement predictable from racial-ethnic group membership and their families' socioeconomic status

Source of prediction	% of variance
SES, independent of ethnic group	12
Ethnic group, independent of SES	11
Both SES and ethnic group	13
Total predicted variance	36
Variance within groups	64
Total	100

Source: Based on Mayeske et al., 1972.

It is equally correct to say that 24 percent of the variance is predictable from racial-group membership, and an additional 12 percent from SES. The neutral way of describing the situation, shown in the table, seems preferable since it begs fewer questions.

This is not a purely academic issue. Writers in this area have often drawn rather strong conclusions based on an a priori allocation of joint variance in one direction or the other. An example is provided by Mayeske et al. (1973, p. 126) in another analysis of the Coleman Report data. They show that most of the variance in student achievement that is predictable from racial-ethnic group membership could be predicted instead by a collection of other variables correlated with ethnic-group membership, including socioeconomic status, family structure, attitudes toward achievement, and the properties of the student body of the school the student attends. This amounts to saying there is a large joint component of variance that is causally ambiguous: the other variables could be predicting achievement because they predict racial-ethnic group membership; racial-ethnic group membership could be predicting achievement because it predicts the other variables; both could be predicting some third variable that in turn predicts achievement; or any combination of these in any degree could be involved. Mayeske and his associates, however, take only one of these possibilities into account in their interpretation and unhesitatingly allocate the joint variation to socioeconomic rather than racial-ethnic factors.

But such questions aside, perhaps the most important fact to be noted in Table 25.1 is that nearly two-thirds of the total variance lies within groups. A small proportion of this represents error of measurement, but most of it means simply that the children within any given social-class and racial-ethnic group differ tremendously in level of academic performance—a fact that is all too easily overlooked when differences between groups are at the center of attention.

THE GENES AND SOCIAL CLASS

It must be emphasized that the variables of racial-ethnic group membership and of socioeconomic status do not coincide with the genes and the environment, respectively. Both variables cut across the heredity-environment distinction. It has for a good while been obvious to social scientists that being born and reared in a particular subculture carries with it many distinctive environmental inputs, as well as a share in a distinctive gene pool. It has not always been so obvious to social scientists that belonging to a particular social status may have genetic as well as environmental implications. However, several recent presentations of this view are available (Burt, 1961; Young and Gibson, 1963; Gottesman, 1963, 1968; Eckland, 1967; Herrnstein, 1971, 1973). Briefly, the argument runs as follows: if status mobility exists within a society and is in part a function of individual differences in ability, and if individual differences in ability are in part genetic, then status differences in that society will tend to be associated, to some degree, with genetic differences. This is not an assertion of hereditary castes, as in an artistocracy—quite the contrary, since social mobility is the key to the genetic sorting-out process in each generation.

Indeed, one direct prediction of such a model concerns social-status *differences* between parent and child: those offspring with an advantageous selection from the family gene pool should tend to rise in social status, and those with an unlucky draw should tend to fall, leaving only the "average" child at the level of his parents when status stabilizes in the next generation. Recent evidence in support of such a model has been reported by Waller (1971). Studied were 131 Minnesota fathers and 170 of their sons, drawn from the extensive data of Reed and Reed (1965). Social status was indexed by questionnaire data on education and occupation, and intelligence by IQ scores from school records, for both generations. Of 27 sons higher by 23 or more IQ points than their fathers, 20 moved up in social status; of 11 sons lower by 23 or more IQ points, 9 moved down. The same trends were present, although to a less marked degree, for fathers and sons differing by 8 to 22 IQ points. Similar data have also been reported from Great Britain (Young and Gibson, 1963; Gibson, 1970).

According to such a social-mobility model, children from families of different social status should differ less in average IQ than their parents do, although they would still be expected to differ appreciably. Then as the children mature and move to their own statuses through the educational and occupational sorting-out process, they should reestablish the higher IQ-status correlation of the parental generation.

A social-mobility model is not inherently a genetic model; one could presumably make parallel deductions from a model based on differential early experience. However, to the extent that the evidence for the association of genetic differences and individual ability differences is valid, a social-mobility model tends to predict some degree of association between SES and the genes.

Of course nothing in such a model implies that social status does not also have important *environmental* consequences for the developing child. We have every reason to believe that variables associated with SES have both genetic and environmental implications; indeed, that these are deeply intertwined, in that the genetic consequences are affected to a considerable extent by the environmental mechanism of social mobility, and that the different environmental inputs children of different social classes receive are in part due to genetic differences between their parents.

Do such processes operate to the same extent for minority-group members in our society? *A priori*, it is difficult to say. On the one hand, limitation of occupational and educational opportunities for members of minority groups might well restrict the operation of social-mobility mechanisms, and thus lower correlations between IQ and status. On the other hand, education might be an even more critical route to social advancement for a minority-group member than for a member of the majority, which could tend to elevate the correlation between status and IQ.

What is the evidence?

IQ AND SOCIAL STATUS IN DIFFERENT U.S. RACIAL-ETHNIC GROUPS

Much of the available data on ability and social status in U.S. minority groups is based on children, and as we have noted, the social-mobility model predicts that correlations will be weaker among children than among their parents. We can, however, begin by citing a few correlations for black and white adults.

Duncan (1968) presents correlations between Armed Forces Qualifying Test scores and level of educational attainment for young adult black and white males, based on the extensive Selective Service data tabulated by Karpinos (1966). A correlation of .59 was obtained for whites, and .62 for blacks—very similar correlations between ability and education despite substantial average differences of the two groups on both. Level of educational attainment also shows a similar relation to income in both groups: for black and white males in 1969 the correlations were .42 and .41, respectively (Farley, 1971, Bureau of the Census data), again similar correlations within both groups, despite average between-group differences on both measures. (For women, the education-income correlation was actually somewhat higher for blacks: .50 versus .33). The correlation between education and occupational level, on the other hand, may be somewhat lower for blacks than for whites, at least for males. Duncan, Featherman, and Duncan (1972, Tables A.1 and A.3) report correlations of .41 for blacks and .61 for nonblacks, based on large samples of men 25–64 years old in the U.S. civilian labor force in 1962. Among the fathers of these men the correlations between education and occupational level were lower, but the difference was in the same direction: the correlations were .35 for the blacks and .49 for the nonblacks. The difference in correlations between blacks and whites appear to be most attributable to a relative restriction of range in occupational status among the blacks.

Taken together, these data suggest that the relation of mental ability to SES-related variables is similar for U.S. blacks and whites, although the education-occupation relationship may be slightly weaker for blacks.

Let us turn to the somewhat more numerous studies relating children's IQs and SES. Some recent correlations for U.S. black samples are given in Table 25.2. The average correlation between child's IQ and family SES in the table falls in the neighborhood of .30. This is close to the value found in some large-scale recent studies of white populations (Duncan, 1968; Sewell et al., 1970). At best, of course, comparisons such as these are indirect, since many details of sampling and measurement differ across

Table 25.2

Some correlations between children's IQ and family socio-economic-status measures in recent U.S. black samples

Sample* and test	Correlation	Study
New York City, Stanford-Binet & PPVT	.22†	Palmer (1970)
5 southeastern states, Stanford-Binet	.27	Kennedy et al. (1963)
New York City, Lorge-Thorndike	.37	Whiteman & Deutsch (1968)
Riverside, Calif., WISC	.41‡	Mercer (1971)

* First study preschool, others elementary grades.
† Mean of 6 correlations for three age groups.
‡ Multiple correlation based on 5 best of 16 SES indicators ($N = 339$). Some shrinkage would therefore be expected on cross-validation.

researches. Let us turn to some studies in which direct comparisons between blacks and whites are possible.

For example, Nichols's (1970) study of 4-year-old sibling pairs from the Collaborative Study sample yielded a correlation of .24 among blacks between IQ and an SES index. The corresponding correlation for whites in this sample was a bit higher, .33. Nichols also reports correlations for SES with 13 measures obtained at age 7 years from his sample, including 7 WISC subtests and miscellaneous ability and achievement measures. The median correlations of these measures with the SES index were .18 for blacks and .26 for whites; for 12 of the 13 individual measures the correlation was higher in the white sample (Nichols, 1970, Table 21).

A similar direct comparison, in this case among several racial-ethnic groups, can be made from the data of the Coleman Report (Coleman et al., 1966) as shown in Table 25.3. In this instance, the black and white

Table 25.3

Correlation of sixth-grade nonverbal intelligence measure with four SES indicators, for various U.S. racial-ethnic groups

Variable	White	Black	Mexican American	Oriental American	American Indian	Puerto Rican
Reading material in home*	.21	.25	.24	.45	.16	.23
Items in home†	.26	.28	.31	.51	.22	.35
Parent's education	.21	.19	.10	.19	.00	.01
Small no. of siblings	.06	.07	.05	.32	.05	.11

Source: Data from Coleman et al., 1966, Suppl. Appendix.
* Dictionary, encyclopedia, daily newspaper.
† TV, telephone, record player, refrigerator, automobile, vacuum cleaner.

ability-SES correlations are intermediate in size, and roughly comparable. The strongest association between SES indicators and the nonverbal ability measure is found for the Oriental American group, and the weakest for the American Indian group. However, somewhat less confidence can be placed in the correlations for the groups other than blacks and whites, because of smaller and probably less representative samples.

The Mayeske analysis of the Coleman data used a composite of ability and achievement measures and a more broadly based SES score, and obtained a slightly higher correlation between the two for whites, .46, than for blacks, .39. The correlations in the other minority groups ranged from .30 to .38 (Mayeske et al., 1973, p. 16).

Other studies examining the relation of children's IQ, racial-ethnic group, and SES, present their data in terms of differences in group means, rather than in correlational form. Sometimes the question is asked, are average differences in IQ between racial-ethnic groups the same at different SES levels? Several relevant studies were summarized by Shuey (1966) as indicating a somewhat larger black-white difference for higher than lower SES groups. Her averaged figures are presented in Table 25.4, along with results from a number of more recent studies that offer comparisons on this point. The different studies differ in how the SES groups

Table 25.4

Comparison of average IQs for a higher and a lower social-class group defined in the same way for black and white samples in various studies

Study*	Average IQ				W-B IQ difference, within class		H-L IQ difference, within race	
	LB	LW	HB	HW	L	H	B	W
Six earlier studies†	82	94	92	112	12	20	10	18
Wilson (1967)	94	101	95	109	7	14	1	8
Tulkin (1968)	91	94	108	113	3	5	17	19
Sitkei & Meyers (1969)	77	93	96	106	16	10	19	13
Nichols (1970)	92	97	102	107	5	5	10	10
Scarr-Salapatek (1971a)‡	82	88	87	101	6	14	5	13
Nichols & Anderson (1973)	101	102	103	111	1	8	2	9
Nichols & Anderson (1973)	91	94	96	104	3	8	5	10

* Tests and samples: (Wilson) Henmon-Nelson, 6th grade, professional and white-collar vs. skilled & unskilled labor; (Tulkin) Lorge-Thorndike, 5th & 6th grade, Hollingshead I & II vs. V; (Sitkei) PPVT, 4-year-old, middle vs. lower class; (Nichols) Stanford-Binet, 4-year-old sib pairs from Collaborative Study, upper-middle vs. lower-middle class hospitals; (Scarr-Salapatek) various aptitude tests, school-age twins, above- vs. below-median census tracts; (Nichols & Anderson) Stanford-Binet, 4-year-old children from Collaborative Study, Boston and Baltimore-Philadelphia samples, SES index above 60 vs. below 40. In some instances, two or more IQs from original sources averaged (unweighted means).
† Reported by various authors between 1948 and 1964, averaged by Shuey (1966).
‡ IQ equivalents calculated from standard scores, using IQ $\sigma = 15$.

were defined, but in each instance there was a relatively higher and a relatively lower SES group, defined by the same criteria for blacks and whites, for which an average IQ was available or could be estimated. Use of the same classification criteria does not guarantee exact equality of the groups compared, if individuals are distributed differently within the categories, as is probably true for these data. It should, however, serve to attenuate considerably the SES differences in the racial comparisons. Since the definitions of the SES groups differ from study to study, and since some represent more extreme SES comparisons than others, simple conclusions cannot be drawn concerning the relative size of the ethnic-group and social-class differences. (Though on the whole they seem comparable.) The racial-ethnic differences within social-class groups (5th and 6th columns) appear in general to run somewhat smaller in recent studies than in the earlier ones summarized in the first row.

On the whole the differences between blacks and whites in recent studies tend to confirm the trend observed by Shuey of being larger at higher SES levels. In five of the seven recent samples, there was a difference in that direction, in one there was no difference, and in one (Sitkei and Meyers) there was the opposite outcome, with a larger difference for the lower SES group.

It should also be noted that the basic data of Table 25.4 can be looked at from a different perspective (last two columns), as testing the hypothesis that IQs are more differentiated by social class among white children than among black children. This would be consistent with a social-mobility mechanism that worked more effectively within the white than within the black population (Duncan et al., 1972). Again, the tendency in this direction in the earlier studies receives some, but not uniform, support in the more recent studies.

This is perhaps a good time to reemphasize the point that the overwhelming proportion of total ability differences lies *within*, not between these groups. A child's race or his family's social status is a much poorer predictor of his intellectual competence than an IQ test given to the child himself.

Besides the Coleman Report data mentioned above, some limited information is available concerning the relation of IQ to SES indices in U.S. minority groups other than blacks. Mercer (1971) reports a multiple correlation of WISC IQ with five SES indicators that is about the same for Mexican American children as for black children: .37 versus .41. Christiansen and Livermore (1970) found about the same IQ difference between middle- and lower-class groups for Spanish American as for Anglo American children: 20 versus 17 IQ points, again on the WISC. The study of Lesser, Fifer, and Clark (1965) compared first-grade New York children from four ethnic groups on four ability measures. On the whole, social-class differences occurred consistently across verbal, reasoning, number, and spatial abilities in all of the groups, with middle-class children exceeding lower-class children in average performance; the social-class differences were largest for black children and smallest for Chinese Americans, with Jews and Puerto Ricans intermediate. A replication in Boston of the difference between black and Chinese American children has been reported (Stodolsky and Lesser, 1967), but there were some problems in matching SES groups in this study (Lesser, personal communication). Note that these results are somewhat at odds with the Coleman data, in which Oriental Americans showed a stronger association than blacks between ability and SES measures.

Finally, Backman (1972), studying twelfth-grade students of different ethnic groups in the large Project TALENT sample, found only a very slight tendency for the relation between ability and SES to differ among different ethnic groups. This tendency, although at a conventional level of statistical significance in this large sample, was judged too weak to be of any real practical importance. On the whole, the differences between ethnic groups (Jewish and non-Jewish white, black, and Oriental American) were larger than those between SES groups (upper- and lower-middle class) in Backman's data. Obviously, the SES comparisons were not very extreme.

On the whole, then, we may safely conclude that an association between SES and measured intelligence holds within different minority groups in the U.S. as well as within the white majority; however, the data do not yet permit us to draw strong conclusions about differences, if any, in the relative degree of correlation between ability and SES in different U.S. racial-ethnic groups. Some of the studies we have reviewed suggest a slightly weaker association between SES and intelligence among U.S. blacks than whites, but other studies suggest essentially no difference.

Ethnic Differences in Profile of Abilities

In light of the fact that different racial-ethnic subpopulations represent somewhat different gene pools that have evolved under somewhat different environmental circumstances, it has frequently been suggested that such groups should display differences from one another primarily in the *pattern* of abilities they display rather than in any generalized level of ability. Such a hypothesis has a measure of biological plausibility, and it also has the comforting feature of avoiding some of the more socially unacceptable aspects of hypotheses that imply a generalized intellectual inferiority or superiority of different groups. The argument proceeds essentially as follows: if there are genetically determined differences between groups that have been in relative breeding isolation, one would expect these variations to be influenced by differences in selection pressure determined by different environments. Thus, each group should be somewhat better adapted to the unique demands of its own average environment. The natural result of this would be that each group should display distinctive superiorities over other groups in certain settings but no group should display a generalized superiority in all settings. Such an argument does not avoid all hazards—for example, a thoroughgoing racist might happily concede that the talents of blacks are better suited to the African jungle than to Western society—but it has undoubtedly been a factor in focusing interest on the possibility of distinctive patterns or profiles of abilities in different racial-ethnic groups. In this light, it is understandable that several observers (e.g., Dreger and Miller, 1960, 1968) have called for more studies of specific components of mental ability, and that a number of studies have been carried out that attempt to identify such differences in intellectual performance.

STUDIES COMPARING SEVERAL RACIAL-ETHNIC GROUPS

Two main questions can be asked of data from a battery of ability tests given to a number of ethnic groups. First, are the relationships among these measures similar in the different ethnic groups; that is, is it meaningful to speak of the same underlying dimensions of ability in each case? And second, if so, how do the groups compare along these dimensions, in the average performance of individuals, the range of variation, or the like?

A number of studies have examined the first of these two questions, and have found the interrelationships of different ability measures to be similar across ethnic groups. An early study by Michael (1949) found a generally similar factor structure among ability measures on black and white Air Force cadets. A study of 5–9-year-old children by Semler and Iscoe (1966) also obtained similar though not identical ability factor structures among blacks and whites. A recent study by Flaugher and Rock (1972) found similar factor structures in a battery of 9 ability measures administered to black, white, Mexican American, and Oriental American high-school males from low-income groups in Los Angeles. In a Hawaiian study, DeFries and others (1974) administered a battery of 15 cognitive tests to samples of persons of European and of Japanese ancestry. They obtained almost identical factor structures in the two samples. In each, four factors were identified: spatial visualization, verbal ability, perceptual speed and accuracy, and visual memory. A study by Humphreys and Taber (1973) investigated the factor structure of 21 ability measures from the Project TALENT test battery for large samples of ninth-grade boys in the top and bottom fourths on SES, and found the same six factors in each group. The relation of tests to factors showed virtually no differences by SES. (The boys in the study were not separately identified by race, but in this population the high and low SES groups would be expected to differ in ethnic composition as well.) Finally,... very similar subtest intercorrelation patterns were found by Scarr-Salapatek (1971a) and Nichols (1970) in U.S. black and white samples. Thus all these studies agree in suggesting that the underlying dimensions of ability vary little if at all across U.S. racial-ethnic groups.

The standings of different groups on these dimensions may differ, however. A number of studies have compared the average performance of members of different U.S. racial-ethnic groups on measures of cognitive abilities.

An ambitious and influential study by Lesser, Fifer, and Clark (1965) investigated the level and pattern of mental abilities in Chinese American, Jewish, black, and Puerto Rican children of middle- and lower-class background in New York City. A total of 320 first-grade children were studied, with an equal number (20) of subjects in each sex, class, and ethnic group. Mental abilities were assessed by means of a modified version of the Hunter College Aptitude Scales for Gifted Children, which included four scales, each intended to measure a different dimension or component of mental ability. The tests were revised to make them more fair to the past experience of all subjects, and tests were administered under conditions intended to minimize group difference in test-taking experience, rapport, and such. Testers were of ethnic groups corresponding to the children tested, and testing was done either in English or the native language, as appropriate to the individual child.

The major results of the study are summarized in Table 25.5, which presents the average performance for each of the ethnic groups in each social class on the four subtests. It is clear that there are marked ethnic differences in overall level of ability, and there are also differences in the pattern of performance on the various tests among these groups. Social class had marked effects on the level of performance but did not appear to influence the pattern of abilities. Differences in the pattern of ability between ethnic groups are more easily visible in Figure 25.1 where the four tests are averaged across social classes and placed on a comparable scale.

A partial replication of the Lesser, Fifer, and Clark study was conducted by Stodolsky and Lesser (1967) in Boston. This study used the same tests but smaller groups of black and Chinese American children of middle-class and lower-class background. The main findings were quite similar to those obtained in New York. An additional group of Irish-Catholic children was included in this study but the results here failed to show either a distinctive ethnic-group pattern of abilities or distinctive social-class differences within this group.

In general the findings of the New York and Boston studies provide evidence suggesting that Chinese American subjects did least well in verbal tests and best on numerical, spatial, and reasoning tests. Black subjects performed best on verbal tasks and were poorest in numerical performance. Jewish subjects were best in verbal tasks and poorest in spatial tasks, and their performance in the numerical area was next to highest. The Puerto Rican children showed less variability between abilities than the other groups but their best ability was spatial and their poorest was verbal.

. . .

Table 25.5

Scores on ability scale; mean scores are listed
in the bottom rows and righthand columns

	Verbal				
	Chinese	Jewish	Negro	Puerto Rican	
Middle	76.8	96.7	85.7	69.6	82.2
Lower	65.3	84.0	62.9	54.3	66.6
	71.1	90.4	74.3	61.9	74.4

	Reasoning				
	Chinese	Jewish	Negro	Puerto Rican	
Middle	27.7	28.8	26.0	21.8	26.1
Lower	24.2	21.6	14.8	16.0	19.1
	25.9	25.2	20.4	18.9	22.6

	Number				
	Chinese	Jewish	Negro	Puerto Rican	
Middle	30.0	33.4	24.7	22.6	27.7
Lower	26.2	23.5	12.1	15.7	19.4
	28.1	28.5	18.4	19.1	23.5

	Space				
	Chinese	Jewish	Negro	Puerto Rican	
Middle	44.9	44.6	41.8	37.4	42.2
Lower	40.4	35.1	27.1	32.8	33.8
	42.7	39.8	34.4	35.1	38.0

Source: From Lesser, Fifer, and Clark, 1965.

A study by Leifer (1972) compared 4-year-old disadvantaged New York children from Chinese, Italian, black, and Puerto Rican backgrounds on four tests requiring construction of mosaics, understanding of body parts, copying of geometric figures, and verbal ideational fluency. Relative to the

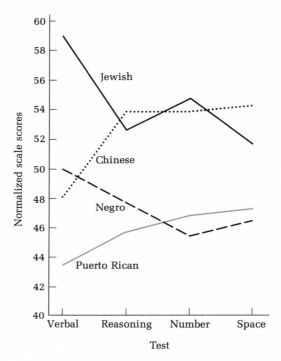

Figure 25.1

Patterns of Normalized Ability Scores for four ethnic groups (from Lesser, Fifer, and Clark, 1965).

other three groups, the Chinese American children were high on the first two tests and low on the verbal-fluency measure. There were no significant group differences on the figure-copying task.

The results for the Chinese Americans seem generally consistent with Lesser's findings, although one might have also predicted this group to perform well on figure copying. The relatively good verbal performance of the Puerto Rican children is somewhat at odds with Lesser's study; the fact that the verbal measure was one that emphasized fluent verbal production may be relevant here.

A study by Backman (1971, 1972), utilizing data from Project TALENT, compared Jewish whites (1236), non-Jewish whites (1051), blacks (488) and Oriental Americans (150) in performance on six mental-ability factors. The factors studied were: verbal knowledge, English language, mathematics, visual (spatial) reasoning, perceptual speed and accuracy, and memory. The subjects were all in the 12th grade and they were classified as upper-middle class or lower-middle class, and included males and females.

The most marked differences in the profile of scores were attributable to the sex of the subjects, with ethnicity and social class appearing to have much less influence upon the ability profile. "Considering differences in shape alone, sex accounted for 69 percent of the total variance, ethnicity 9 percent and SES 1 percent" (1971, p. 511).... Descriptively it appears that the Jewish sample was relatively superior in verbal knowledge and mathematics, the non-Jewish white subjects displayed on the average a relatively flat profile, the black subjects showed least disadvantage on perceptual speed and accuracy and memory, and the Oriental American subjects were distinctively high in mathematics.

It is clear that ethnic differences in profile are less dramatic than in the Lesser studies and it is also clear that direct comparisons between the studies are difficult both because of the different ability measures employed and because of considerable differences between the samples in age, ethnic background, and socioeconomic status. Nonetheless, several of the differences observed appear to be congruent with the findings reported by Lesser and his colleagues.

Another study involving several racial-ethnic groups used the Primary Mental Abilities Test, which measures verbal, reasoning, spatial, perceptual, and numerical factors. The study was conducted by Werner and her associates (1968, 1971), on a large sample ($N = 635$) of 10-year-old Hawaiian children classified according to ancestry as Japanese, part- and full-Hawaiian, Filipino, Portuguese, and Anglo-Saxon Caucasian. The general results are summarized in Figure 25.2, and indicate marked ethnic differences on the individual scales, except for scale P (Perceptual Acuity and Speed). The profile or pattern differences are less striking but generally consistent with the results reported by Lesser and co-workers where comparisons appear possible, e.g., Caucasian subjects performed best on verbal comprehension, and Oriental American subjects in both studies were relatively high-scoring on spatial, numerical, and reasoning factors.

While our chief interest is in U.S. racial-ethnic comparisons, we may note in passing a Canadian study by Marjoribanks (1972), which tested 11-year-old boys from five ethnic groups, and found differences both in level and pattern of abilities. In general, the Jewish group averaged highest on the tests, and the French Canadians and the Canadian Indians lowest. The profile for the Jewish group, with Verbal and Numerical abilities exceeding Reasoning and Spatial abilities, was similar to that found in Lesser's and Backman's U.S. studies. Marjoribanks also assessed cultural and family environmental factors in these groups, and found more cultural emphasis on intellectual achievement in the higher-performing groups. As is usually the case in studies of intact groups in natural settings, there is inherent ambiguity between cultural and genetic factors here: the development of different traditions could in part be a function of differences in gene frequencies in the groups—which could in turn have been influenced by earlier cultural conditions.

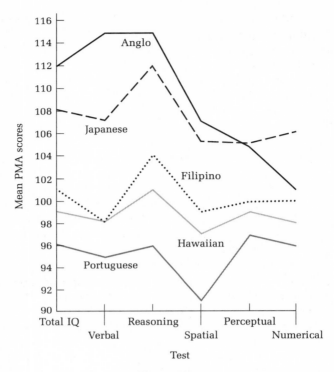

Figure 25.2

Patterns of Primary Mental Abilities for five ethnic
groups (from Werner et al., 1968).

STUDIES COMPARING ABILITY PROFILES IN U.S. BLACKS AND WHITES

As usual, the majority of U.S. studies involving racial-ethnic groups have
confined their comparisons to blacks and whites. Easily the largest
number of studies conducted with a single instrument are those employing various forms of the Wechsler tests of intelligence. Most of these
studies have focused upon comparisons of blacks and whites, or else have
compared the verbal and nonverbal performance of black subjects. The
findings from a number of studies of the latter variety are summarized in
Table 25.6. Although the results are by no means invariant, in about two-
thirds of the samples black subjects have relatively higher scores on the
verbal scale than on the performance scale, which is consistent with Lesser's results.

. . .

An extensive study of black and white children in the rural south by
Baughman and Dahlstrom (1968), employing Thurstone's Primary Mental
Abilities Test, produced findings that diverge from the Wechsler studies.

Table 25.6

Wechsler verbal and performance IQs in U.S. black samples*

Study	Ages	Number	Verbal IQ	Performance IQ
Osborne (1965)†	5–6	50	90	85
Semler & Iscoe (1963)	5–9	60	95	92
Nichols & Anderson (1973)	7	490	99	101
Nichols & Anderson (1973)	7	4091	91	93
Sartin (1950)†	8–9	45	86	97
Caldwell & Smith (1968)	6–12	420	91	83
Young & Pitts (1951)	6–16	40	79	67
Tuttle (1964)†	9–11	25	89	87
Young & Bright (1954)	10–13	81	74	67
Grandison (1951)†	11–12	21	109	95
Bonner & Belden (1970)	16–17	31	101	95
Wysocki & Wysocki (1969)	21–26	110	94	91
Fortson (1956)†	Grads.	50	106	101
Young & Collins (1954)	av. 26	52	82	83
Scarborough (1956)	av. 29	59	80	80

* Samples of neurotics, delinquents, venereal disease patients, retarded, etc., are excluded, although some normal control groups matched to such subjects are included.
† Unpublished, cited in Shuey (1966).

Black subjects appeared to perform more poorly on a verbal scale (Verbal Meaning) than on two nonverbal scales (Perceptual Speed, Number Facility).

In an analysis of Stanford-Binet items, Nichols (1970) found blacks to score relatively higher on items requiring concentration and memory, and whites relatively high on items requiring judgment and reasoning at age 4 years.

Still another measure, the Lorge-Thorndike Intelligence Test, was employed by Tulkin (1968) in a study of 389 fifth- and sixth-grade black and white subjects. In both upper- and lower-socioeconomic-status group black subjects had very similar verbal and nonverbal IQs. White subjects were significantly higher than black subjects in nonverbal IQ for both social classes and for verbal IQ in upper social class.

A somewhat different approach to the study of differences in the patterning or structure of intelligence in ethnic groups was made by Sitkei and Meyers (1969). They studied 100 black and white subjects of middle- and lower-class backgrounds, each of whom was within 6 months of his or her fourth birthday. The study employed 22 specific tests that for the most part were intended to assess six general factors: verbal comprehension, ideational fluency, perceptual speed, figural reasoning, memory span, and picture memory.

The results indicated significant ethnic and social-class differences on verbal comprehension and a general lack of such differences on other factors when measured independently of verbal comprehension. While these results appear somewhat discrepant from others that have been cited, it is not clear whether it is the difference in age level of the subjects, the test battery, the method of analysis, or some other variable that is responsible.

SUMMARY AND CONCLUSIONS: PROFILES OF ABILITIES

What conclusions, then, can be drawn from studies comparing U.S. racial-ethnic groups in terms of different patterns or profiles of abilities?

First, the interrelationships among ability measures have repeatedly been found to be similar across racial-ethnic groups, suggesting a similar underlying structure of abilities. However, the average levels of performance of different groups on such dimensions often differ. These results are far from entirely consistent. While most studies have obtained some significant subpopulation differences, there are inconsistencies in the particular traits involved. It is difficult to evaluate these discrepancies in view of the differences in measuring instruments and populations studied. Only in the black-white comparisons on the Wechsler scales is there a substantial number of studies using the same instruments, and here, although there is some variation in the findings, there appears to be a tendency for black subjects to do relatively better on the verbal scales than on the nonverbal scales. Other findings that show up in more than one study are the relatively good performance of groups of Oriental ancestry on quantitative tasks and the strong verbal and numerical performance of Jewish groups.

Second, the majority of studies find differences in level of performance as well as in pattern of abilities, among the ethnic groups studied. While such differences in level can be made to look larger or smaller by altering the relative weight given to different elements of the profile, in most cases it would not be easy to make them disappear by this means.

In short, most of the studies we have reviewed are not at all decisive on the question of the possible genetic or environmental basis of observed differences in ability patterns among U.S. racial-ethnic groups. This is not to argue that studies of this type are inherently powerless to shed light on the issue of genetic versus environmental influences. On the contrary, a multidimensional pattern of ability differences places much more severe constraints on the particular genetic or environmental hypotheses that may be adduced to explain it than does a difference in average performance on a single dimension. It is merely that so far the empirical results are not sufficiently strong or consistent to provide much help in differentiating among competing theories about their origin.

Bibliography

Alanen, Y. O. 1966. The family in the pathogenesis of schizophrenic and neurotic disorders. *Acta Psychiatrica Scandinavica* 42: Suppl. 189.

Alanen, Y. O. 1968. From the mothers of schizophrenic patients to interactional family dynamics. In *The transmission of schizophrenia,* eds. D. Rosenthal and S. S. Kety, pp. 201–212. Oxford: Pergamon.

Albert, R. S. 1971. Cognitive development and parental loss among the gifted, the exceptionally gifted, and the creative. *Psychological Reports* 29:19–26.

Albert, R. S. 1973. *Genius, eminence and creative behavior.* Fort Lee, N.J.: Behavioral Sciences Tape Library.

Alexander, F. 1930. The neurotic character. *Int. J. Psychoanal.* 11:292.

Alker, H. A. 1972. Is personality situationally specific or intrapsychically consistent? *J. Personality* 40:1–16.

Allen, G. 1958. Patterns of discovery in the genetics of mental deficiency. *Amer. J. Mental Deficiency* 62:840–849.

Allport, G. W. 1937. *Personality: A psychological interpretation.* New York: Holt.

Allport, G. W. 1966. Traits revisited. *Amer. Psychologist* 21:1–10.

Allport, G. W., and Odbert, H. S. 1936. Trait-names: A psycholexical study. *Psychol. Monographs* 47 (1, Whole No. 211).

American Psychiatric Association. 1968. *DSMII: Diagnostic and statistical manual of mental disorders,* 2nd ed. Washington, D.C.: APA.

Anderson, J., and Bower, G. 1973. *Human associative memory.* New York: Academic Press.

Anderson, K. E., ed. 1961. *Research on the academically talented student.* Washington, D.C.: National Education Association.

Annan, N. G. 1955. The intellectual aristocracy. In *Studies in social history,* ed. J. H. Plumb. London: Longmans Green.

Annin, E., Boring, E., and Watson, R. L. 1968. Important psychologists, 1600–1967. *J. Hist. Behav. Sciences* 4:303–315.

Argyle, M. and Little, B. R. 1972. Do personality traits apply to social behavior? *J. Theory of Soc. Behav.* 2:1–35.

Atkinson, R. C. 1968. Computerized instruction and the learning process. *Amer. Psychologist* 23:225–239.

Atkinson, R. C., Fletcher, J. D., Chetin, H. C., and Stauffer, C. M. 1971. Instruction in initial reading under computer control: The Stanford Project. In *Computers in education,* ed. A. Romano and S. Rossi. Bari, Italy: Adriatica Editrice.

Atkinson, R. C., and Fletcher, J. D. 1972. Teaching children to read using a computer. *The Reading Teacher* 25:319–327.

Atkinson, R. C., and Paulson, J. A. 1972. An approach to the psychology of instruction. *Psychol. Bull.* 78:49–61.

Atkinson, R. C., and Shiffrin, R. M. 1968. Human Memory: A proposed system and its control processes. In *The psychology of learning and motivation: Advances in research and theory* (II), ed. K. W. Spence and J. T. Spence. New York: Academic Press.

Atkinson, R. C., and Westcourt, K. 1974. Some remarks on a theory of memory. *Acta Psychologica* (in press).

Averill, J. R. 1973. The dis-position of psychological dispositions. *J. Exper. Res. Personality* 6:275–282.

Backman, M. E. 1971. Patterns of mental abilities of adolescent males and females from different ethnic and socioeconomic backgrounds. *Proceedings of the 79th Annual Convention of the American Psychological Association* 6:511–512.

Backman, M. E. 1972. Patterns of mental abilities: Ethnic, socioeconomic, and sex differences. *Amer. Ed. Res. J.* 9:1–12.

Bacon, F. 1939. *Novum organum.* In *The English philosophers from Bacon to Mill,* ed. E. A. Burtt. New York: Modern Library.

Bakan, D. 1966. *The duality of human existence.* Chicago: Rand McNally.

Baldwin, J. W. 1962. The relationship between teacher-judged giftedness, a group intelligence test, and kindergarten pupils. *Gifted child Quart.* 6:153–156.

Balla, D., and Zigler, E. 1964. Discrimination and switching learning in normal, familial retarded, and organic retarded children. *J. Abnormal Soc. Psychol.* 69:664–669.

Baltes, P. B. 1968. Longitudinal and cross-sectional sequences in the study of age and generation effects. *Human Devel.* 11:145–171.

Baltes, P. B., and Schaie, K. W. 1974. Aging and IQ: The myth of the twilight years. *Psychol. Today* 7:35–40.

Baltes, P. B., Schaie, K. W., and Nardi, A. H. 1971. Age and experimental mortality in a seven-year longitudinal study of cognitive behavior. *Devel. Psychol.* 5:18–26.

Barron, F. 1969. *Creative person and creative process.* New York: Holt, Rinehart & Winston.

Baughman, E. E., and Dahlstrom, W. G. 1968. *Negro and white children: A psychological study in the rural South.* New York: Academic Press.

Bayley, N. 1955. On the growth of intelligence. *Amer. Psychologist* 10:805–823.

Bayley, N. 1970. Development of mental abilities. In *Carmichael's manual of child psychology,* Vol. 1, ed. P. Mussen, pp. 1163–1209. New York: John Wiley.

Bayley, N., and Oden, M. H. 1955. The maintenance of intellectual ability in gifted adults. *J. Gerontol.* 10:91–107.

Behrman, J., Taubman, P., and Wales, T. 1977. Controlling for the effects of genetics and family environment in equations for schooling and labor market success. In *Kinometrics: The determinants of economic success within and between families,* ed. P. Taubman. North Holland: Elsevier.

Beller, E. 1955. Dependency and independence in young children. *J. Genetic Psychol.* 87:25–35.

Bem, D. J. 1972. Constructing cross-situational consistencies in behavior: Some thoughts on Alker's critique of Mischel. *J. Personality* 40:17–26.

Bem, D. J., and Allen, A. 1974. On predicting some of the people some of the time: The search for cross-situational consistencies in behavior. *Psychol. Rev.* 81:506–520.

Bem, S. L. 1974. The measurement of psychological androgyny. *J. Consult. Clin. Psychol.* 42:155–162.

Bem, S. L. 1975. Sex role adaptability: One consequence of psychological androgyny. *J. Personality Soc. Psychol.* 31:634–643.

Bem, S. L. In press. Some presumptuous prescriptions for a liberated sexual identity. In *The future of women: Issues in psychology,* eds. J. Sherman and F. Denmark. New York: Psychological Dimensions.

Bem, S. L., and Lenney, E. 1976. Sex typing and the avoidance of cross-sex behavior. *J. Personality Soc. Psychol.* 33:48–54.

Berdie, R. F. 1961. Intra-individual variability and predictability. *Ed. Psychol. Measurement* 21:663–676.

Berkowitz, A., and Zigler, E. 1965. Effects of preliminary positive and negative interactions and delay conditions on children's responsiveness to social reinforcement. *J. Personality Soc. Psychol.* 2:500–505.

Berkowitz, H., Butterfield, E. C., and Zigler, E. 1965. The effectiveness of social reinforcers on persistence and learning tasks following positive and negative social interactions. *J. Personality Soc. Psychol.* 2:706–714.

Berlit, B. 1931. Erblichkeitsuntersuchungen bei Psychopathen. *Z. Ges. Neurol. Psychiat.* 134:382.

Bernard, J. 1964. *Academic women.* University Park: Pennsylvania State University Press.

Binet, A., and Henri, V. 1896. La psychologie individuelle. *L'Annee Psychologique* 2:411–465.

Birch, H. G. 1972. Malnutrition, learning, and intelligence. *Amer. J. Public Health* 62:773–784.

Birren, J. E., and Morrison, D. F. 1961. Analysis of the WAIS subjects in relation to age and education. *J. Gerontol.* 16:363–369.

Bish, C. E. 1963. Underachievement of gifted students. In *Educating the academically able: A book of readings,* eds. L. D. Crow and Alice Crow, pp. 226–229. New York: David McKay Co.

Block, J. H. 1973. Conceptions of sex role: Some cross-cultural and longitudinal perspectives. *Amer. Psychol.* 28:512–526.

Block, J., Levine, L., and McNemar, Q. 1951. Testing for the significance of psychometric patterns. *J. Abnormal Soc. Psychol.* 46:356–359.

Bloom, B. S. 1963. Report on creativity research by the examiner's office of the University of Chicago. In *Scientific creativity: Its recognition and development,* eds. C. W. Taylor and F. Barron. New York: John Wiley.

Bonner, M. W., and Belden, B. R. 1970. A comparative study of the performance of Negro seniors of Oklahoma City high schools on The Wechsler Adult Intelligence Scale and the Peabody Picture Vocabulary Test. *J. Negro Ed.* 39:354–358.

Botwinick, J. 1967. *Cognitive processes in maturity and old age.* New York: Springer.

Bowers, K. S. 1973. Situationism in psychology: An analysis and a critique. *Psychol. Rev.* 80:307–336.

Bowlby, J. 1951. *Maternal care and mental health.* Geneva: World Health Organization (WHO Monograph Series, No. 2).

Bradway, K. P., Thompson, C. W., and Cravens, R. B. 1958. Preschool IQs after twenty-five years. *J. Ed. Psychol.* 49:278–281.

Brandwein, P. F. 1965. *The gifted student as future scientist.* New York: Harcourt Brace Jovanovich.

Broverman, D. M., Klaiber, E. L., Kobayashi, Y., and Vogel, W. 1968. Roles of activation and inhibition in sex differences in cognitive abilities. *Psychol. Rev.* 75:23–50.

Bugelski, B. R. 1962. Presentation time, total time, and mediation in paired-associate learning. *J. Exper. Psychol.* 63:409–412.

Buros, O. K., ed. 1972. *Seventh mental measurements yearbook,* Vol. 1. Highland Park, N.J.: Gryphon Press.

Burt, C. 1958. The inheritance of mental ability. *Amer. Psychologist* 13:1–15.

Burt, C. 1961. Intelligence and social mobility. *Brit. J. Statistical Psychol.* 14:3–24.

Burt, C. 1962. The psychology of creative ability: A review of Getzels and Jackson's Creativity and Intelligence. *Brit. J. Ed. Psychol.* 32:292–298.

Burt, C., and Howard, M. 1956. The multifactorial theory of inheritance and its application to intelligence. *Brit. J. Statistical Psychol.* 9:95–131.

Burt, C., and Howard, M. 1957. Heredity and intelligence: A reply to criticisms. *Brit. J. Statistical Psychol.* 10:33–63.

Butcher, J. J. 1968. *Human intelligence: Its nature and assessment.* London: Methuen.

Caldwell, M. B., and Smith, T. A. 1968. Intellectual structure of Southern Negro children. *Psychol. Rep.* 23:63–71.

Caldwell, T. E. 1967. Can pupil performance rates tell us when a student teacher is ready for her own class? Unpublished doctoral dissertation, University of Kansas.

Campus, N. 1974. Transituational consistency as a dimension of personality. *J. Personality Soc. Psychol.* 29:593–600.

Cappa, D., and Schubert, D. 1962. Do parents help gifted children read? *J. Ed. Res.* 56:33–36.

Carlson, E. R., and Carlson, R. 1960. Male and female subjects in personality research. *J. Abnormal Soc. Psychol.* 61:482–483.

Carlson, R. 1971. Where is the person in personality research? *Psychol. Bull.* 75:203–219.

Carlson, R., and Levy, N. 1968. A brief method for assessing social-personal orientation. *Psychol. Rep.* 23:911–914.

Carlson, R., and Levy, N. 1970. Self, values, and affects: Derivations from Tomkins' polarity theory. *J. Personality Soc. Psychol.* 16:338–345.

Carroll, J. B. 1962. The predication of success in intensive language training. In *Training research and education,* ed. R. Glaser, pp. 87–136. Pittsburgh: University of Pittsburgh Press.

Carroll, J. B. 1963. A model of school learning. *Teachers Coll. Rec.* 64:723–733.

Carroll, J. B. 1974. A new "structure of intellect." For presentation at the LDRC Conference on the Nature of Intelligence. Pittsburgh March 4–6.

Cattell, R. B. 1971. *Abilities: their structure, growth and action.* Boston: Houghton Mifflin.

Chall, J. 1967. *Learning to read: The great debate.* New York: McGraw-Hill.

Chapman, L. J., and Chapman, J. P. 1969. Illusory correlations as an obstacle to the use of valid psycho-diagnostic signs. *J. Abnormal Psychol.* 74:271–280.

Christensen, P. R., Guilford, J. P., Merrifield, P. R., and Wilson, R. C. 1960. *Alternate uses.* Beverly Hills: Sheridan Supply Co.

Christiansen, T., and Livermore, G. A. 1970. Comparison of Anglo-American and Spanish-American children on the WISC. *J. Soc. Psychol.* 81:9–14.

Clark, H., and Chase, W. 1972. On the process of comparing sentences against pictures. *Cognitive Psychol.* 3:472–517.

Clark, K. 1969. *Civilization: A personal view.* New York: Harper & Row.

Clark, K. E. 1957. *America's psychologists: A survey of a growing profession.* Washington, D.C.: American Psychological Association.

Clarke, A. D. B. 1968. Problems in assessing the later effects of early experience. In *Foundations of child psychiatry,* ed. E. Miller. Oxford: Pergamon.

Clarke, A. D. B. and Clarke, A. M. 1954. Cognitive changes in the feebleminded. *Brit. J. Psychol.* 45:173–179.

Clausen, J. A. 1959. The sociology of mental illness. In *Sociology today, problems and prospects,* eds. R. K. Merton, L. Broom, and L. S. Cottrell, Jr. pp. 485–508. New York: Basic Books.

Cochran, W. G. 1963. *Sampling techniques,* 2d ed. New York: Holt, Rinehart & Winston.

Cole, J., and Cole, S. 1973. *Social stratification in science.* Chicago: University of Chicago Press.

Cole, S., and Cole, J. R. 1967. Scientific output and recognition: A study in operation of the reward system in science. *Amer. Sociol. Rev.* 32:377–390.

Coleman, J. S., et al. 1966. *Equality of educational opportunity.* Washington, D.C.: U.S. Government Printing Office.

Cooper, L. A., and Shepard, R. N. 1973. The time required to prepare for a rotated stimulus. *Memory and cognition* 1:246–250.

Court Brown, W. M. 1968. Males with an XYY sex chromosome complement. *J. Med. Genetics* 5:341.

Cox, C. 1926. *The early mental traits of three hundred geniuses: Genetic studies of genius,* Vol. 2. Stanford, Calif: Stanford University Press.

Craft, M. 1966. *Psychopathic disorders.* Oxford: Pergamon.

Cravioto, J., DeLicardie, E. R., and Birch, H. G. Nutrition, growth, and neuro-integrative development: An experimental and ecologic study. *Pediatrics* 38:319–372.

Cromwell, R. L. 1963. A social learning approach to mental retardation. In *Handbook of mental deficiency,* ed. N. R. Ellis, pp. 41–91. New York: McGraw-Hill.

Cronbach, L. J. *Essentials of psychological testing.* New York: Harper & Row, 1970.

Cropley, A. J. 1968. A note on the Wallach-Kogan tests of creativity. *Brit. J. Ed. Psychol.* 38:197–200.

Cropley, A. J., and Maslany, G. W. 1969. Reliability and factorial validity of the Wallach-Kogan creativity test. *Brit. J. Psychol.* 60:395–398.

Crouse, J. 1977. Effects of academic ability. In *Ability, IQ, and earnings,* ed. P. Taubman. Unpublished manuscript.

Cruikshank, W. M. 1947. Qualitative analysis of intelligence test responses. *J. Clin. Psychol.* 3:381–386.

Cunningham, W. R. 1974. Age changes in human abilities. Master's thesis, University of Southern California, Los Angeles.

Curran, D., and Mallinson, P. 1944. Psychopathic personality. *J. Mental Science* 90:266.

Darwin, C., 1896. *The life and letters of Charles Darwin*, Vol. 4, ed. Francis Darwin. New York: Appleton-Century-Crofts.

Datta, L. E. 1963. Test instructions and identification of creative scientific talent. *Psychol. Rep.* 13:495–500.

Dearborn, G. V. 1898. A study of imagination. *Amer. J. Psychol.* 9:183–190.

DeFries, J. C., et al. 1974. Near identity of cognitive structure in two ethnic groups. *Science* 183:338–339.

DeHaan, R. F., and Havighurst, R. J. 1961. *Educating gifted children*. Chicago: University of Chicago Press.

Dellas, M., and Gaier, E. L. 1970. Identification of creativity: The individual. *Psychol. Bull.* 73:55–73.

Denenberg, V. 1969. Experimental programming of life histories in the rat. In *Stimulation in early infancy*, ed. A. Ambrose, pp. 21–33. London: Academic Press.

Dennis, W. 1954(a). Bibliographies of eminent psychologists. *Amer. Psychologist* 9:35–62.

Dennis, W. 1954(b). Bibliographies of eminent scientists. *Scientific Monthly* 79:180–183.

Deutsch, H. 1944. *The psychology of women: A psychoanalytic interpretation*. New York: Grune & Stratton.

Doll, E. E. 1962. A historical survey of research and management of mental retardation in the United States. In *Readings on the exceptional child*, eds. E. P. Trapp and P. Himelstein, pp. 21–68. New York: Appleton-Century-Crofts.

Domino, G. 1970. The identification of potentially creative persons from the Adjective Check List. *J. Consult. Clin. Psychol.* 35:48–51.

Doppelt, J. E. 1956. Estimating the full scale score on the Wechsler Adult Intelligence Scale from scores on four subtests. *J. Consulting Psychol.* 20:63–66.

Douvan, E., and Adelson, J. 1966. *The adolescent experience*. New York: John Wiley.

Dreger, R., and Miller, K. S. 1960. Comparative psychological studies of Negroes and whites in the United States. *Psychol. Bull.* 57:361–402.

Dreger, R. M., and Miller, K. S. 1968. Comparative psychological studies of Negroes and whites in the United States: 1959–1965. *Psychol. Bull. Monograph Suppl.* 70: (3, pt. 2).

Dudycha, G. J. 1936. An objective study of punctuality in relation to personality and achievement. *Arch. Psychol.* 204:1–319.

Duncan, Ann Dell. 1967. Self-control in teenagers. Unpublished manuscript. University of Kansas.

Duncan, O. D. 1968. Ability and achievement. *Eugenics Quart.* 15:1–11.

Duncan, O. D., Featherman, D. L., and Duncan, B. 1972. *Socioeconomic background and achievement*. New York: Seminar Press.

Dyer, H. S. 1960. A psychometrician views human ability. *Teachers Coll. Rec.* 61:394–403.

Eckland, B. K. 1967. Genetics and sociology: A reconsideration. *Amer. Sociol. Rev.* 32:173–194.

Edwards, A. L. 1970. *The measurement of personality traits*. New York: Holt, Rinehart & Winston.

Edwards, J. S. 1967. It happens all the time. Unpublished manuscript, University of Kansas.

Eissler, K. R. 1963. *Goethe: A psychoanalytic study 1775–1786*, Vol. 1. Detroit: Wayne State University Press.

Ekehammar, B. 1974. Interactionism in personality from a historical perspective. *Psychol. Bull.* 81:1026–1048.

Ellenberger, H. 1970. *The discovery of the unconscious.* New York: Basic Books.

Ellis, N. R. 1963. The stimulus trace and behavioral inadequacy. In *Handbook of mental deficiency*, ed. N. R. Ellis, pp. 134–158. New York: McGraw-Hill.

Ellmann, R. 1959. *James Joyce.* New York: Oxford University Press.

Endler, N. S. 1973(a). The case for person-situation interactions. Paper presented at the meeting of the American Psychological Association, Montreal, August.

Endler, N. S. 1973(b). The person versus the situation—A pseudo issue? A response to Alker. *J. Personality* 41:287–303.

Endler, N. S., and Hunt, J. McV. 1968. S-R inventories of hostility and comparisons of the proportions of variance from persons, responses, and situations for hostility and anxiousness. *J. Personality Soc. Psychol.* 9:309–315.

Erikson, E. H. 1950. *Childhood and society.* New York: W. W. Norton.

Erikson, E. H. 1964. Inner and outer space: Reflections on womanhood. *Daedalus,* 93:582–606.

Erlenmeyer-Kimling, L., and Jarvik, L. F. 1963. Genetics and intelligence: A review. *Science,* 142:1477–1479.

Estes, W. K. 1972. Interactions of signal and background variables in visual processing. *Perception and Psychophysics* 12:278–286.

The excitement and fascination of science: A collection of autobiographical and philosophical essays. Palo Alto, Calif.: Annual Reviews, 1965.

Fägerlind, I. 1975. *Formal education and adult earnings.* Stockholm: Almquist & Wiksell.

Falconer, D. S. 1960. *Quantitative genetics.* New York: Ronald Press.

Farley, R. 1971. Indications of recent demographic change among blacks. *Social Biology* 18:341–358.

Fenigstein, A., Scheier, M., and Buss, A. H. 1975. Public and private self-consciousness: Assessment and theory. *J. Consult. Clin. Psychol.* 43:522–527.

Fiske, D. W., and Butler, J. M. 1963. The experimental conditions for measuring individual differences. *Ed. Psychol. Measurement* 23:249–266.

Fishbein, M., and Ajzen, I. 1974. Attitudes towards objects as predictors of single and multiple behavioral criteria. *Psychol. Rev.* 81:59–74.

Flanagan, J. C., et al. 1962. *Characteristics of high school youth*, Vol. 2. Boston: Houghton Mifflin.

Flaugher, R. L., and Rock, D. A. 1972. Patterns of ability factors among four ethnic groups. *Proceedings of the 80th Annual Convention of the American Psychological Association* 7:27–28.

Fliegler, L. A., ed. 1961. *Curriculum planning for the gifted.* Englewood Cliffs, N.J.: Prentice-Hall.

Flescher, I. 1963. Anxiety and achievement of intellectually gifted and creatively gifted children. *J. Psychol.* 56:251–268.

French, J. L., ed. 1964. *Educating the gifted: The book of readings.* New York: Holt, Rinehart, & Winston.

Freud, S. 1969. *A general introduction to psychoanalysis* (1933). New York: Clarion Books.

Freud, S. 1955. *Moses and monotheism* (1938). New York: Vintage Books.

Furry, C. A., and Baltes, P. B. 1973. The effect of age differences in ability extraneous performance variables on the assessment of intelligence in children, adults, and the elderly. *J. Gerontol.* 28:73–80.

Gallagher, J. J. 1964. *Teaching the gifted child.* Boston: Allyn & Bacon.

Gallagher, J. J., and Crowder, T. 1957. The adjustment of gifted children in the regular classroom. *Exceptional Children* 23:306–312; 317–319.

Galton, F. 1869. *Hereditary genius.* New York: Macmillan.

Garai, J., and Scheinfeld, A. 1968. Sex differences in mental and behavioral traits. *Genetic Psychol. Monographs* 77:169–299.

Garfield, E. 1970. Citation indexing for studying science. *Nature* 222:669–670.

Garmezy, N. 1974. Children at risk: The search for the antecedents of schizophrenia. Part II: Ongoing research programs, issues, and intervention. *Schizophrenia Bull.* No. 8:55–125.

Garmezy, N., with Streitman, S. 1974. Children at risk: The search for the antecedents of schizophrenia. Part I. Conceptual models and research methods. *Schizophrenia Bull.* No. 9:14–90.

Gewirtz, J. 1954. Three determinants of attention seeking in young children. *Monographs of the Society for Research in Child Development* No. 59:19(2).

Ghiselin, B. 1963. Ultimate criteria for two levels of creativity. In *Scientific creativity: Its recognition and development,* eds. C. W. Taylor and F. Barron. New York: John Wiley.

Gibson, J. B. 1970. Biological aspects of a high socio-economic group. I. IQ, education and social mobility. *J. Biosocial Science* 2:1–16.

Gold, M. 1963. *Divergent production performance as affected by type of task and length of test.* Doctoral dissertation, George Peabody College for Teachers. Ann Arbor, Mich.: University Microfilms, No. 63-7816.

Goldberg, Miriam, et al. 1959. A three-year experimental program at DeWitt Clinton High School to help bright underachievers. *High Points* 41:5–35.

Gottesman, I. L. 1963. Genetic aspects of intelligent behavior. In *Handbook of mental deficiency,* ed. N. R. Ellis, pp. 253–296. New York: McGraw-Hill.

Gottesman, I. 1968. Biogenetics of race and class. In *Social class, race and psychological development,* eds. M. Deutsch, I. Katz, and A. R. Jensen, pp. 11–51. New York: Holt, Rinehart, & Winston.

Gottesman, I. I., and Shields, J. 1972. *Schizophrenia and genetics: A twin study vantage point.* New York: Academic Press.

Gottesman, I. I., and Shields, J. 1976. A critical review of recent adoption twin, and family studies of schizophrenia: Behavioral genetics perspectives. *Schizophrenia Bull.* 2(3):360–401.

Gough, H. G. 1952. *The Adjective Check List.* Palo Alto, Calif.: Consulting Psychologists Press.

Gough, H. G. 1956. *California Psychological Inventory.* Palo Alto, Calif. Consulting Psychologists Press.

Gough, H. G. 1957. *Manual for the California Psychological Inventory.* Palo Alto, Calif.: Consulting Psychologists Press.

Gough, H. G. 1968. *An interpreter's syllabus for the California Psychological Inventory.* Palo Alto, Calif.: Consulting Psychologists Press.

Gough, H. G., and Heilbrun, A. B. 1965. *The Adjective Check List Manual.* Palo Alto, Calif.: Consulting Psychologists Press.

Gowan, J. C. 1965. *Annotated bibliography on creativity and giftedness.* Northridge, Calif.: San Fernando Valley State Teachers College Foundation.

Granick, S., and Friedman, A. S. 1973. Educational experience and maintenance of intellectual functioning by the aged: An overview. In *Intellectual functioning in adults*, eds. L. F. Jarvik, C. Eisdorfer, and J. E. Blum, pp. 59–64. New York: Springer.

Graves, W. L., Freeman, M. G., and Thompson, J. D. 1968. Culturally related reproductive factors in mental retardation. Paper read at Conference on Sociocultural Aspects of Mental Retardation, Peabody College, Nashville, Tenn., June.

Green, C., and Zigler, E. 1962. Social deprivation and the performance of retarded and normal children on a satiation type task. *Child Development* 33:499–508.

Green, R. F. 1969. Age-intelligence relationship between ages sixteen and sixty-four: A rising trend. *Developmental Psychol.* 1:618–627.

Greenacre, P. 1945. Conscience in the psychopath. *Amer. J. Orthopsychiat.* 15:495.

Grilliches, Z., and Mason, W. M. 1972. Education, income and ability. *J. Political Economy* 80:S74–S103.

Guilford, J. P., Christensen, P. R., Frick, J. W., and Merrifield, P. R. 1957. The relations of creative-thinking aptitudes to non-aptitude personality traits. *Reports from the Psychological Laboratory*, University of Southern California, 20.

Guilford, J. P., and Hoepfner, R. 1971. *The analysis of intelligence*. New York: McGraw-Hill.

Gutmann, D. 1965. Women and the conception of ego strength. *Merrill Palmer Quart.* 11:229–240.

Hamburg, D. A., and Lunde, D. T. 1966. Sex hormones in the development of sex differences in human behavior. In *The development of sex differences*, ed. E. Maccoby. Stanford, Calif.: Stanford University Press, 1966.

Hanson, N. R. 1958. *Patterns of discovery*. Cambridge, Mass.: Cambridge University Press.

Harmon, L. R. 1963. The development of a criterion of scientific competence. In *Scientific creativity: Its recognition and development*, eds. C. W. Taylor and F. Barron. New York: John Wiley.

Harré, R., and Secord, P. F. 1972. *The explanation of social behavior*. Oxford: Basil, Blackwell, & Mott.

Harrington, D. M. 1972. Effects of instructions to "Be Creative" on three tests of divergent thinking abilities. Unpublished doctoral dissertation, University of California, Berkeley.

Hartshorne, H., and May, M. A. 1928. *Studies in the nature of character*. Vol. 1, *Studies in deceit*. New York: Macmillan.

Hartshorne, H., and May, M. A. 1929. *Studies in the nature of character*. Vol. 2, *Studies in service and self-control*. New York: Macmillan.

Hartshorne, H., May, M. A., and Shuttleworth, F. K. 1930. *Studies in the nature of character*. Vol. 3, *Studies in the organization of character*. New York: Macmillan.

Havighurst, R. J., Hersey, J., Meister, M., Cornog, W. H., and Terman, L. M. 1958. The importance of education for the gifted. In *Education for the gifted: Fifty-seventh yearbook of the national society for the study of education*, ed. N. B. Henry. Chicago: University of Chicago Press.

Hays, W. L. 1963. *Statistics for psychologists*. New York: Holt, Rinehart & Winston.

Hazard, P. 1953. *The European mind 1685–1715*. New Haven, Conn.: Yale University Press.

Heathers, G. 1955. Emotional dependence and independence in nursery school play. *J. Genetic Psychol.* 87:37–57.

Heilbrun, A. B. 1976. Measurement of masculine and feminine sex role identities as independent dimensions. *J. Consult. Clin. Psychol.* 44:183–190.

Helson, R., and Crutchfield, R. S. 1970. Mathematicians: The creative researcher and the average Ph.D. *J. Consult. Clin. Psychol.* 34:250–256.

Henderson, D. K. 1939. *Psychopathic states.* New York: W. W. Norton

Herrnstein, R. 1971. I.Q. *The Atlantic* 228(3):43–64.

Herrnstein, R. J. 1973. *I.Q. in the meritocracy.* Boston: Little, Brown.

Hertzig, M. E., Birch, H. G., Richardson, S. A., and Tizard, J. 1972. Intellectual levels of school children severely malnourished during the first two years of life. *Pediatrics* 48:814–824.

Heston, L. L. 1966. Psychiatric disorders in foster home reared children of schizophrenic mothers. *Brit. J. Psychiat.* 112:819–825.

Hildreth, Gertrude H. 1966. *Introduction to the gifted.* New York: McGraw-Hill.

Hirsch, J. 1963. Behavior genetics and individuality understood. *Science* 142:1436–1442.

Hirsch, S. R., and Leff, J. P. 1975. *Abnormalities in parents of schizophrenics.* New York: Oxford University Press.

Hirsh, E. A. 1959. The adaptive significance of commonly described behavior of the mentally retarded. *Amer. J. Mental Deficiency* 63:639–646.

Hollingshead, A. B. 1957. The two-factor index of social position. Unpublished manuscript.

Hollingworth, L. S. 1926. *Gifted children: Their nature and nurture.* New York: Macmillan.

Hollingworth, L. 1942. *Children above 180 IQ.* Yonkers-on-Hudson, N.Y.: World Book.

Holt, E. E. 1960. *A selected and annotated bibliography on the gifted.* Columbus, Ohio: Heer Publishing Co.

Holton, G. 1971. On trying to understand scientific genius. *American Scholar* 41(1):95–110.

Hong, C. Y. 1970. *Pediatric diagnosis and treatment.* Korea: Yongrin.

Honzik, M. P. 1972. Abstracted in *Abstract guide, XXth international congress of psychology,* 224.

Howells, J. G. 1972. Family psychopathology and schizophrenia. In *Modern perspectives in world psychiatry,* ed. J. G. Howells, p. 414. New York: Brunner/Mazel, Inc.

Humphreys, L. G., and Taber, T. 1973. Ability factors as a function of advantaged and disadvantaged groups. *J. Ed. Measurement* 10:107–115.

Hunt, E. B. 1971. What kind of computer is man? *Cognitive Psychol.* 2:57–98.

Hunt, E. B. 1973. The memory we must have. In *Computer models of thought and language.* eds. R. Schank and K. Colby. San Francisco: Freeman.

Hunt, E. B., Frost, N., and Lunneborg, C. L. 1973. Individual differences in cognition: A new approach to intelligence. In *Advances in learning and motivation,* Vol. 7, ed. G. Bower. New York: Academic Press.

Hunt, E. B., and Poltrock, S. 1974. The mechanics of thought. In *Human information processing: Tutorials in performance and cognition,* ed. B. Kantowitz. Potomac, Md.: Erlbaum.

Hurst, C. C. 1932. A genetic formula for the inheritance of intelligence in man. *Proceedings of the Royal Society of London* Serial B 112:80–97.

Jaccard, J. J. 1974. Predicting social behavior from personality traits. *J. Res. Personality* 7:358–367.

Janik, A., and Toulmin, S. 1973. *Wittgenstein's Vienna*. New York: Simon & Schuster.

Jamison, D., Fletcher, J. D., Suppes, P., and Atkinson, R. C. 1973. Cost and performance of computer assisted instruction for education of disadvantaged children. In *Education as an industry*, eds. J. Froomkin and R. Radner. New York: Columbia University Press.

Jarvik, L. F., and Falek, A. 1963. Intellectual stability and survival in the aged. *J. Gerontol.* 18:173–176.

Jastak, J. F., and Jastak, S. R. 1965. *The wide range achievement test*. Wilmington, Del.: Guidance Associates.

Jencks, C. 1972. *Inequality: A reassessment of the effects of family and schooling in America*. New York: Basic Books.

Jencks, C., and Brown, M. 1977. Genes and social stratification. In *Ability, IQ, and earnings*, ed. P. Taubman. Unpublished manuscript.

Jencks, C., Smith, M., Acland, H., Bane, M. J., Cohen, D., Gintis, H., Heyns, B., and Michelson, S. 1972. *Inequality*. New York: Basic Books.

Jensen, A. R. 1969. How much can we boost IQ and scholastic achievement? *Harvard Ed. Rev.* 39:1–123.

Jensen, A. R. 1974(a). Cumulative deficit: A testable hypothesis? *Developmental Psychol.* 10:996–1019.

Jensen, A. R. 1974(b). How biased are culture-loaded tests? *Genetic Psychol. Monographs* 90:185–244.

Jensen, A. R. 1976. Culture bias and construct validity. *Phi Delta Kappan* 57:340–346.

Jervis, G. A. 1959. Biomedical types of mental deficiency. In *American handbook of psychiatry*, ed. S. Arieti, pp. 463–473. New York: Basic Books.

Johnson, N. J. A. 1967(a). Acceleration by a student teacher of both the planned and performed rates of primary, learning-disabled pupils. Unpublished master's thesis, University of Kansas.

Johnson, N. J. A. 1967(b). A comparison of arithmetic performance of students identified as gifted with that of students identified as average and below average. *Kansas Studies in Education* 17:7–9.

Jones, E. E., and David, K. W. 1965. From acts to dispositions: The attribution process in person perception. In *Advances in experimental psychology*, Vol. 2, ed. L. Berkowitz. New York: Academic Press.

Jones, E. E., and Goethals, G. R. 1971. *Order effects in impression formation: Attribution context and the nature of the entity*. New York: General Learning Press.

Jones, E. E., and Harris, V. A. 1967. The attribution of attitudes. *J. Exper. Soc. Psychol.* 3:1–24.

Jones, E. E., and Nisbett, R. E. 1971. *The actor and observer: Divergent perceptions of the causes of behavior*. New York: General Learning Press.

Jones, F. E. 1964. Predictor variables for creativity in industrial science. *J. Appl. Psychol.* 48:134–136.

Jones, H. E. 1959. Intelligence and problem-solving. In *Handbook of Aging and the Individual*, ed. J. E. Birren, pp. 700–738. Chicago: University of Chicago Press.

Kagan, J., and Moss, H. A. 1962. *Birth to maturity*. New York: John Wiley.

Kahn, F. 1931. *Psychopathic personalities*. New Haven, Conn.: Yale Universit Press.

Kangas, J., and Bradway, K. 1971. Intelligence at middle age: A thirty-eight-yea follow-up. *Developmental Psychol.* 5:333–339.

Karpinos, B. D. 1966. The mental test qualifications of American youths for mili tary service and its relationship to educational attainment. *Proceedings of th 126th Annual Meeting of the American Statistical Association*, pp. 92–111.

Karpman, B. 1947–1948. The myth of the psychopathic personality. *Amer. Psychiat.* 104:523.

Keele, S. 1973. *Attention and human performance*. Los Angeles: Goodyear.

Kelley, H. H. 1967. Attribution theory in social psychology. In *Nebraska Sym posium on Motivation: 1967*. ed. D. Levine. Lincoln: University of Nebrask Press.

Kelley, H. H., and Stahelski, A. J. 1970. Social interaction basis of cooperators' an competitors' beliefs about others. *J. Personality Soc. Psychol.* 16:66–91.

Kelley, T. L. 1923. *Statistical method*. New York: Macmillan.

Kelley, T. L., Madden, R., Gardner, E. G., and Rudman, H. C. 1964. *Stanfor Achievement Test: Directions for administering*. New York: Harcourt Brac Jovanovich.

Kelly, G. A. 1955. *The psychology of personal constructs* (2 vols). New York: W. W Norton.

Kennedy, W. A., Van De Riet, V., and White, J. C., Jr. 1963. A normative sample o intelligence and achievement of Negro elementary school children in th Southeastern United States. *Monographs of the Society for Research in Chil Development* 28:No. 90.

Kety, S. S. 1959. Biochemical theories of schizophrenia. A two-part critical review of current theories and of the evidence used to support them. *Science* 129:1528–1532; 1590–1596.

Kety, S. S., Rosenthal, D., Wender, P. H., and Schulsinger, F. 1968. The types and prevalence of mental illness in the biological families of adopted schizophre nics. In *The transmission of schizophrenia*, eds. D. Rosenthal and S. S. Kety, p 345. Oxford: Pergamon.

Kety, S. S., Rosenthal, D., Wender, P. H., Schulsinger, F., and Jacobsen, B. 1975. Mental illness in the biological and adoptive families of adopted individuals who have become schizophrenic: A preliminary report based upon psychiat ric interviews. In *Genetic Research in Psychiatry*, eds. R. Fieve, D. Rosenthal, and M. Brill, pp. 147–165. Baltimore: The Johns Hopkins University Press.

Kim, H. 1971. Mastery learning in the Korean middle schools. *UNESCO Regional Office for Education in Asia* 6:55–60.

Kinney, D., and Jacobsen, B. 1976. Environmental factors in schizophrenia: Adop tion study evidence. Paper read at the Second Rochester International Confer ence on Schizophrenia, Rochester, N.Y., May 3.

Klausmeier, H. J., and Loughlin, L. T. 1961. Behavior during problem-solving among children of low, average, and high intelligence. *J. Ed. Psychol.* 52:148–152.

Kleemeier, R. W. 1962. Intellectual change in the senium. *Proceedings of the Social Statistics Section of The American Statistical Association*, pp. 290–295.

Klineberg, O. 1931. Genius. *Encyclopaedia of the social sciences*, Vol. 6. New York: Macmillan.

och, J. I. A. 1891. *Die psychopathische minderwertigkeiten.* Ravensburg: Maier.

oenig, C. H. 1967. Precision teaching with emotionally disturbed children. Unpublished manuscript, University of Kansas.

ogan, N. 1973. Creativity and cognitive style: A life span perspective. In *Life-span development psychology,* eds. P. R. Baltes and K. W. Schaie. New York: Academic Press.

ohlberg, L. 1966. A cognitive-developmental analysis of children's sex-role concepts and attitudes. In *The development of sex differences,* ed. E. Maccoby. Stanford, Calif.: Stanford University Press.

ohn, M. L. 1968. Social class and schizophrenia: A critical review. In *The transmission of schizophrenia,* ed. D. Rosenthal and S. S. Kety. New York: Pergamon.

ounin, J. 1941(a). Experimental studies of rigidity: I. The measurement of rigidity in normal and feebleminded persons. *Character and Personality* 9:251–273.

ounin, J. 1941(b). Experimental studies of rigidity: II. The explanatory power of the concept of rigidity as applied to feeblemindedness. *Character and Personality* 9:273–282.

raepelin, F. 1915. *Psychiatrie,* 8th ed., Vol. 4. Leipzig: Barth.

uhn, T. S. 1962. *The structure of scientific revolutions.* Chicago: University of Chicago Press.

ushlick, A. 1966. Assessing the size of the problem of subnormality. In *Genetic and environmental factors in human ability,* eds. J. E. Meade and A. S. Parkes, pp. 121–147. New York: Plenum Press.

avin, D. E. 1965. *The prediction of academic performance.* New York: Russel Sage.

aycock, F., and Caylor, J. S. 1964. Physiques of gifted children and their less gifted siblings. *Child Development* 35:63–74.

ehman, H. C. 1947. National differences in creativity. *Amer. J. Sociol.* 52:475–488.

ehman, H. C. 1953. *Age and achievement.* Princeton, N.J.: Princeton University Press.

eibowitz, A. 1977. Family background and economic success. In *Ability, IQ, and earnings,* ed. P. Taubman. Unpublished manuscript.

eifer, A. 1972. Ethnic patterns in cognitive tasks. *Proceedings of the 80th Annual Convention of the American Psychological Association* 7:73–74.

ekachman, R. 1968. *The age of Keynes.* New York: Vintage Books.

esser, G. S., Fifer, G., and Clark, D. H. 1965. Mental abilities of children from different social-class and cultural groups. *Monographs of the Society for Research in Child Development* 30:No. 4.

evine, S. 1969. An endocrine theory of infantile stimulation. In *Stimulation in early infancy,* ed. A. Ambrose, pp. 45–54. London: Academic Press.

evitsky, D. A., and Barnes, R. H. 1972. Nutritional and environmental interactions in the behavioral development of the rat: Long-term effects. *Science* 176:68–71.

ewin, K. 1936. *A dynamic theory of personality.* New York: McGraw-Hill.

idz, T. 1972. The nature and origins of schizophrenic disorders. *Ann. Intern. Med.* 77:639–645.

idz, T. 1976. Commentary on "A critical review of recent adoption, twin and family studies of schizophrenia: Behavioral genetics perspectives." *Schizophrenia Bull.* 2(3):402–412.

Lidz, T., Cornelison, A. R., Fleck, S., and Terry, D. 1957(a). Intrafamilial environment of the schizophrenic patient. I: The father. *Psychiatry* 20:329–342.

Lidz, T., Cornelison, A. R., Fleck, S., and Terry, D. 1957(b). The intrafamilia
environment of the schizophrenic patient. II: Marital schism and marita
skew. *Amer. J. Psychiat.* 114:241–248.

Lindsley, O. R. 1964. Direct measurement and prostheses of retarded behavior. *J
Ed.* 147:62–81.

Lindsley, O. R. 1966(a). An experiment with parents handling behavior at home
Paper presented at the Johnstone Training Center, Bordentown, New Jersey
December.

Lindsley, O. R. 1966(b). Experimental analysis of cooperation and competition. I
The experimental analysis of behavior, ed. T. Verhave. New York: Appleton
Century-Crofts.

Lohnes, P. R. 1966. *Measuring adolescent personality.* Interim Report I to th
United States Office of Education: Cooperative Research Project No. 3051
Pittsburgh: Project TALENT Office, University of Pittsburgh.

Luria, A. R. 1963. Psychological studies of mental deficiency in the Soviet Union
In *Handbook of mental deficiency,* N. R. Ellis, pp. 353–387. New York
McGraw-Hill.

Maccoby, E., ed. *The development of sex differences.* Stanford, Calif.: Stanford
University Press.

MacKinnon, D. W. 1962. The nature and nurture of creative talent. *Amer. Psychologist* 17:484–495.

MacKinnon, D. W. 1966. Illustrative material for some reflections on the curren
status of personality assessment with special references to the assessment c
creative persons. Paper presented to graduate students, Department o
Psychology, University of Utah, Salt Lake City.

MacKinnon, D. W. (1968). Selecting students with creative potential. In *The creative college student: An unmet challenge,* ed. P. Heist. San Francisco: Jossey
Bass.

Mackworth, J. F. 1963. The relation between the visual image and post perceptua
immediate memory. *J. Verbal Learn. Verbal Behav.* 2:75–85.

Maher, B. 1976. Etiology of schizophrenia. *Science* 192:879.

Marjoribanks, K. 1972. Ethnic and environmental influences on mental abilities
Amer. J. Sociol. 78:333–337.

Martinson, R., and Lessinger, L. 1960. Problems in the identification of intellectu
ally gifted children. *Exceptional Children* 26:227–231.

Masland, R. L. 1959. Methodological approaches to research on etiology. *Am. J
Mental Deficiency* 64:305–310.

Masling, J., and Harris, S. 1969. Sexual aspects of TAT administration. *J. Consul
Clin. Psychol.* 33:166–169.

Matarazzo, J. B. 1972. *Wechsler's measurement and appraisal of adult intelligence.* Baltimore: Williams & Wilkins.

Mayeske, G. W., et al. 1972. *A study of our nation's schools.* DHEW Publicatio
No. (OE) 72-142. Washington, D.C.: U.S. Government Printing Office.

Mayeske, G. W., et al. 1973. *A study of the achievement of our nation's students
DHEW Publication No. (OE) 72-131. Washington, D.C.: U.S. Governmen
Printing Office.

McCall, R. B., Applebaum, M. I., and Hogarty, P. S. 1973. Developmental change in mental performance. *Monographs of the Society for Research in Child Development* 38:(3, Serial No. 150).

McClearn, G. E. 1962. The inheritance of behavior. In *Psychology in the making,* ed. L. Postman, pp. 144–252. New York: Knopf.

McCoy, N., and Zigler, E. 1965. Social reinforcer effectiveness as a function of the relationship between child and adult. *J. Personality Soc. Psychol.* 1:604–612.

McGuire, C., and White, G. 1952. The measurement of social status. Research Paper in Human Development, No. 3 (revised), University of Texas, Austin, May.

McNemar, Q. 1969. *Psychological statistics,* 4th ed. New York: John Wiley.

Mercer, J. R. 1971. Pluralistic diagnosis in the evaluation of Black and Chicano children: A procedure for taking sociocultural variables into account in clinical assessment. Paper presented at the Annual Meeting of the American Psychological Association, Washington, D.C., September.

Merton, R. K. 1961. Singletons and multiples in scientific discovery. *Proceedings of the American Philosophical Society* 105:470–486.

Meschkowski, H. 1964. *Ways of thought of great mathematicians.* San Francisco: Holden-Day.

Michael, W. B. 1949. Factor analysis of tests and criteria: A comparative study of two AAF pilot populations. *Psychological Monographs* 63:(Whole No. 298).

Milgram, N. A., and Furth, H. G. 1963. The influence of language on concept attainment in educable retarded children. *Amer. J. Mental Deficiency* 67:733–739.

Mischel, W. 1966. A social-learning view of sex differences in behavior. In *The development of sex differences,* ed. E. Maccoby. Stanford, Calif.: Stanford University Press.

Mischel, W. 1968. *Personality and assessment.* New York: John Wiley.

Mischel, W. 1969. Continuity and change in personality. *Amer. Psychologist* 24:1012–1018.

Mischel, W. 1973(a). On the empirical dilemmas of psychodynamic approaches: Issues and alternatives. *J. Abnormal Psychol.* 82:335–344.

Mischel, W. 1973(b). Toward a cognitive social learning reconceptualization of personality. *Psychol. Rev.* 80:252–283.

Mishler, E. G., and Waxler, N. E. 1968. Family interaction and schizophrenia: Alternative frameworks of interpretation. In *The Transmission of Schizophrenia,* eds. D. Rosenthal and S. Kety. Oxford: Pergamon.

Moos, R. H. 1969. Sources of variance in responses to questionnaires and in behavior. *J. Abnormal Psychol.* 74:405–412.

Nahm, M. 1957. *The artist as creator.* Baltimore: The Johns Hopkins Press.

Newcomb, T. M. 1929. *Consistency of certain extrovert-introvert behavior patterns in 51 problem boys.* New York: Columbia University, Teachers College, Bureau of Publications.

Newell, A., and Simon, H. A. 1972. *Human problem solving.* Englewood Cliffs, N.J.: Prentice-Hall.

Newkirk, P. R. 1957. Psychopathic traits are inheritable. *Dis. Nerv. Syst.* 18:52.

Nichols, P. L. 1970. The effects of heredity and environment on intelligence test performance in 4 and 7 year white and negro sibling pairs. Doctoral dissertation, University of Minnesota. Ann Arbor, Mich.: University Microfilms, No. 71-18, 874.

Nichols, P. L., and Anderson, V. E. 1973. Intellectual performance, race, and socio-economic status. *Social Biology* 20:367–374.

Nielsen, J., Stürup, G., Tsuboi, T., and Romano, D. 1969. Prevalence of the XYY syndrome in an institution for psychologically abnormal criminals. *Acta Psychiatrica Scand.* 45.

Nisbet, J. D. 1957. IV.-Intelligence and age: Retesting with twenty-four years' interval. *Brit. J. Ed. Psychol.* 27:190–198.

Nunnally, J. C. 1967. *Psychometric theory.* New York: McGraw-Hill.

O'Connor, N., and Hermelin, B. 1959. Discrimination and reversal learning in imbeciles. *J. Abnormal Soc. Psychol.* 59:409–413.

Oden, M. H. 1968. The fulfillment of promise: 40-year follow-up of the Terman gifted group. *Genetic Psychology Monographs* 77:3–93.

Osborne, R. T. 1966. Stability of factor structure of the WISC for normal Negro children from pre-school level to first grade. *Psychol. Rep.* 18:655–664.

Owens, W. A., Jr. 1953. Age and mental abilities: A longitudinal study. *Genetic Psychology Monographs* 48:3–54.

Owens, W. A., Jr. 1966. Age and mental abilities: A second adult follow-up. *J. Ed. Psychol.* 51:311–325.

Palmer, F. H. 1970. Socioeconomic status and intellective performance among Negro preschool boys. *Developmental Psychol.* 3:1–9.

Parsons, T., and Bales, R. F. 1955. *Family, socialization and interaction process.* New York: Free Press.

Partridge, G. E. 1930. Current conceptions of psychopathic personality. *Amer. J. Psychiat.* 10:53.

Passini, F. T., and Norman, W. T. 1966. A universal conception of personality structure? *J. Personality Soc. Psychol.* 4:44–49.

Passow, A. H. 1958. Enrichment of education for the gifted. In *Education for the gifted: Fifty-seventh yearbook of the national society for the study of education,* ed. N. B. Henry. Chicago: University of Chicago Press.

Pearson, K. 1914. *The life, letters, and labours of Francis Galton,* Vol. 1. Cambridge: Cambridge University Press.

Pearson, K. 1930–1931. On the inheritance of mental disease. *Ann. Eugenics* 4:362–380.

Pearson, K., and Jaederholm, C. A. 1913–14. *On the continuity of mental defect.* Vol. 2 in the set *Mendelism and the problem of mental defect.* London: Dulau & Co.

Pegnato, C. W., and Birch, J. W. 1959. Locating gifted children in junior high schools: A comparison of methods. *Exceptional Children* 25:300–304.

Penrose, L. S. 1939. Intelligence test scores of mentally defective patients and their relatives. *Brit. J. Psychol.* 30.

Penrose, L. S. 1963. *The biology of mental defect.* London: Sidgwick & Jackson.

Peterson, D. R. 1968. *The clinical study of social behavior.* New York: Appleton-Century-Crofts.

Peterson, L., and Peterson, M. J. 1959. Short term retention of individual verbal items. *J. Exper. Psychol.* 58:193–198.

Pickford, R. W. 1949. The genetics of intelligence. *J. Psychol.* 28:129–145.

Pinneau, S. R. 1955. The infantile disorders of hospitalism and anaclitic depression. *Psychol. Bull.* 52:429–452.

Plumb, H. H. 1969. *The death of the past.* London: Macmillan.

Polanyi, M. 1955. From Copernicus to Einstein. *Encounter* (Winter)54–63.

Posner, M. I., Boies, S. J., Eichelman, W. H., and Taylor, R. L. 1969. Retention of visual and name codes of single letters. *J. Exper. Psychol.* (Monograph) 79:1–16.

Raskin, E. A. 1936. Comparison of scientific and literary ability: A biological study of eminent scientists and men of letters of the nineteenth century. *J. Abnormal Soc. Psychol.* 31:20–35.

Reed, E. W., and Reed, S. C. 1965. *Mental retardation: A family study.* Philadelphia: W. B. Saunders.

Reed, T. E. 1969. Caucasian genes in American Negroes. *Science* 165:762–768.

Reiter, H. 1930. Aus wirkung von Anlage und Milieu, unterfucht an Adoptierten uneheliche Geborenen. *Klin. Wschr.* 9:2358.

Renaud, H., and Estess, F. 1961. Life history interviews with one hundred normal American males. *Amer. J. Orthopsychiatry* 31:786–802.

Rieber, M. 1964. Verbal mediation in normal and retarded children. *Amer. J. Mental Deficiency* 68:634–641.

Riedel, H. 1937. Zur enpirischen Erbprognose der Psychopathie. *Z. Ges. Neurol. Psychiat.* 59:648.

Riegel, K. F., Riegel, R. M., and Meyer, M. 1967. A study of the dropout rate in longitudinal research on aging and the prediction of death. *J. Personality Soc. Psychol.* 5:342–348.

Robb, G. P., Bernardoni, L. C., and Johnson, R. W. 1972. *Assessment of individual mental ability.* Scranton, Pa.: Intext Educational Publishers.

Roberts, J. A. F. 1940. Studies on a child population. V. The resemblance in intelligence between sibs. *Ann. Eugenics* 10:293–312.

Roberts, J. A. F. 1952. The genetics of mental deficiency. *Eugenics Rev.* 44:71–83.

Roe, A. 1952. *The making of a scientist.* New York: Dodd, Mead.

Rosenthal, D. 1962. Familial concordance by sex with respect to schizophrenia. *Psychol. Bull.* 59:401–421.

Rosenthal, D., and Kety, S. S., eds. 1968. *The transmission of schizophrenia.* New York: Pergamon.

Sanford, N. 1970. *Issues in personality theory.* San Francisco: Jossey-Bass.

Scarborough, B. B. 1956. Some mental characteristics of Southern colored and white veneral disease patients as measured by the Wechsler-Bellevue test. *J. Soc. Psychol.* 43:313–321.

Scarr-Salapatek, S. 1971. Race, social class, and IQ. *Science* 174:1285–1295.

Scarr, S., and Weinberg, R. A. 1976. IQ test performance of black children adopted by white families. *Amer. Psychologist* 31:726–739.

Scarr, S., and Weinberg, R. A. 1977(a). Intellectual similarities within families of both adopted and biological children. *Intelligence* 1:170–191.

Scarr, S., and Weinberg, R. A. 1977(b). Nature and nurture strike (out) again. *Intelligence* (in press).

Schaie, K. W. 1958. Rigidity-flexibility and intelligence: A cross-sectional study of the adult life-span from 20 to 70. *Psychol. Monographs* 72:(9, Whole No. 462).

Schaie, K. W. 1965. A general model for the study of developmental problems. *Psychol. Bull.* 64:92–107.

Schaie, K. W., and Labouvie-Vief, G. 1974. Generational versus ontogenetic components of change in adult cognitive behavior: A fourteen-year cross-sequential study. *Developmental Psychol.* 10:305–320.

Schaie, K. W., Labouvie, G. V., and Buech, B. U. 1973. Generational and cohort-specific differences in adult cognitive functioning: A fourteen-year study of independent samples. *Developmental Psychol.* 9:151–166.

Schaie, K. W., and Strother, C. R. 1968. A cross-sequential study of age changes in cognitive behavior. *Psychol. Bull.* 70:671–680.

Schank, R. 1973. Identification of conceptualizations underlying natural language. In *Computer models of thought and language,* eds. R. Shank and K. Colby. San Francisco: Freeman.

Schlipp, P. A., ed. 1949. *Albert Einstein: Philosopher-scientist.* Evanston, Ill.: Library of Living Philosophers.

Schneider, D. J. 1973. Implicit personality theory: A review. *Psychol. Bull.* 79:294–309.

Schneider, K. 1934. *Die psychopathischen persönlichkeiten.* Leipzig: Thieme.

Schopler, E., and Loflin, J. 1969. Thought disorder in parents of psychotic children: A function of past anxiety. *Archives of General Psychiatry* 20:174–181.

Semler, I. J., and Iscoe, I. 1963. Comparative and developmental study of the learning abilities of Negro and white children under four conditions. *J. Ed. Psychol.* 54:38–44.

Sewell, W. H., Hallow, A. D., and Ohlendorf, G. W. 1970. The educational and early occupational status attainment process: Replication and revision. *Amer. Sociol. Rev.* 35:1014–1027.

Sewell, W. H., and Hauser, R. M. 1975. *Education, occupation, and earnings: Achievement in the early career.* New York: Academic Press.

Shakow, D., and Rapaport, D. 1968. *The influence of Freud on American psychology.* Cleveland, Ohio: World Publishing Co.

Shallenberger, P., and Zigler, E. 1961. Rigidity, negative reaction tendencies, and cosatiation effects in normal and feebleminded children. *J. Abnormal Soc. Psychol.* 63:20–26.

Shaycoft, M. F. 1967. *The high school years: Growth in cognitive skills.* Pittsburgh: American Institutes for Research and University of Pittsburgh, Project TALENT Office.

Shepps, R., and Zigler, E. 1962. Social deprivation and rigidity in the performance of organic and familial retardates. *Amer. J. Mental Deficiency* 67:262–268.

Sheridan Supply Company. 1962. *Plot Titles.* Beverly Hills: Sheridan Supply Company.

Shuey, A. M. 1966. *The testing of Negro intelligence.* New York: Social Science Press.

Sitkei, E. G., and Meyers, C. E. 1969. Comparative structure of intellect in middle- and lower-class four-year-olds of two ethnic groups. *Developmental Psychol.* 1:592–604.

Skinner, B. F. 1938. *The behavior of organisms: An experimental analysis.* New York: Appleton-Century-Crofts.

Skinner, B. F. 1953. *Science and human behavior.* New York: Macmillan.

Skinner, B. F. 1961. Teaching machines. *Scientific American* 205:90–102.

Skinner, B. F. 1966. Operant behavior. In *Operant behavior: Areas of research and development,* ed. W. Honig. New York: Appleton-Century-Crofts.

Smart, M. S., and Smart, R. C. 1970. Self-esteem, social-personal orientation of Indian 12- and 18-year-olds. *Psychol. Rep.* 27:107–115.

Smith, J. M., and Schaefer, C. F. 1969. Development of a creativity scale for the Adjective Check List. *Psychol. Rep.* 25:87–92.

Sontag, L. W., Baker, C. T., and Nelson, V. L. 1958. Mental growth and personality development: A longitudinal study. *Monographs of the Society for Research in Child Development* 23:No. 68, 1–143.

Spache, G. D. 1963. *Diagnostic reading scale.* Monterey, Calif.: California Test Bureau.

Spence, J. T., Helmreich, R., and Stapp, J. 1975. Ratings of self and peers on sex-role attributes and their relation of self-esteem and conceptions of masculinity and femininity. *J. Personality Soc. Psychol.* 32:29–39.

Sperling, G. 1960. The information available in brief visual presentations. *Psychological Monographs* 74:(Whole No. 498).

Spitz, H. H. 1963. Field theory in mental deficiency. In *Handbook of mental deficiency*, ed. N. R. Ellis, pp. 11–40. New York: McGraw-Hill.

Spitz, R. A. 1945. Hospitalism: A follow-up report. *Psychoanalytic Study of the Child* 1:53–74.

Spivack, G. 1963. Perceptual processes. In *Handbook of mental deficiency*. ed. N. R. Ellis, pp. 480–511. New York: McGraw-Hill.

Stagner, R. 1937. *Psychology of personality.* New York: McGraw-Hill.

Stagner, R. 1973. Traits are relevant-logical and empirical analysis. Paper presented at the meeting of the American Psychological Association, Montreal, August.

Sternberg, S. 1965. High speed scanning in human memory. *Science* 153:652–654.

Sternberg, S. 1975. Memory Scanning: New findings and current controversies. *Quarterly J. Exper. Psychol.* 27:1–32.

Stevenson, H., and Fahel, L. 1961. The effect of social reinforcement on the performance of institutionalized and noninstitutionalized normal and retarded children. *J. Personality* 29:136–147.

Stoch, M. B., and Smythe, P. M. 1963. Does undernutrition during infancy inhibit brain growth and subsequent intellectual development? *Arch. Dis. Childhood* 38:546–552.

Stodolsky, S. S., and Lesser, G. 1967. Learning patterns in the disadvantaged *Harvard Ed. Rev.* 37:546–593.

Strömgren, E. 1975. Genetic factors in the origin of schizophrenia. In *On the origin of schizophrenic psychoses,* ed. H. N. Van Praag. Amsterdam: DeErven Bohn BV.

Stumpfl, F. 1936. *Die Unsprunge des Verbrechens an Lebenslauf von Zwilligen.* Leipzig: George Thieme Verlag.

Sumpton, M. R., and Lueckling, E. M. 1960. *Education of the gifted.* New York: Ronald Press.

Svalastoga, K. 1959. *Prestige, chaos, and mobility.* Copenhagen: Gyldendal.

Taft, R., and Gilchrist, M. B. Creative attitudes and creative productivity: A comparison of two aspects of creativity among students. *Journal of Educational Psychology,* 1970, 61:136–143.

Tannenbaum, A. J. 1958. History of interest in the gifted. In *Education for the gifted: Fifty-seventh yearbook of the national society for the study of education,* ed. N. B. Henry. Chicago: University of Chicago Press.

Taubman, P. 1976. The determinants of earnings: Genetics, family, and other environment; a study of white, male twins. *Amer. Economic Res.* 66:858–870.

Taubman, P. 1977. *Ability, IQ, and earnings.* Unpublished manuscript.

Taubman, P., and Wales, T. 1972. *Mental ability and higher educational attainment in the twentieth century.* Berkeley, Calif.: NBER-Carnegie.

Taubman, P., and Wales, T. 1974. *Higher educations and earnings.* New York: McGraw-Hill.

Taylor, E. W., and Holland, J. L. 1962. Development and application of tests of creativity. *Rev. Ed. Res.* 32:91–102.

Tellegen, A., and Briggs, P. F. 1967. Old wine in new skins: Grouping Wechsler subtests into new scales. *J. Consult. Psychol.* 31:499–506.

Terman, L. M. 1954. The discovery and encouragement of exceptional talent. *Amer. Psychologist* 9:221–230.

Terman, L. M., et al. 1925. *Genetic studies of genius.* Vol. 1, *Mental and physical traits of a thousand gifted children.* Stanford, Calif: Stanford University Press.

Terman, L. M., and Oden, Melita H. 1947. *The gifted child grows up.* Stanford, Calif.: Stanford University Press.

Thorndike, R. L. 1973. *Reading comprehension education in fifteen countries: International studies in evaluation: III.* New York: John Wiley.

Tomkins, S. S. 1962–1963. *Affect, imagery, consciousness,* 2 vols. New York: Springer.

Torrance, E. P. 1966. *Thinking creatively with words.* Booklets A and B. Lexington, Mass.: Personnel Press.

Trabasso, T. 1972. Mental operations in language comprehension. In *Language comprehension and the acquisition of knowledge,* eds. J. B. Carroll and R. V. Freedle. Washington, D.C.: Winston-Wiley.

Trabasso, T., Rollins, H., and Shaunessey, E. 1971. Storage and verification stages in processing concepts. *Cognitive Psychol.* 2:239–289.

Tuddenham, R. D., Blumenkrantz, J., and Wilkin, W. R. 1968. Age changes on AGCT: A longitudinal study of average adults. *J. Consult. Clin. Psychol.* 32:659–663.

Tulkin, S. R. 1968. Race, class, family, and school achievement. *J. Personality Soc. Psychol.* 9:31–37.

Turner, R. G., and Peterson, M. 1977. Public and private self-consciousness and emotional expressivity. *J. Consult. Clin. Psychol.* 45:490–491.

Turnure, J., and Zigler, E. 1964. Outer-directedness in the problem solving of normal and retarded children. *J. Abnormal Soc. Psychol.* 69:427–436.

Tyson, A., and Strachey, J. 1956. A chronological hand-list of Freud's works. *Int. J. Psycho-analysis* 57:19–33.

Vale, J. R., and Vale, G. R. 1969. Individual difference and general laws in psychology: A reconciliation. *Amer. Psychologist* 24:1093–1108.

Vanggaard, T. 1968. Neurose og psykopati, *Nord psykiat.* 22:277.

Van Zelst, R. H., and Kerr, W. A. 1954. Personality and self-assessment of scientific and technical personnel. *J. Appl. Psychol.* 38:145–147.

Vernon, P. E. 1964. *Personality assessment: A critical survey.* New York: John Wiley.

Vernon, P. E. 1971. Effects of administration and scoring on divergent thinking tests. *Brit. J. Ed. Psychol.* 41:245–247.

Wachtel, P. 1973. Psychodynamics, behavior therapy, and the implacable experimenter: An inquiry into the consistency of personality. *J. Abnormal Psychol.* 82:324–334.

Walker, J. 1966. Pregnancy and perinatal association with mental subnormality. In *Genetic and environmental factors in human ability,* eds. J. E. Meade and A. S. Parkes, pp. 105–119. New York: Plenum Press.

Wall, W. D. 1960. Highly intelligent children: The psychology of the gifted. *Ed. Res.* 2:101–110.

Wallace, J. 1966. An abilities conception of personality: Some implications for personality measurement. *Amer. Psychologist* 21:132–138.

Wallach, M. A. 1971. *The intelligence/creativity distinction.* New York & Morristown, N.J.: General Learning Press.

Wallach, M. A., and Leggett, M. I. 1972. Testing the hypothesis that a person will be consistent: Stylistic consistency versus situational specificity in size of children's drawing. *Personality* 40:309–330.

Wallach, M. A., and Wing, C. W., Jr. 1969. *The talented student: A validation of the creativity-intelligence distinction.* New York: Holt, Rinehart, & Winston.

Waller, J. H. 1971. Achievement and social mobility: Relationships among IQ score, education, and occupation in two generations. *Social Biology* 18:252–259.

Warner, W. L., et al. 1949. *Social class in America: A manual of procedure for the measurement of social status.* Chicago: Science Research Associates.

Wason, P., and Johnson-Laird, P. 1972. *Psychology of reasoning.* Cambridge, Mass.: Harvard University Press.

Watson, J. D. 1968. *The double helix.* New York: Atheneum.

Wechsler, D. 1955. *Wechsler adult intelligence scale.* New York: Psychological Corporation.

Wechsler, D. 1958. *The measurement and appraisal of adult intelligence,* 4th ed. Baltimore: Williams & Wilkins.

Weil, E. 1960. *Albert Einstein: A bibliography of his scientific papers.* London.

Wellman, B. L. 1938. Guiding mental development. *Childhood Education* 15:108–112.

Wender, P. H., Rosenthal, D., and Kety, S. S. 1968. A psychiatric assessment of the adoptive parents of schizophrenics. In *The transmission of schizophrenia,* eds. D. Rosenthal and S. S. Kety. New York: Pergamon.

Wender, P. H., Rosenthal, D., Kety, S. S., Schulsinger, F., and Welner, J. 1973. Social class and psychopathology in adoptees. *Archives of General Psychiatry* 28:318–325.

Wender, P. H., Rosenthal, D., Kety, S. S., Schulsinger, F., and Welner, J. 1974. Cross fostering: A research strategy for clarifying the role of genetic and experiential factors in the etiology of schizophrenia. *Archives of General Psychiatry* 30:121–128.

Werner, E. E., Bierman, J. M., and French, F. E. 1971. *The children of Kauai: A longitudinal study from the prenatal period to age ten.* Honolulu: University of Hawaii Press.

Whipple, G. T. 1915. *Manual of mental and physical tests. Part II: Complex processes.* Baltimore: Warwick & York.

White, K. 1968. Anxiety, extraversion-intraversion and divergent thinking ability. *J. Creative Behav.* 2:119–127.

White, S. H. 1965. Evidence for a hierarchical arrangement of learning processes. In *Advances in child development and behavior,* eds. L. P. Lipsitt and C. C. Spiker, pp. 187–220. New York: Academic Press.

Whiteman, M., and Deutsch, M. 1968. Social disadvantage as related to intellective and language development. In *Social class, race, and psychological development,* eds. M. Deutsch, I. Katz, and A. R. Jensen, pp. 86–114. New York: Holt, Rinehart, & Winston.

Wickens, D. D. 1972. Characteristics of word encoding. In *Coding processes in human memory*, eds. A. Melton and E. Martin. Washington, D.C.: V. H. Winston and Sons.

Willerman, L., Turner, R. G., and Peterson, M. 1976. A comparison of the predictive validity of typical and maximal personality measures. *J. Res. Personality* 10:482–492.

Wilson, A. B. 1967. Educational consequences of segregation in a California community. In *Report of U.S. Commission on Civil Rights, Racial isolation in the public schools*. Vol. 2, *Appendices*. Washington, D.C.: U.S. Government Printing Office.

Wing, J. K. 1975. By schism or by skew. *Times Literary Supplement*. London, September, 19, 1975.

Witty, P. A. 1940. Some considerations in the education of gifted children. *Educational Admin. Supervision* 26:512–521.

Woodward, M. 1960. Early experiences and later social responses of severely subnormal children. *Brit. J. Med. Psychol.* 33:123–132.

Wynne, L. C. 1968. Methodologic and conceptual issues in the study of schizophrenics and their family. In *The transmission of schizophrenia*, eds. D. Rosenthal and S. Kety. Oxford: Pergamon.

Wysocki, B. A., and Wysocki, A. C. 1909. Cultural differences as reflected in Wechsler-Bellevue Intelligence (WBII) Test. *Psychol. Rep.* 25:95–101.

Young, F. M., and Bright, H. A. 1954. Results of testing 81 Negro rural juveniles with the Wechsler Intelligence Scale for Children. *J. Soc. Psychol.* 39:219–226.

Young, F. M., and Collins, J. J. 1954. Results of testing Negro contact-syphilitics with the Wechsler-Bellevue Intelligence Scale. *J. Soc. Psychol.* 39:93–98.

Young, M., and Gibson, J. 1963. In search of an explanation of social mobility. *Brit. J. Statistical Psychol.* 16:27–36.

Young, F. M., and Pitts, V. A. 1951. The performance of congenital syphilitics on the Wechsler Intelligence Scale for Children. *J. Consult. Psychol.* 15:239–242.

Zigler, E. 1958. The effect of pre-institutional social deprivation on the performance of feebleminded children. Unpublished dissertation, University of Texas at Austin.

Zigler, E. 1961. Social deprivation and rigidity in the performance of feebleminded children. *J. Abnormal Soc. Psychol.* 62:413–421.

Zigler, E. 1963. Rigidity and social reinforcement effects in the performance of institutionalized and noninstitutionalized normal and retarded children. *J. Personality* 31:258–269.

Zigler, E. 1963. Social reinforcement, environmental conditions and the child. *Amer. J. Orthopsychiat.* 33:614–623.

Zigler, E. 1966. Mental retardation: Current issues and approaches. In *Review of Child Development Research*, eds. M. L. Hoffman and L. W. Hoffman. New York: Russell Sage Foundation.

Zigler, E., and Child, I. L. 1968. Socialization. In *Handbook of social psychology*, Vol. 3 (2d ed.), eds. G. Lindzey and E. Aronson. Reading, Mass.: Addison-Wesley.

Zigler, E., and deLabry, J. 1962. Concept-switching in middle-class, lower-class, and retarded children. *J. Abnormal Soc. Psychol.* 65:267–273.

Zigler, E., Hodgden, L., and Stevensen, H. 1958. The effect of support on the performance of normal and feebleminded children. *J. Personality* 26:106–122.

Zigler, E., and Unell, E. 1962. Concept-switching in normal and feebleminded children as a function of reinforcement. *Amer. J. Mental Deficiency* 66:651–657.

Zigler, E., and Williams, J. 1963. Institutionalization and the effectiveness of social reinforcement: A three year follow-up study. *J. Abnormal Soc. Psychol.* 66:191–205.

Zuckerman, H. 1967(a). The sociology of the Nobel Prizes. *Scientific American* 217, 5:25–33.

Zuckerman, H. 1967(b). Nobel laureates in science: Patterns of production, collaboration and authorship. *Amer. Sociol. Rev.* 32:391–403.

Name Index

Subject Index